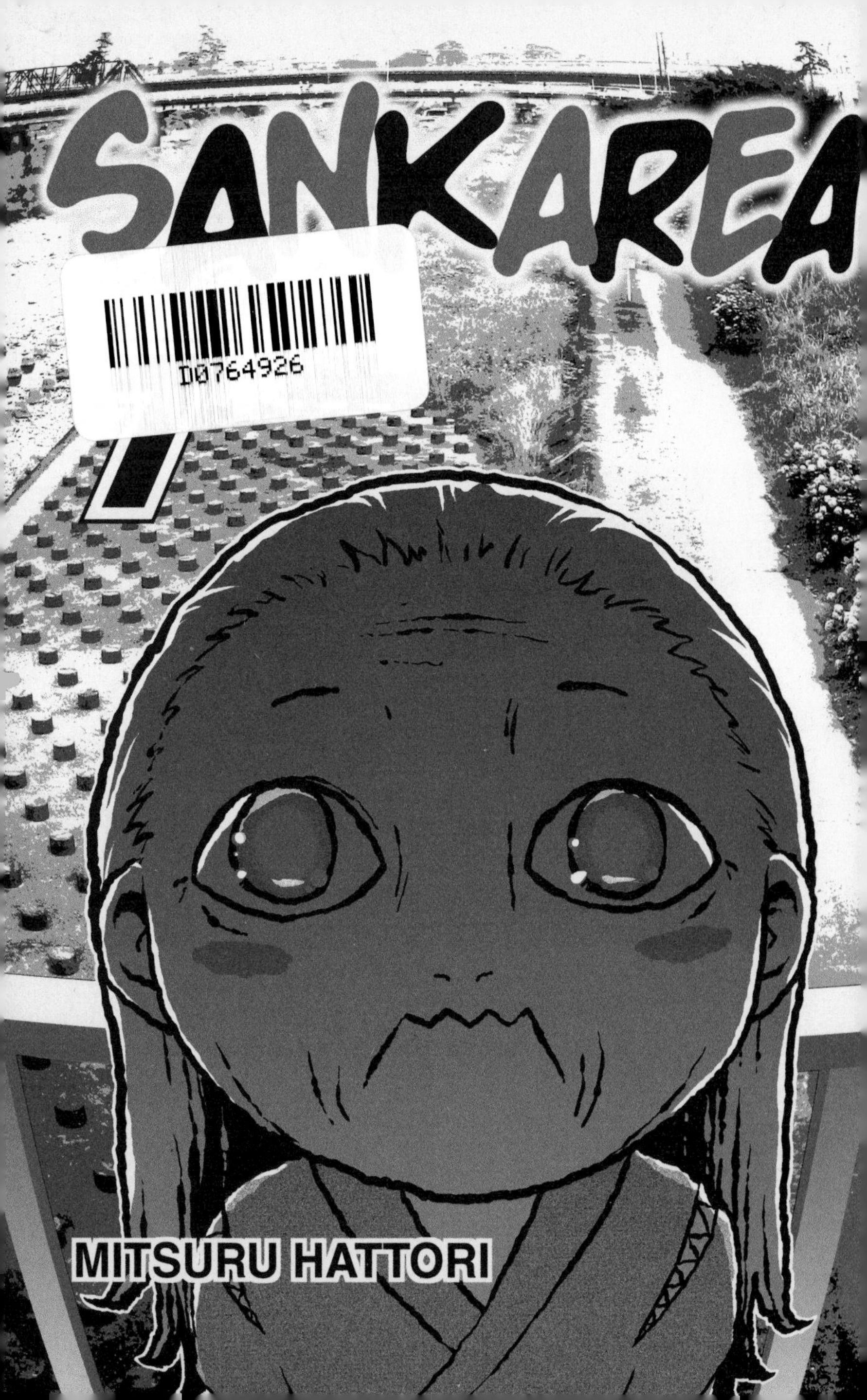
SANKAREA
7
MITSURU HATTORI

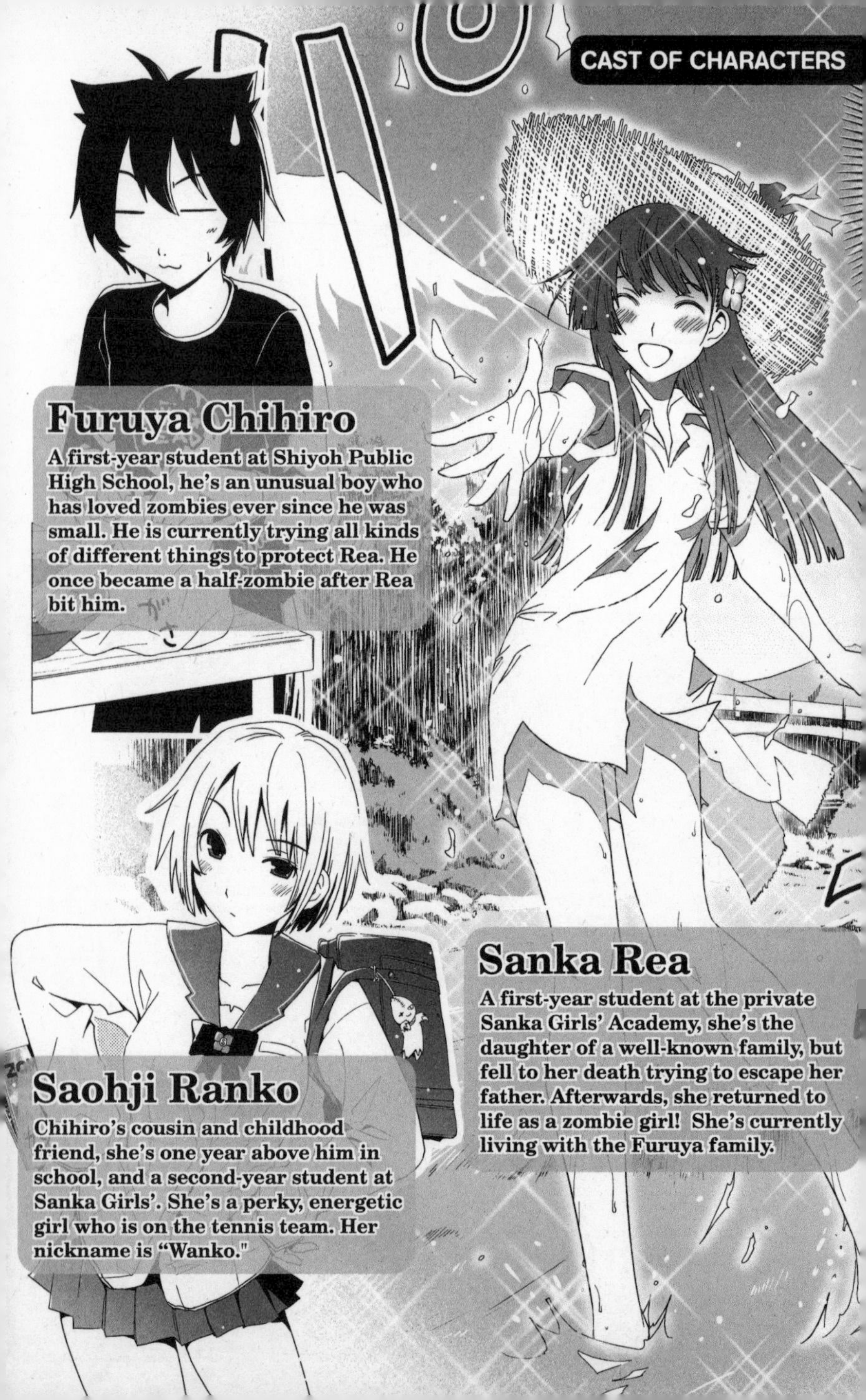

CAST OF CHARACTERS

Furuya Chihiro

A first-year student at Shiyoh Public High School, he's an unusual boy who has loved zombies ever since he was small. He is currently trying all kinds of different things to protect Rea. He once became a half-zombie after Rea bit him.

Sanka Rea

A first-year student at the private Sanka Girls' Academy, she's the daughter of a well-known family, but fell to her death trying to escape her father. Afterwards, she returned to life as a zombie girl! She's currently living with the Furuya family.

Saohji Ranko

Chihiro's cousin and childhood friend, she's one year above him in school, and a second-year student at Sanka Girls'. She's a perky, energetic girl who is on the tennis team. Her nickname is "Wanko."

Kurumiya Darin Arciento

An expert in zombie research who came to Japan from the southern islands to visit "Professor Boyle" (Grandpa). She has a strange passion for her research. Despite her looks, she's younger than Rea.

18

Darin's faithful pet. It's been zombified and half-mechanized.

THE FURUYA FAMILY

Dad

His real name is Furuya Dohn. He's the head priest at Shiryohji Temple. He agreed to Rea and Darin living in their home, saying only, "Should be fine, right?"

Grandpa

The most mysterious organism (?) of all in "Sankarea". Apparently he has studied zombies at an overseas research facility in the past...

Bub

He was hit by a car and died, but came back to life thanks to the elixir Chihiro and Rea made.

Furuya Mero

A reliable first-year middle school student, she manages all the housework for the Furuya family. She loves to read the Heart Sutra.

STORY

Without acknowledging the changes in Rea's rationality after the ruins, the Furuya household seems to have regained their tranquility. But with Bub's symptoms growing worse, Chihiro is shocked to discover him cannibalizing his cat friends, and is then attacked by Bub! The attack is repelled by Towa, but Bub's situation has taken a tragic turn. Troubled by this, Chihiro tries to cremate Bub, but is rendered speechless by Rea, who, in a fit of desperation, says she "wants to be together until the end." Furthermore, he is notified that Rea suddenly took off for ZoMA with Darin...

MITSURU HATTORI presents

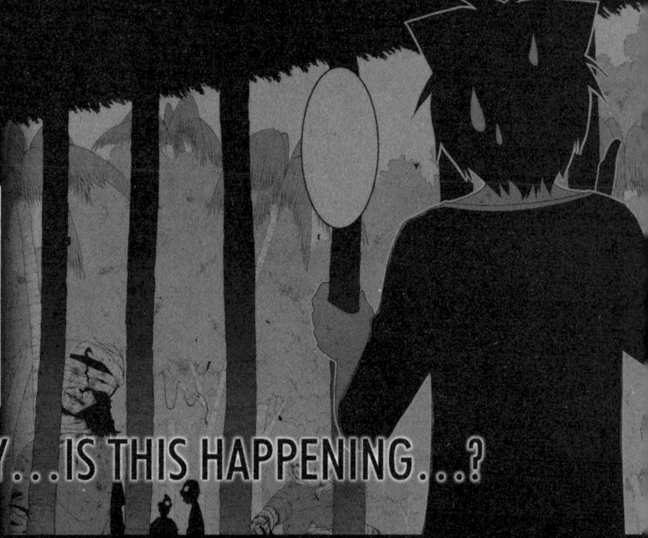
WHY...IS THIS HAPPENING...?

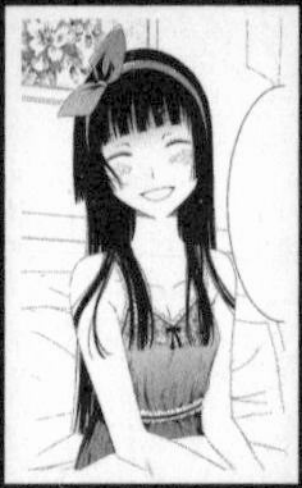

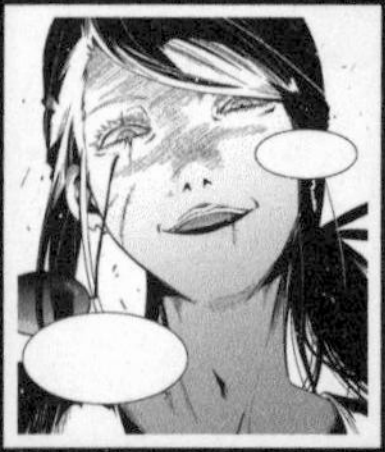

CONTENTS

SERIALIZED IN BESSATSU SHONEN MAGAZINE, JULY 2012 – NOVEMBER 2012.

SANKAREA 7

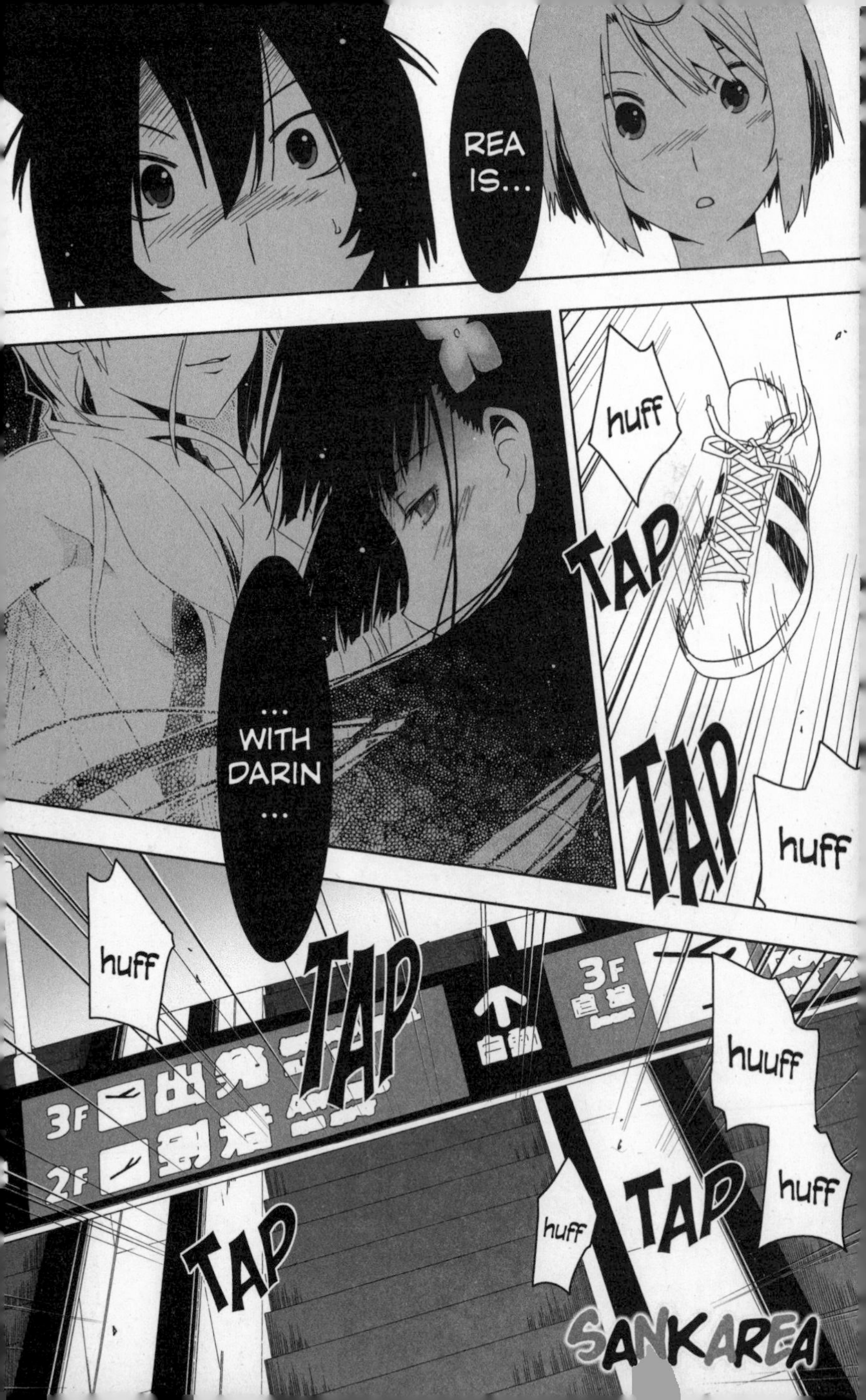
REA IS...
huff
TAP
TAP
huff
... WITH DARIN ...
huuff
huff
TAP
huff
TAP
huff
TAP
SANKAREA

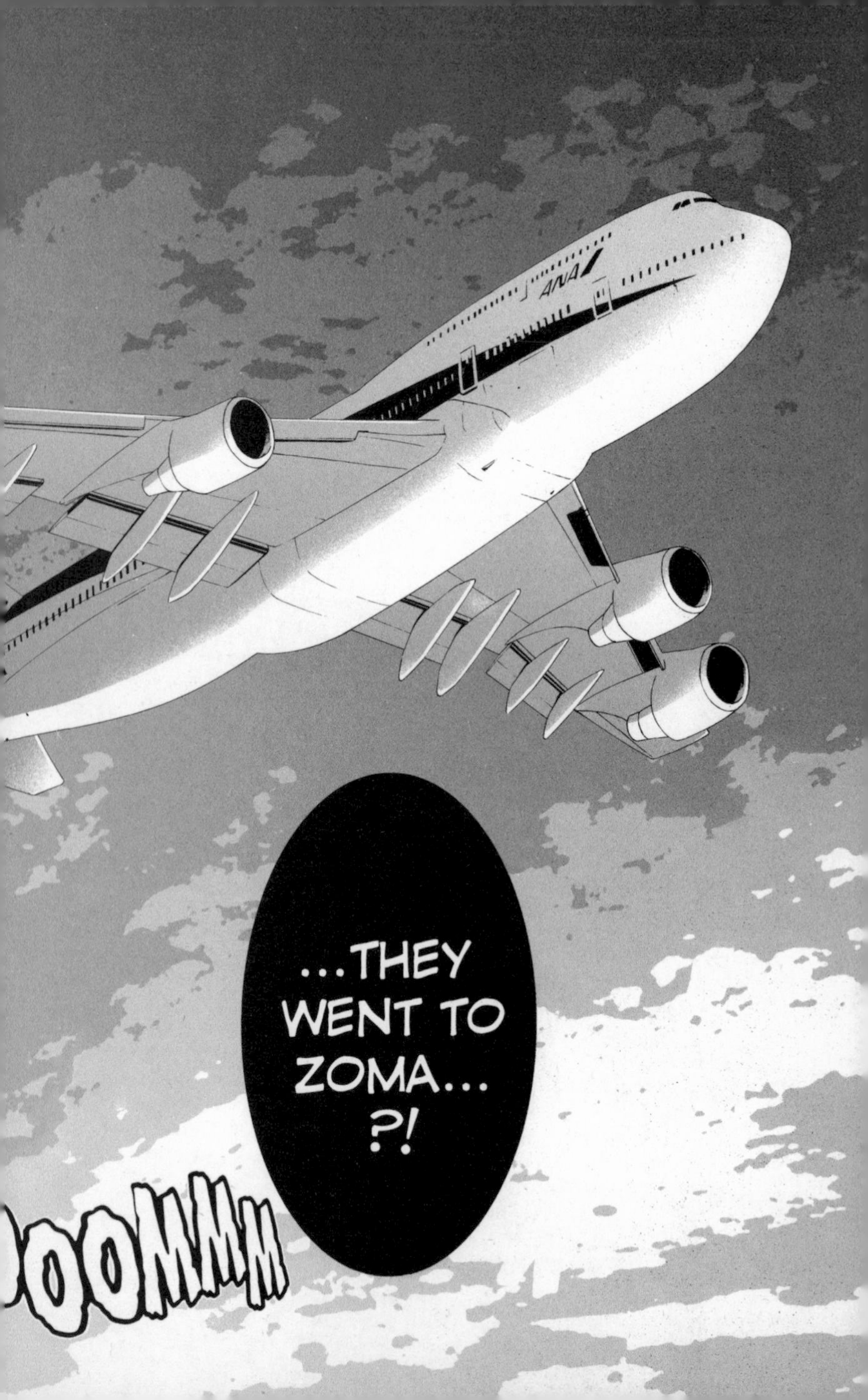
...THEY WENT TO ZOMA... ?!
OOOMMM

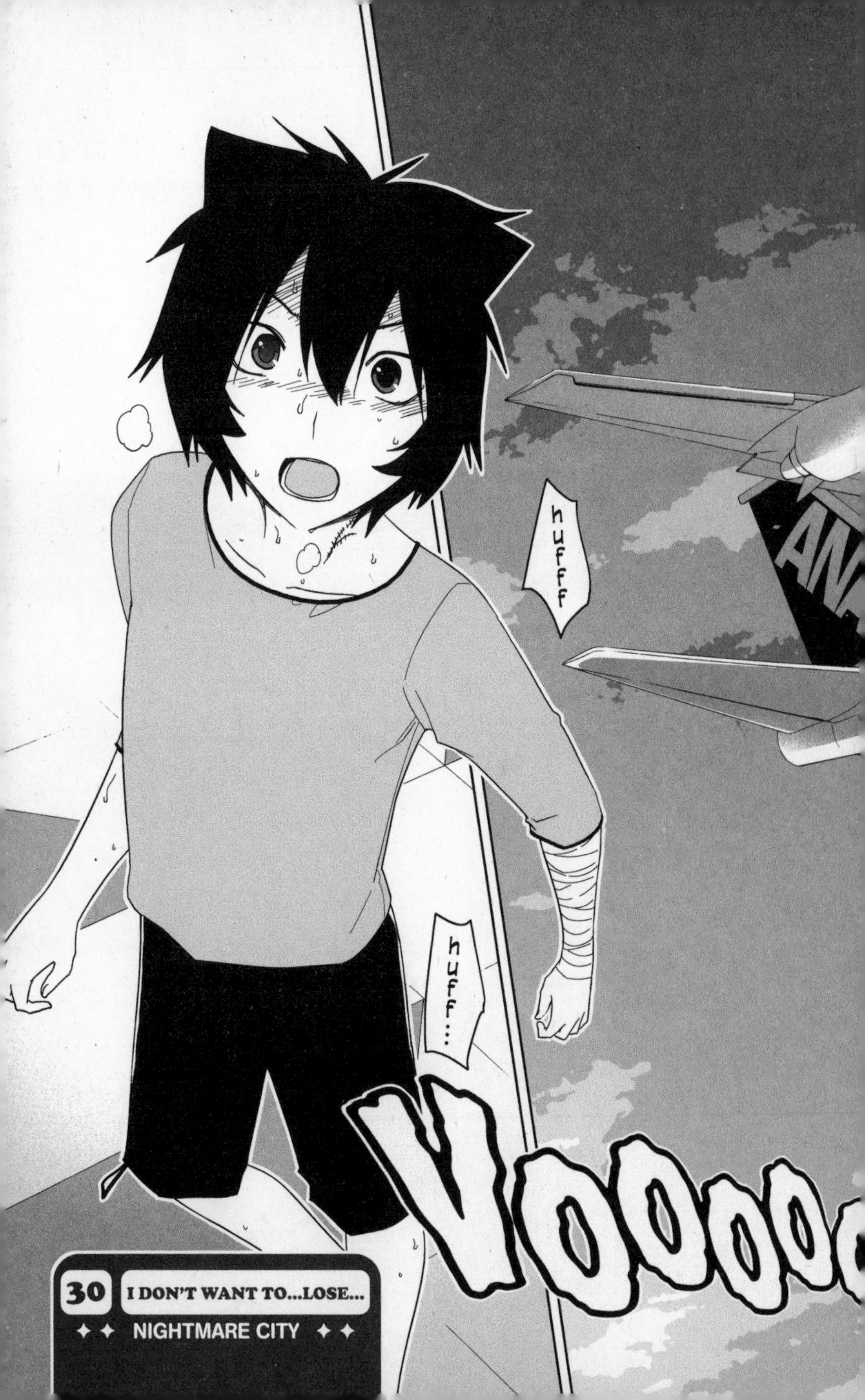
huff
huff...
VOOOO
30 I DON'T WANT TO...LOSE...
✦✦ NIGHTMARE CITY ✦✦

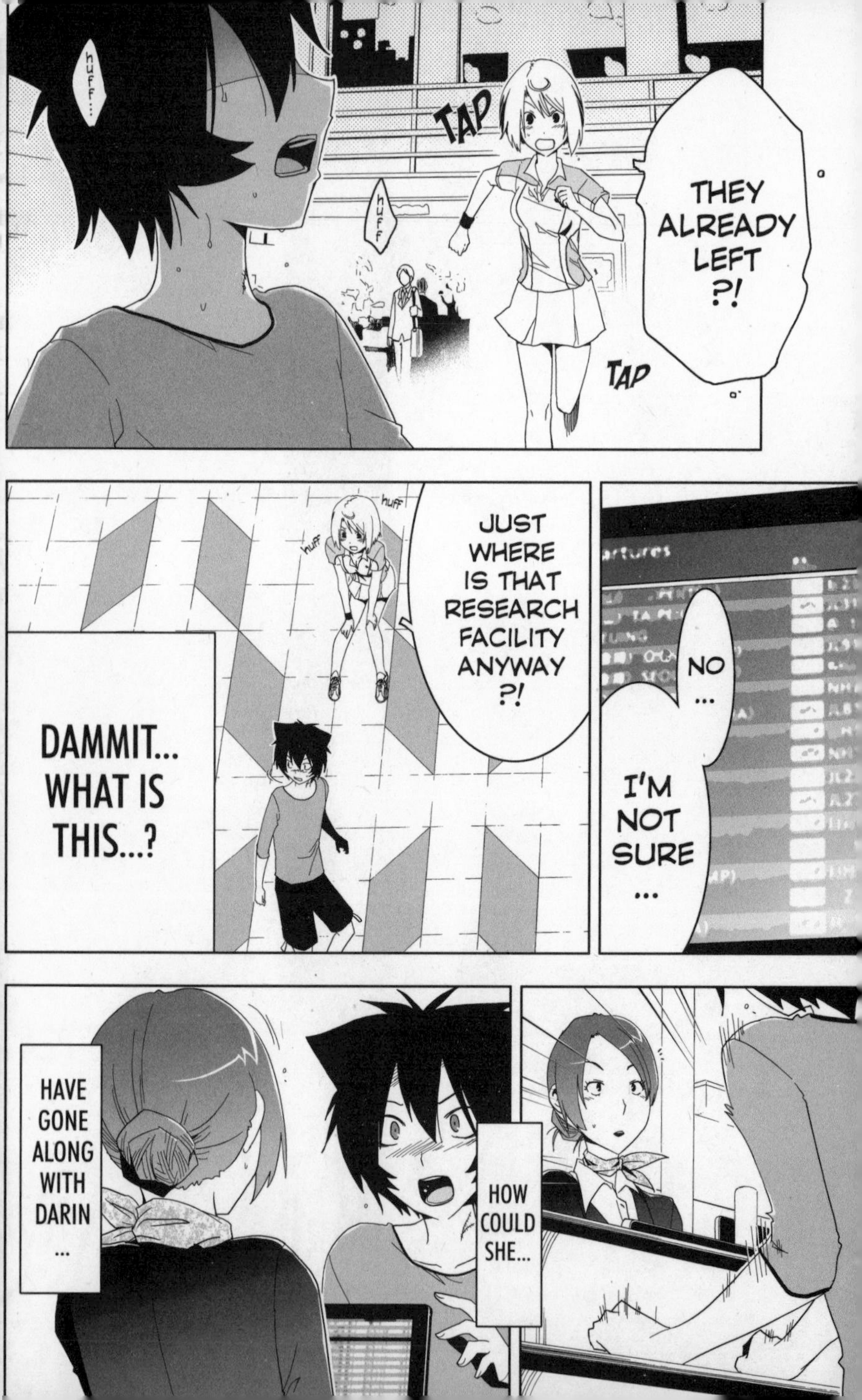
THEY ALREADY LEFT ?!
TAP
huff...
huff
TAP
NO ...
I'M NOT SURE ...
JUST WHERE IS THAT RESEARCH FACILITY ANYWAY ?!
huff
huff
DAMMIT... WHAT IS THIS...?
HOW COULD SHE...
HAVE GONE ALONG WITH DARIN ...

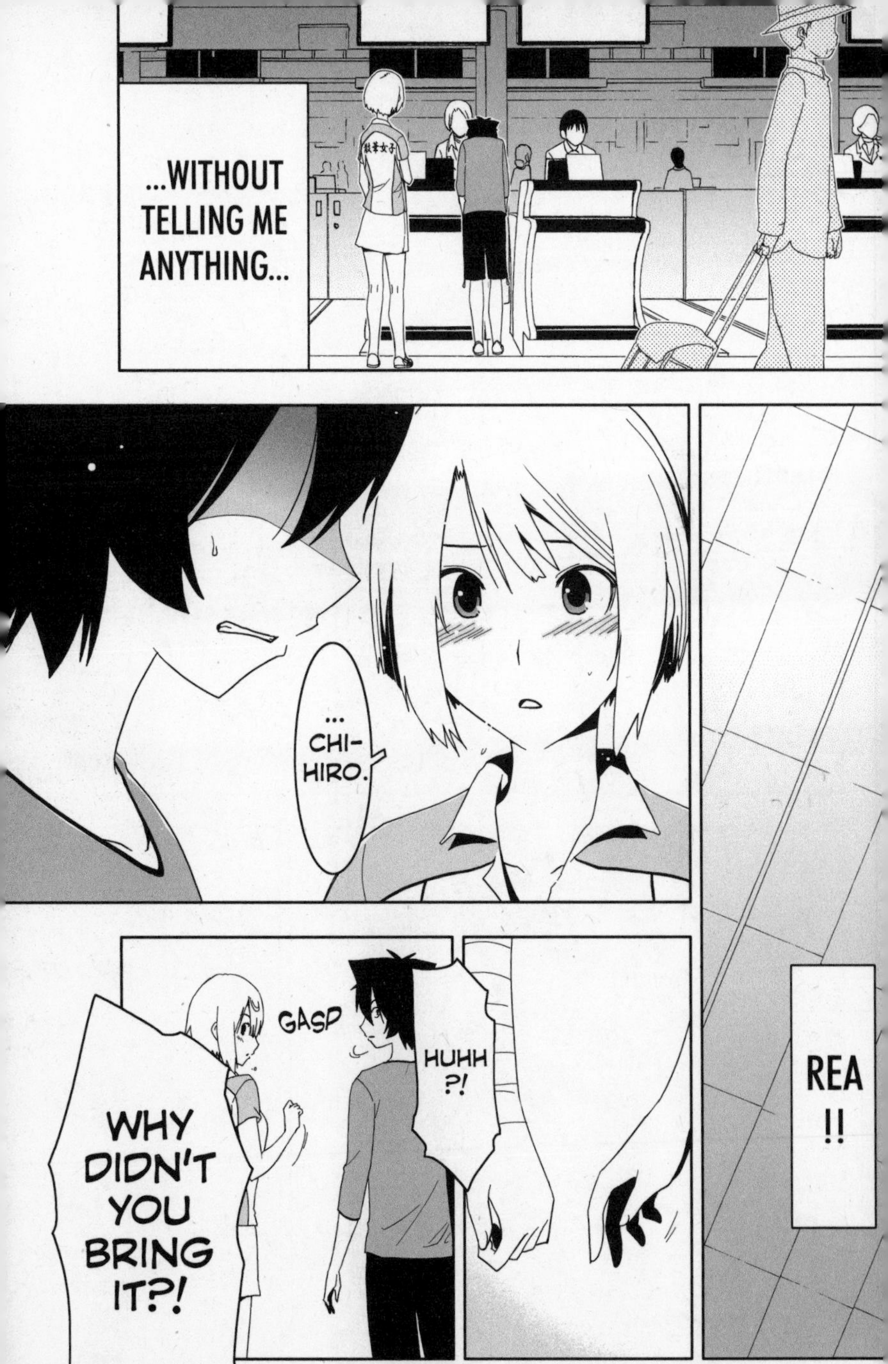
...WITHOUT TELLING ME ANYTHING...
REA !!
... CHI-HIRO.
HUHH ?!
GASP
WHY DIDN'T YOU BRING IT?!

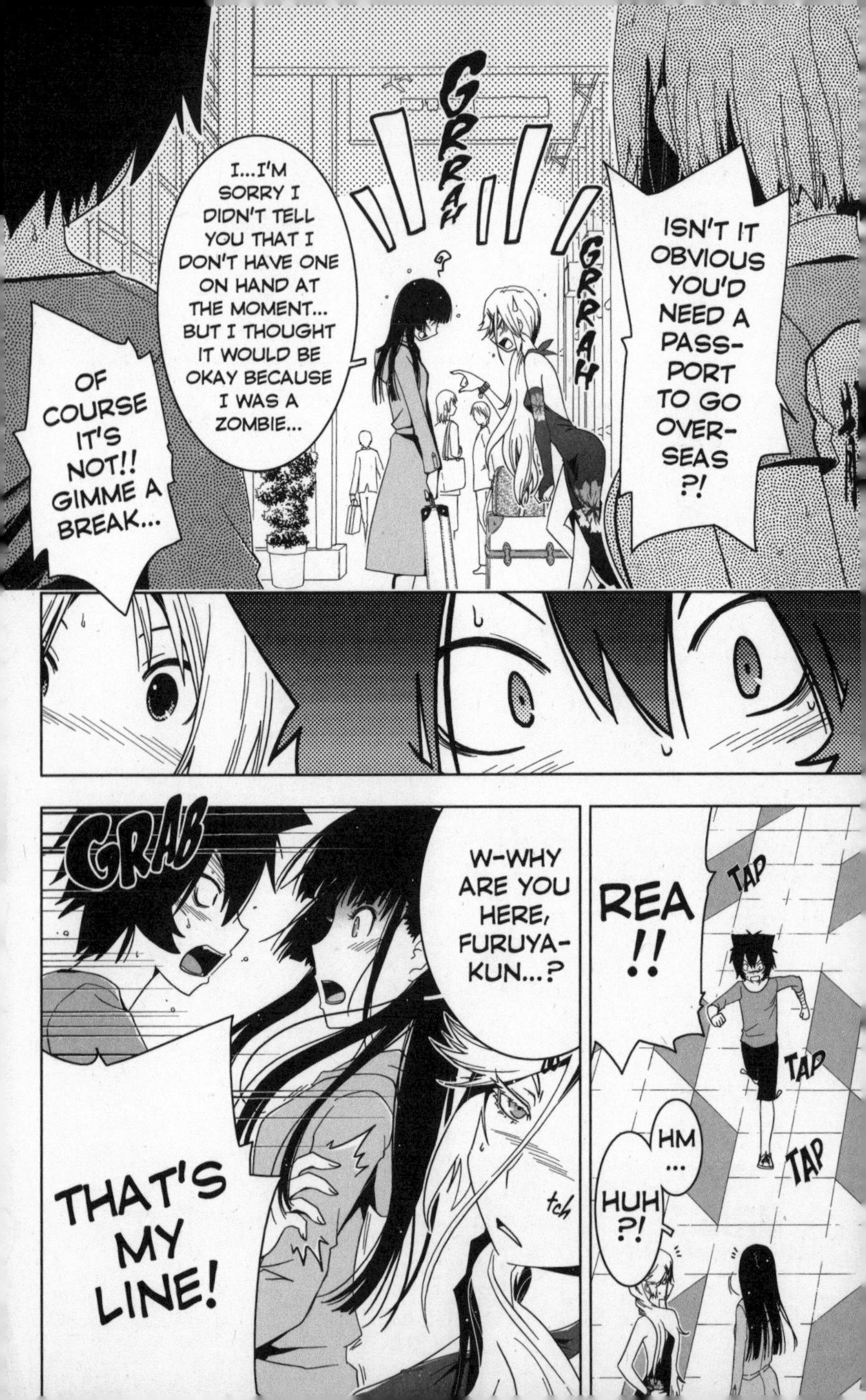
ISN'T IT OBVIOUS YOU'D NEED A PASSPORT TO GO OVERSEAS?!
GRRAH
GRRAH
I...I'M SORRY I DIDN'T TELL YOU THAT I DON'T HAVE ONE ON HAND AT THE MOMENT... BUT I THOUGHT IT WOULD BE OKAY BECAUSE I WAS A ZOMBIE...
OF COURSE IT'S NOT!! GIMME A BREAK...
TAP
REA!!
TAP
TAP
HM...
HUH?!
W-WHY ARE YOU HERE, FURUYA-KUN...?
GRAB
tch
THAT'S MY LINE!

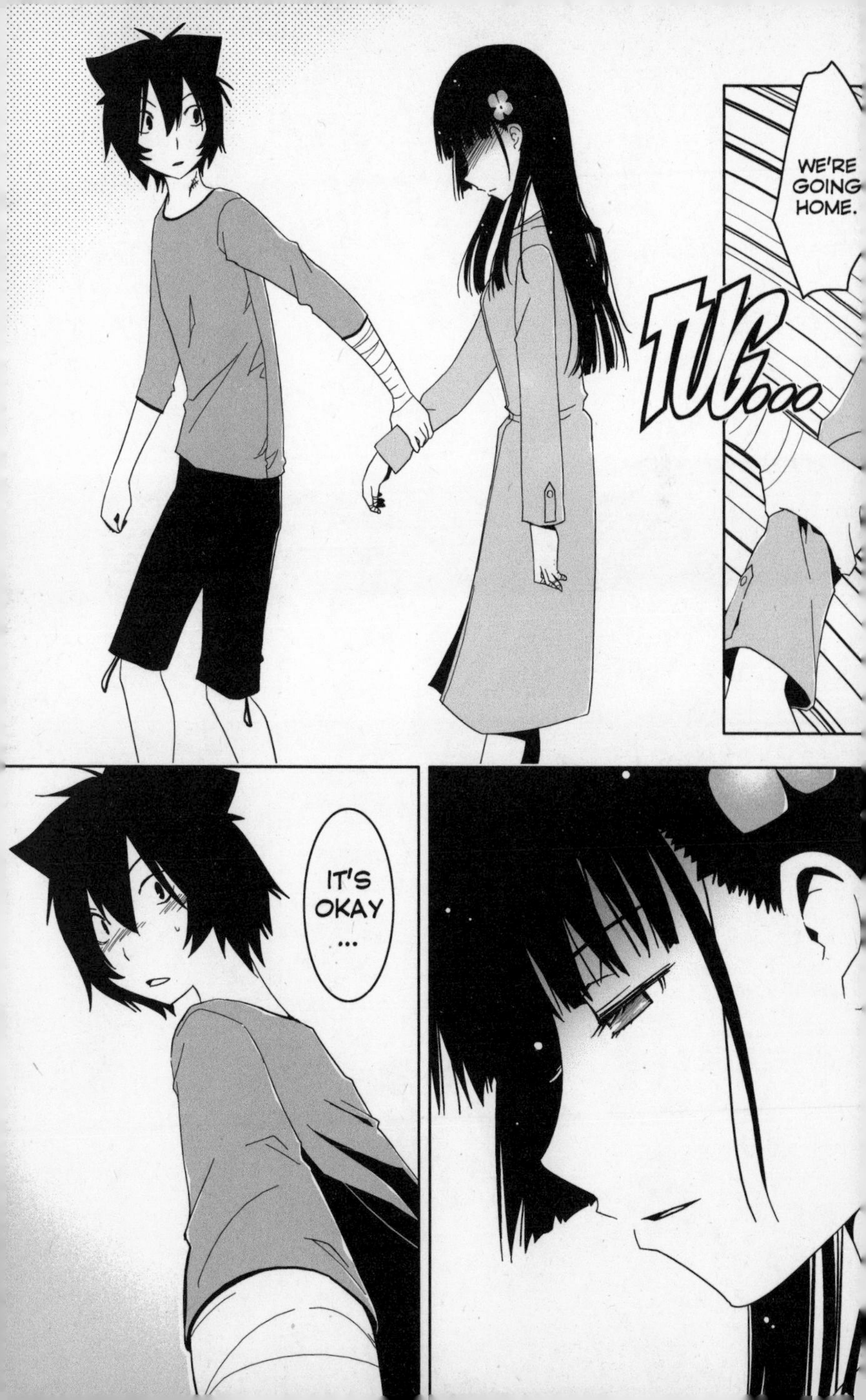
WE'RE GOING HOME.
TUG...
IT'S OKAY ...

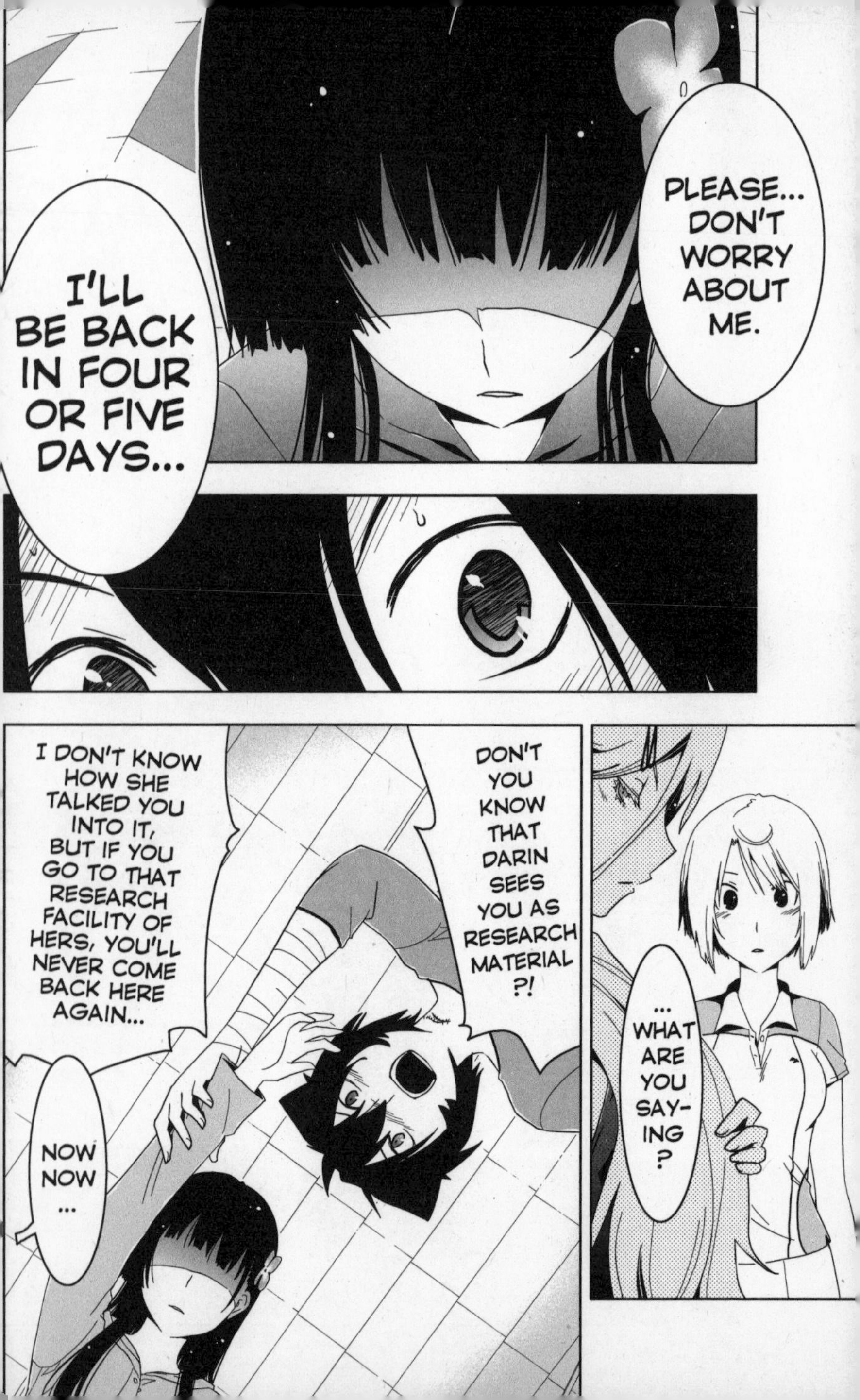
PLEASE... DON'T WORRY ABOUT ME.
I'LL BE BACK IN FOUR OR FIVE DAYS...
...WHAT ARE YOU SAY-ING?
DON'T YOU KNOW THAT DARIN SEES YOU AS RESEARCH MATERIAL?!
I DON'T KNOW HOW SHE TALKED YOU INTO IT, BUT IF YOU GO TO THAT RESEARCH FACILITY OF HERS, YOU'LL NEVER COME BACK HERE AGAIN...
NOW NOW...

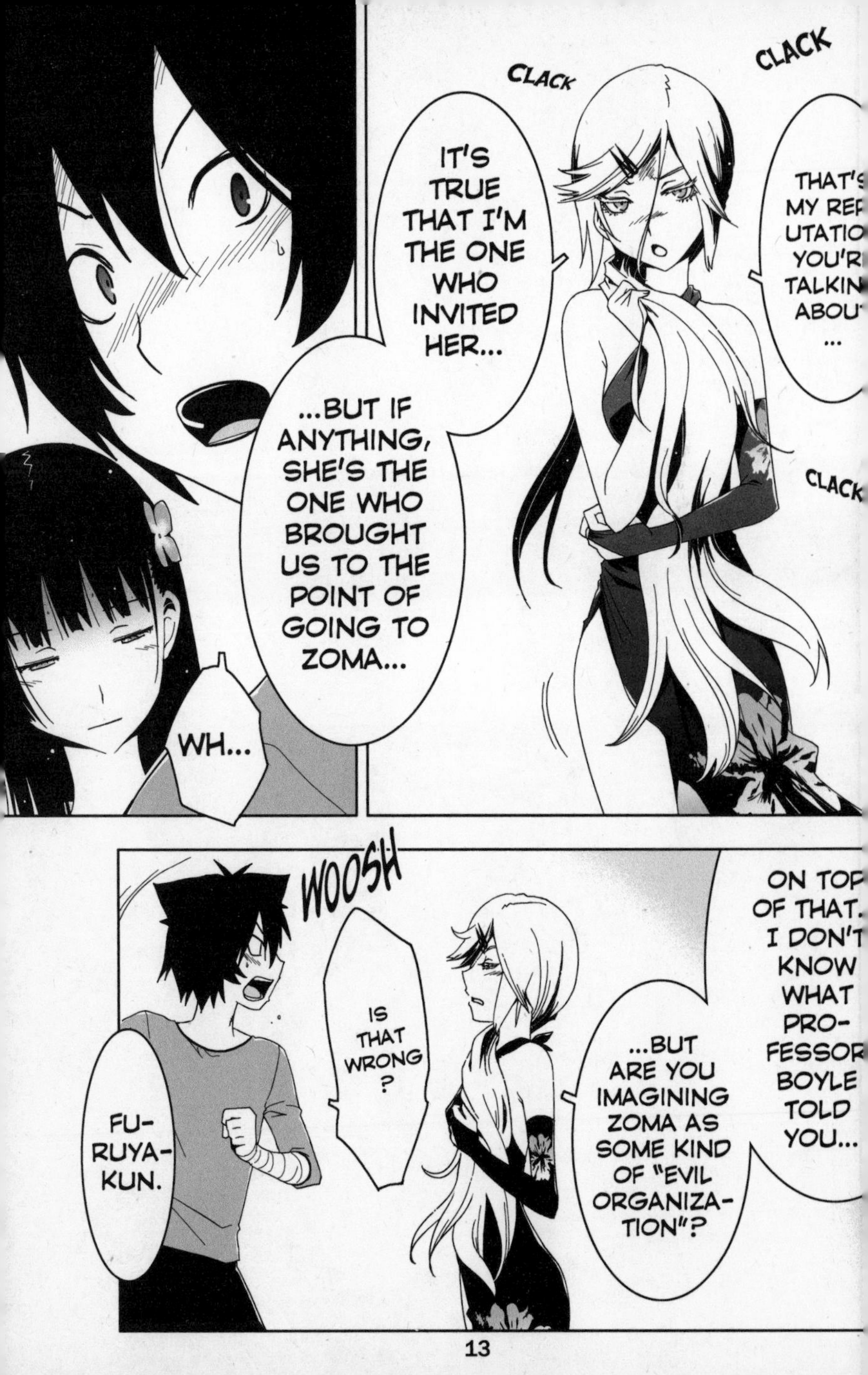
CLACK
CLACK
THAT'S MY REPUTATIO YOU'R TALKIN ABOU ...
IT'S TRUE THAT I'M THE ONE WHO INVITED HER...
...BUT IF ANYTHING, SHE'S THE ONE WHO BROUGHT US TO THE POINT OF GOING TO ZOMA...
CLACK
WH...
ON TOP OF THAT. I DON'T KNOW WHAT PRO-FESSOR BOYLE TOLD YOU...
...BUT ARE YOU IMAGINING ZOMA AS SOME KIND OF "EVIL ORGANIZA-TION"?
WOOSH
IS THAT WRONG?
FU-RUYA-KUN.

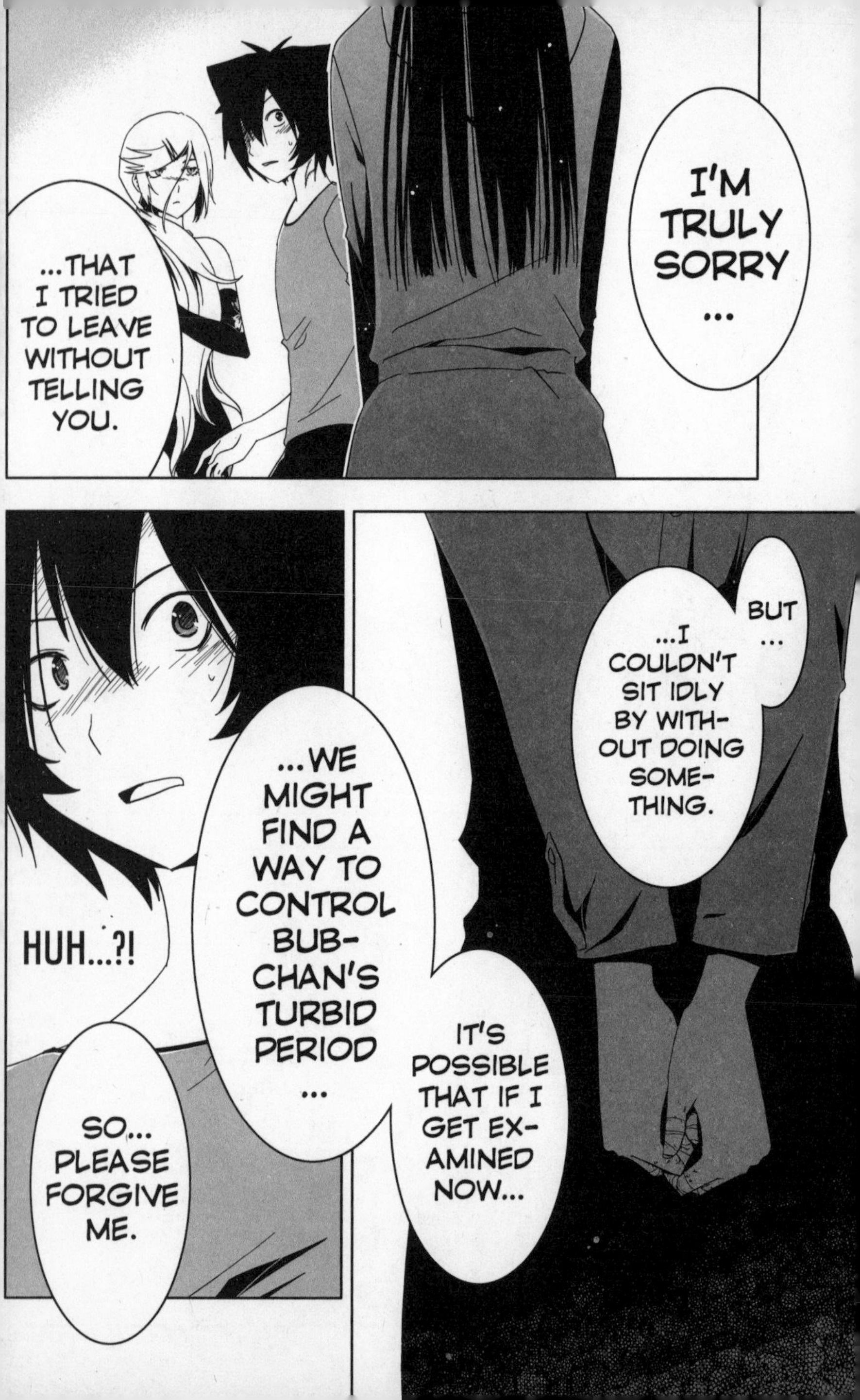

I'M TRULY SORRY ...
...THAT I TRIED TO LEAVE WITHOUT TELLING YOU.
BUT ...
...I COULDN'T SIT IDLY BY WITH-OUT DOING SOME-THING.
IT'S POSSIBLE THAT IF I GET EX-AMINED NOW...
...WE MIGHT FIND A WAY TO CONTROL BUB-CHAN'S TURBID PERIOD ...
SO... PLEASE FORGIVE ME.
HUH...?!

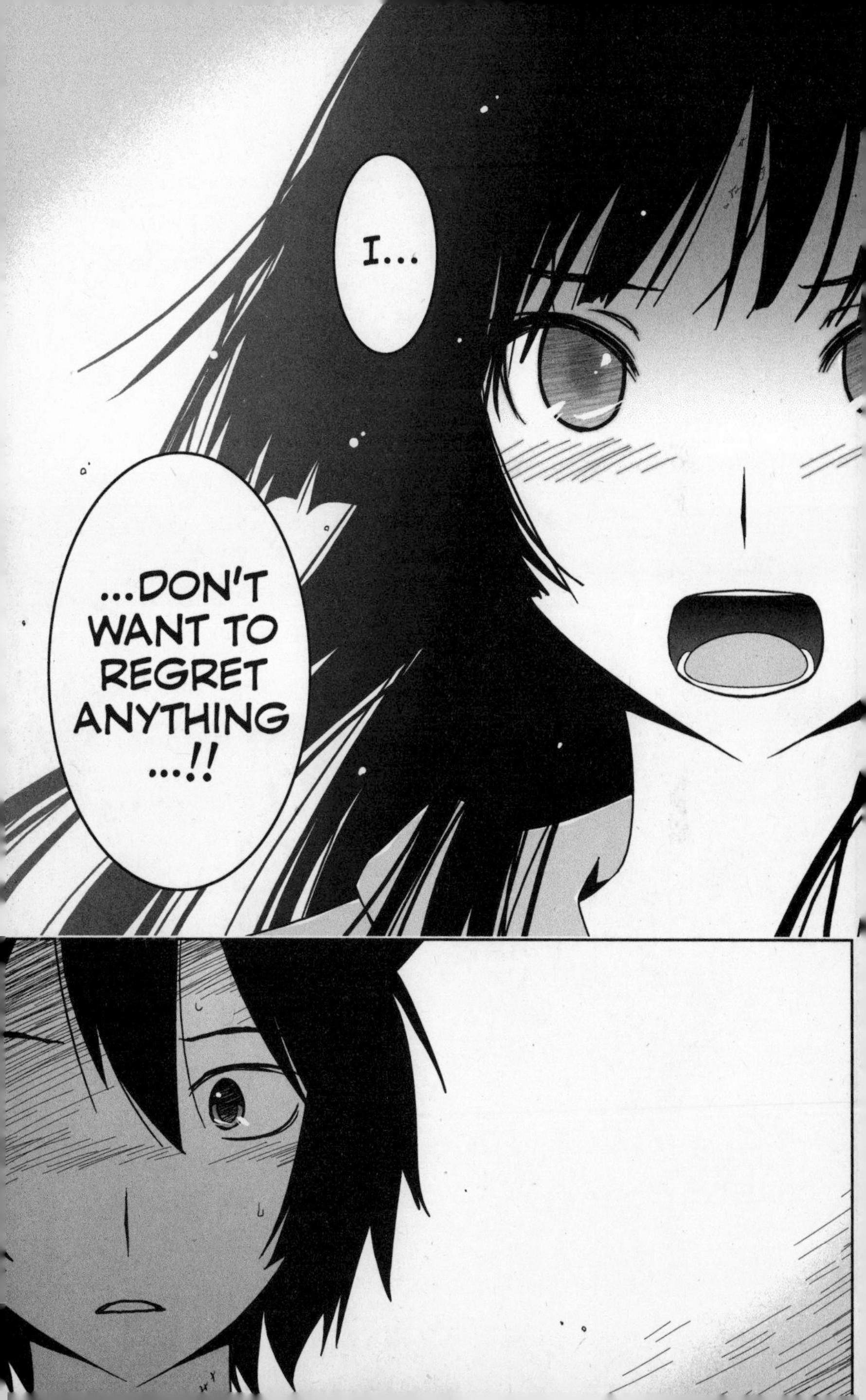
I...
...DON'T WANT TO REGRET ANYTHING ...!!

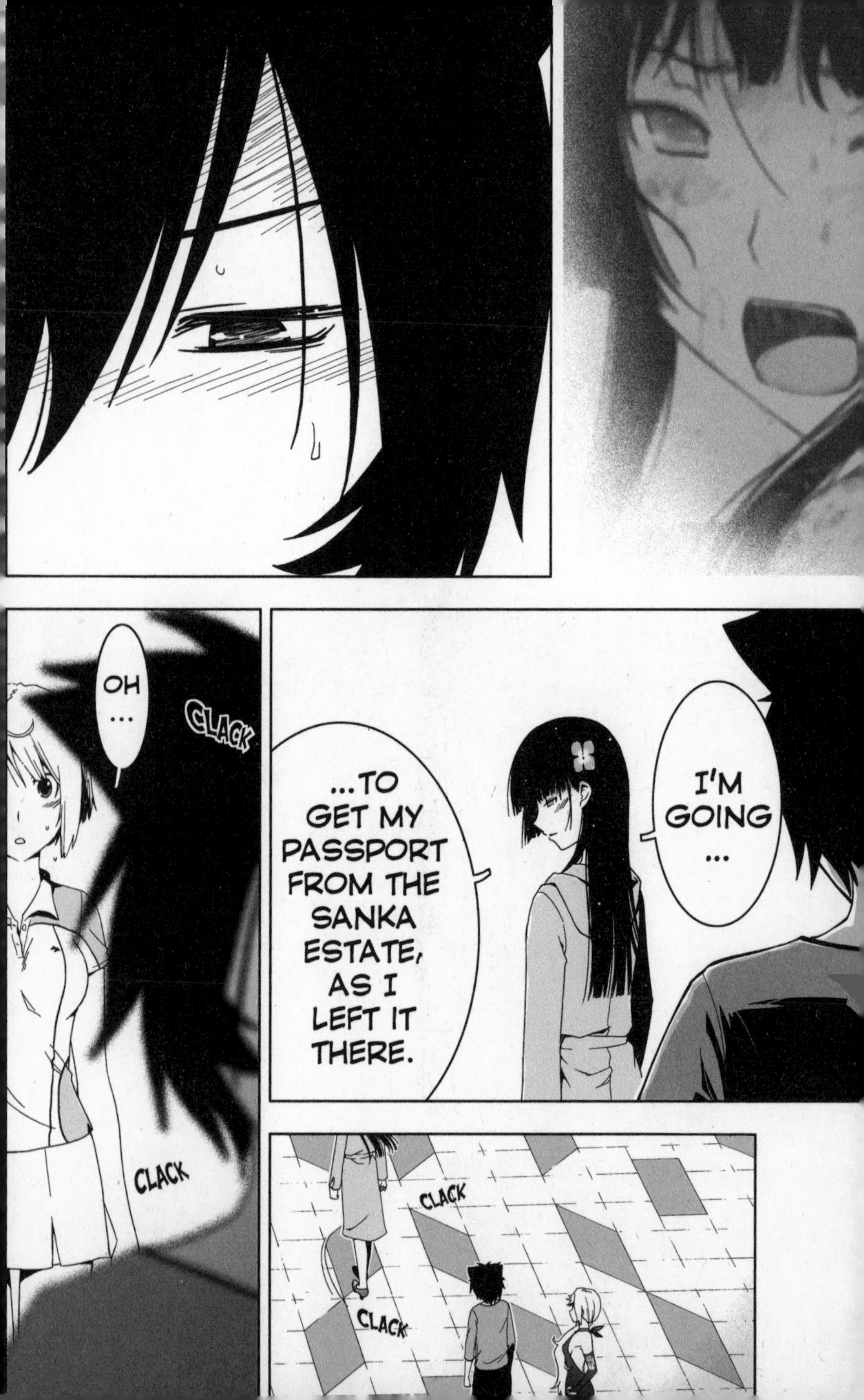
I'M GOING ...
...TO GET MY PASSPORT FROM THE SANKA ESTATE, AS I LEFT IT THERE.
CLACK
CLACK
OH ...
CLACK
CLACK

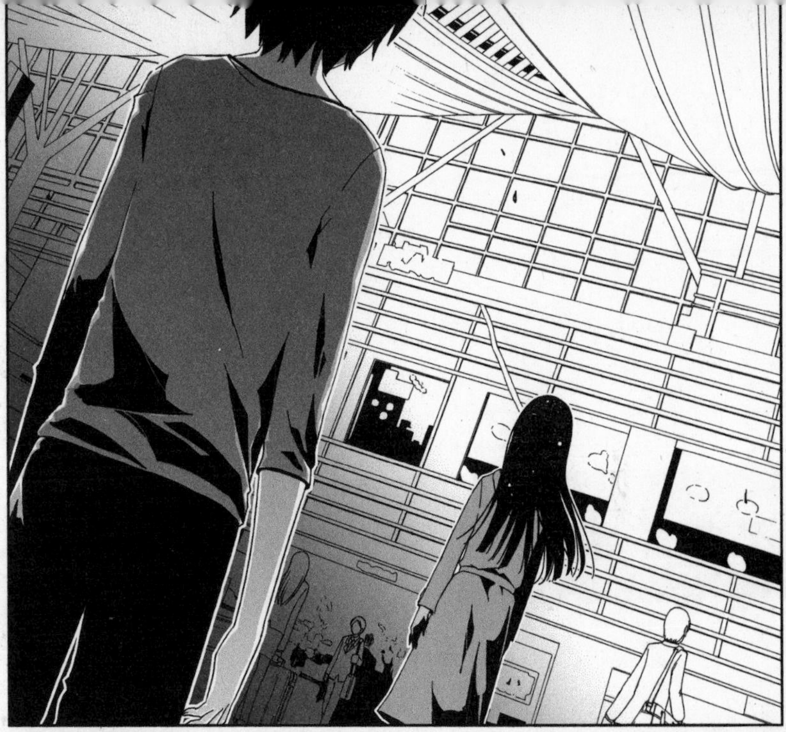
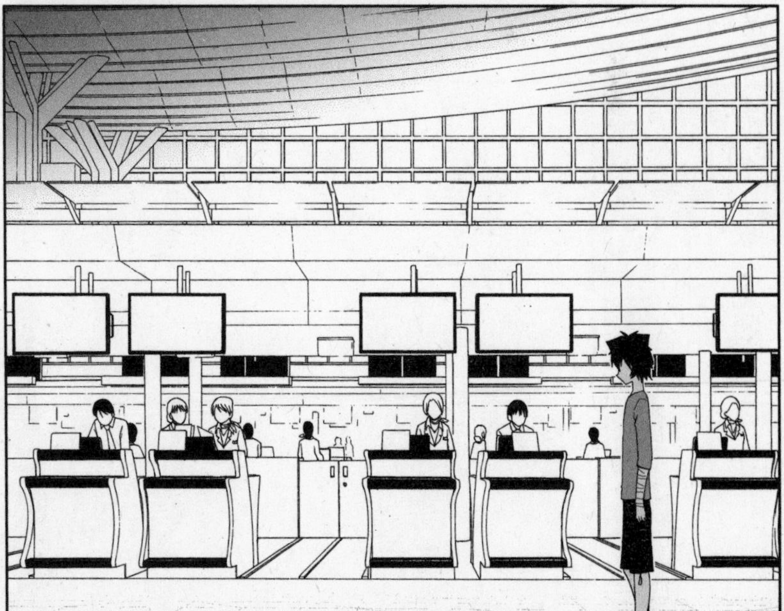

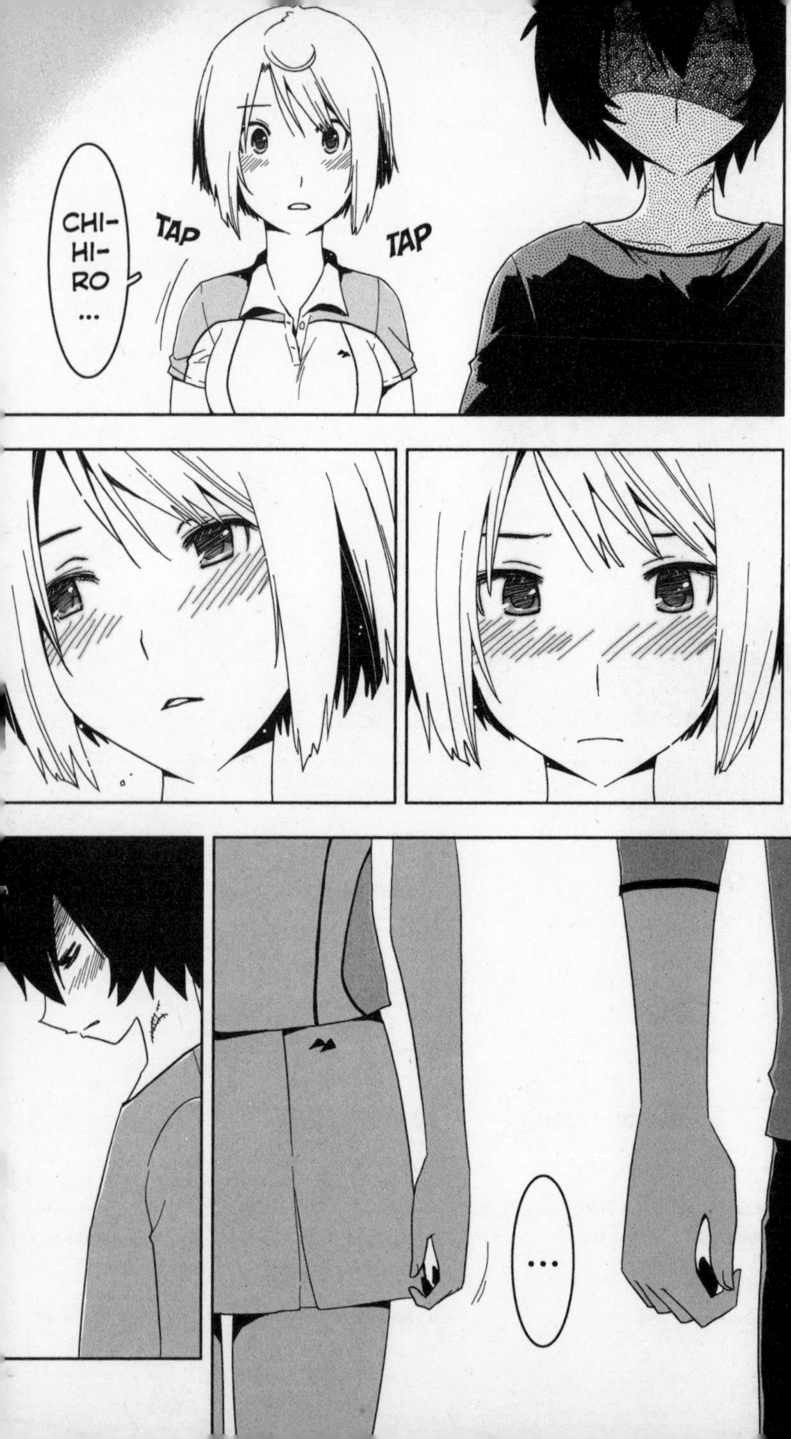
TAP
TAP
CHI-HI-RO ...
...

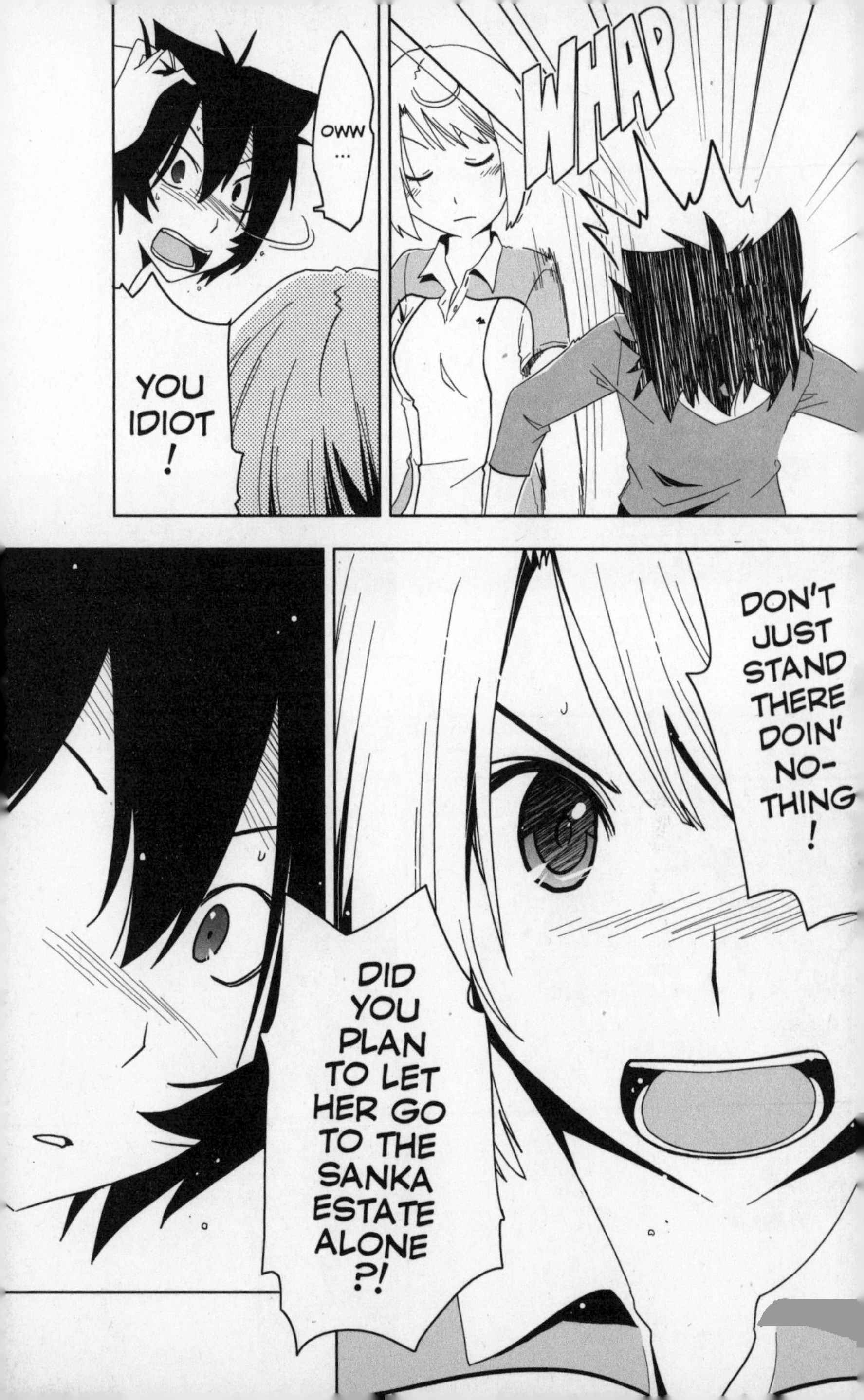
WHAP
OWW ...
YOU IDIOT !
DON'T JUST STAND THERE DOIN' NO-THING !
DID YOU PLAN TO LET HER GO TO THE SANKA ESTATE ALONE ?!

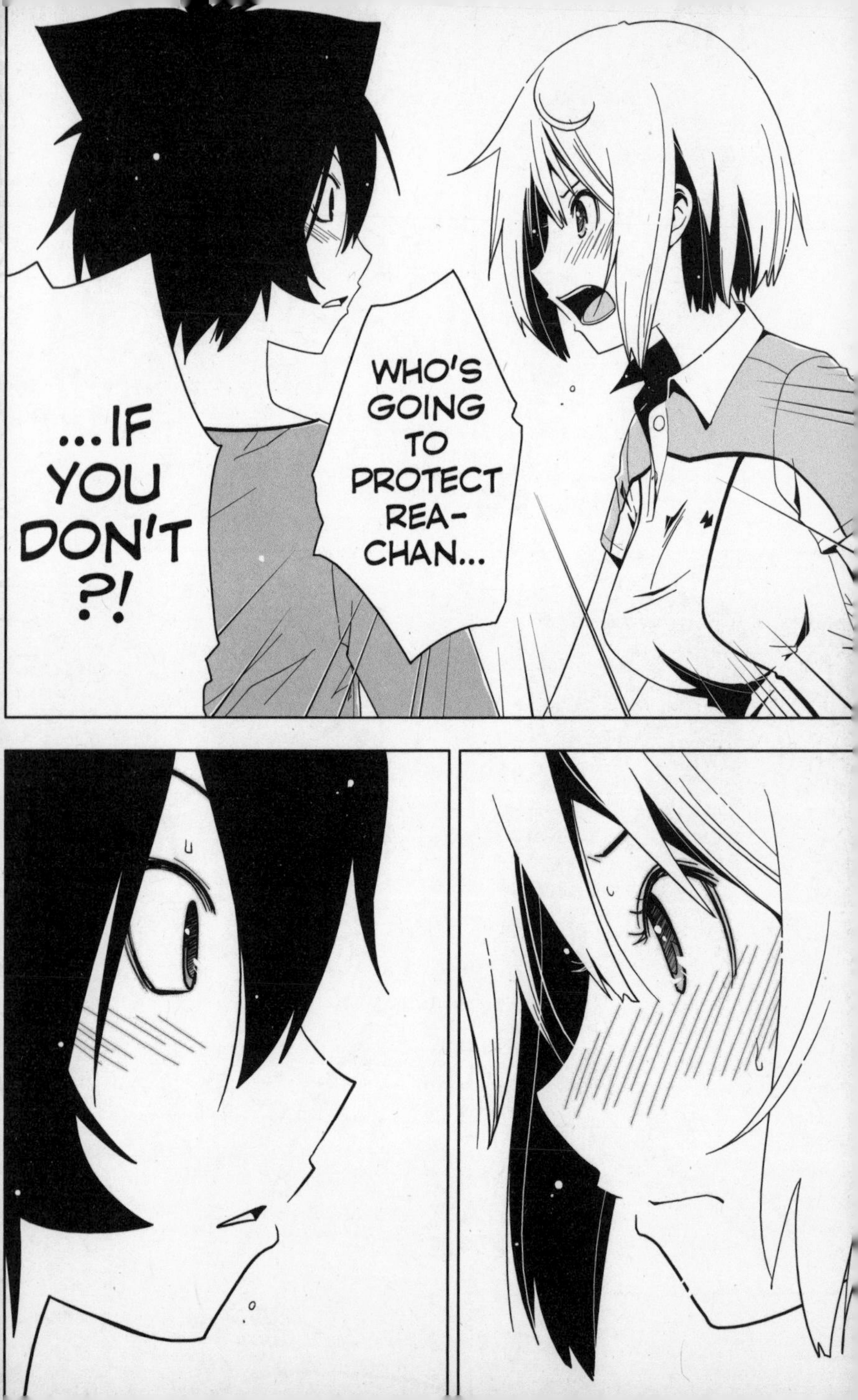
WHO'S GOING TO PROTECT REA-CHAN...
...IF YOU DON'T?!

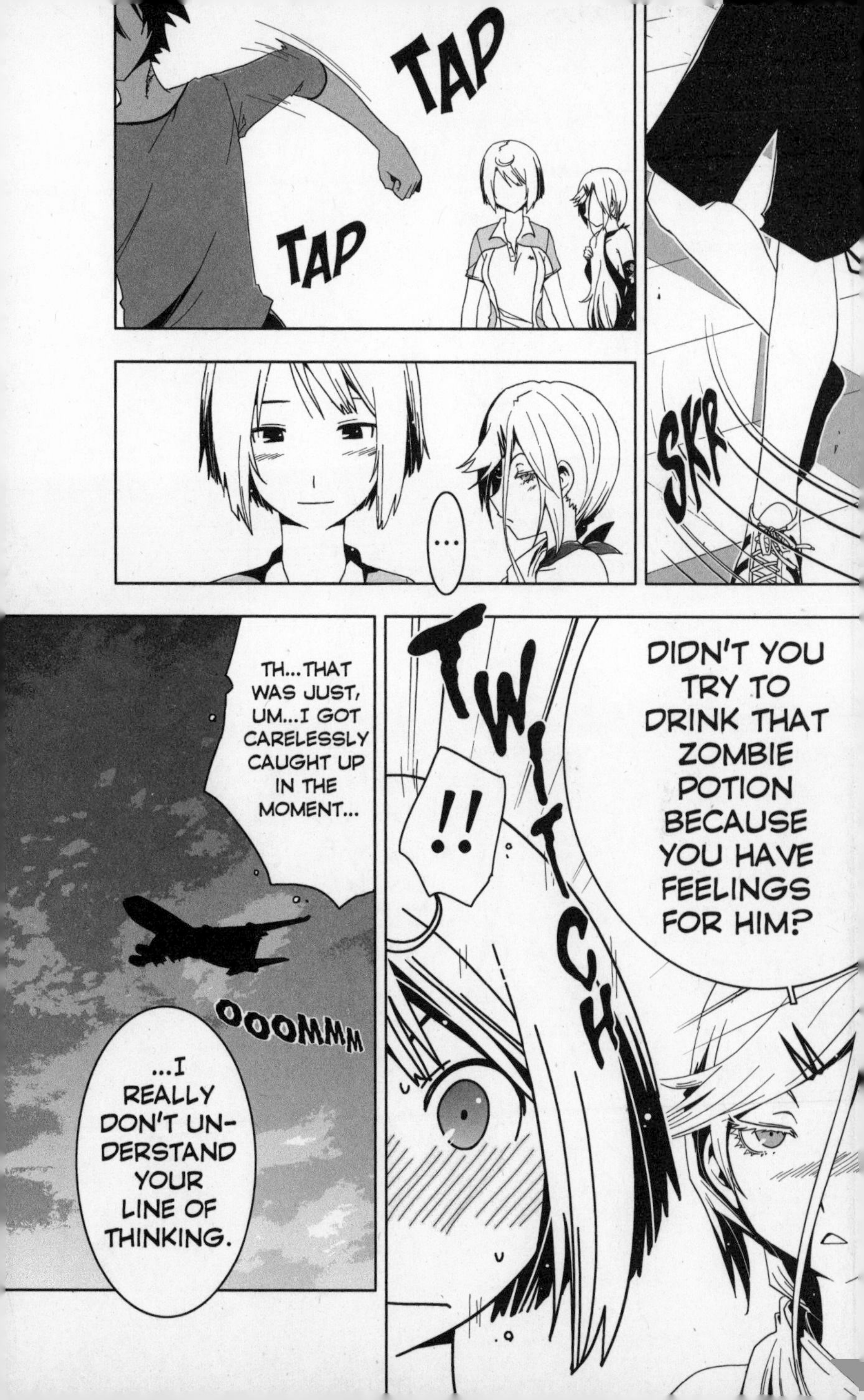
SKR
TAP
TAP
...
DIDN'T YOU TRY TO DRINK THAT ZOMBIE POTION BECAUSE YOU HAVE FEELINGS FOR HIM?
TWITCH
!!
TH...THAT WAS JUST, UM...I GOT CARELESSLY CAUGHT UP IN THE MOMENT...
OOOMMM
...I REALLY DON'T UN-DERSTAND YOUR LINE OF THINKING.

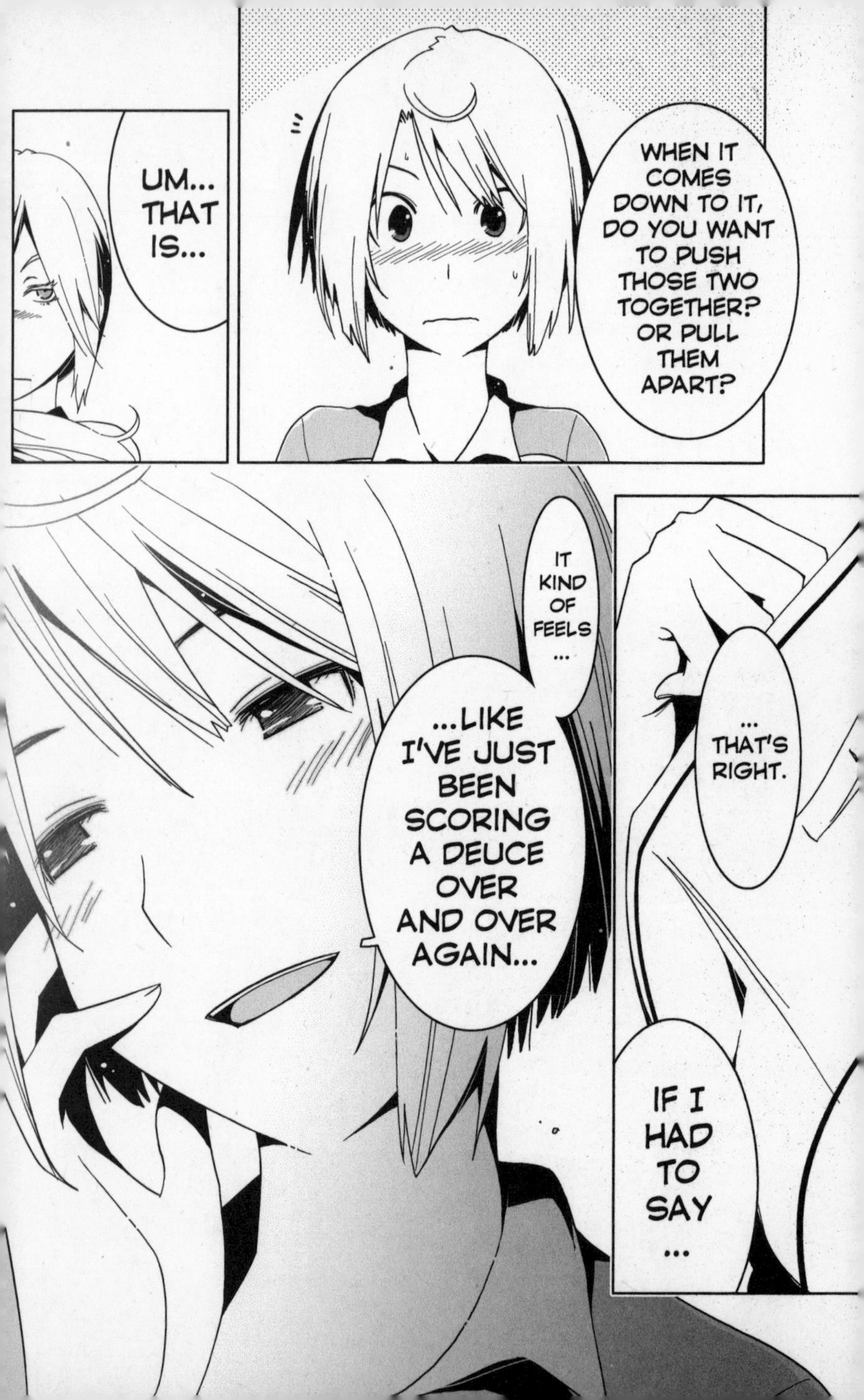
WHEN IT COMES DOWN TO IT, DO YOU WANT TO PUSH THOSE TWO TOGETHER? OR PULL THEM APART?
UM... THAT IS...
... THAT'S RIGHT.
IF I HAD TO SAY ...
IT KIND OF FEELS ...
...LIKE I'VE JUST BEEN SCORING A DEUCE OVER AND OVER AGAIN...

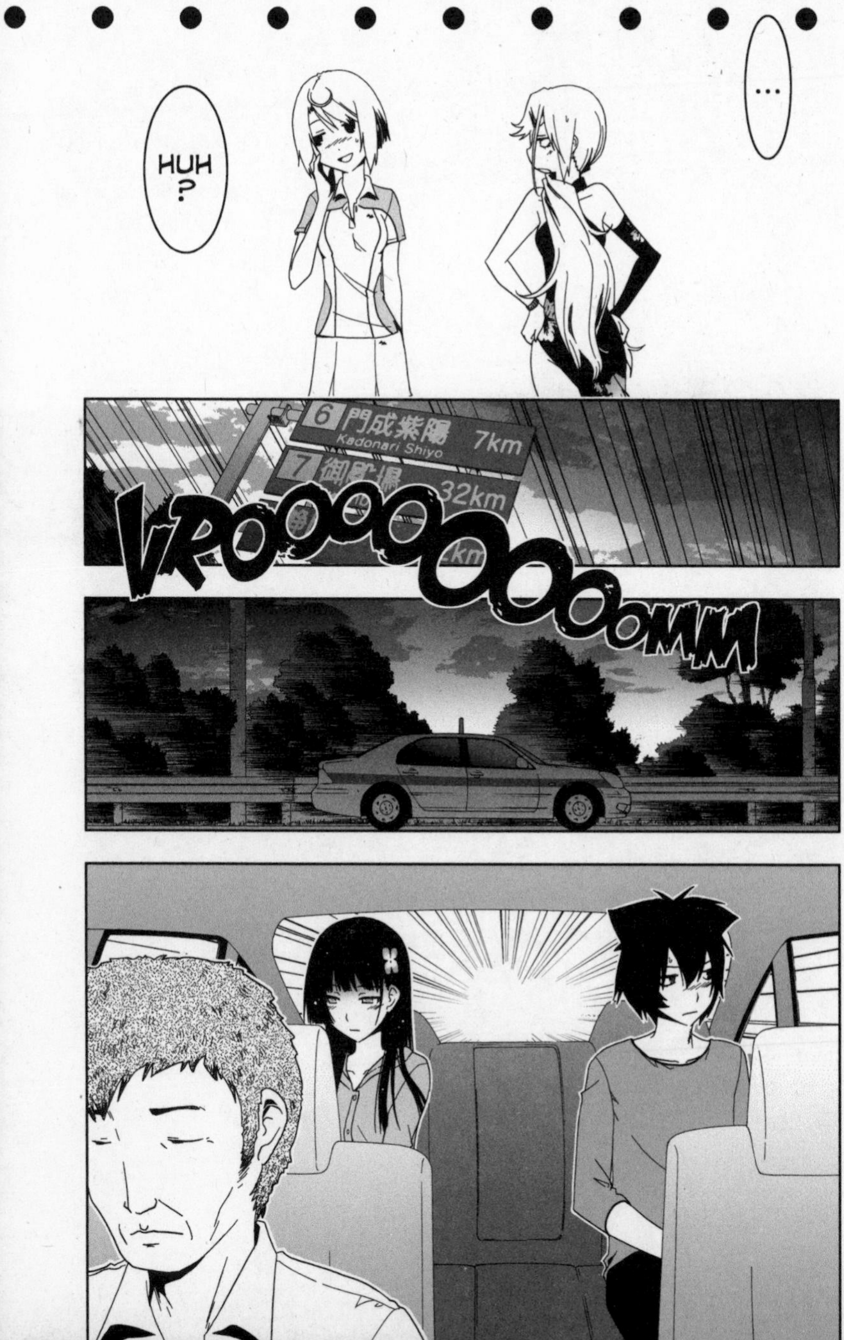
...
HUH ?
6 門成紫陽
Kadonari Shiyo
7km
7
32km
VROOOOOOOOOOOMM

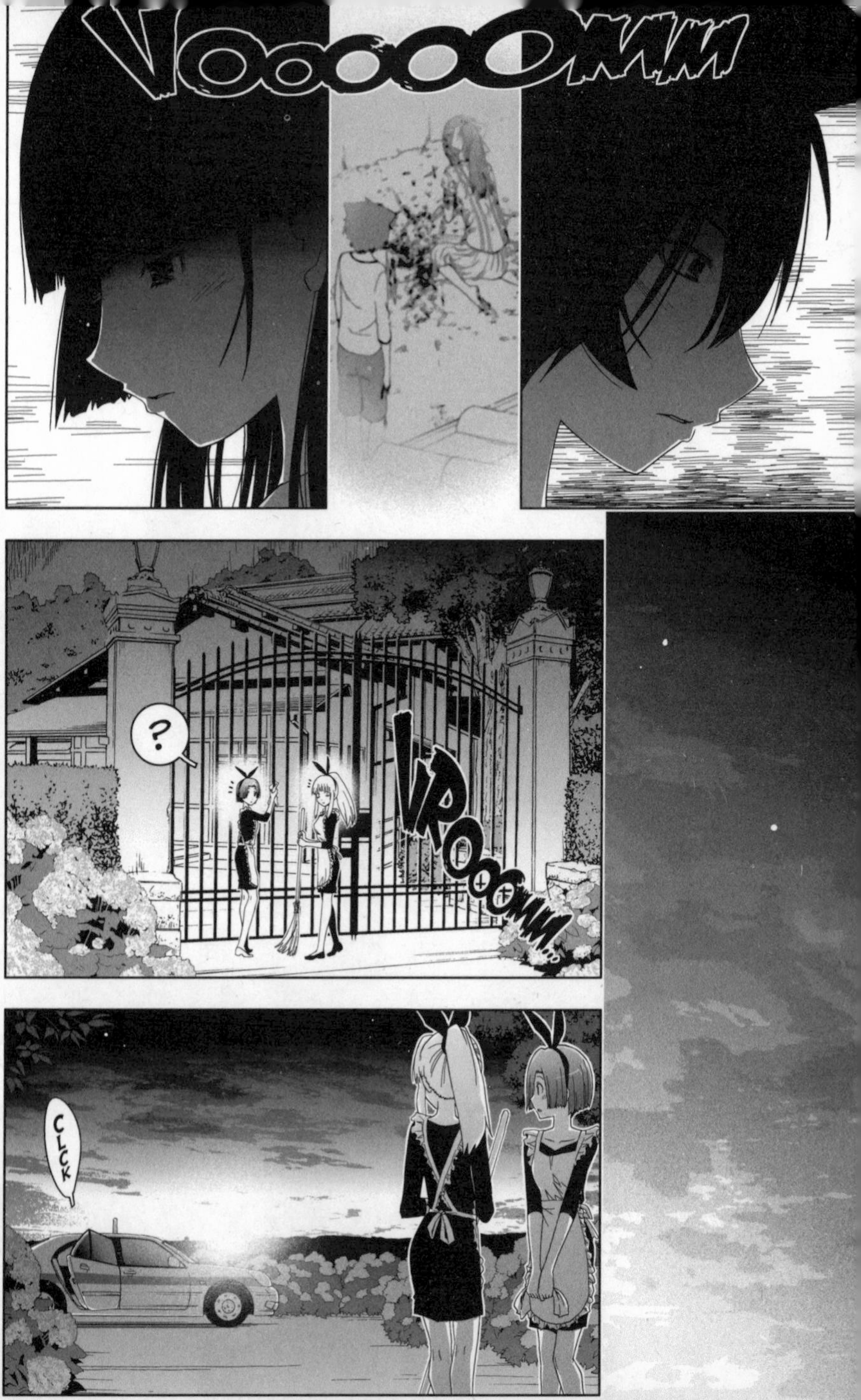
VOOOOOMMM
VROOOOMM...
?
CLCK

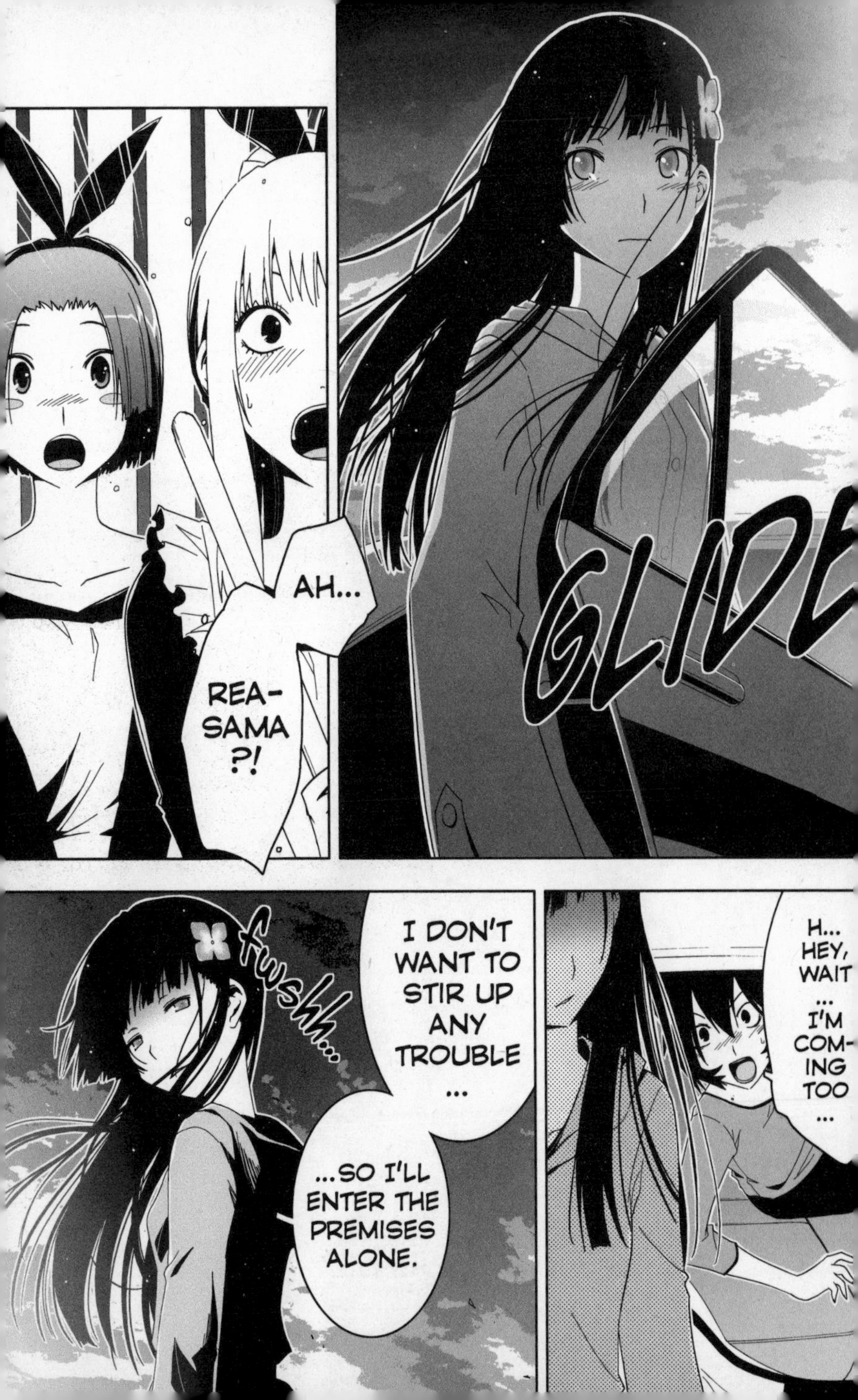
GLIDE
AH...
REA-SAMA?!
H... HEY, WAIT ... I'M COMING TOO ...
fushh...
I DON'T WANT TO STIR UP ANY TROUBLE ...
...SO I'LL ENTER THE PREMISES ALONE.

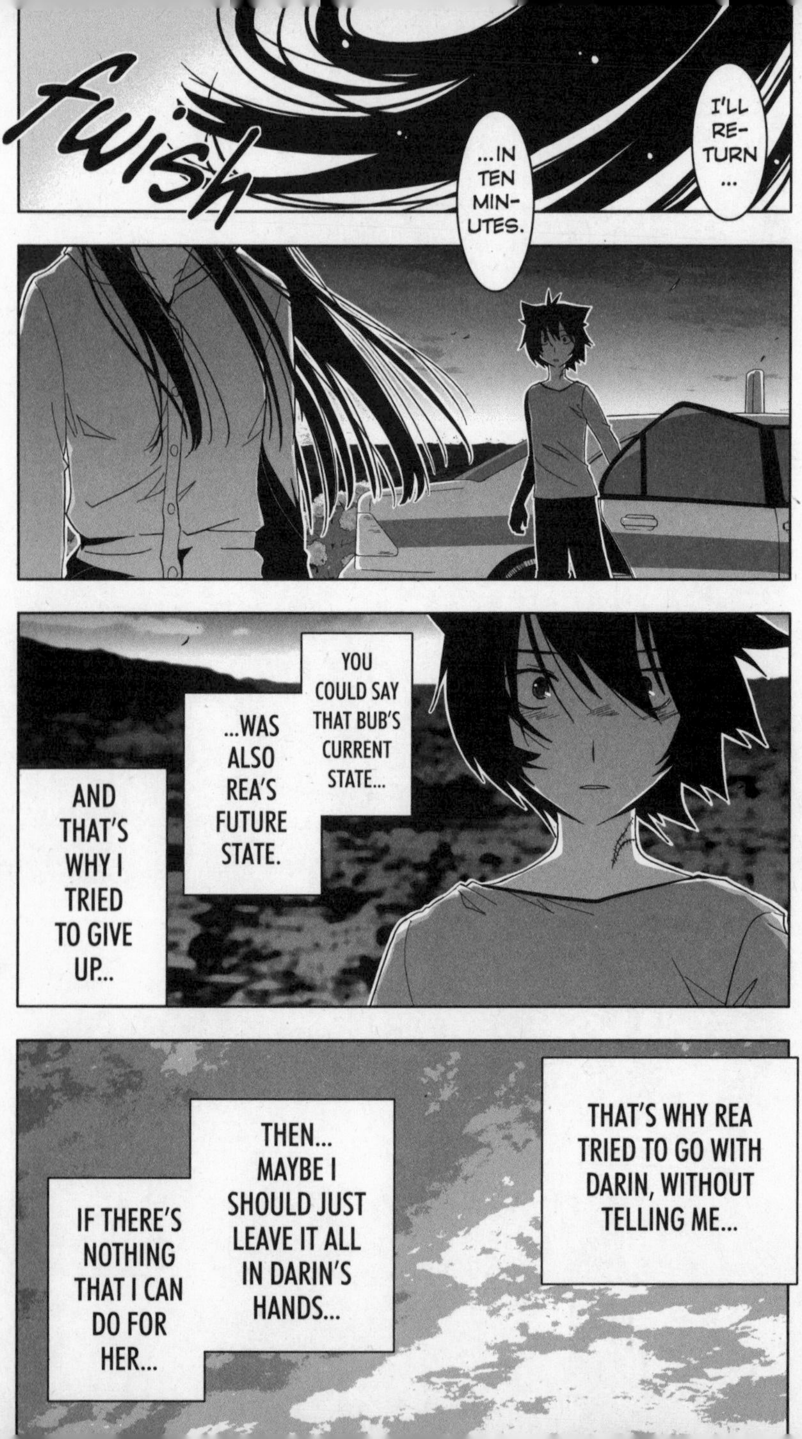
I'LL RE-TURN ...
...IN TEN MIN-UTES.
fwish
YOU COULD SAY THAT BUB'S CURRENT STATE...
...WAS ALSO REA'S FUTURE STATE.
AND THAT'S WHY I TRIED TO GIVE UP...
THAT'S WHY REA TRIED TO GO WITH DARIN, WITHOUT TELLING ME...
THEN... MAYBE I SHOULD JUST LEAVE IT ALL IN DARIN'S HANDS...
IF THERE'S NOTHING THAT I CAN DO FOR HER...

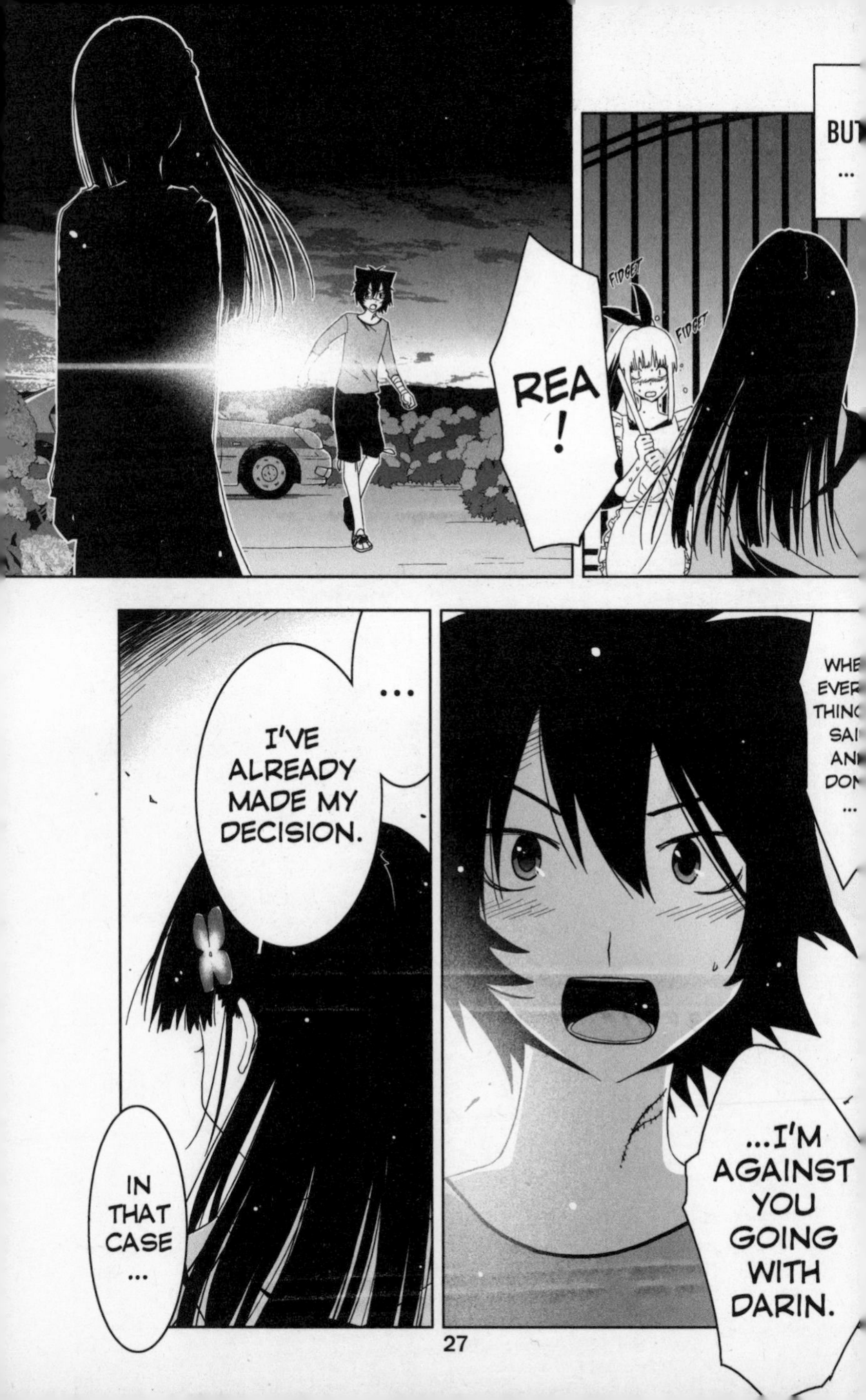
BUT ...
REA!
FIDGET
FIDGET
WHE EVER THING SAI AN DON ...
...I'M AGAINST YOU GOING WITH DARIN.
... I'VE ALREADY MADE MY DECISION.
IN THAT CASE ...

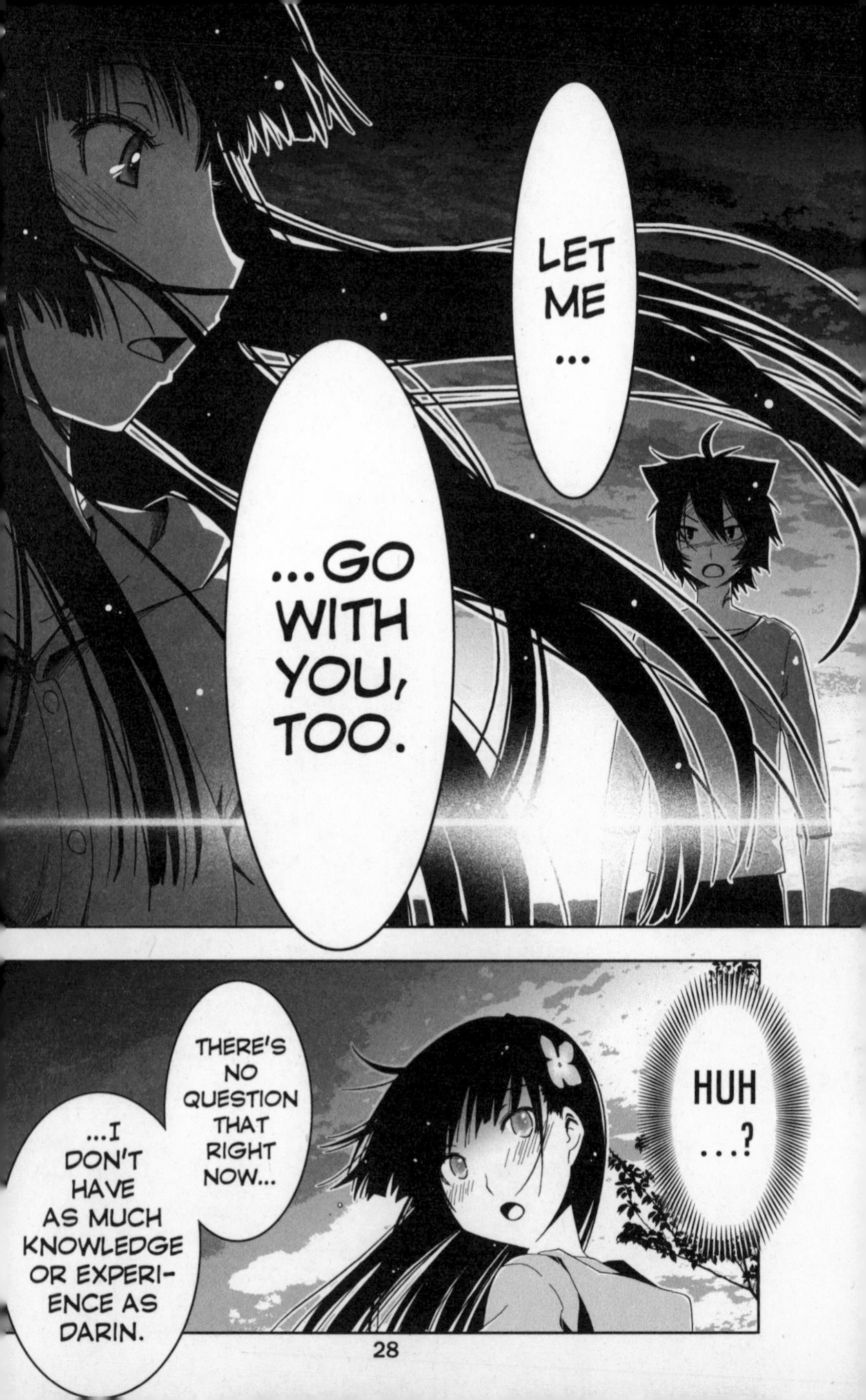
LET ME...
...GO WITH YOU, TOO.
HUH ...?
THERE'S NO QUESTION THAT RIGHT NOW...
...I DON'T HAVE AS MUCH KNOWLEDGE OR EXPERIENCE AS DARIN.

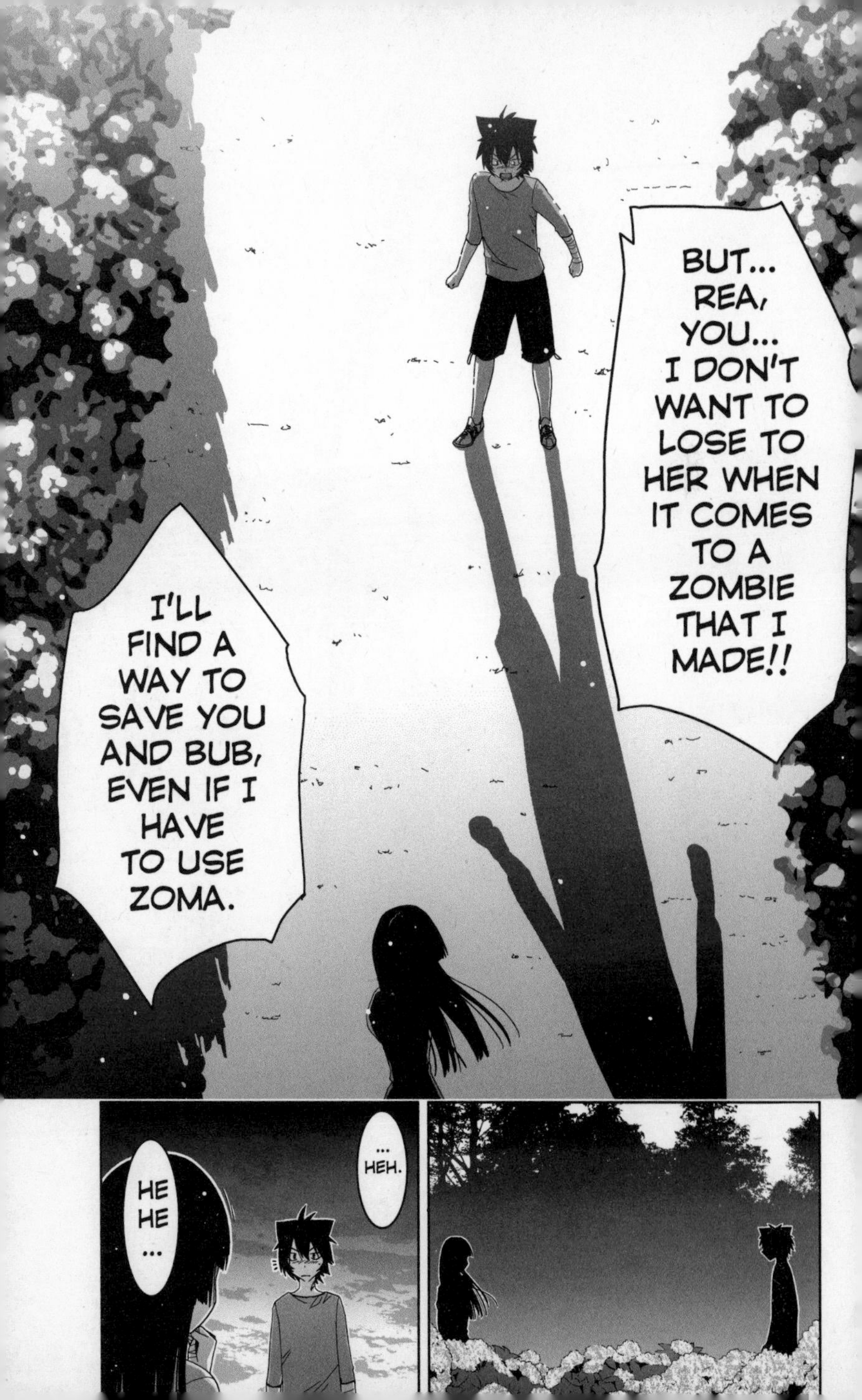
BUT... REA, YOU... I DON'T WANT TO LOSE TO HER WHEN IT COMES TO A ZOMBIE THAT I MADE!!
I'LL FIND A WAY TO SAVE YOU AND BUB, EVEN IF I HAVE TO USE ZOMA.
...HEH.
HE HE ...

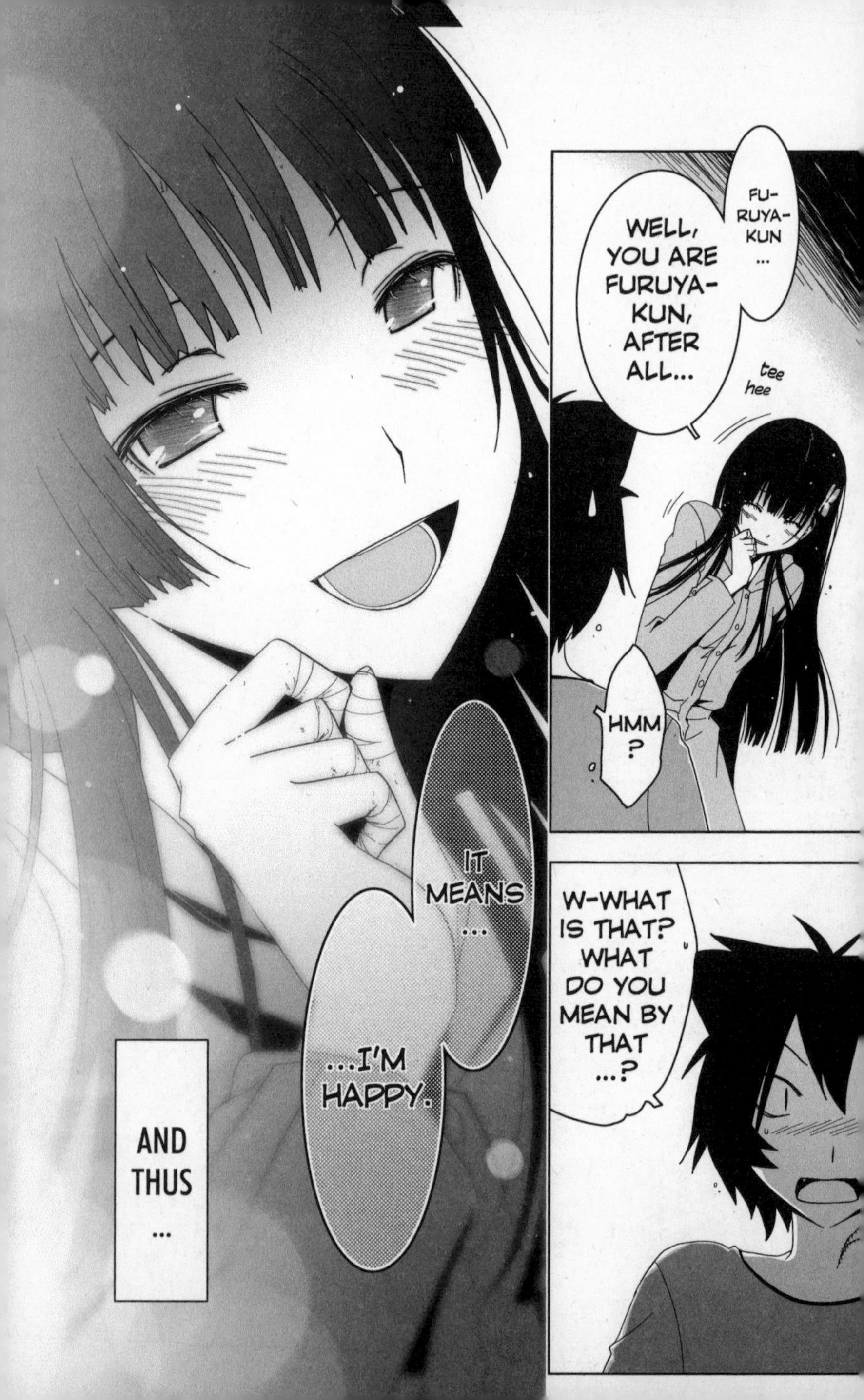
FU-RUYA-KUN ...
WELL, YOU ARE FURUYA-KUN, AFTER ALL...
tee hee
HMM?
W-WHAT IS THAT? WHAT DO YOU MEAN BY THAT ...?
IT MEANS ...
...I'M HAPPY.
AND THUS ...

...WITH A SLIGHT SENSE OF UNEASE, I TRAVELED TO ZOMA, THE PLACE WHERE...
...I...
...WOULD END UP LOSING SOME-THING...
plip
...VERY PRECIOUS.

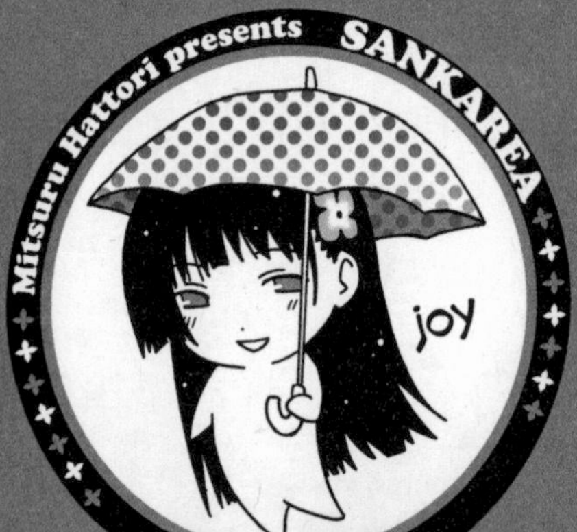
Mitsuru Hattori presents
SANKAREA
joy

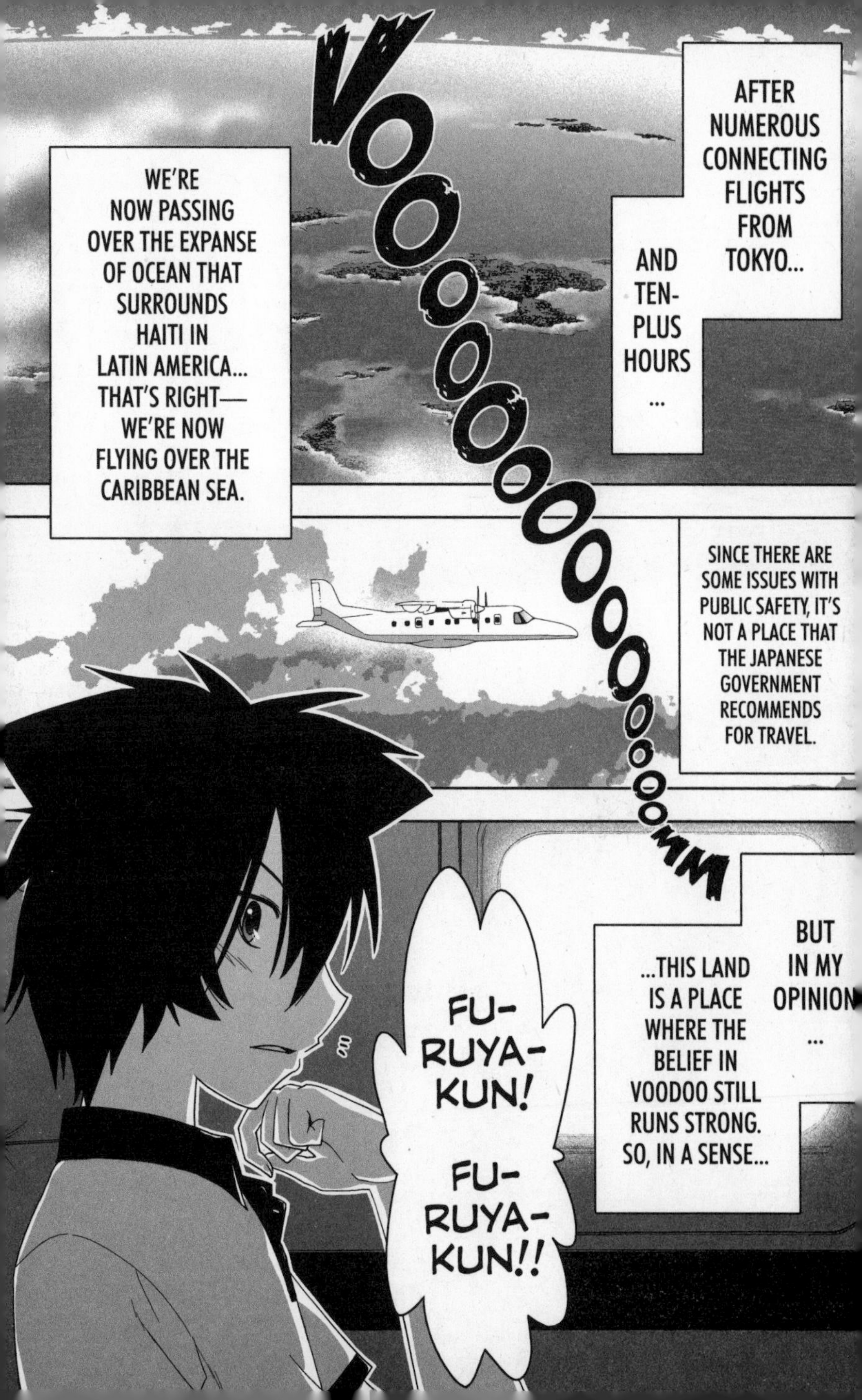

AFTER NUMEROUS CONNECTING FLIGHTS FROM TOKYO...
AND TEN-PLUS HOURS ...
WE'RE NOW PASSING OVER THE EXPANSE OF OCEAN THAT SURROUNDS HAITI IN LATIN AMERICA... THAT'S RIGHT— WE'RE NOW FLYING OVER THE CARIBBEAN SEA.
VOOOOOOOOOOOOOOOOOOOMM
SINCE THERE ARE SOME ISSUES WITH PUBLIC SAFETY, IT'S NOT A PLACE THAT THE JAPANESE GOVERNMENT RECOMMENDS FOR TRAVEL.
BUT IN MY OPINION ...
...THIS LAND IS A PLACE WHERE THE BELIEF IN VOODOO STILL RUNS STRONG. SO, IN A SENSE...
FU-RUYA-KUN!
FU-RUYA-KUN!!
...!

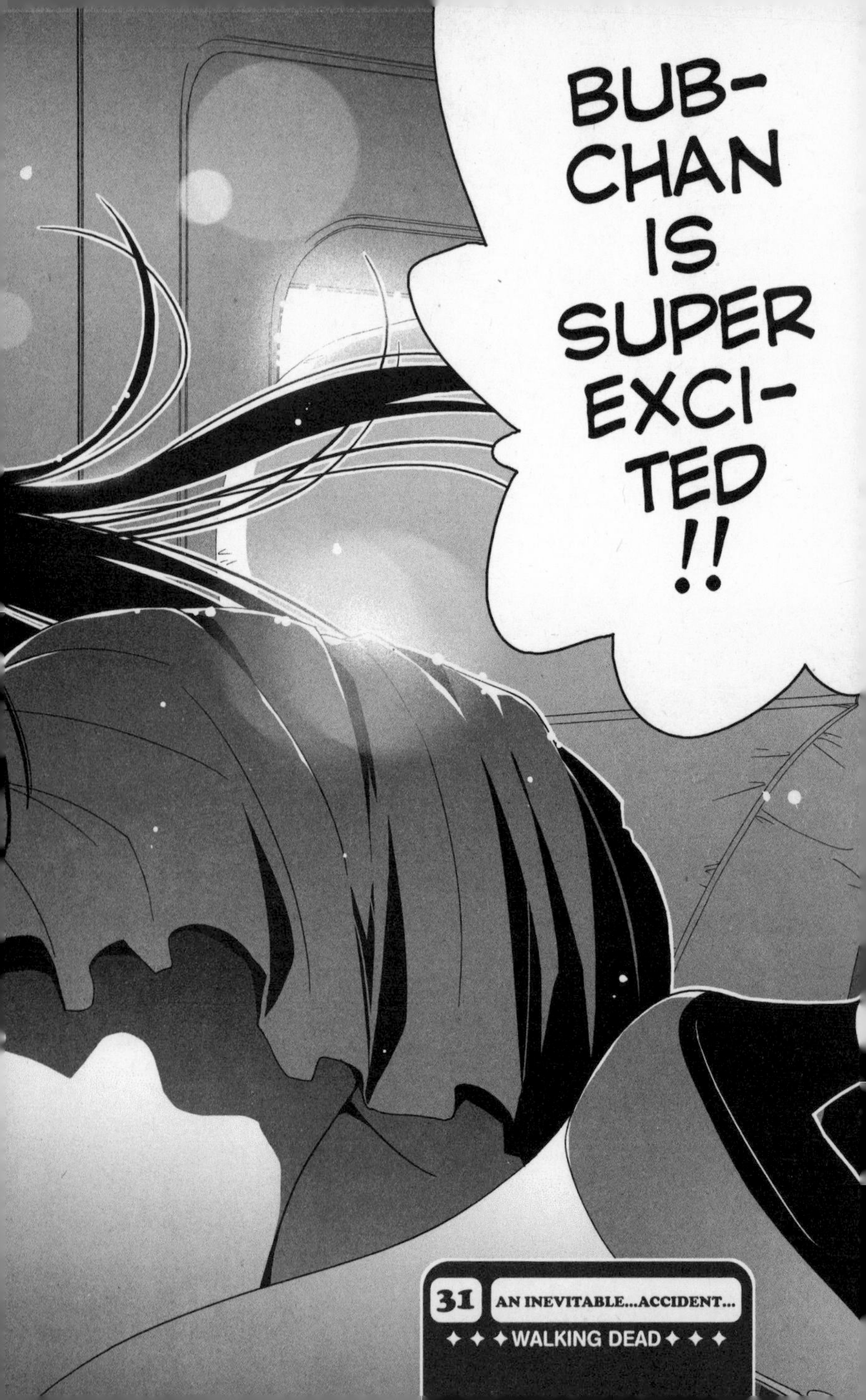
BUB-CHAN IS SUPER EXCI-TED!!
31 AN INEVITABLE...ACCIDENT...
✦✦✦WALKING DEAD✦✦✦

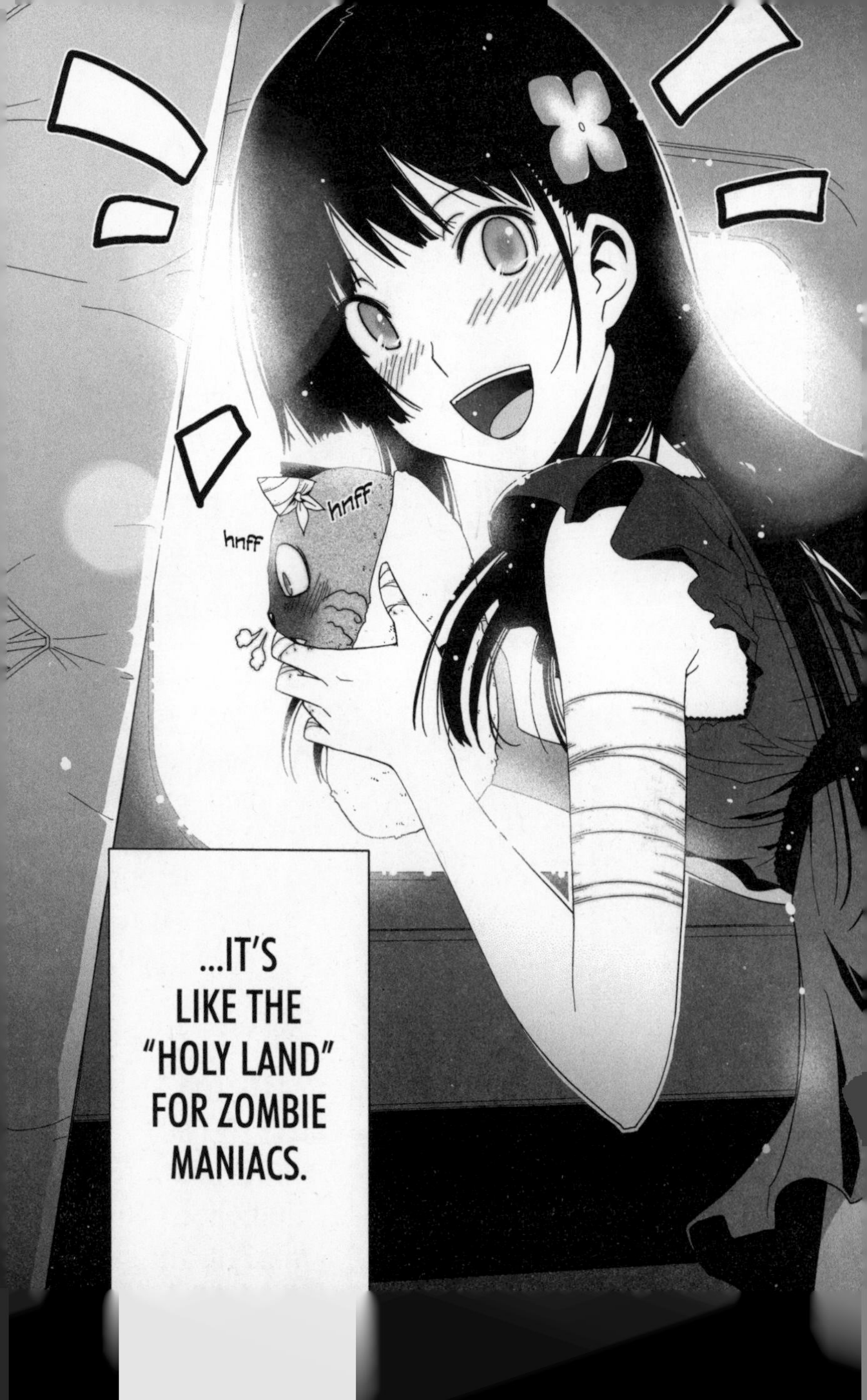
hnff
hnff
...IT'S LIKE THE "HOLY LAND" FOR ZOMBIE MANIACS.

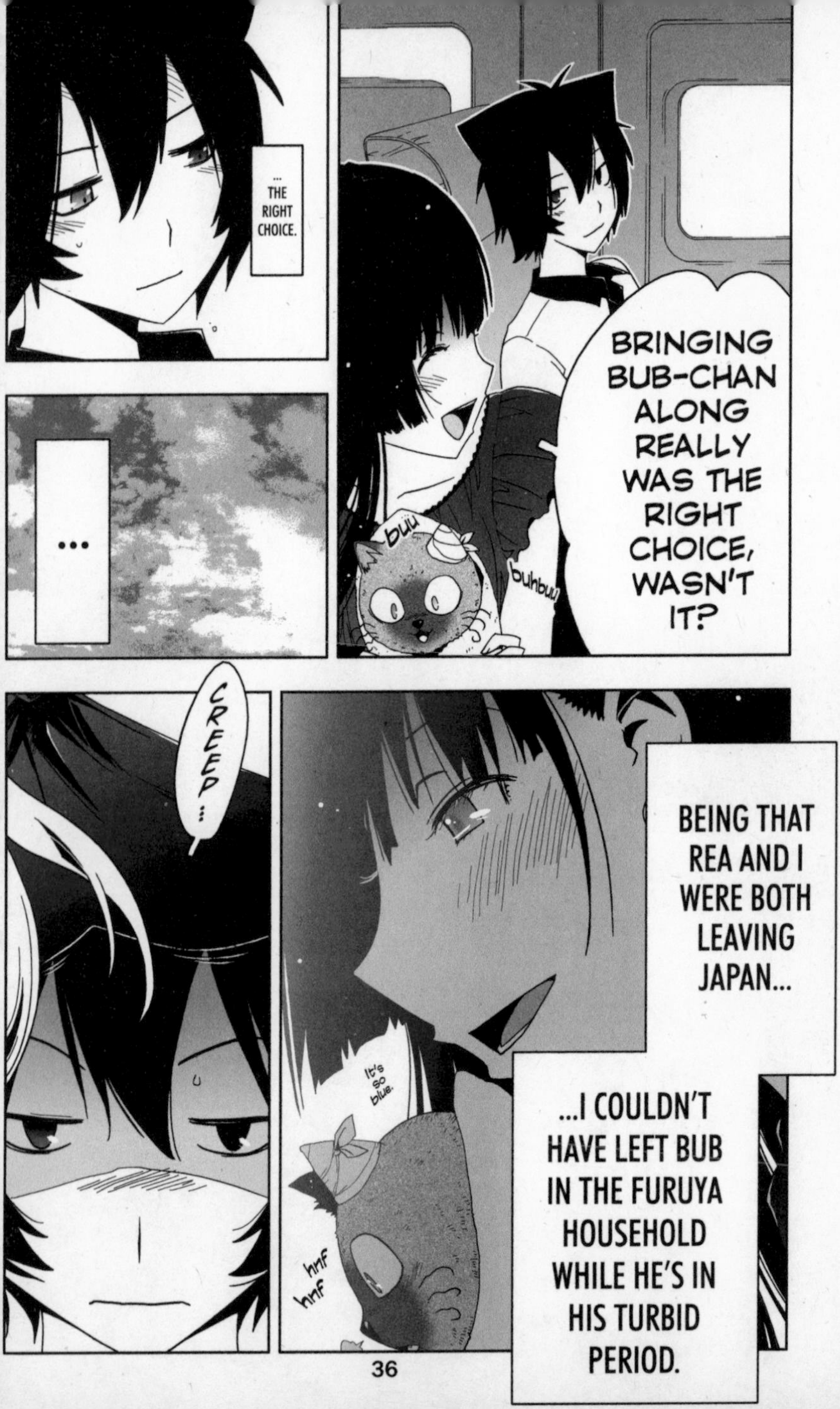
buu
buhbuu
BRINGING BUB-CHAN ALONG REALLY WAS THE RIGHT CHOICE, WASN'T IT?
... THE RIGHT CHOICE.
...
BEING THAT REA AND I WERE BOTH LEAVING JAPAN...
It's so blue.
...I COULDN'T HAVE LEFT BUB IN THE FURUYA HOUSEHOLD WHILE HE'S IN HIS TURBID PERIOD.
hnf hnf
CREEP...

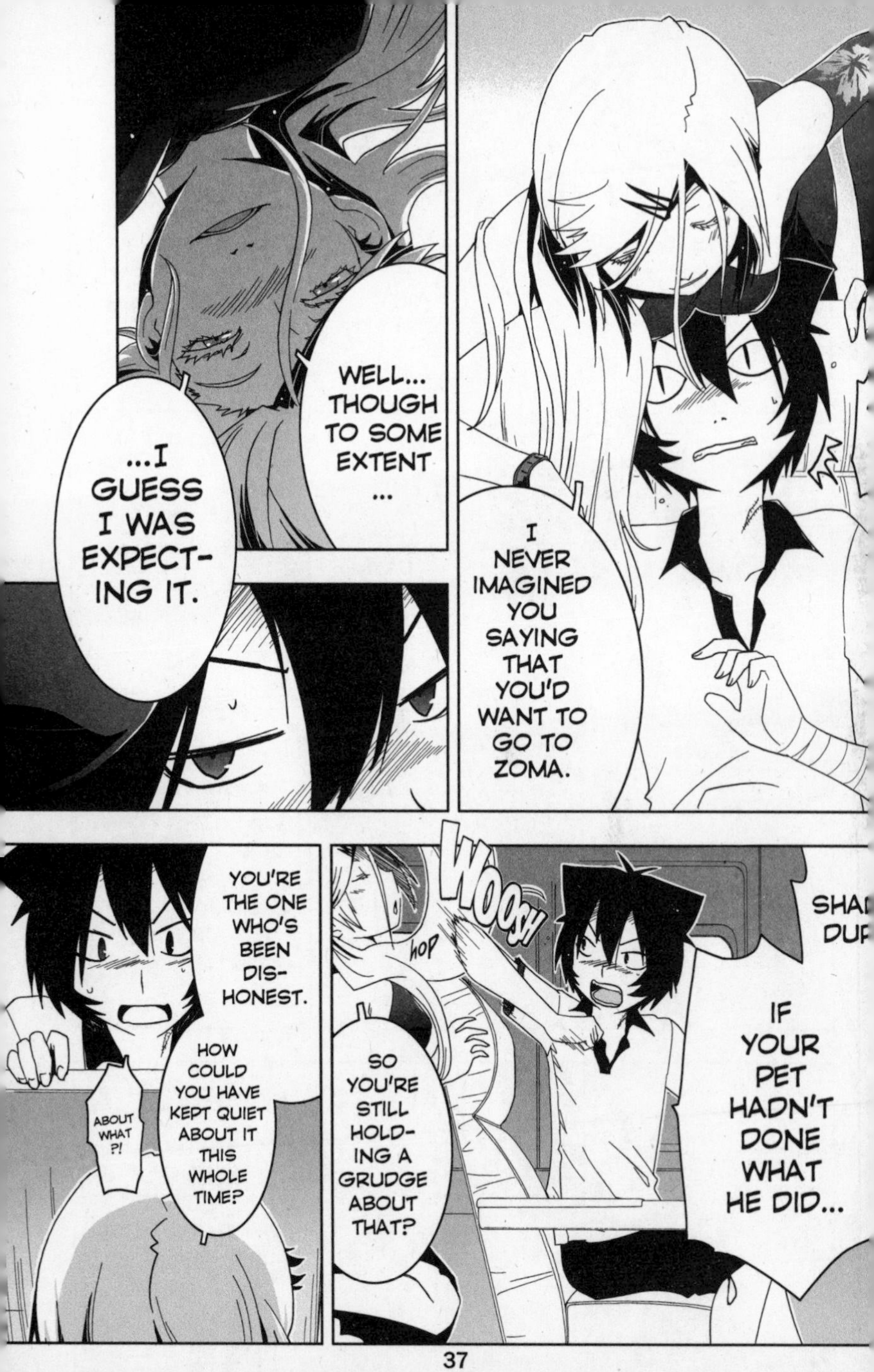
I NEVER IMAGINED YOU SAYING THAT YOU'D WANT TO GO TO ZOMA.
WELL... THOUGH TO SOME EXTENT ...
...I GUESS I WAS EXPECTING IT.
SHAD DUP
IF YOUR PET HADN'T DONE WHAT HE DID...
WOOSH
hop
SO YOU'RE STILL HOLDING A GRUDGE ABOUT THAT?
YOU'RE THE ONE WHO'S BEEN DISHONEST.
HOW COULD YOU HAVE KEPT QUIET ABOUT IT THIS WHOLE TIME?
ABOUT WHAT?!

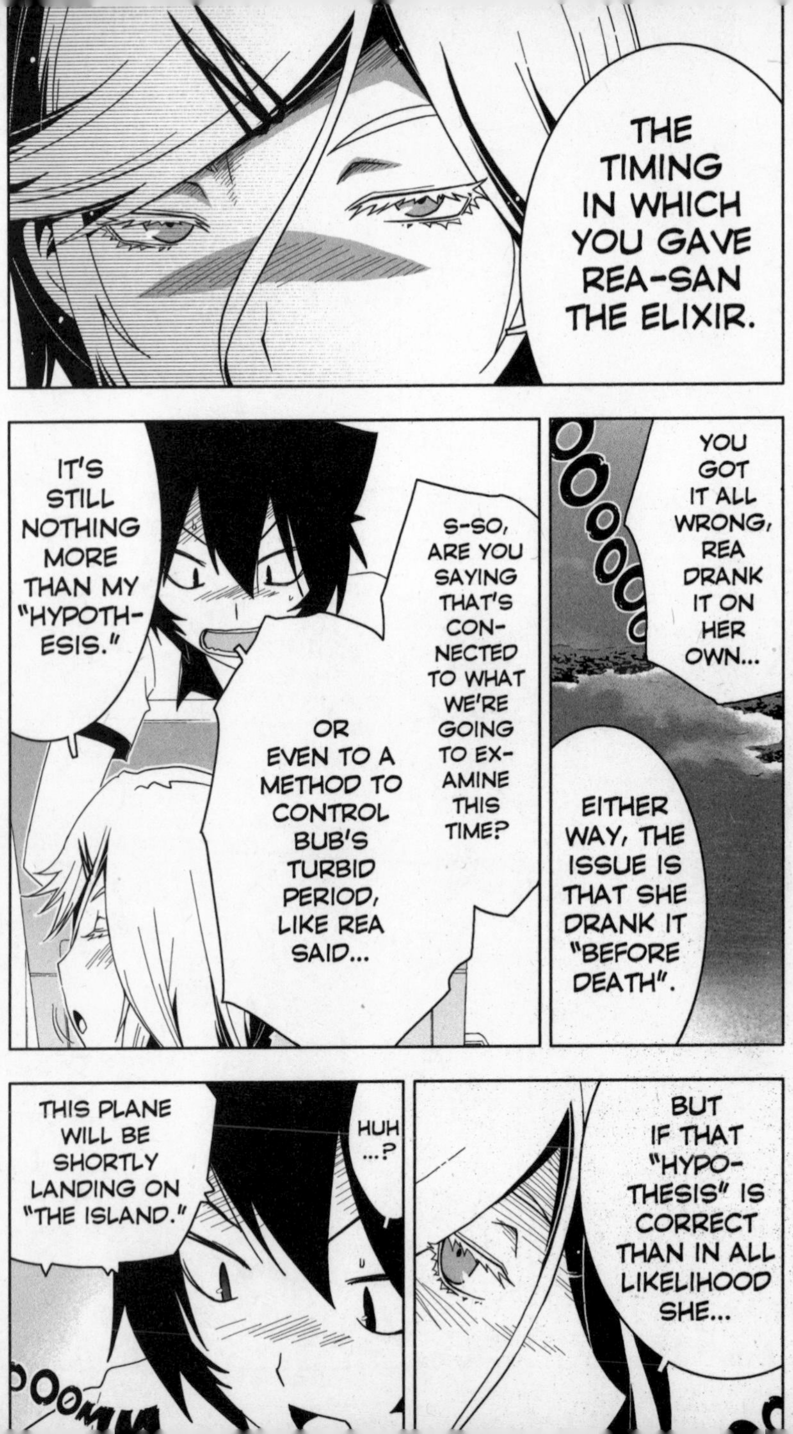
THE TIMING IN WHICH YOU GAVE REA-SAN THE ELIXIR.
YOU GOT IT ALL WRONG, REA DRANK IT ON HER OWN...
EITHER WAY, THE ISSUE IS THAT SHE DRANK IT "BEFORE DEATH".
S-SO, ARE YOU SAYING THAT'S CONNECTED TO WHAT WE'RE GOING TO EXAMINE THIS TIME?
OR EVEN TO A METHOD TO CONTROL BUB'S TURBID PERIOD, LIKE REA SAID...
IT'S STILL NOTHING MORE THAN MY "HYPOTHESIS."
BUT IF THAT "HYPOTHESIS" IS CORRECT THAN IN ALL LIKELIHOOD SHE...
HUH ...?
THIS PLANE WILL BE SHORTLY LANDING ON "THE ISLAND."

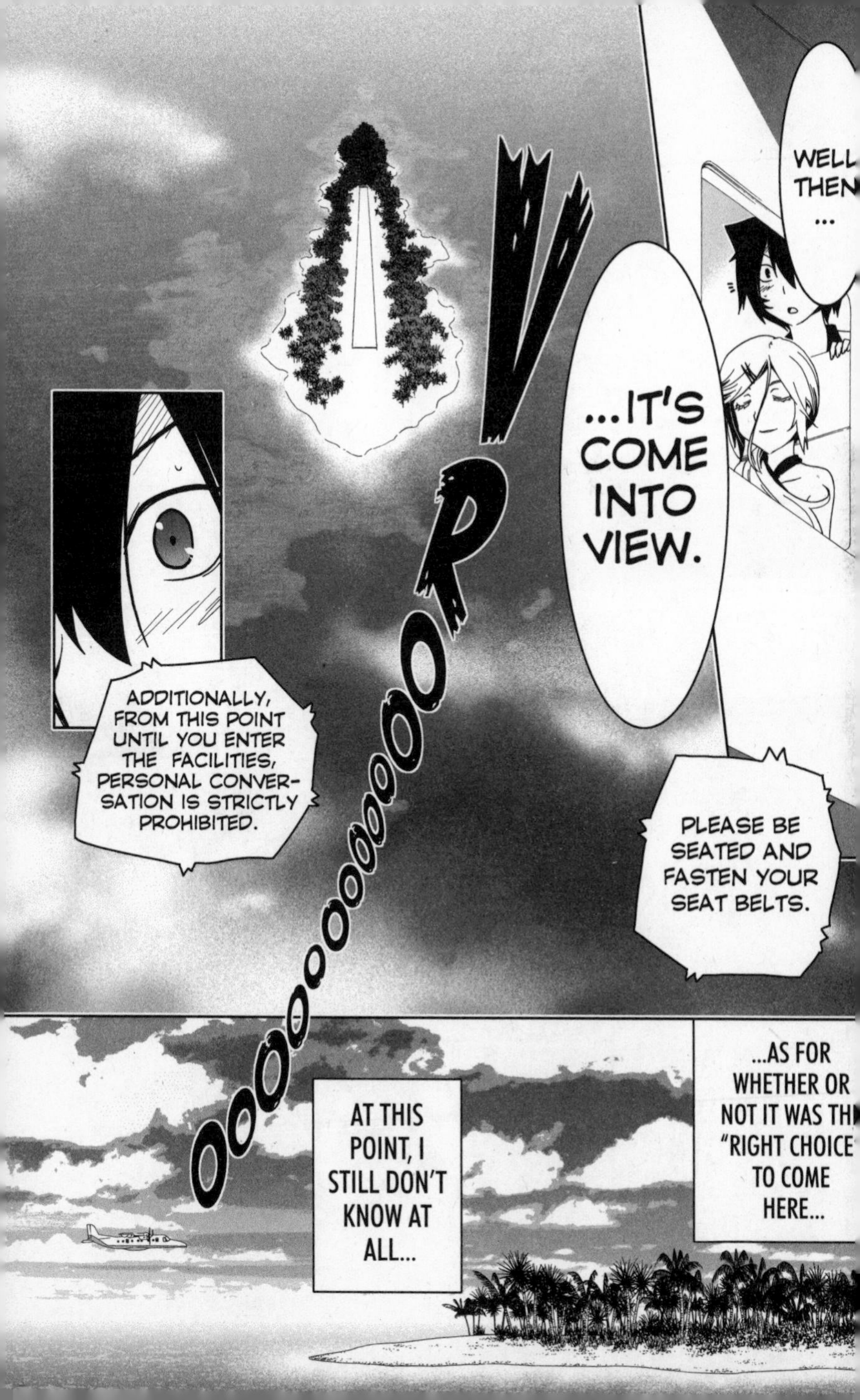
WELL THEN ...
...IT'S COME INTO VIEW.
PLEASE BE SEATED AND FASTEN YOUR SEAT BELTS.
VVROOOOOOOOOOOOOOOOO
ADDITIONALLY, FROM THIS POINT UNTIL YOU ENTER THE FACILITIES, PERSONAL CONVER-SATION IS STRICTLY PROHIBITED.
...AS FOR WHETHER OR NOT IT WAS TH "RIGHT CHOICE TO COME HERE...
AT THIS POINT, I STILL DON'T KNOW AT ALL...

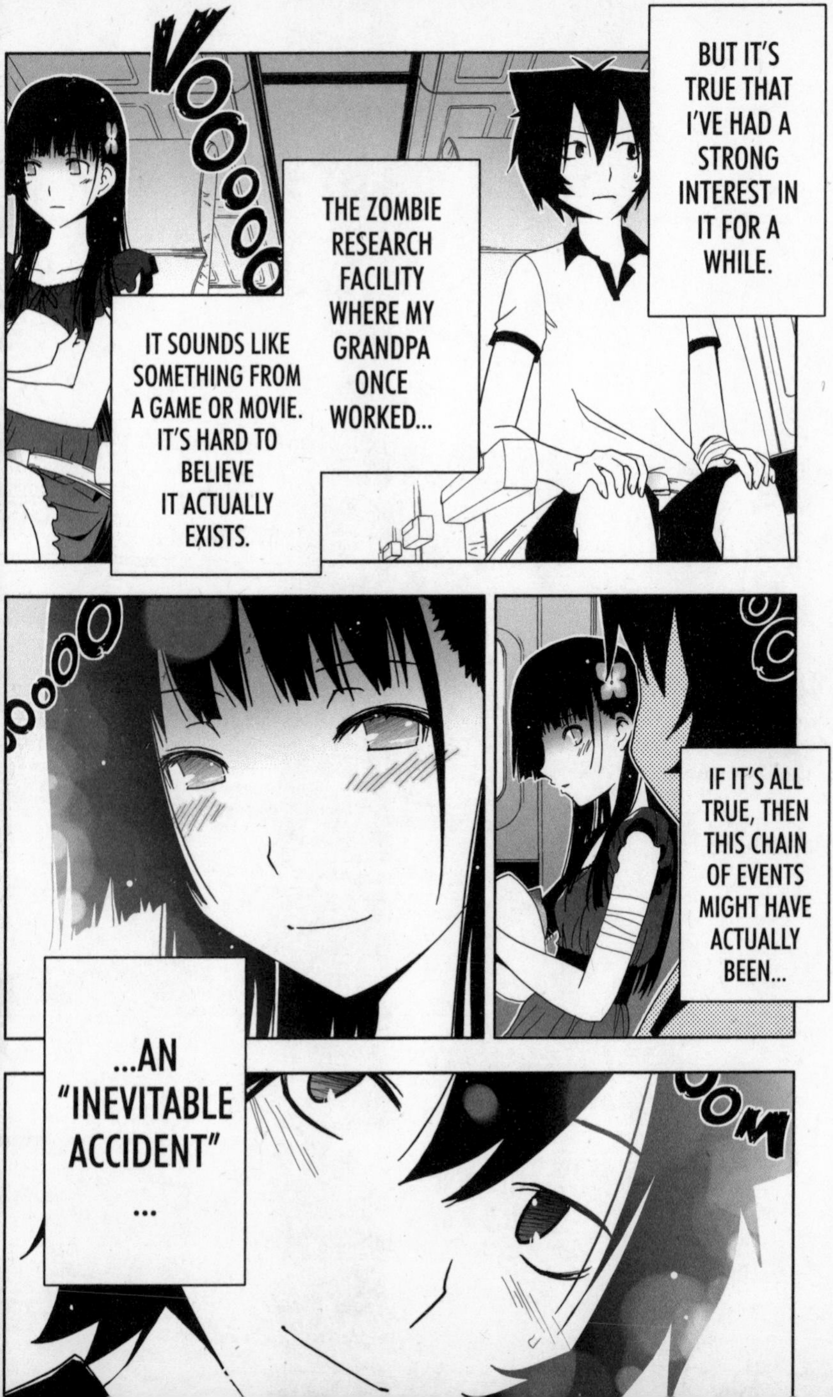
VOOOOOO
BUT IT'S TRUE THAT I'VE HAD A STRONG INTEREST IN IT FOR A WHILE.
THE ZOMBIE RESEARCH FACILITY WHERE MY GRANDPA ONCE WORKED...
IT SOUNDS LIKE SOMETHING FROM A GAME OR MOVIE. IT'S HARD TO BELIEVE IT ACTUALLY EXISTS.
IF IT'S ALL TRUE, THEN THIS CHAIN OF EVENTS MIGHT HAVE ACTUALLY BEEN...
...AN "INEVITABLE ACCIDENT" ...
OOM

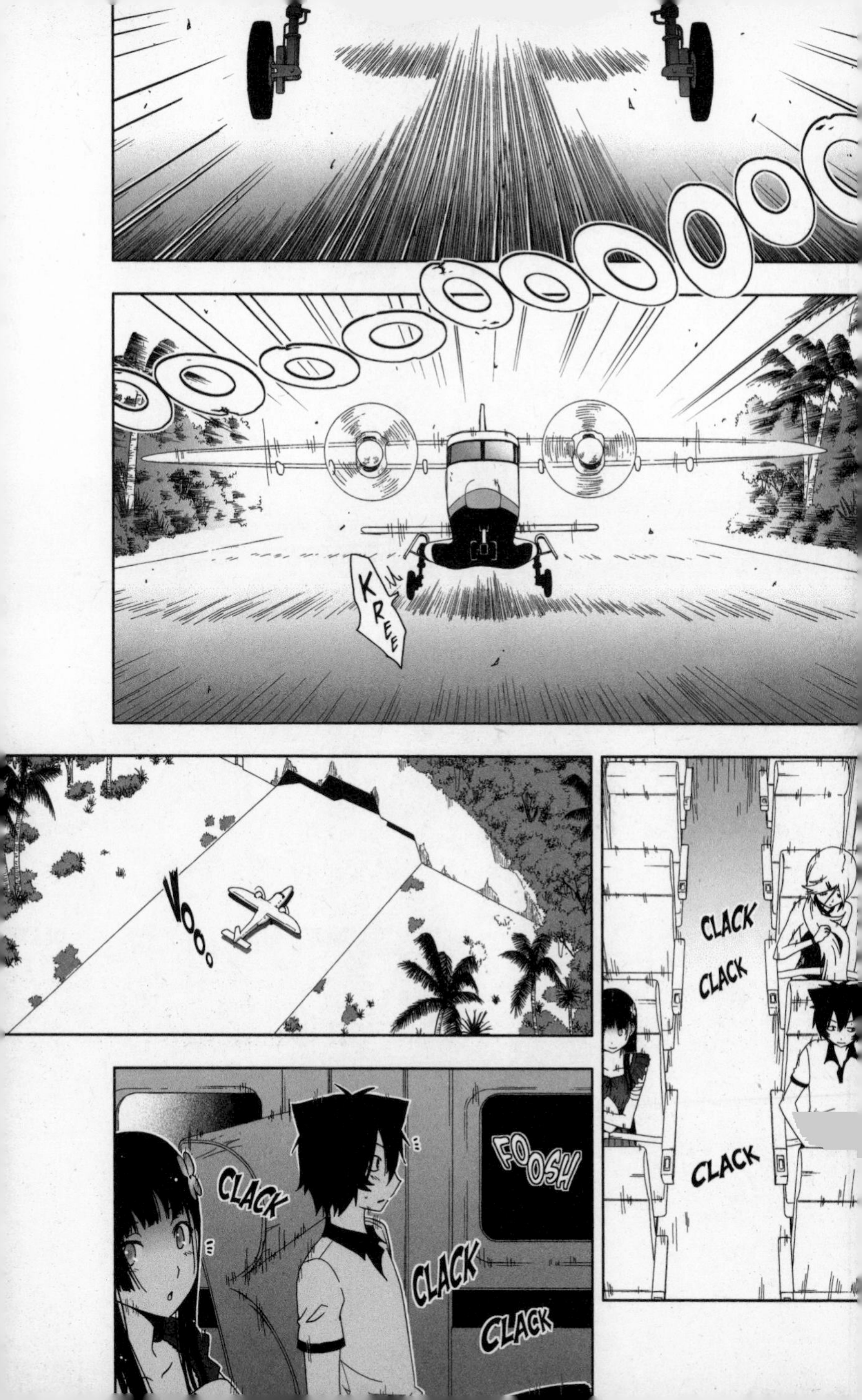
KREEE
CLACK
CLACK
CLACK
VOOO
FOOSH
CLACK
CLACK
CLACK

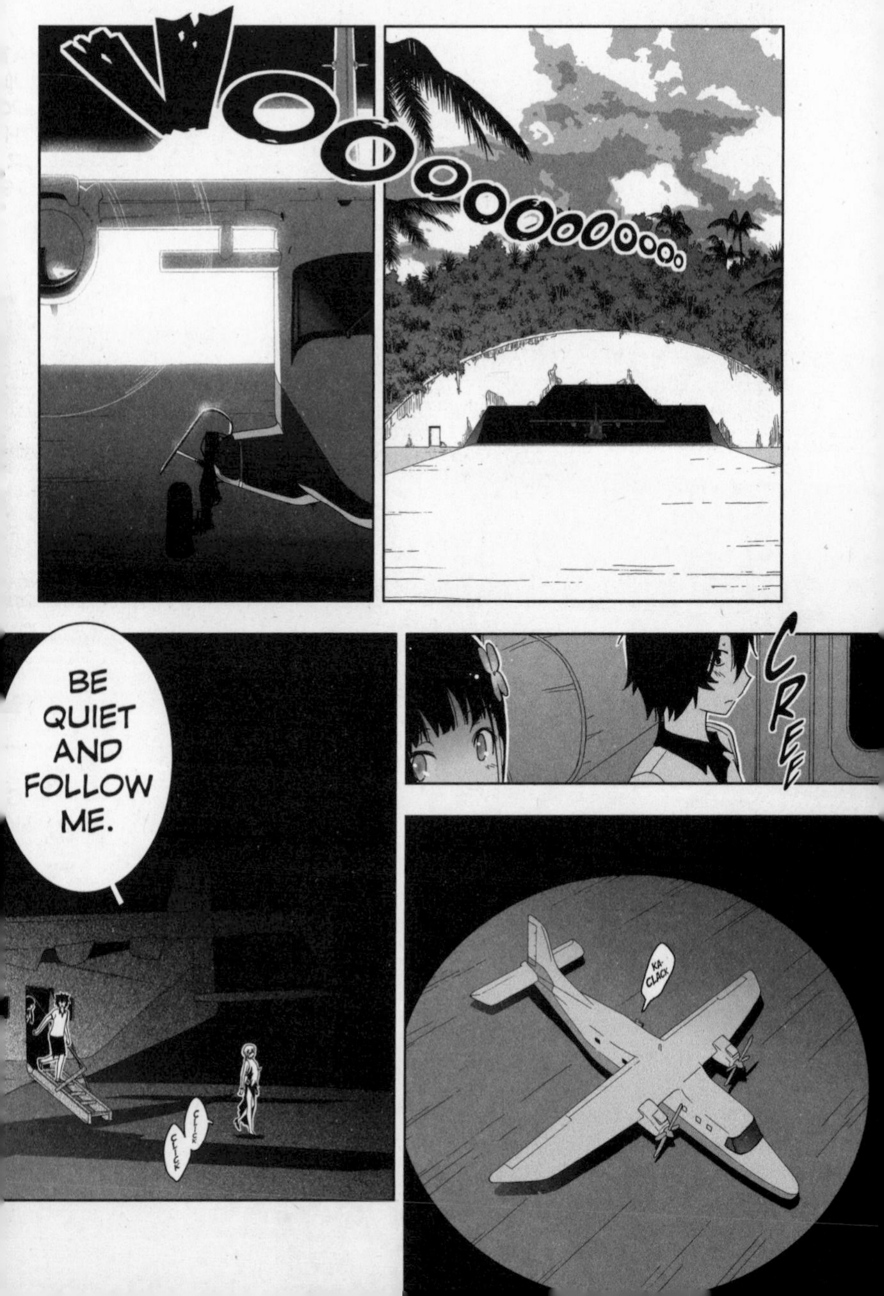
VVOOOOOOOOOOOO
CREE
KA-CLACK
BE QUIET AND FOLLOW ME.
CLICK
CLICK

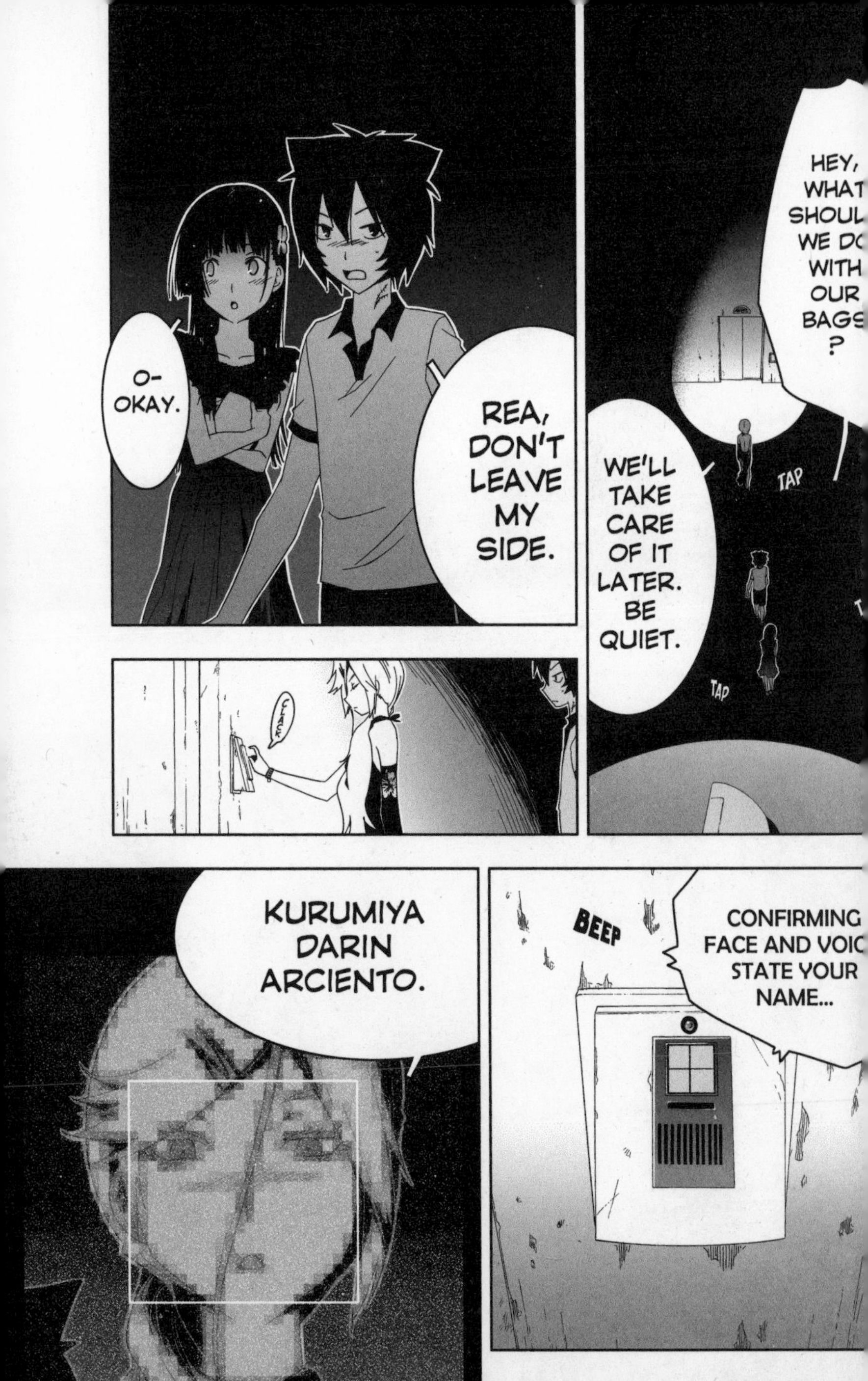
HEY, WHAT SHOUL WE D WITH OUR BAGS ?
WE'LL TAKE CARE OF IT LATER. BE QUIET.
TAP
TAP
REA, DON'T LEAVE MY SIDE.
O- OKAY.
CLACK
BEEP
CONFIRMING FACE AND VOIC STATE YOUR NAME...
KURUMIYA DARIN ARCIENTO.

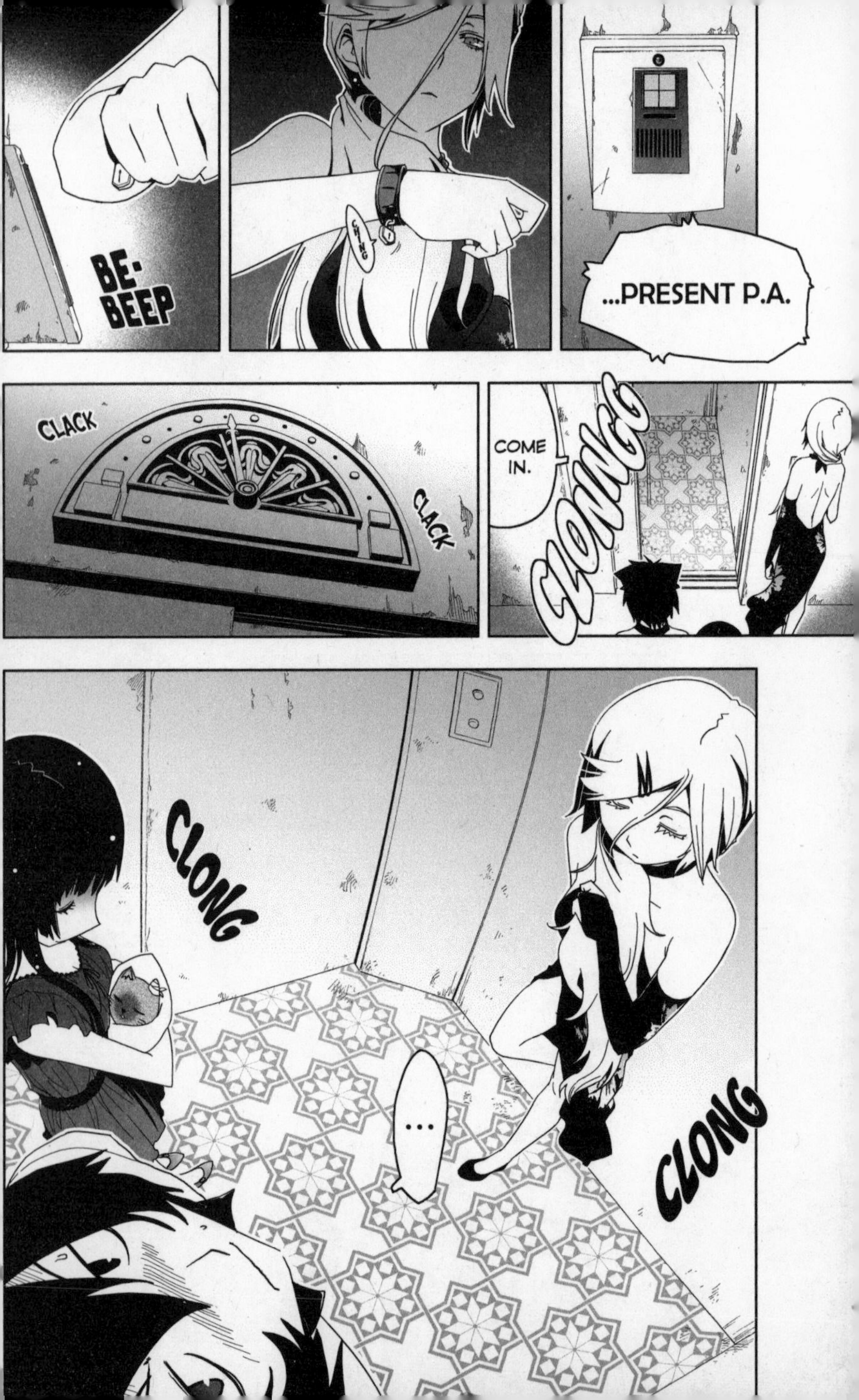
...PRESENT P.A.
CHING
BE-BEEP
COME IN.
CLONNGG
CLACK
CLACK
CLONG
...
CLONG

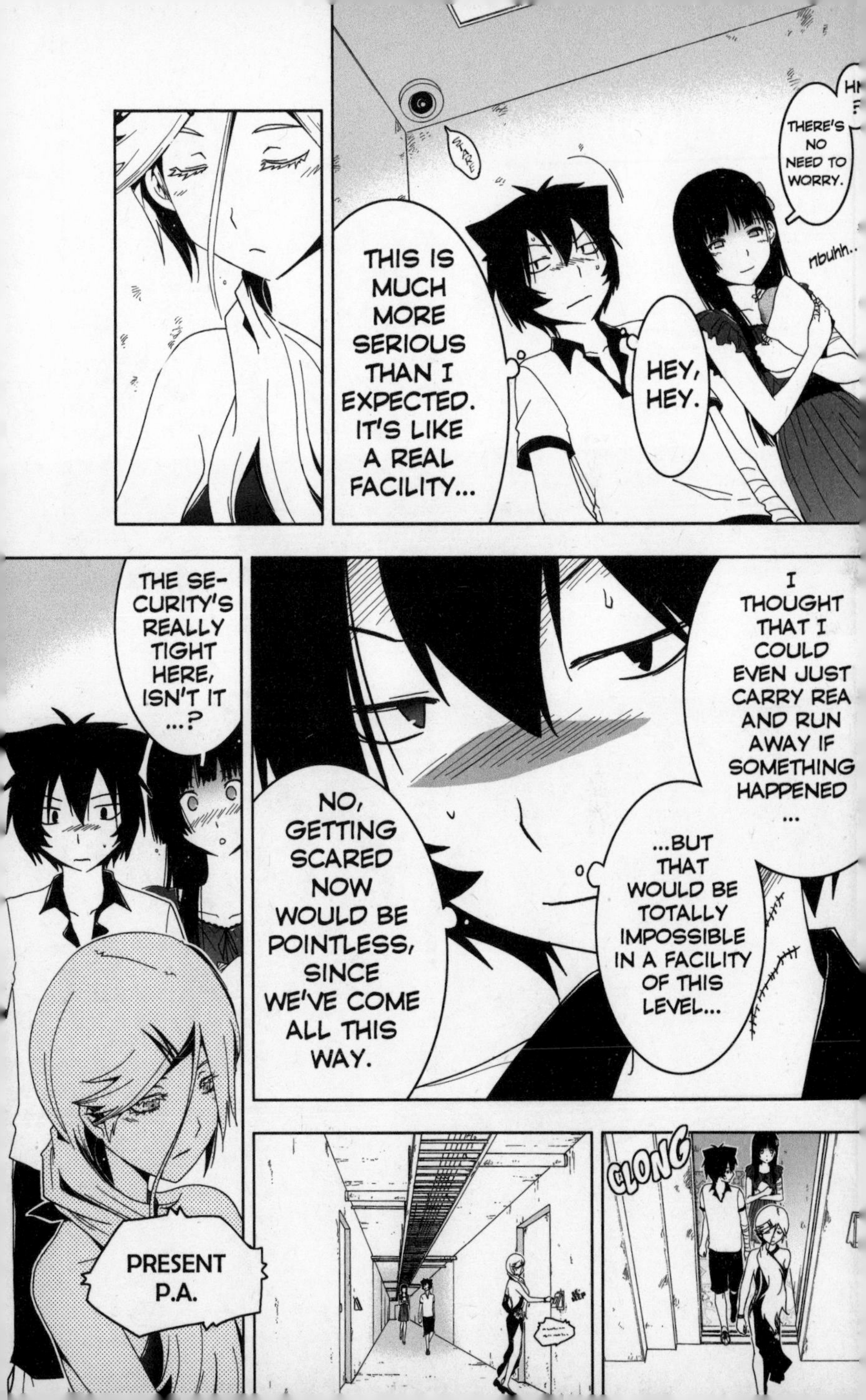
THERE'S NO NEED TO WORRY.
nbuhh..
HEY, HEY.
THIS IS MUCH MORE SERIOUS THAN I EXPECTED. IT'S LIKE A REAL FACILITY...
I THOUGHT THAT I COULD EVEN JUST CARRY REA AND RUN AWAY IF SOMETHING HAPPENED ...
...BUT THAT WOULD BE TOTALLY IMPOSSIBLE IN A FACILITY OF THIS LEVEL...
NO, GETTING SCARED NOW WOULD BE POINTLESS, SINCE WE'VE COME ALL THIS WAY.
CLONG
THE SE-CURITY'S REALLY TIGHT HERE, ISN'T IT ...?
PRESENT P.A.

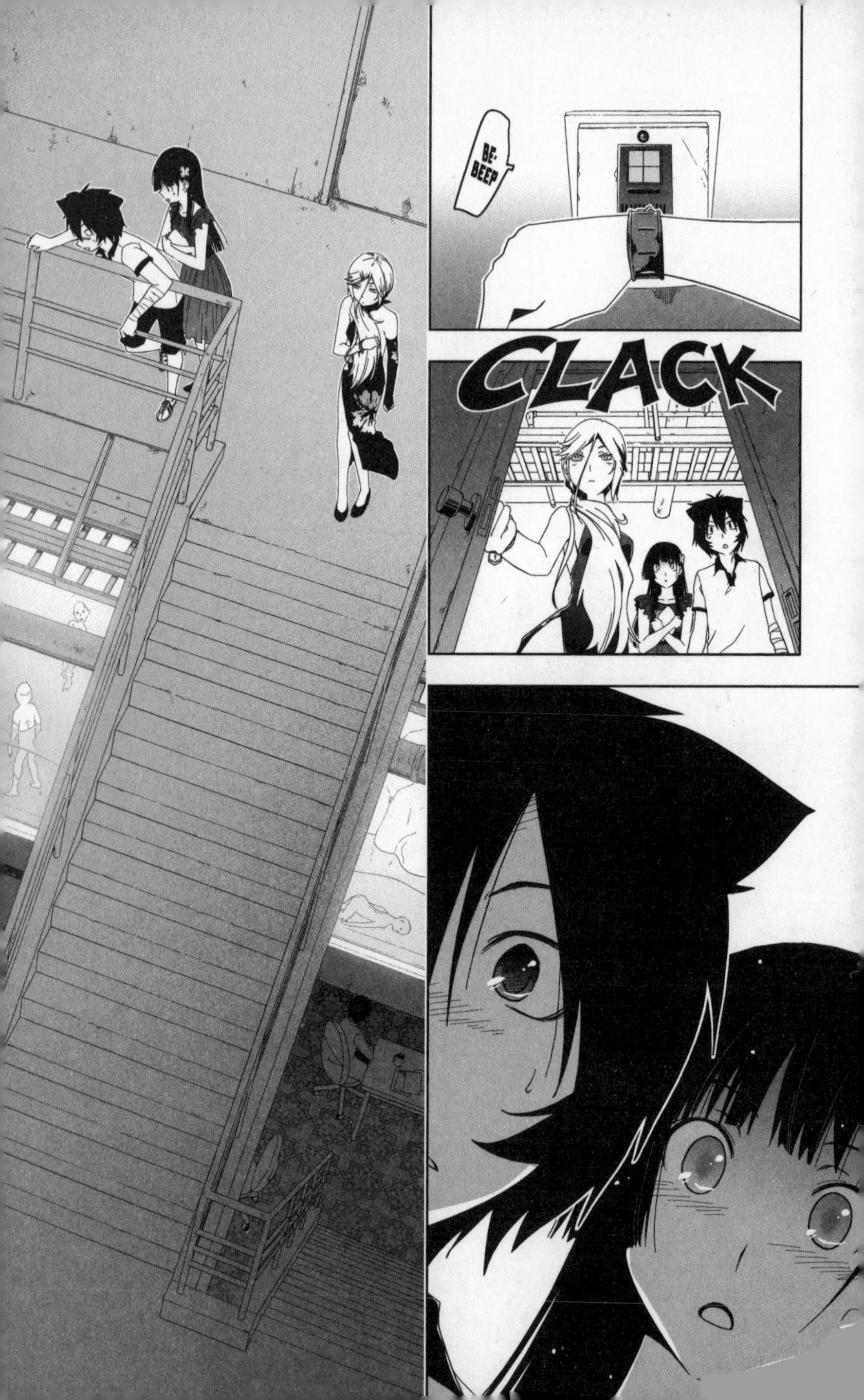
BE-BEEP
CLACK

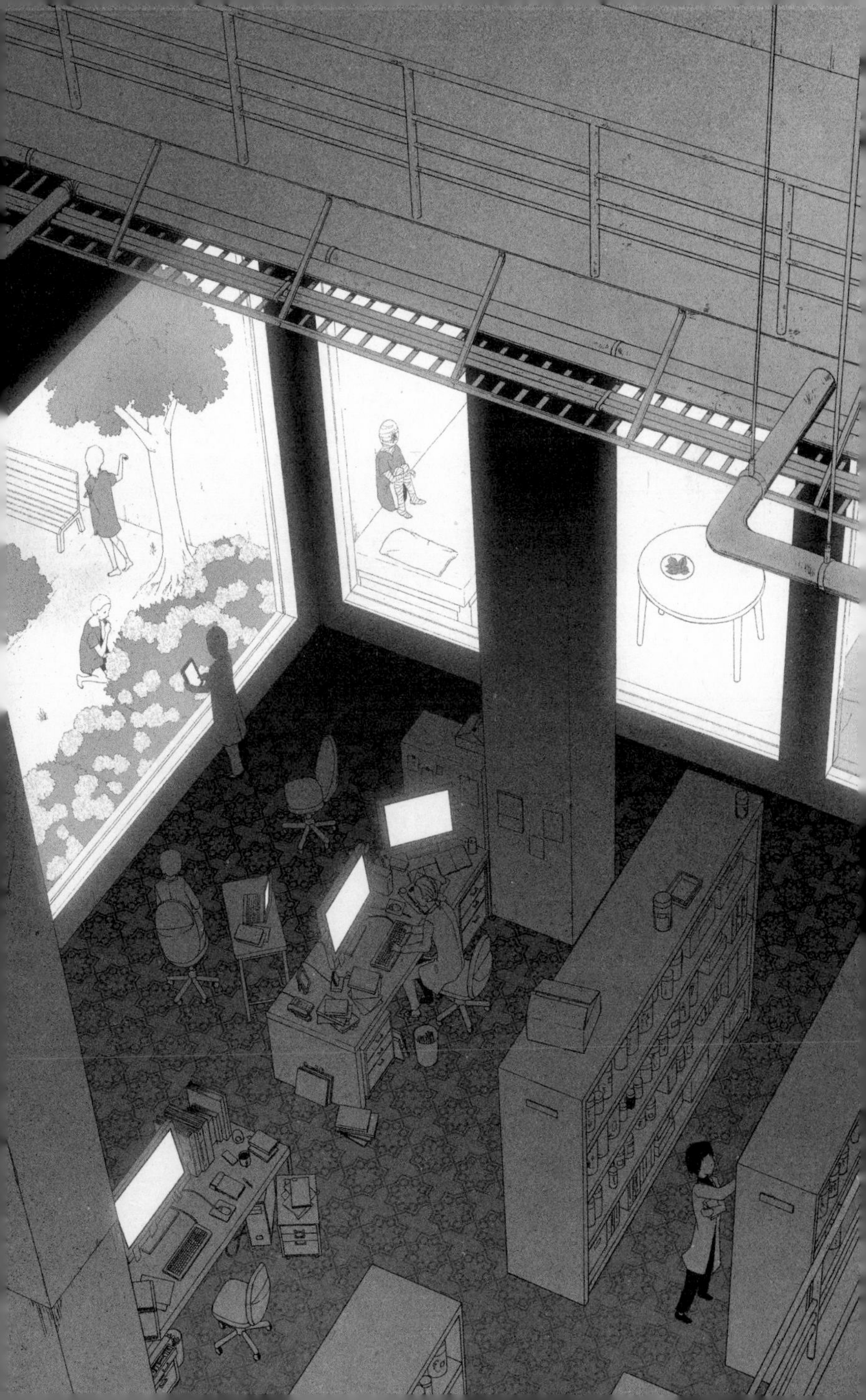

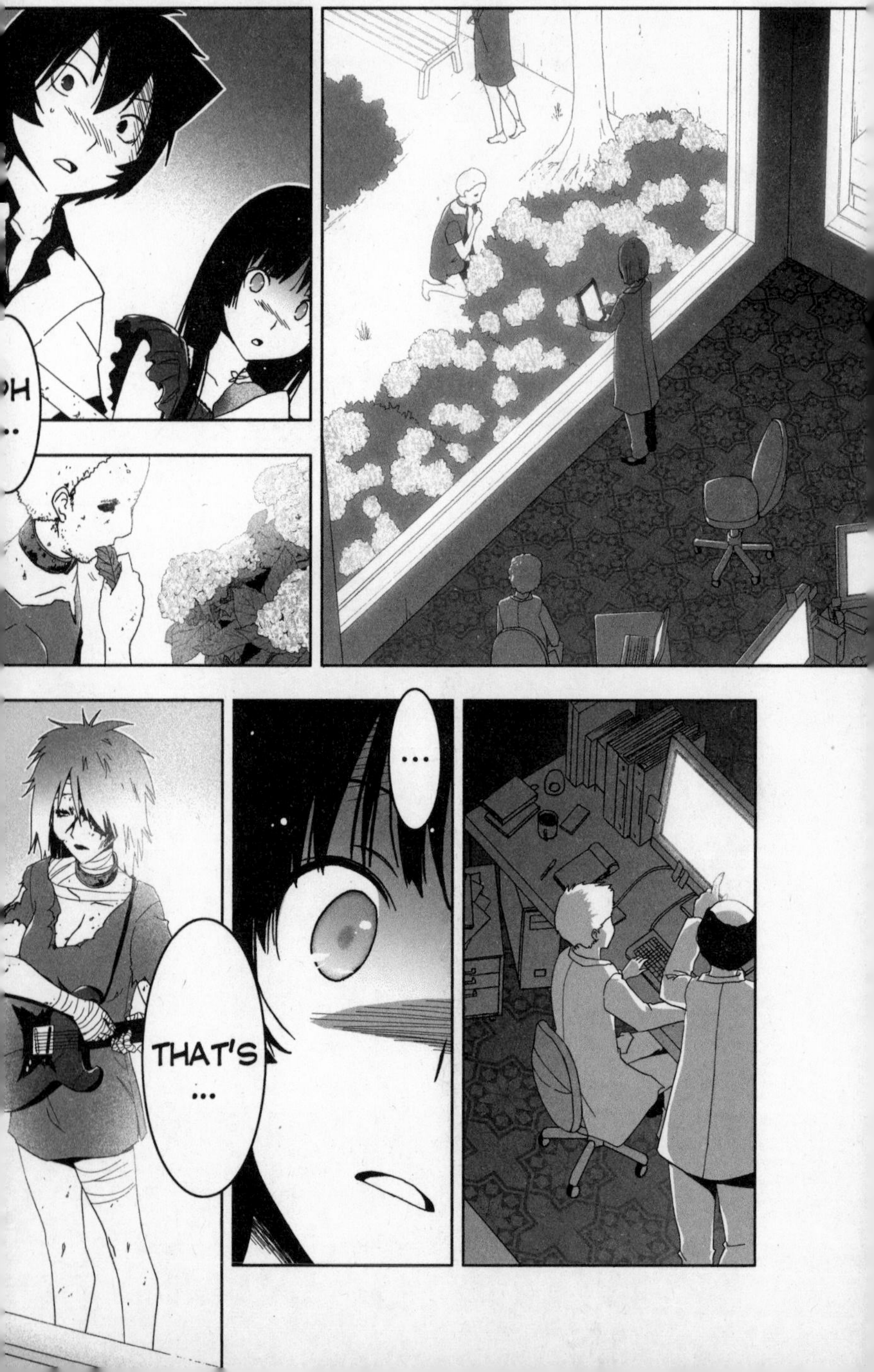
PH
...
...
THAT'S
...

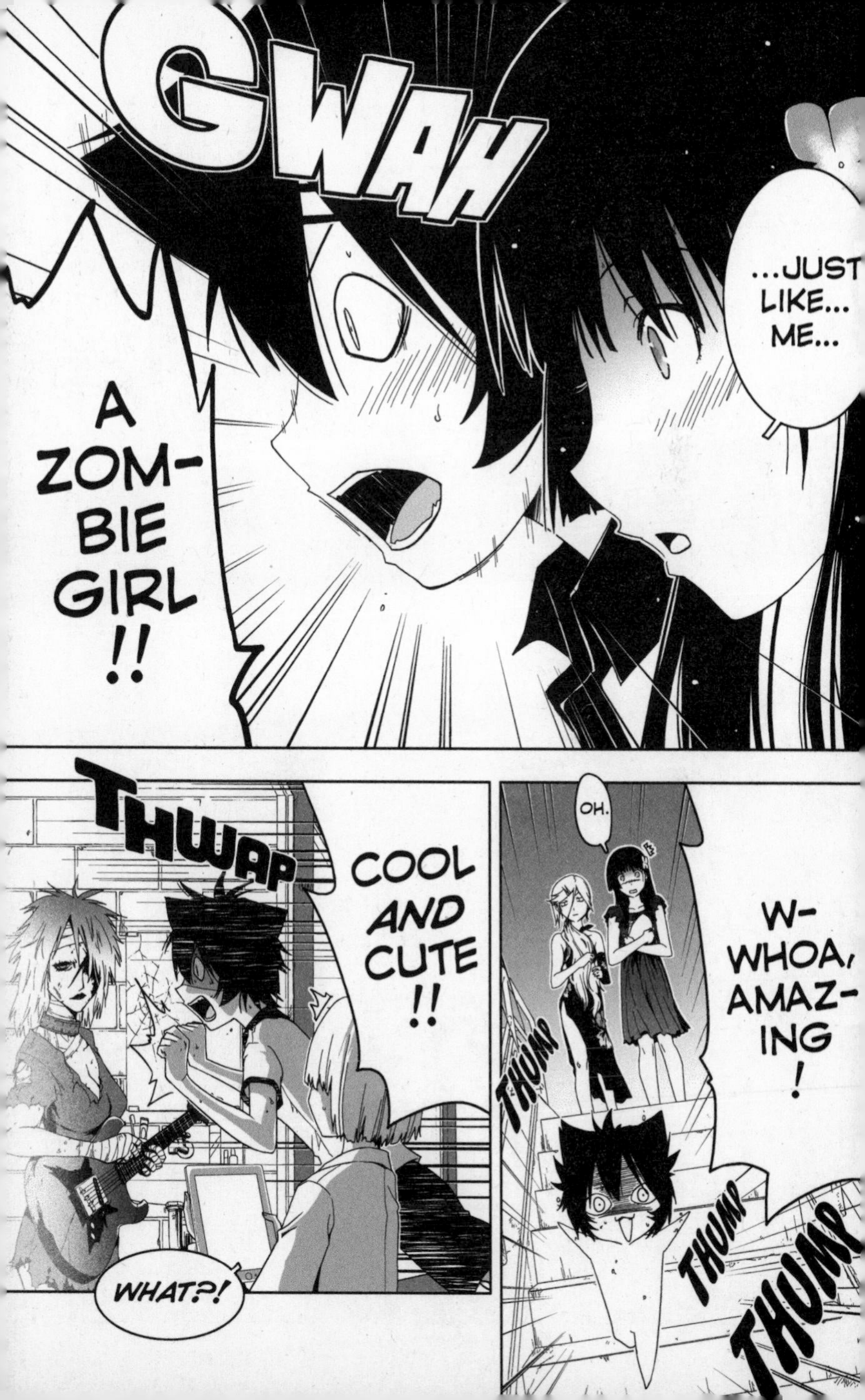
...JUST LIKE... ME...
GWAH
A ZOM-BIE GIRL!!
OH.
W-WHOA, AMAZ-ING!
THUMP
THUMP
THUMP
THUMP
THWAP
COOL AND CUTE!!
WHAT?!

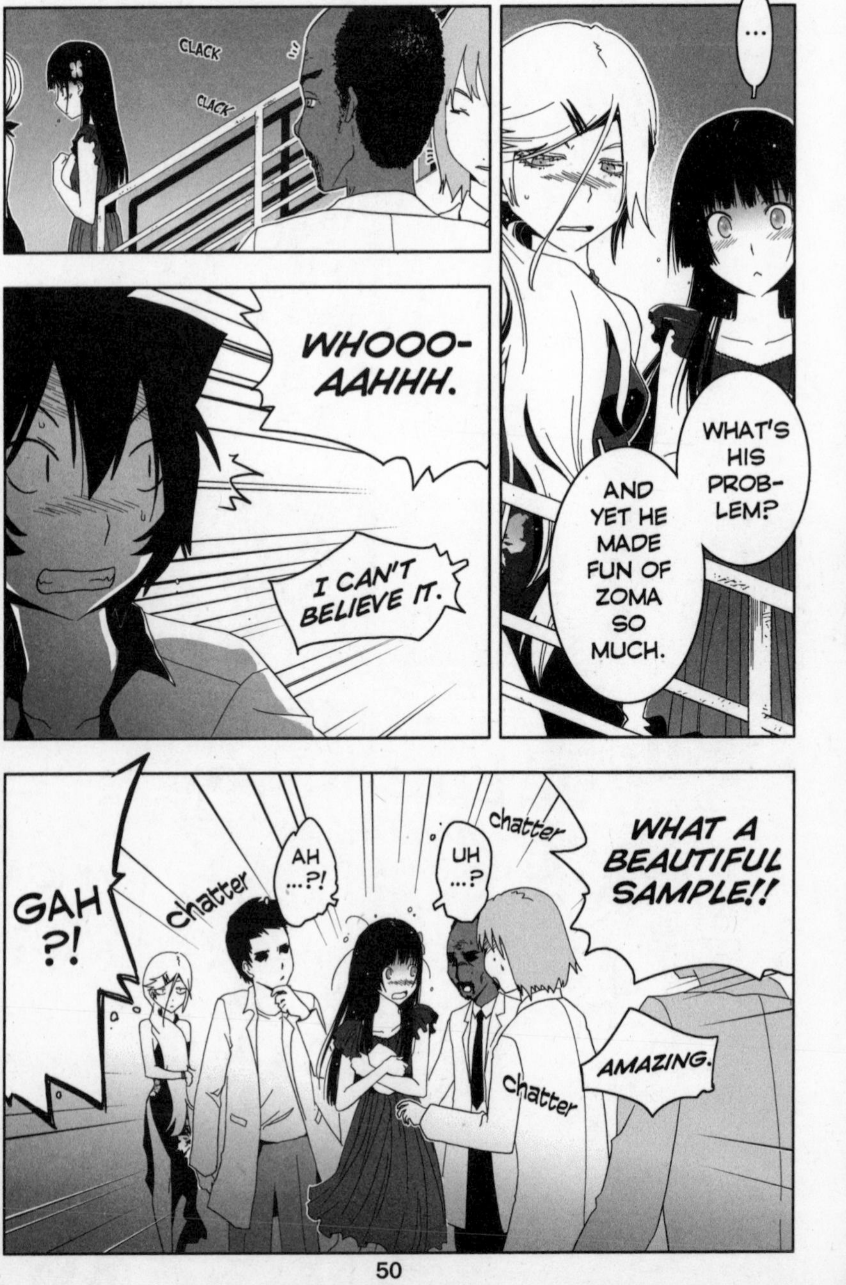
...
WHAT'S HIS PROB-LEM?
AND YET HE MADE FUN OF ZOMA SO MUCH.
CLACK
CLACK
WHOOO-AAHHH.
I CAN'T BELIEVE IT.
WHAT A BEAUTIFUL SAMPLE!!
chatter
UH ...?
AH ...?!
chatter
GAH ?!
AMAZING.
chatter

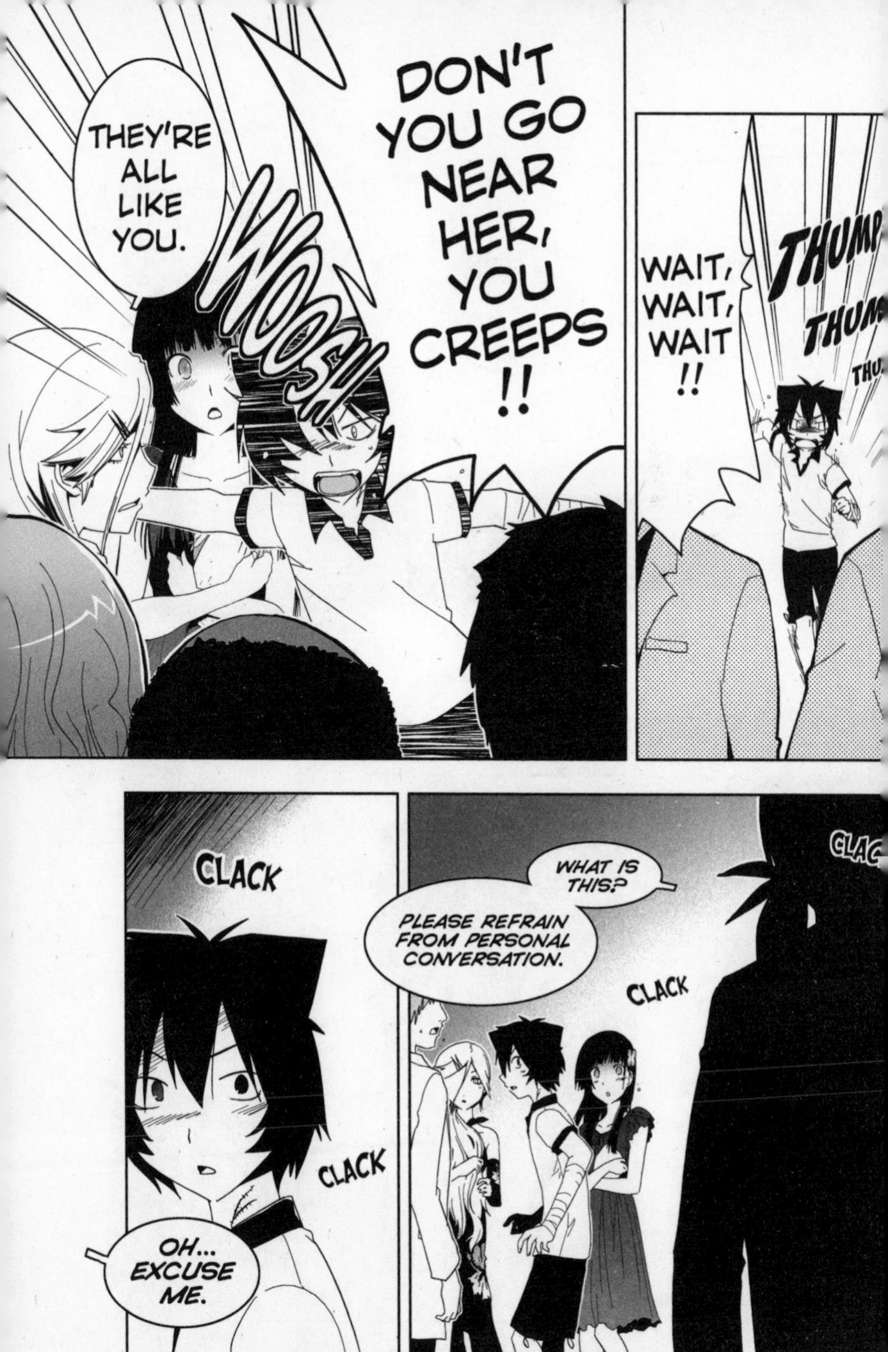
WAIT, WAIT, WAIT!!
THUMP
THUM
THU
DON'T YOU GO NEAR HER, YOU CREEPS!!
WOOSH
THEY'RE ALL LIKE YOU.
CLAC
WHAT IS THIS?
PLEASE REFRAIN FROM PERSONAL CONVERSATION.
CLACK
CLACK
CLACK
OH... EXCUSE ME.

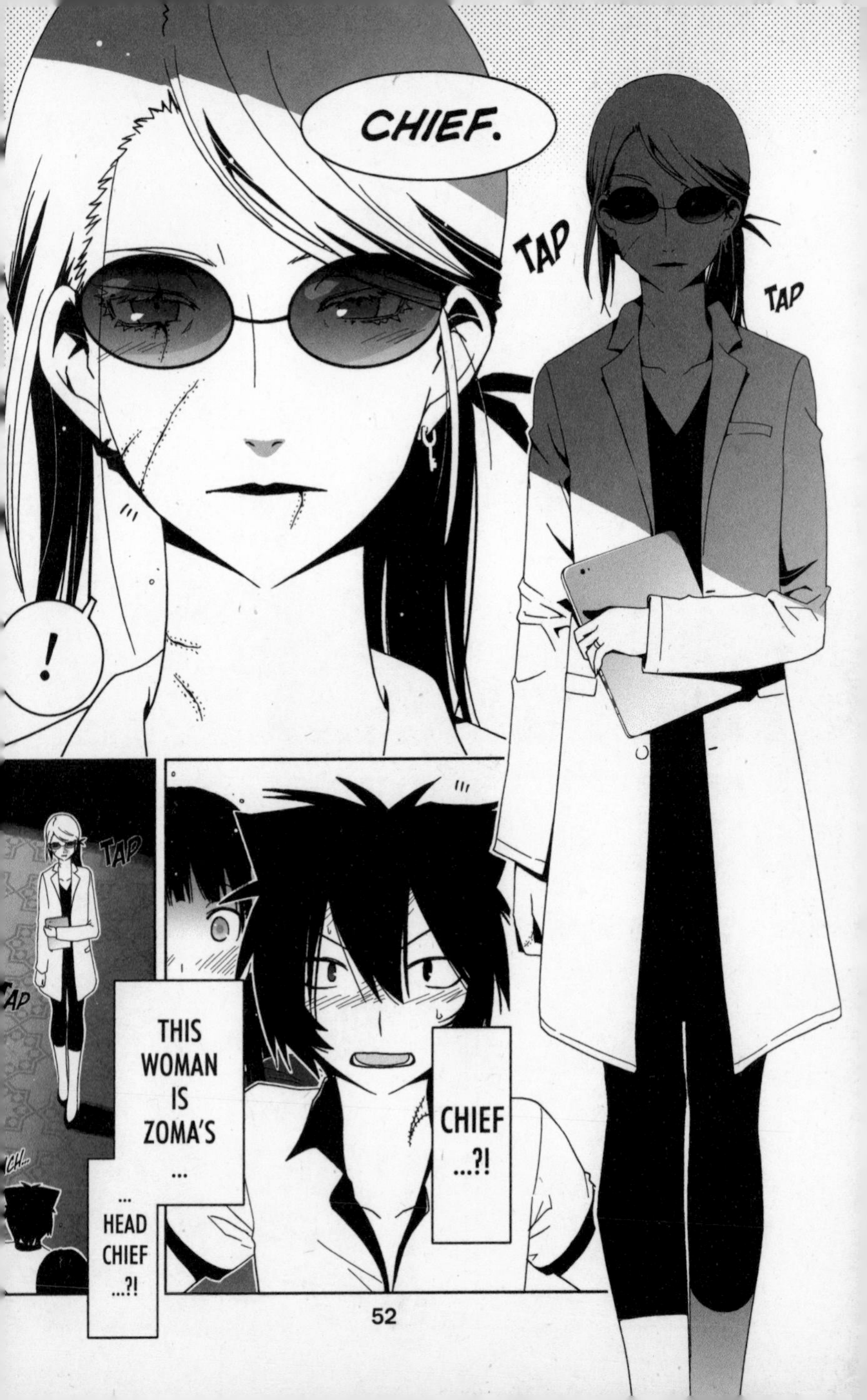
CHIEF.
!
TAP
TAP
CHIEF ...?!
TAP
TAP
THIS WOMAN IS ZOMA'S ...
... HEAD CHIEF ...?!

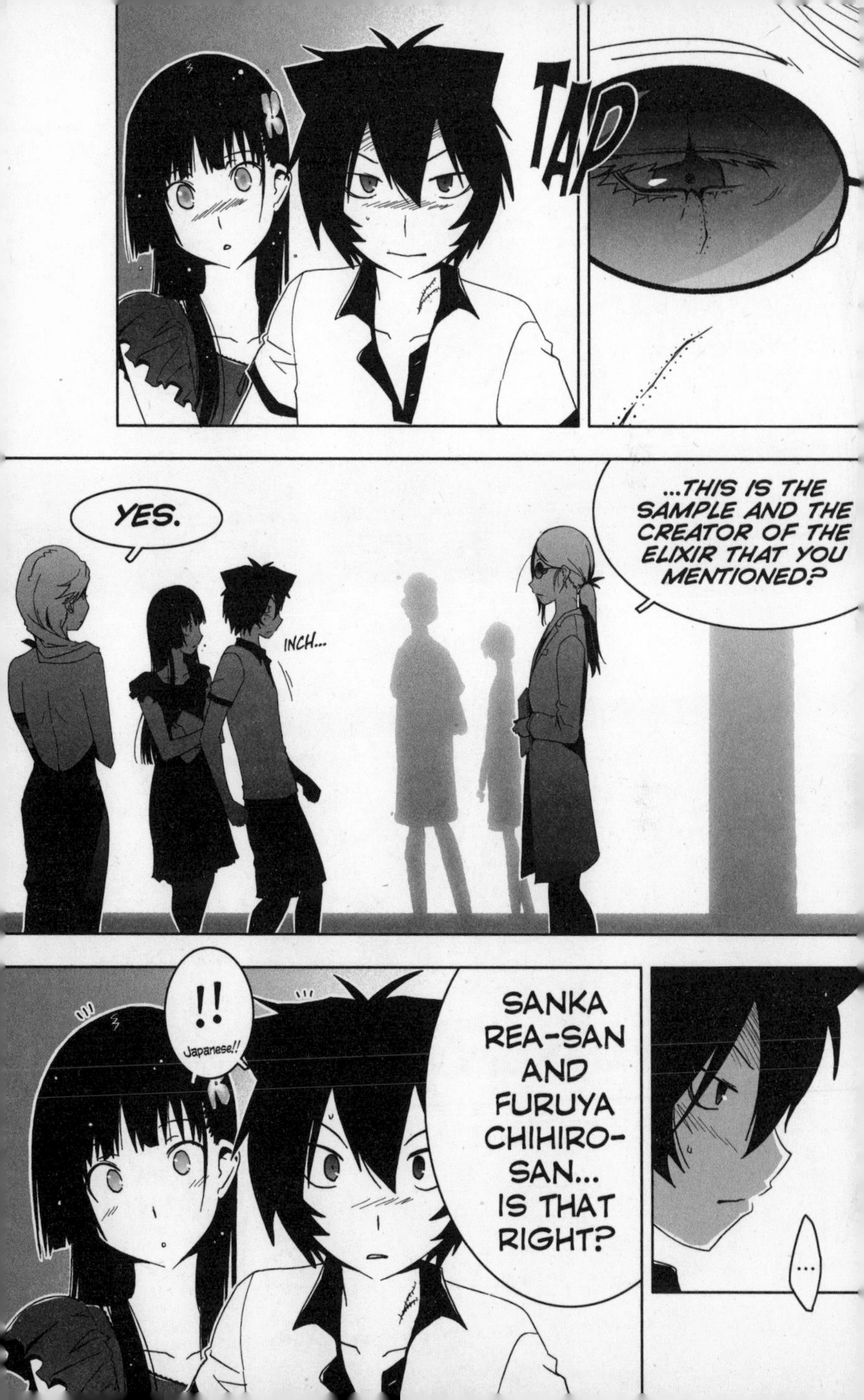
TAP
...THIS IS THE SAMPLE AND THE CREATOR OF THE ELIXIR THAT YOU MENTIONED?
INCH...
YES.
...
SANKA REA-SAN AND FURUYA CHIHIRO-SAN... IS THAT RIGHT?
!!
Japanese!!

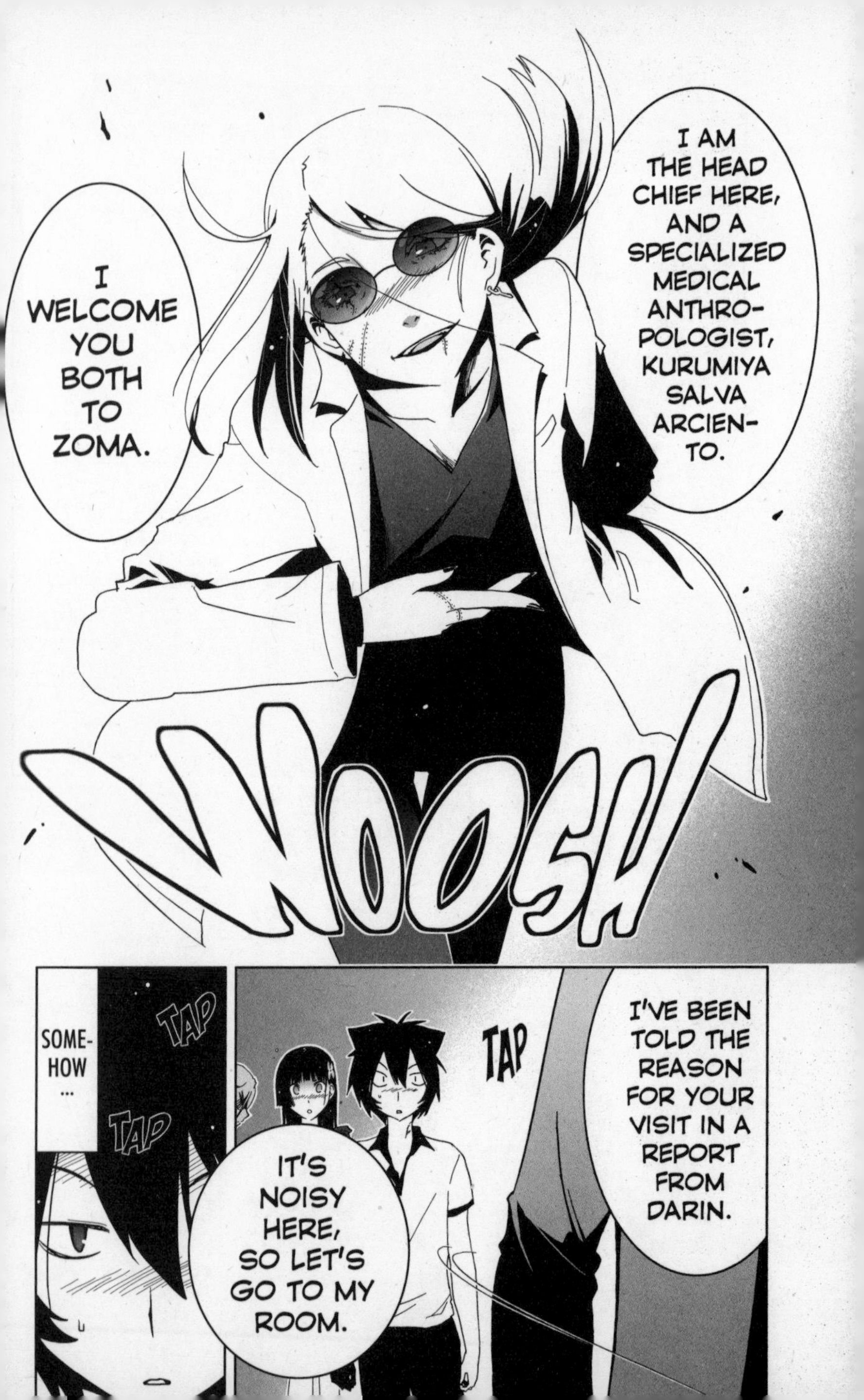
I AM THE HEAD CHIEF HERE, AND A SPECIALIZED MEDICAL ANTHRO-POLOGIST, KURUMIYA SALVA ARCIEN-TO.
I WELCOME YOU BOTH TO ZOMA.
WOOSH
I'VE BEEN TOLD THE REASON FOR YOUR VISIT IN A REPORT FROM DARIN.
TAP
IT'S NOISY HERE, SO LET'S GO TO MY ROOM.
TAP
TAP
SOME-HOW ...

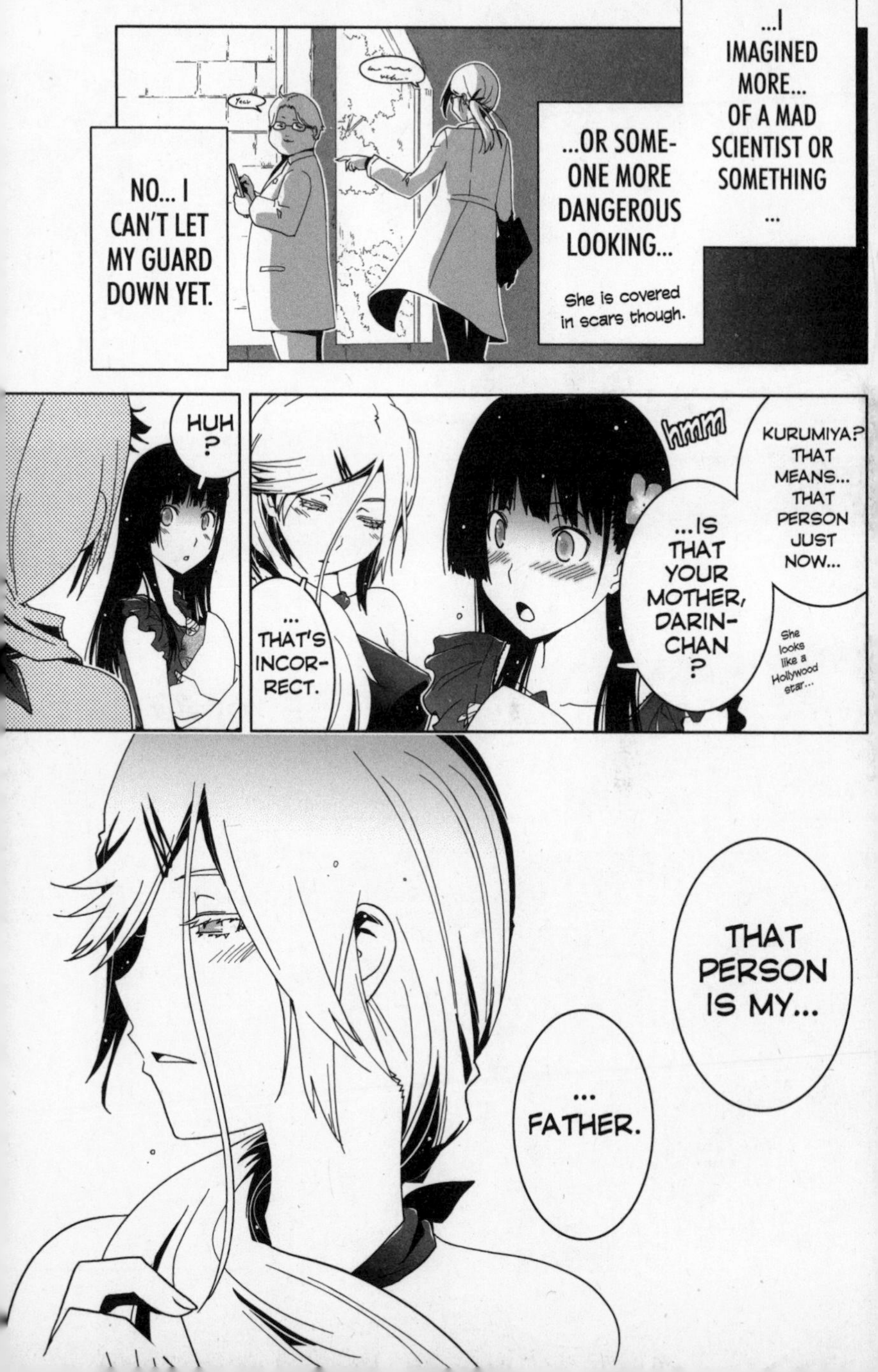
...I IMAGINED MORE... OF A MAD SCIENTIST OR SOMETHING ...
...OR SOME-ONE MORE DANGEROUS LOOKING...
She is covered in scars though.
NO... I CAN'T LET MY GUARD DOWN YET.
KURUMIYA? THAT MEANS... THAT PERSON JUST NOW...
hmm
...IS THAT YOUR MOTHER, DARIN-CHAN?
She looks like a Hollywood star...
... THAT'S INCOR-RECT.
HUH?
THAT PERSON IS MY...
... FATHER.

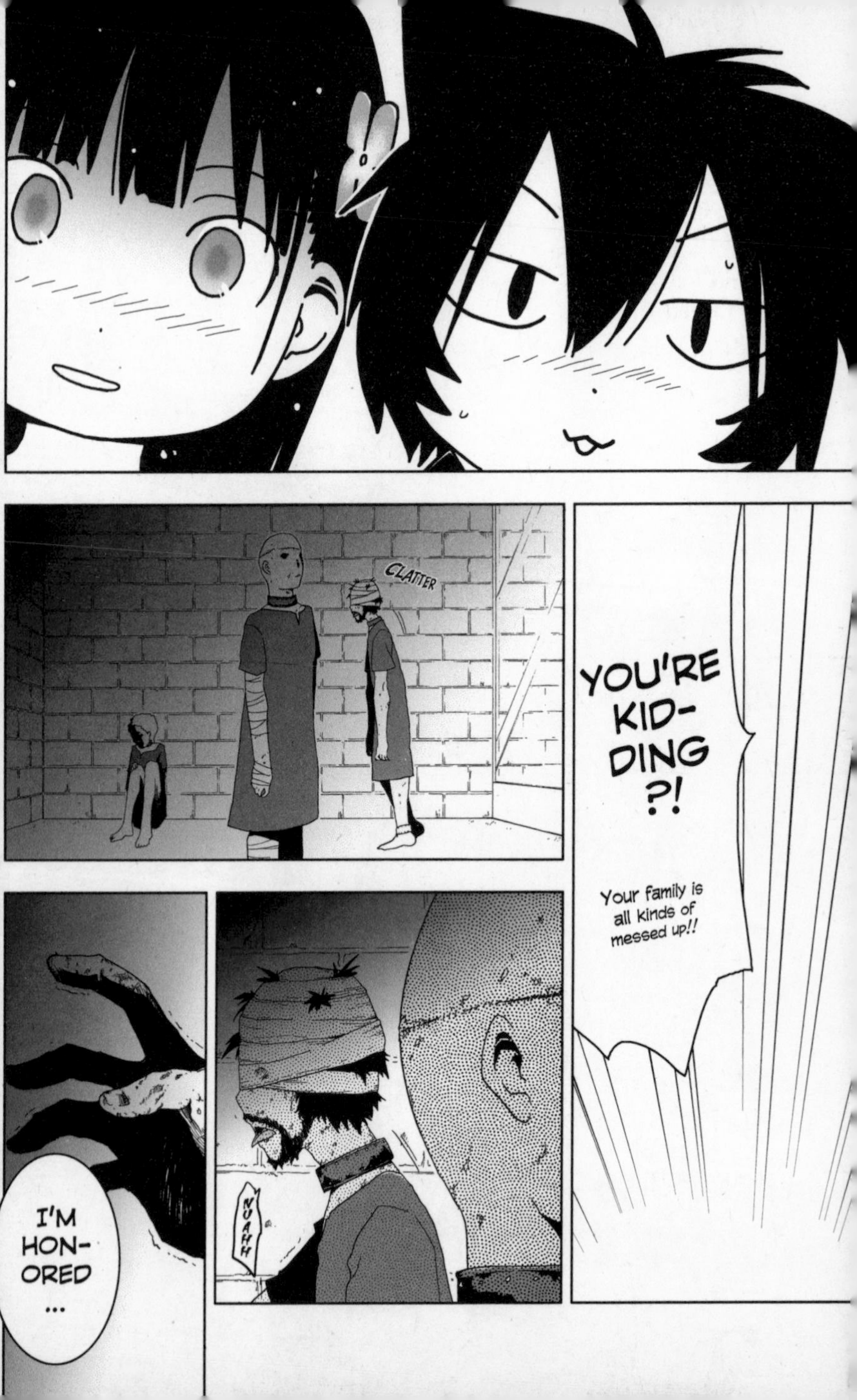
YOU'RE KID-DING?!
Your family is all kinds of messed up!!
CLATTER
NUAHH
I'M HON-ORED...

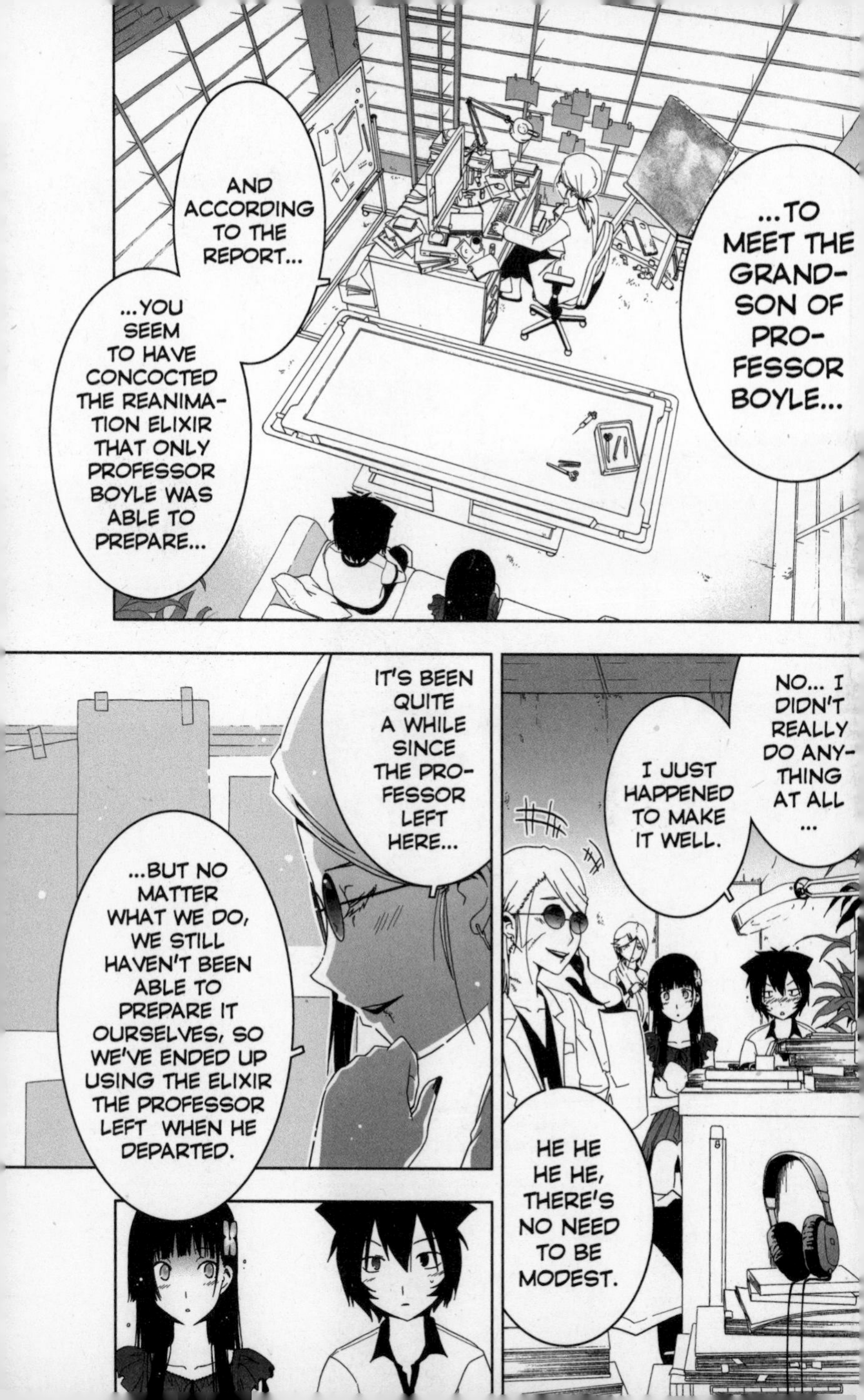
...TO MEET THE GRANDSON OF PROFESSOR BOYLE...
AND ACCORDING TO THE REPORT...
...YOU SEEM TO HAVE CONCOCTED THE REANIMATION ELIXIR THAT ONLY PROFESSOR BOYLE WAS ABLE TO PREPARE...
NO... I DIDN'T REALLY DO ANYTHING AT ALL...
I JUST HAPPENED TO MAKE IT WELL.
HE HE HE HE, THERE'S NO NEED TO BE MODEST.
IT'S BEEN QUITE A WHILE SINCE THE PROFESSOR LEFT HERE...
...BUT NO MATTER WHAT WE DO, WE STILL HAVEN'T BEEN ABLE TO PREPARE IT OURSELVES, SO WE'VE ENDED UP USING THE ELIXIR THE PROFESSOR LEFT WHEN HE DEPARTED.

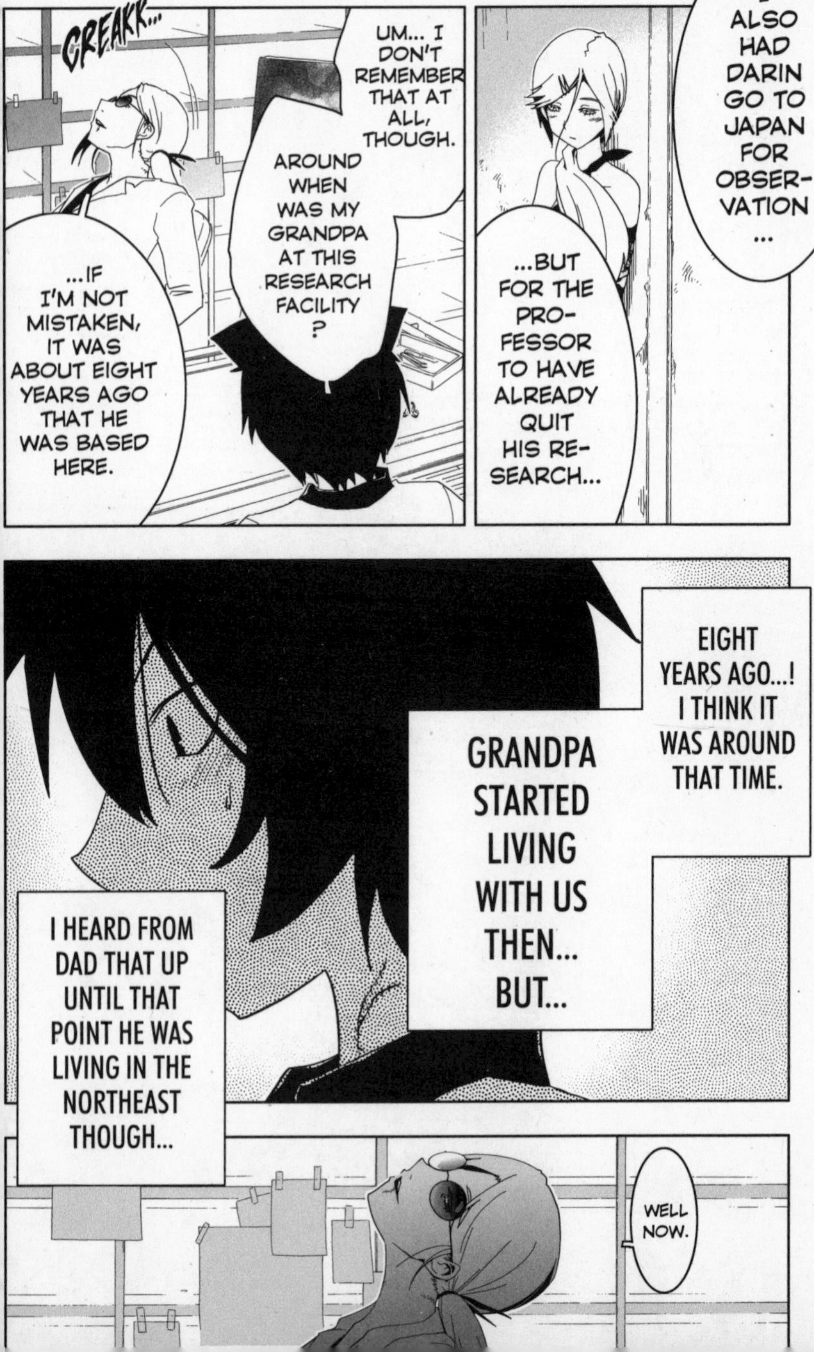
I ALSO HAD DARIN GO TO JAPAN FOR OBSERVATION...
...BUT FOR THE PROFESSOR TO HAVE ALREADY QUIT HIS RESEARCH...
CREAKK...
UM... I DON'T REMEMBER THAT AT ALL, THOUGH.
AROUND WHEN WAS MY GRANDPA AT THIS RESEARCH FACILITY?
...IF I'M NOT MISTAKEN, IT WAS ABOUT EIGHT YEARS AGO THAT HE WAS BASED HERE.
EIGHT YEARS AGO...! I THINK IT WAS AROUND THAT TIME.
GRANDPA STARTED LIVING WITH US THEN... BUT...
I HEARD FROM DAD THAT UP UNTIL THAT POINT HE WAS LIVING IN THE NORTHEAST THOUGH...
WELL NOW.

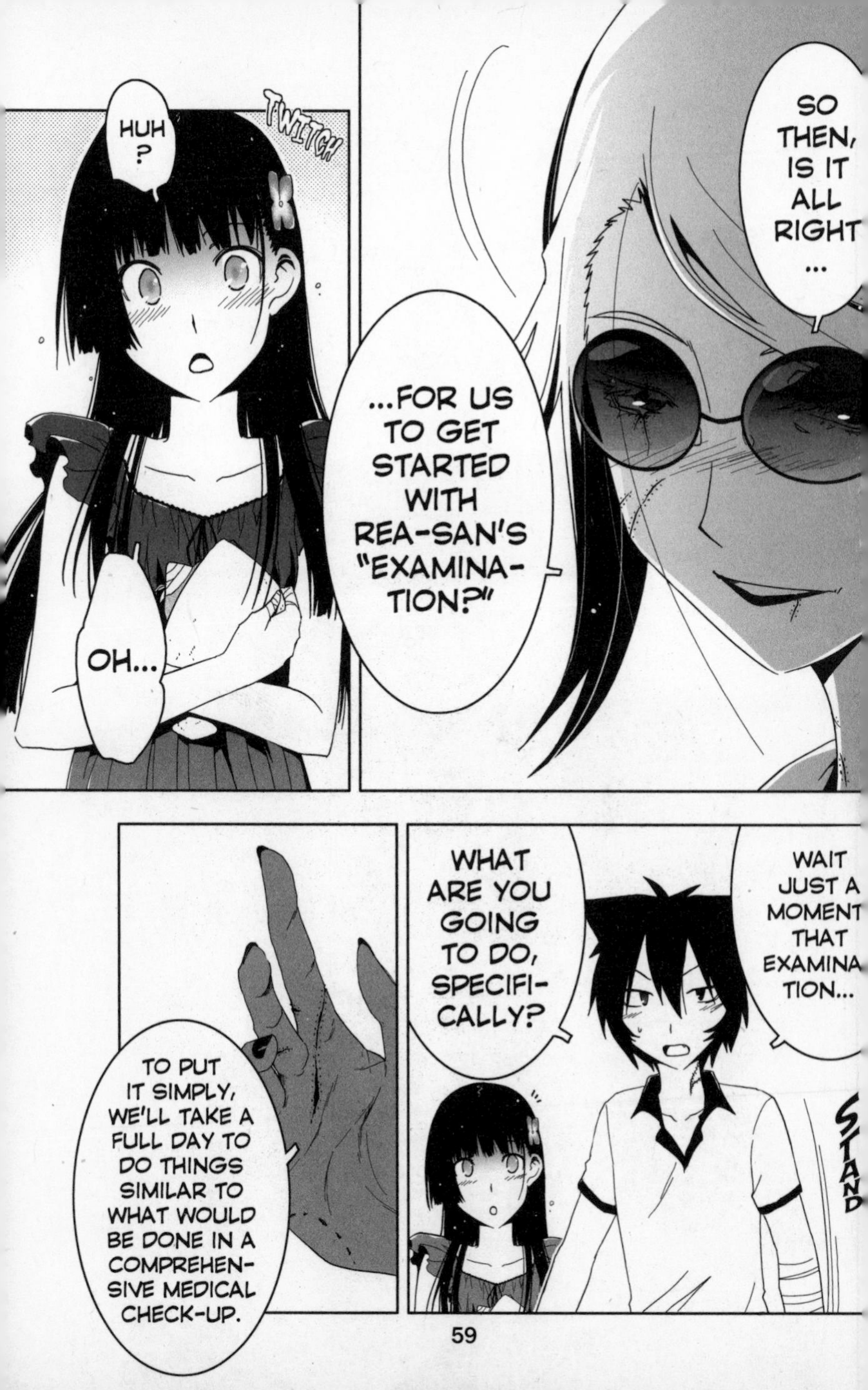
SO THEN, IS IT ALL RIGHT ...
...FOR US TO GET STARTED WITH REA-SAN'S "EXAMINATION?"
HUH ?
T'WITCH
OH...
WAIT JUST A MOMENT THAT EXAMINATION...
STAND
WHAT ARE YOU GOING TO DO, SPECIFICALLY?
TO PUT IT SIMPLY, WE'LL TAKE A FULL DAY TO DO THINGS SIMILAR TO WHAT WOULD BE DONE IN A COMPREHENSIVE MEDICAL CHECK-UP.

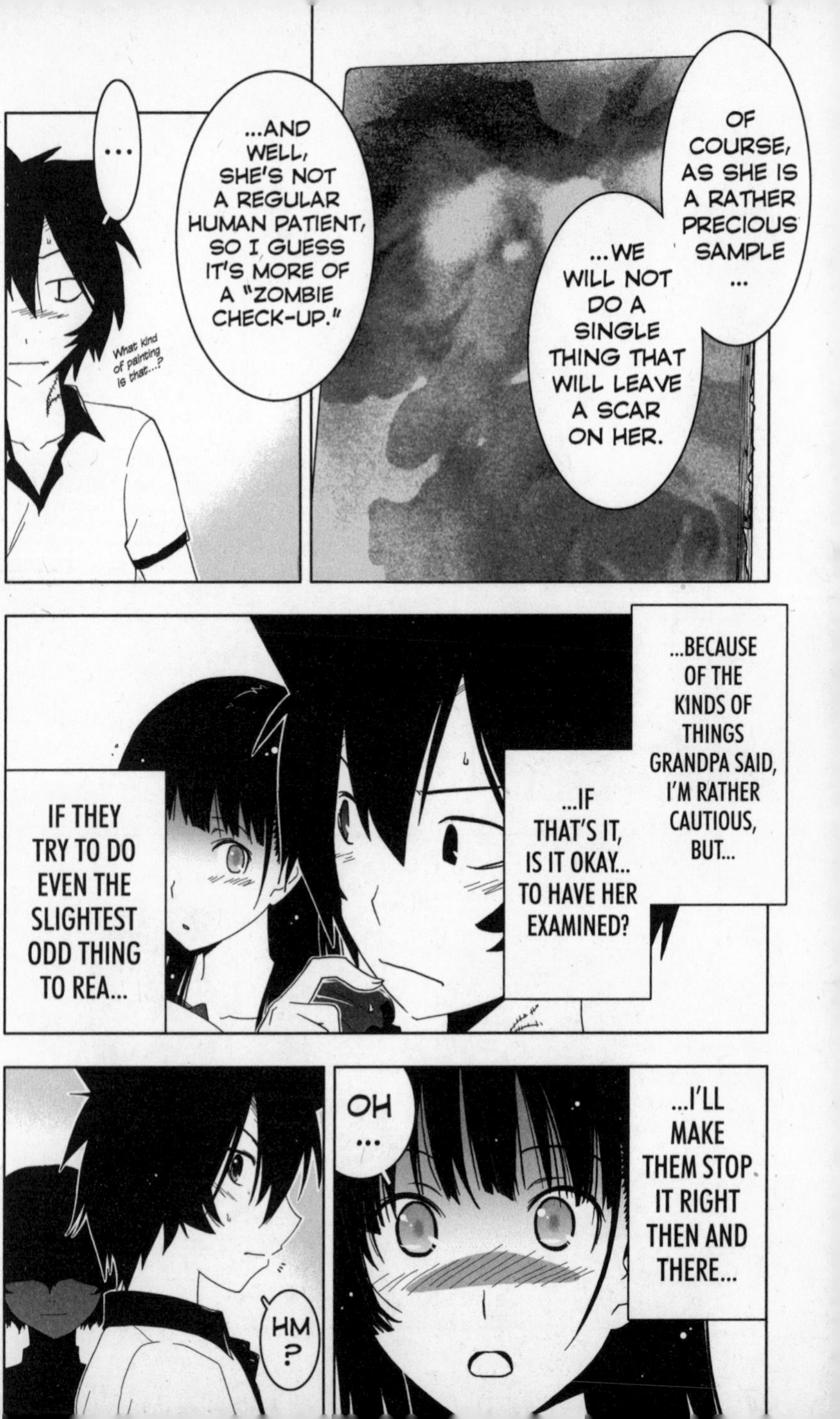
OF COURSE, AS SHE IS A RATHER PRECIOUS SAMPLE ...
...WE WILL NOT DO A SINGLE THING THAT WILL LEAVE A SCAR ON HER.
...AND WELL, SHE'S NOT A REGULAR HUMAN PATIENT, SO I GUESS IT'S MORE OF A "ZOMBIE CHECK-UP."
...
What kind of painting is that...?
...BECAUSE OF THE KINDS OF THINGS GRANDPA SAID, I'M RATHER CAUTIOUS, BUT...
...IF THAT'S IT, IS IT OKAY... TO HAVE HER EXAMINED?
IF THEY TRY TO DO EVEN THE SLIGHTEST ODD THING TO REA...
...I'LL MAKE THEM STOP IT RIGHT THEN AND THERE...
OH ...
HM ?

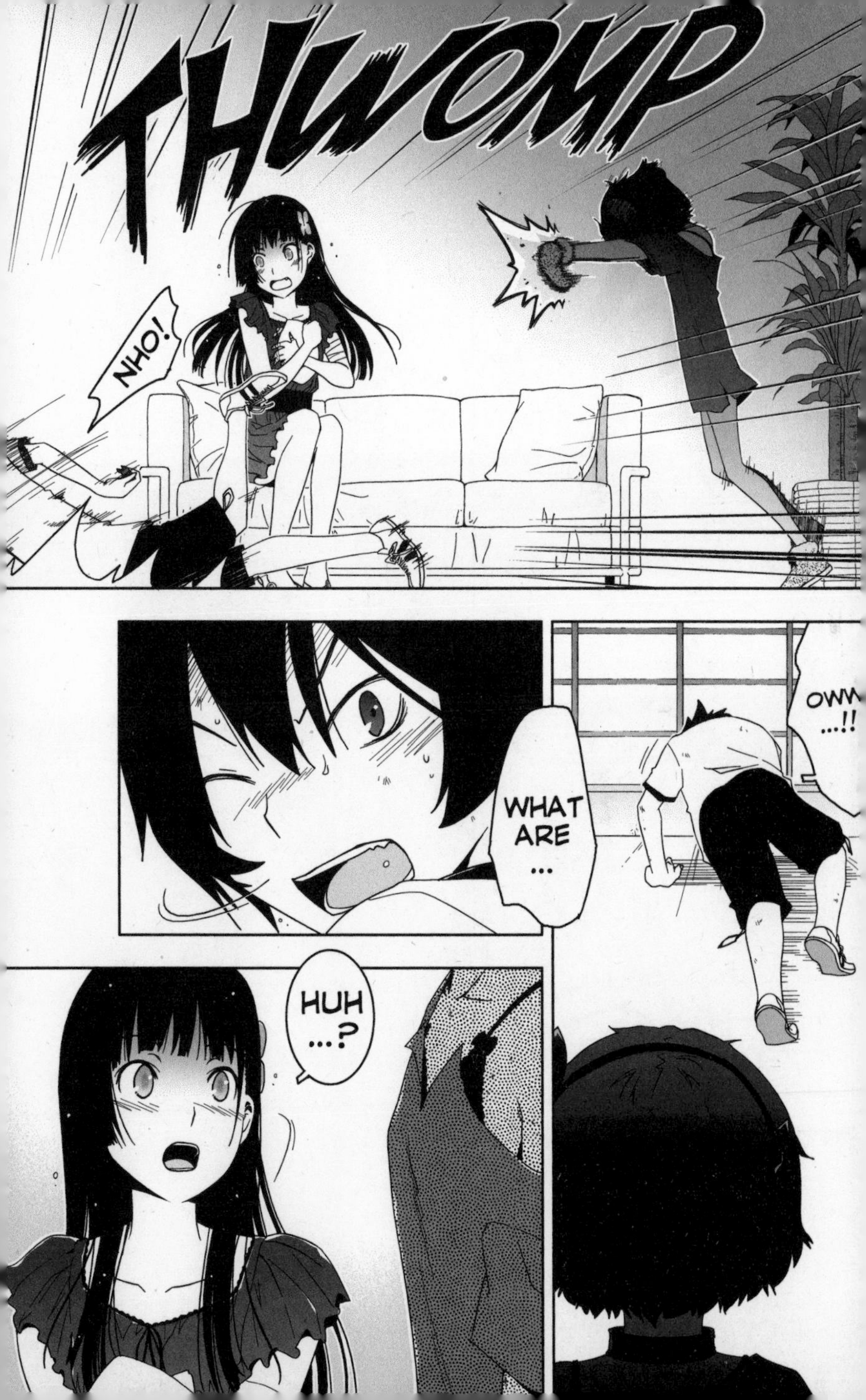
THWOMP
NHO!
OWW ...!!
WHAT ARE ...
HUH ...?

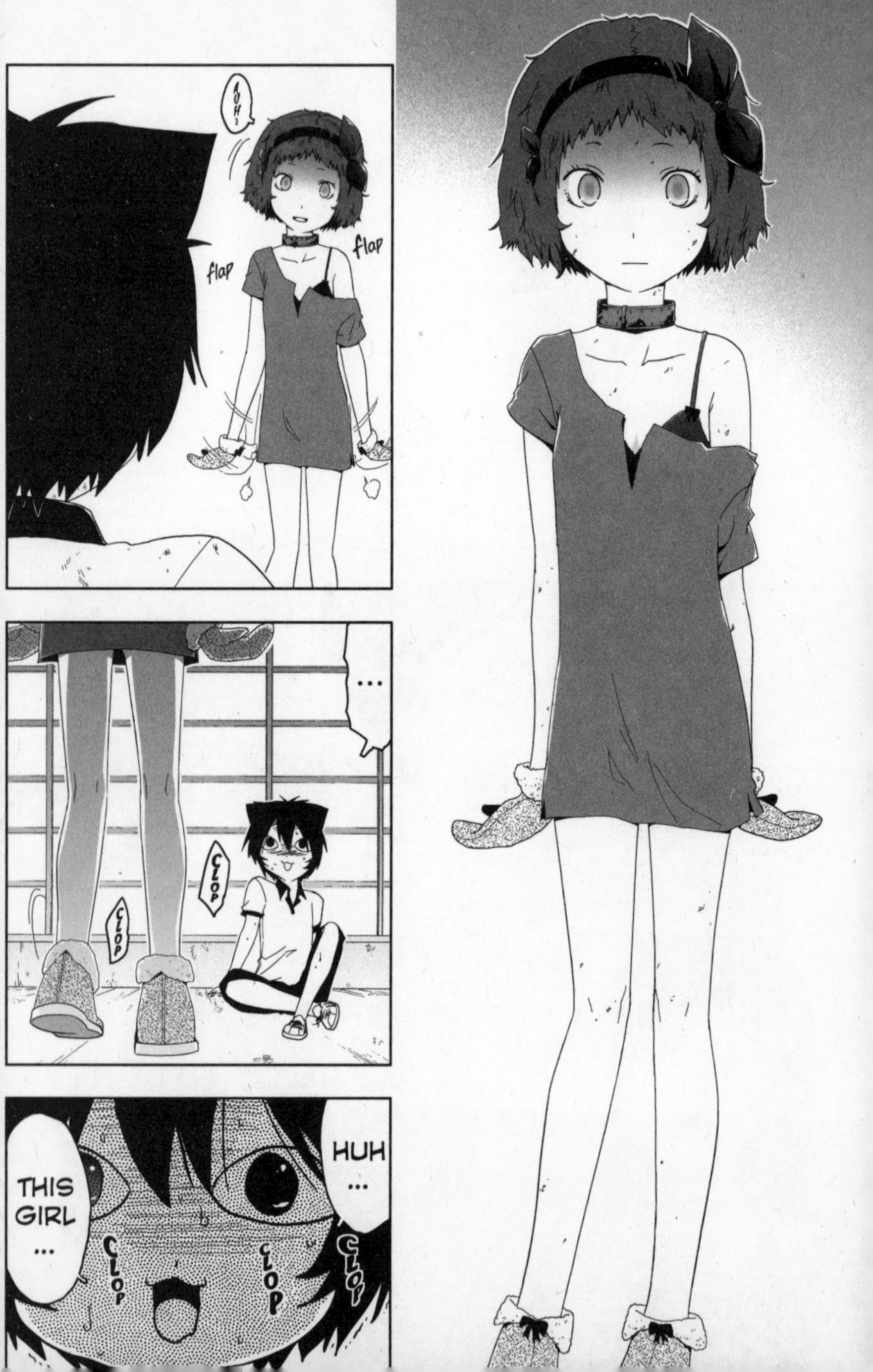
AUH!!
flap
flap
...
CLOP
CLOP
HUH...
CLOP
CLOP
CLOP
THIS GIRL...

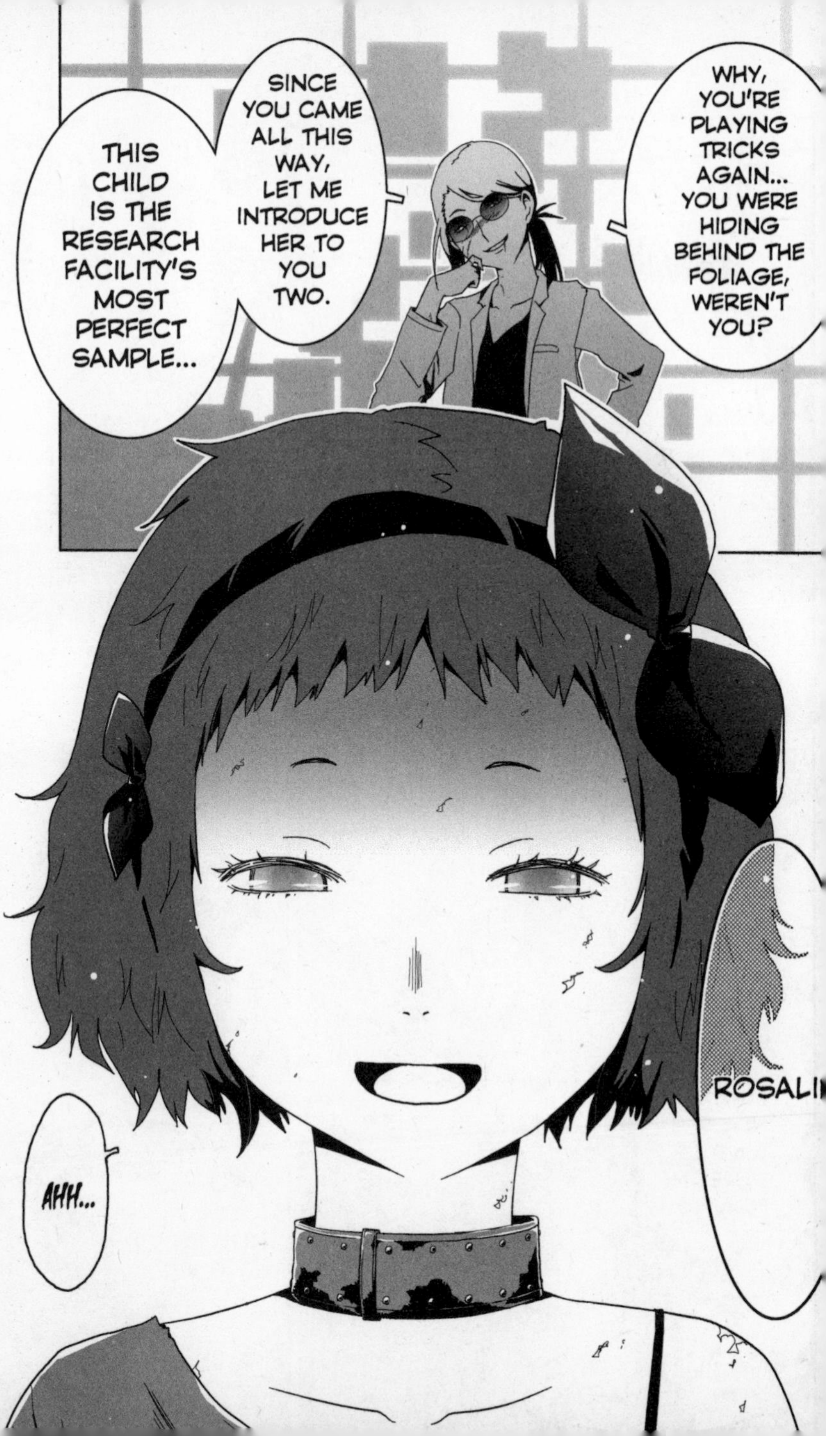
WHY, YOU'RE PLAYING TRICKS AGAIN... YOU WERE HIDING BEHIND THE FOLIAGE, WEREN'T YOU?
SINCE YOU CAME ALL THIS WAY, LET ME INTRODUCE HER TO YOU TWO.
THIS CHILD IS THE RESEARCH FACILITY'S MOST PERFECT SAMPLE...
ROSALI
AHH...

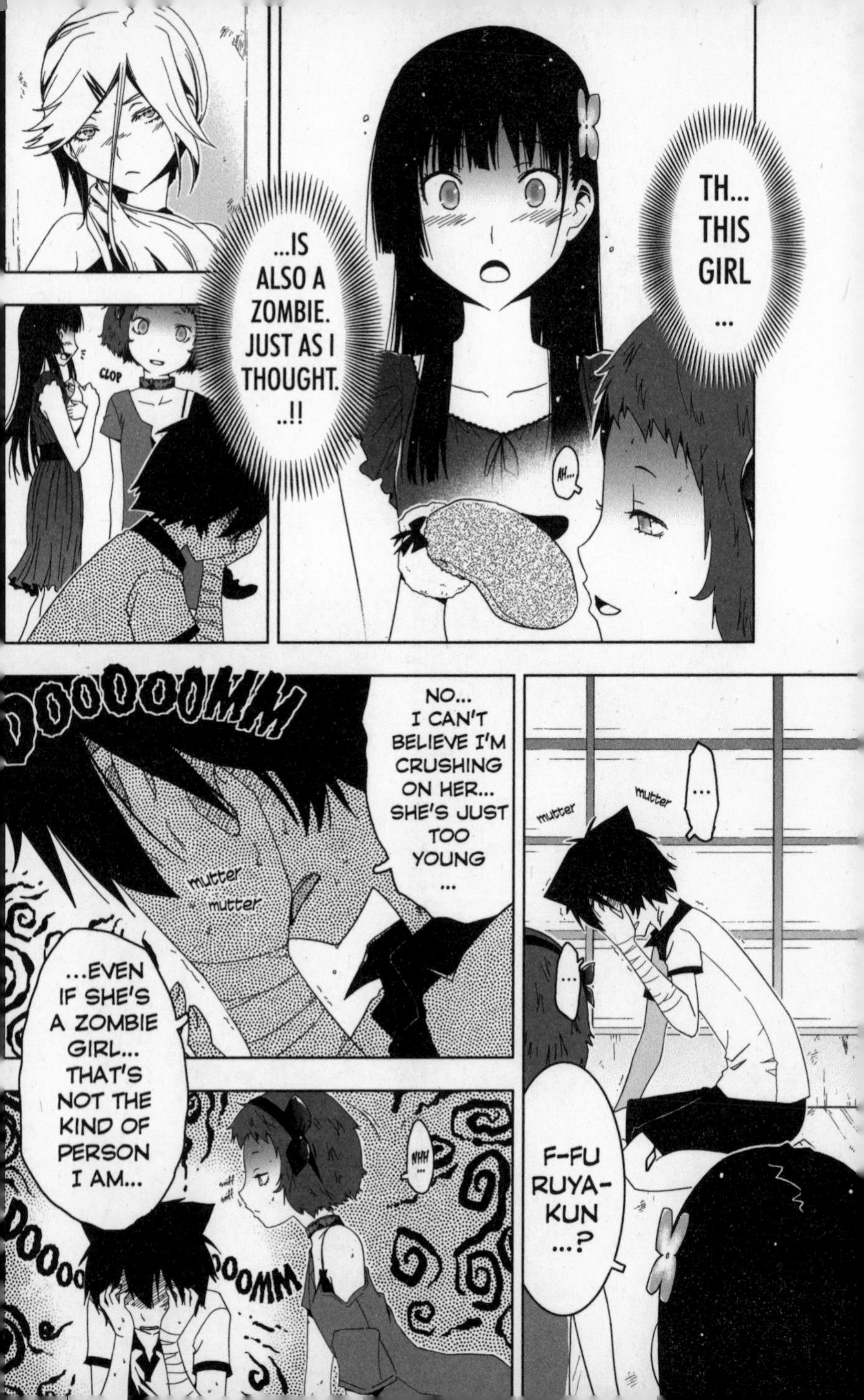

TH... THIS GIRL ...
...IS ALSO A ZOMBIE. JUST AS I THOUGHT. ..!!
AH...
CLOP
mutter
mutter
...
...
F-FURUYA-KUN ...?
DOOOOOOMM
NO... I CAN'T BELIEVE I'M CRUSHING ON HER... SHE'S JUST TOO YOUNG ...
mutter
mutter
...EVEN IF SHE'S A ZOMBIE GIRL... THAT'S NOT THE KIND OF PERSON I AM...
NHH ...
DOOOO
OOMM

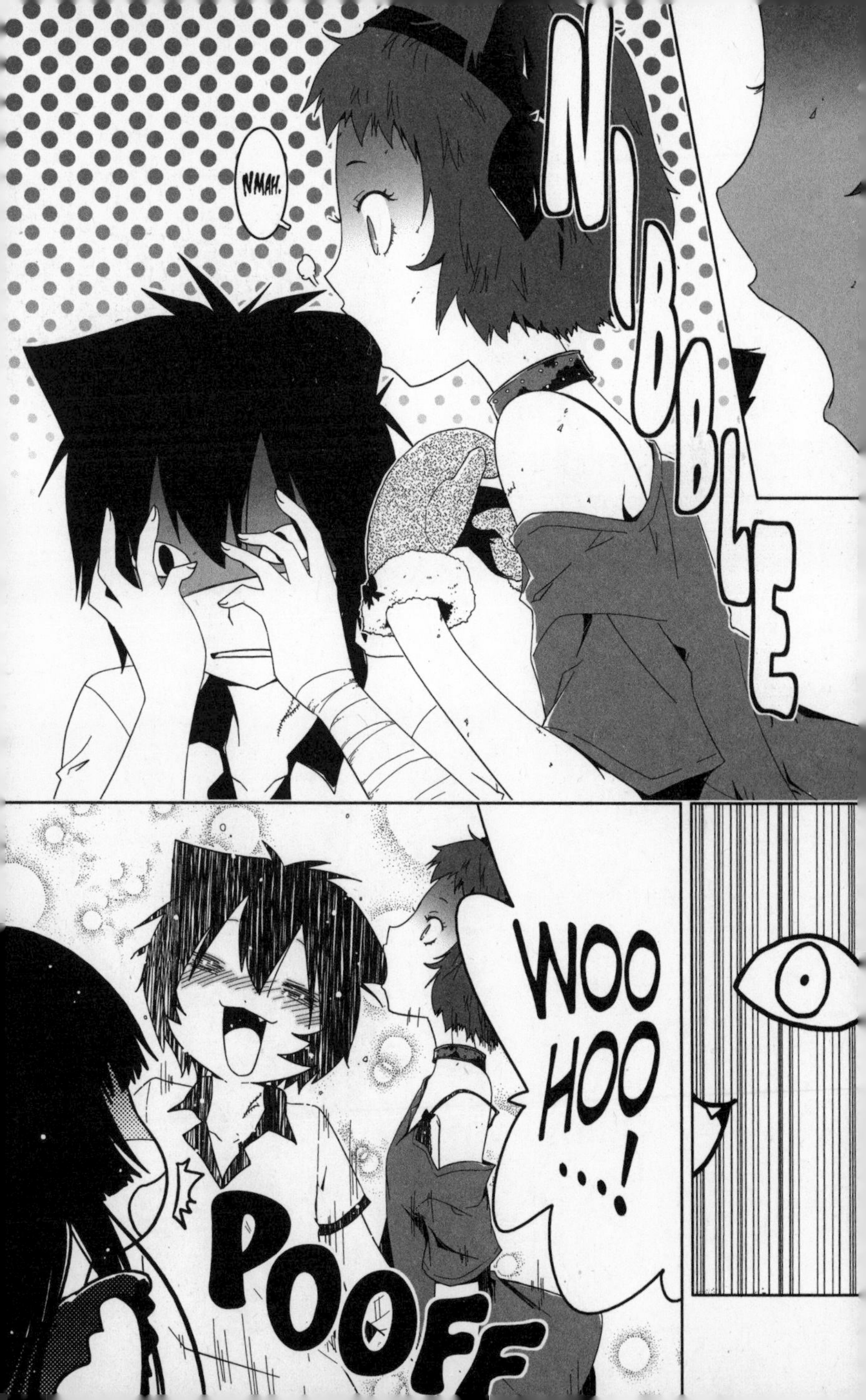
NIBBLE
NMAH.
WOO HOO HOO...!
POOFF

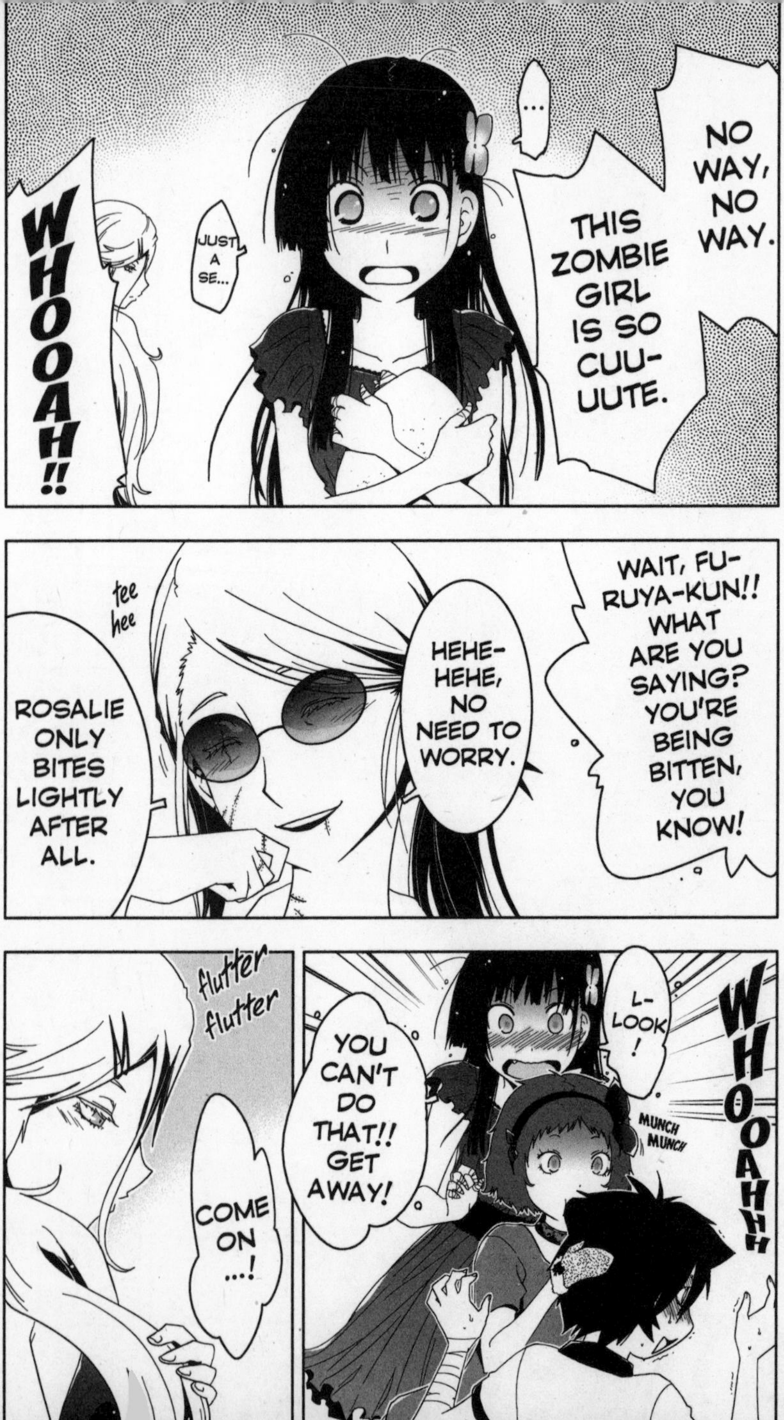
NO WAY, NO WAY.
THIS ZOMBIE GIRL IS SO CUUU-UUTE.
...
JUST A SE...
WHOOAH!!
WAIT, FU-RUYA-KUN!! WHAT ARE YOU SAYING? YOU'RE BEING BITTEN, YOU KNOW!
HEHE-HEHE, NO NEED TO WORRY.
tee hee
ROSALIE ONLY BITES LIGHTLY AFTER ALL.
WHOOAHHH
L-LOOK!
MUNCH MUNCH
YOU CAN'T DO THAT!! GET AWAY!
flutter flutter
COME ON ...!

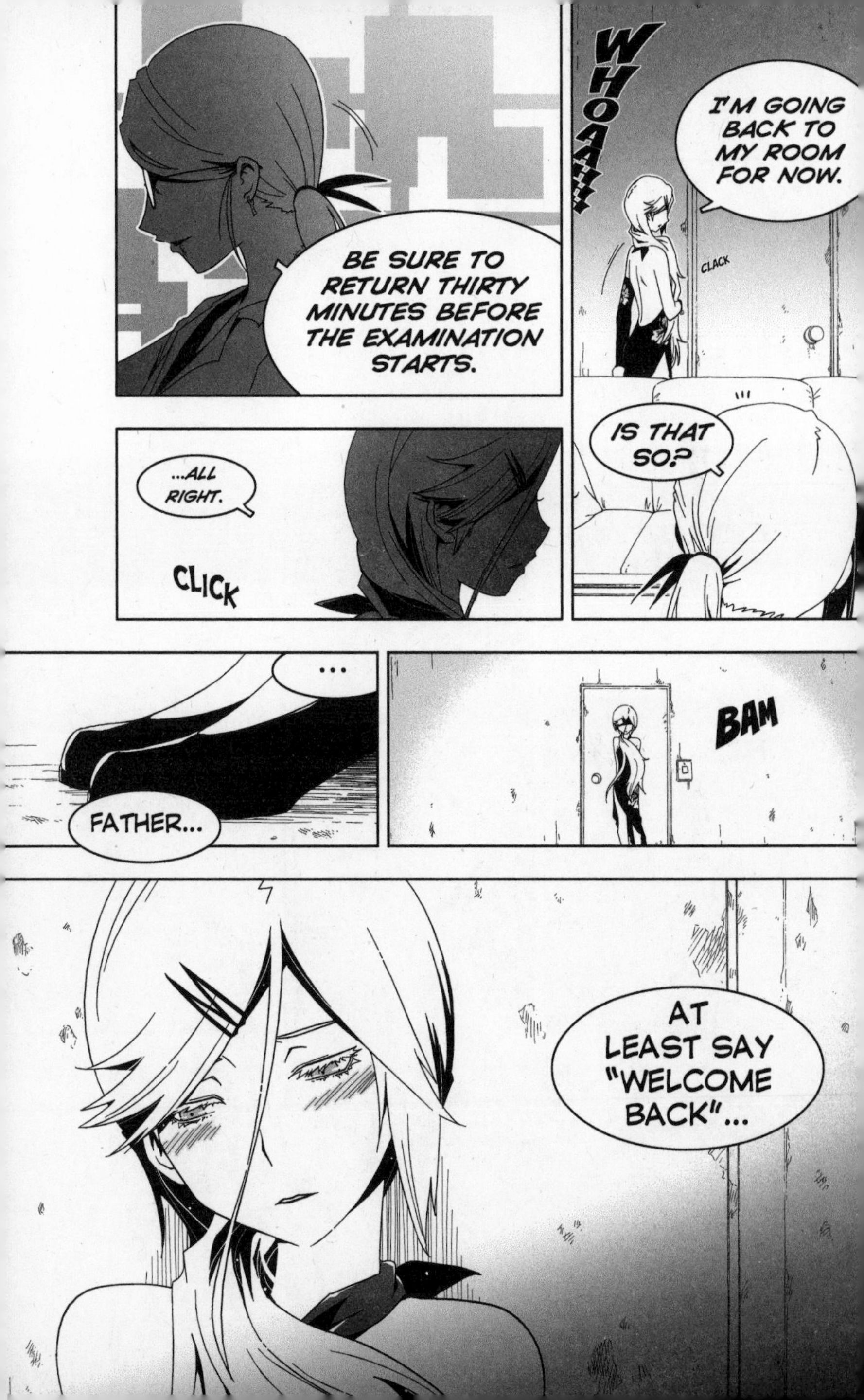
WHOAA
I'M GOING BACK TO MY ROOM FOR NOW.
CLACK
BE SURE TO RETURN THIRTY MINUTES BEFORE THE EXAMINATION STARTS.
IS THAT SO?
...ALL RIGHT.
CLICK
BAM
...
FATHER...
AT LEAST SAY "WELCOME BACK"...

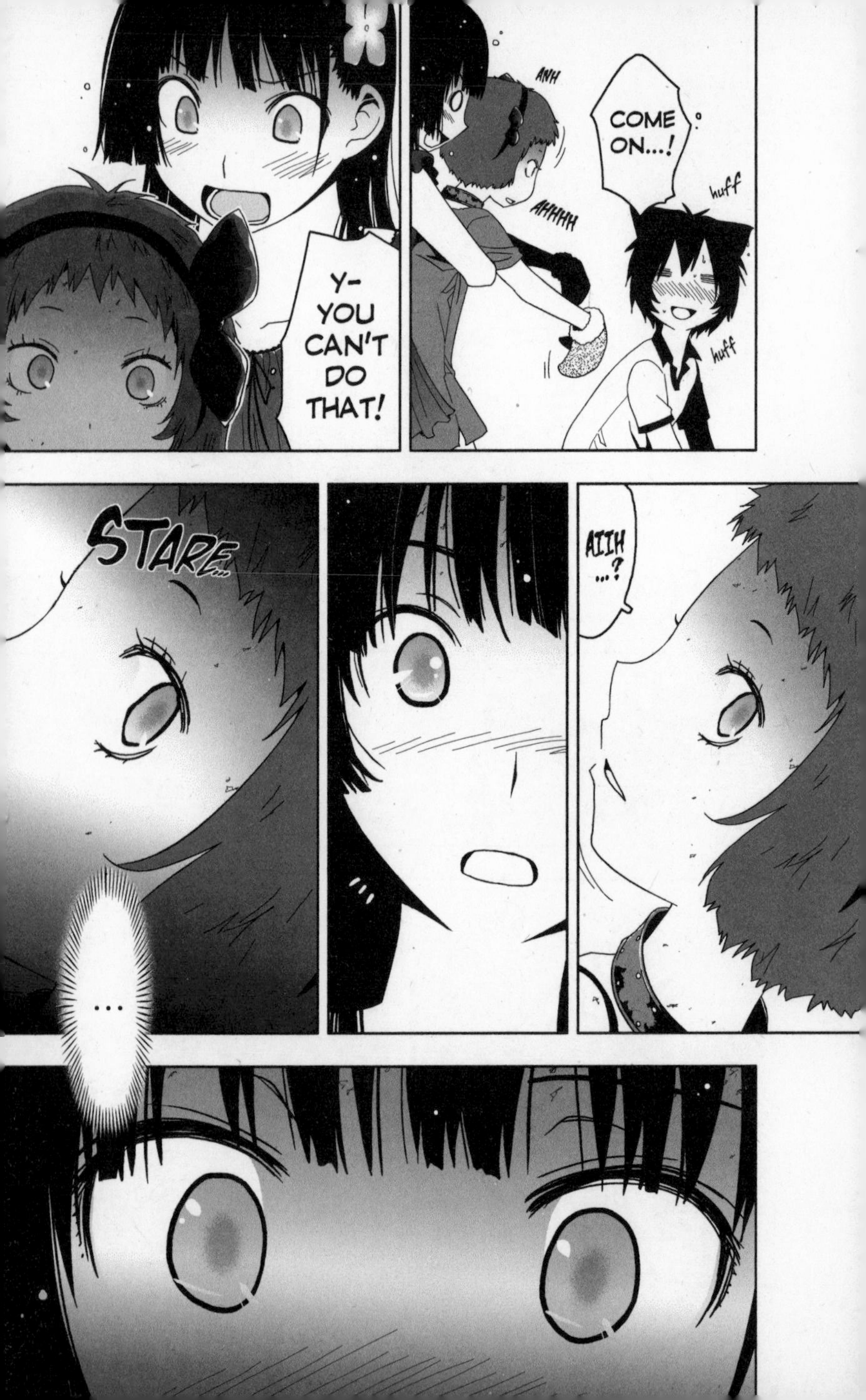

COME ON...!
ANH
huff
AHHHH
huff
Y-YOU CAN'T DO THAT!
AIIH ...?
STARE...
...

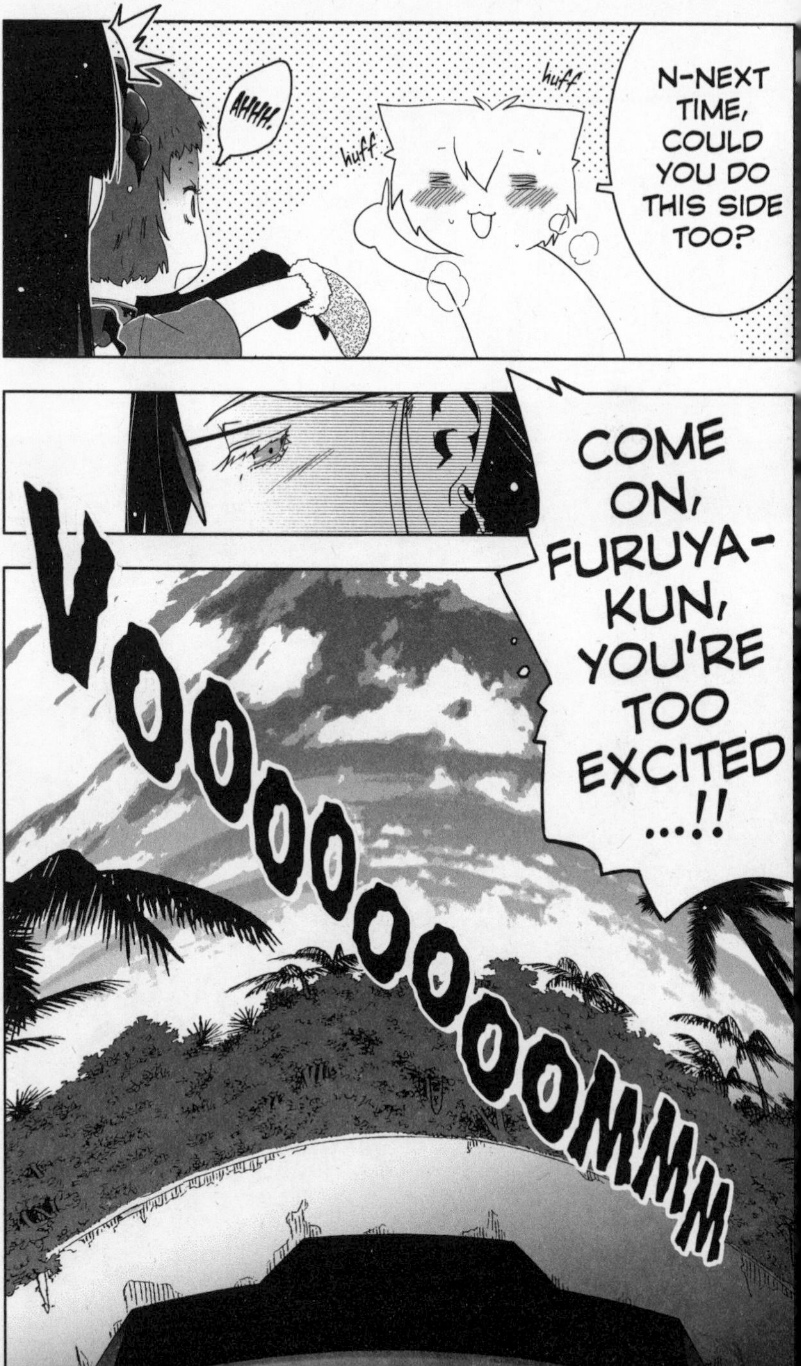
N-NEXT TIME, COULD YOU DO THIS SIDE TOO?
huff
huff
AHHH!
COME ON, FURUYA-KUN, YOU'RE TOO EXCITED ...!!
VOOOOOOOOOOOOMMMM

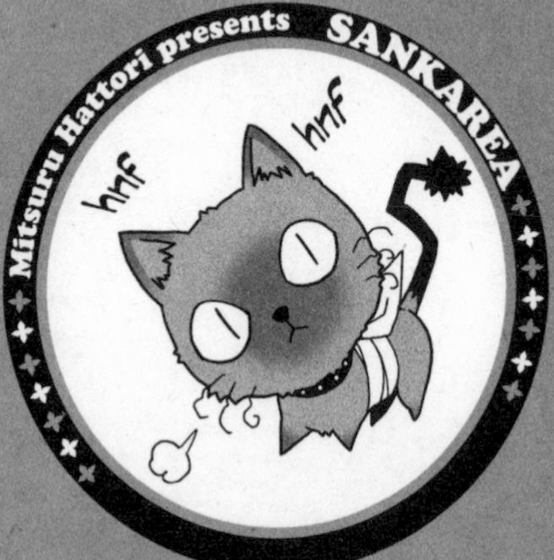
Mitsuru Hattori presents
SANKAREA
hnf
hnf

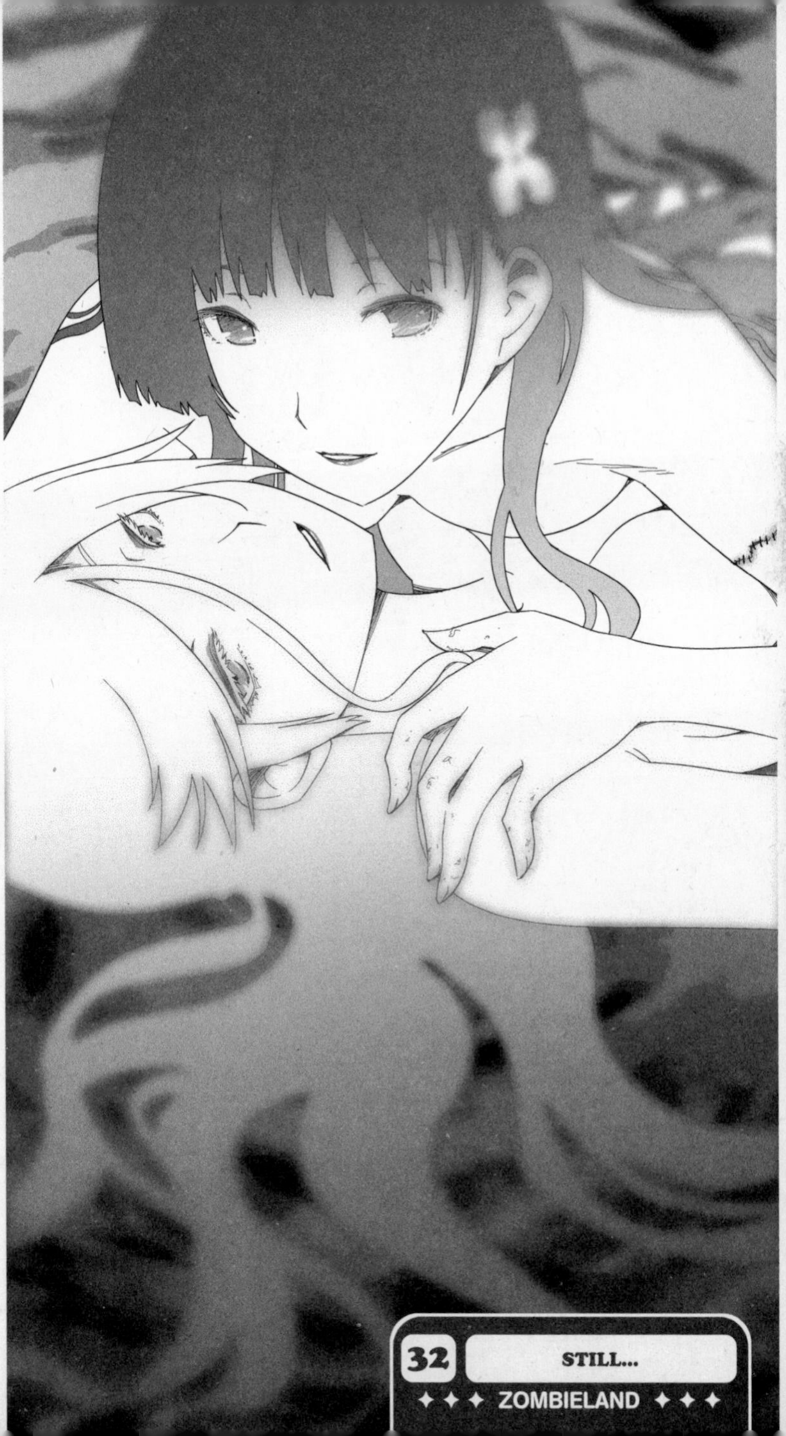
32
STILL...
✦✦✦ ZOMBIELAND ✦✦✦

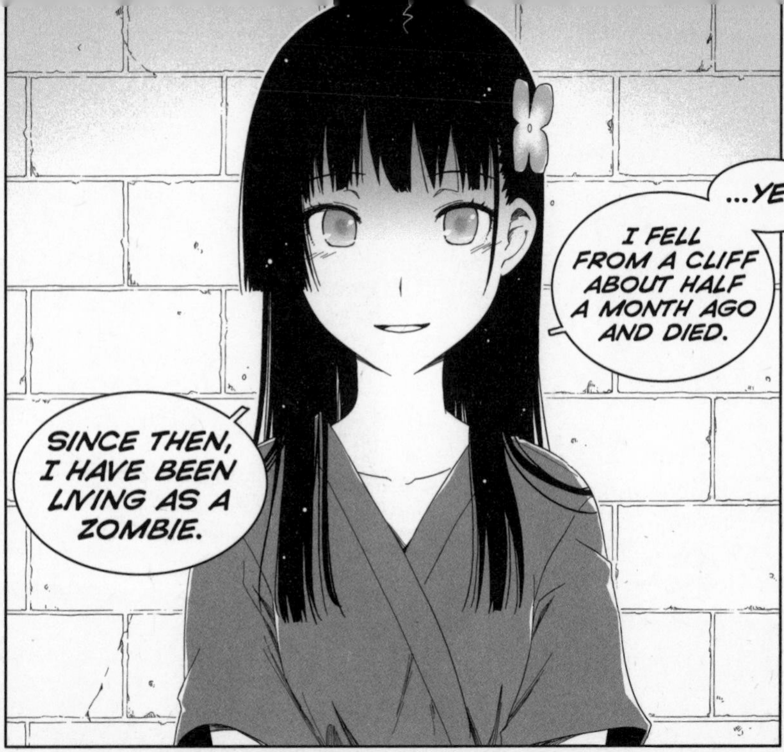
...YES.
I FELL FROM A CLIFF ABOUT HALF A MONTH AGO AND DIED.
SINCE THEN, I HAVE BEEN LIVING AS A ZOMBIE.
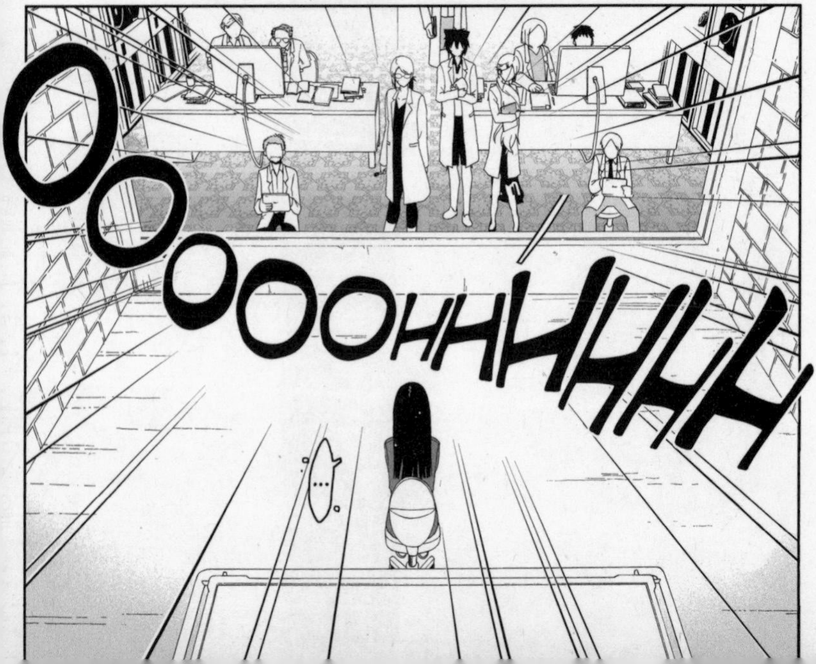
OOOOOHHHHHHH
...

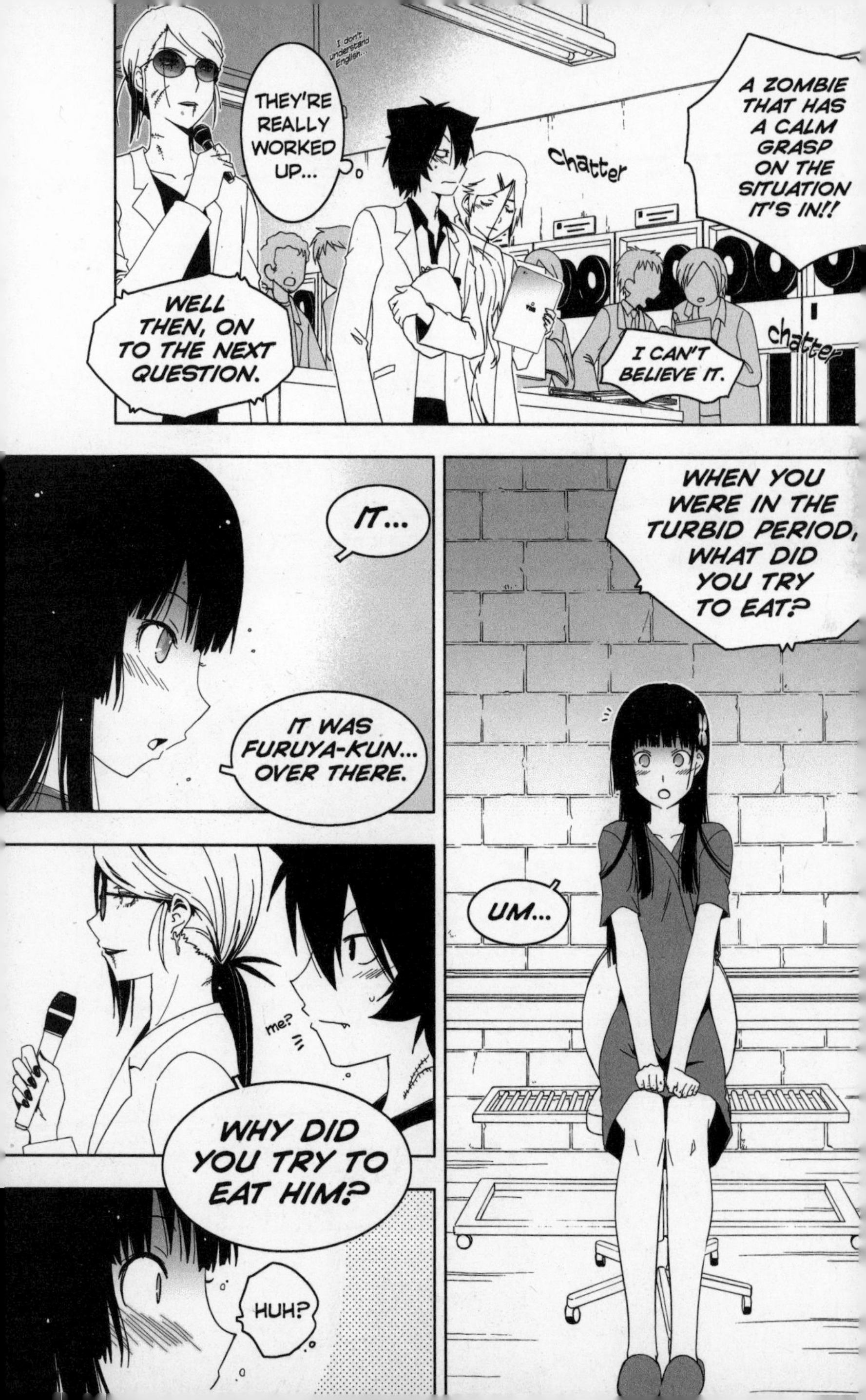
A ZOMBIE THAT HAS A CALM GRASP ON THE SITUATION IT'S IN!!
Chatter
chatter
I CAN'T BELIEVE IT.
THEY'RE REALLY WORKED UP...
I don't understand English...
WELL THEN, ON TO THE NEXT QUESTION.
WHEN YOU WERE IN THE TURBID PERIOD, WHAT DID YOU TRY TO EAT?
UM...
IT...
IT WAS FURUYA-KUN... OVER THERE.
WHY DID YOU TRY TO EAT HIM?
me?
HUH?

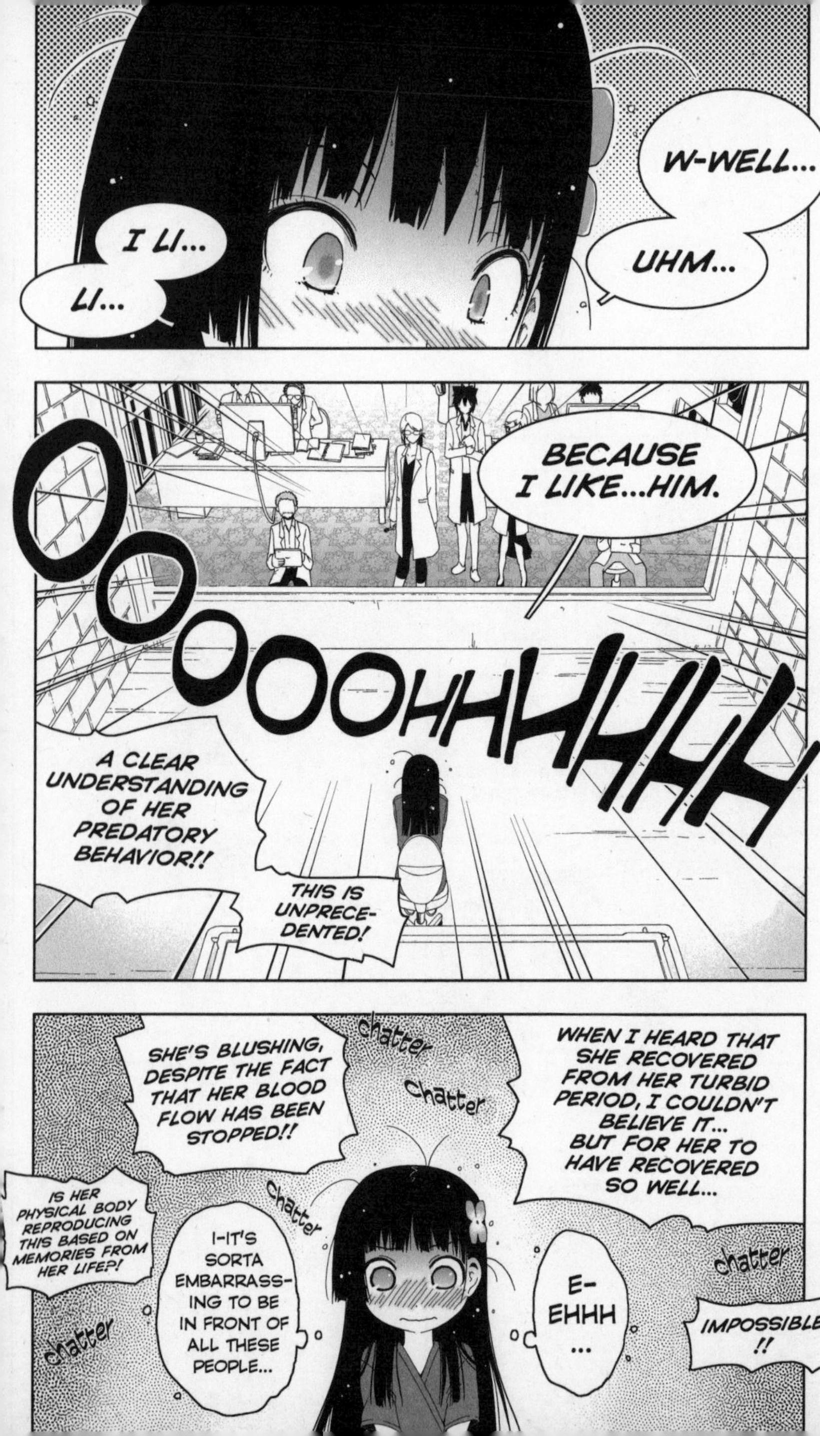

W-WELL...
UHM...
I LI...
LI...
BECAUSE I LIKE...HIM.
OOOOOOHHHHHH
A CLEAR UNDERSTANDING OF HER PREDATORY BEHAVIOR!!
THIS IS UNPRECE-DENTED!
WHEN I HEARD THAT SHE RECOVERED FROM HER TURBID PERIOD, I COULDN'T BELIEVE IT... BUT FOR HER TO HAVE RECOVERED SO WELL...
chatter
chatter
SHE'S BLUSHING, DESPITE THE FACT THAT HER BLOOD FLOW HAS BEEN STOPPED!!
chatter
IMPOSSIBLE!!
E-EHHH...
I-IT'S SORTA EMBARRASS-ING TO BE IN FRONT OF ALL THESE PEOPLE...
IS HER PHYSICAL BODY REPRODUCING THIS BASED ON MEMORIES FROM HER LIFE?!
chatter
chatter

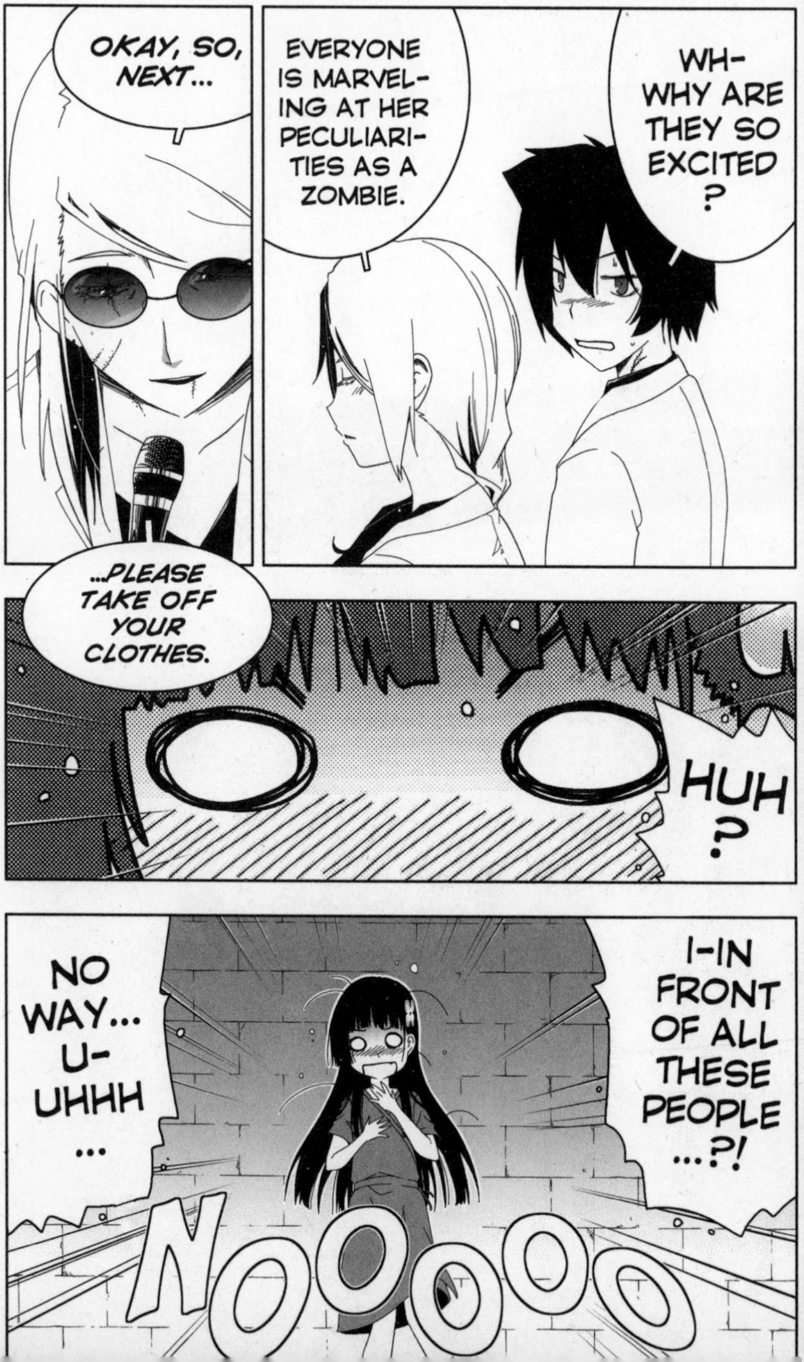
WH- WHY ARE THEY SO EXCITED?
EVERYONE IS MARVEL-ING AT HER PECULIARI-TIES AS A ZOMBIE.
OKAY, SO, NEXT...
...PLEASE TAKE OFF YOUR CLOTHES.
HUH?
I-IN FRONT OF ALL THESE PEOPLE...?!
NO WAY... U-UHHH...
NOOOOO

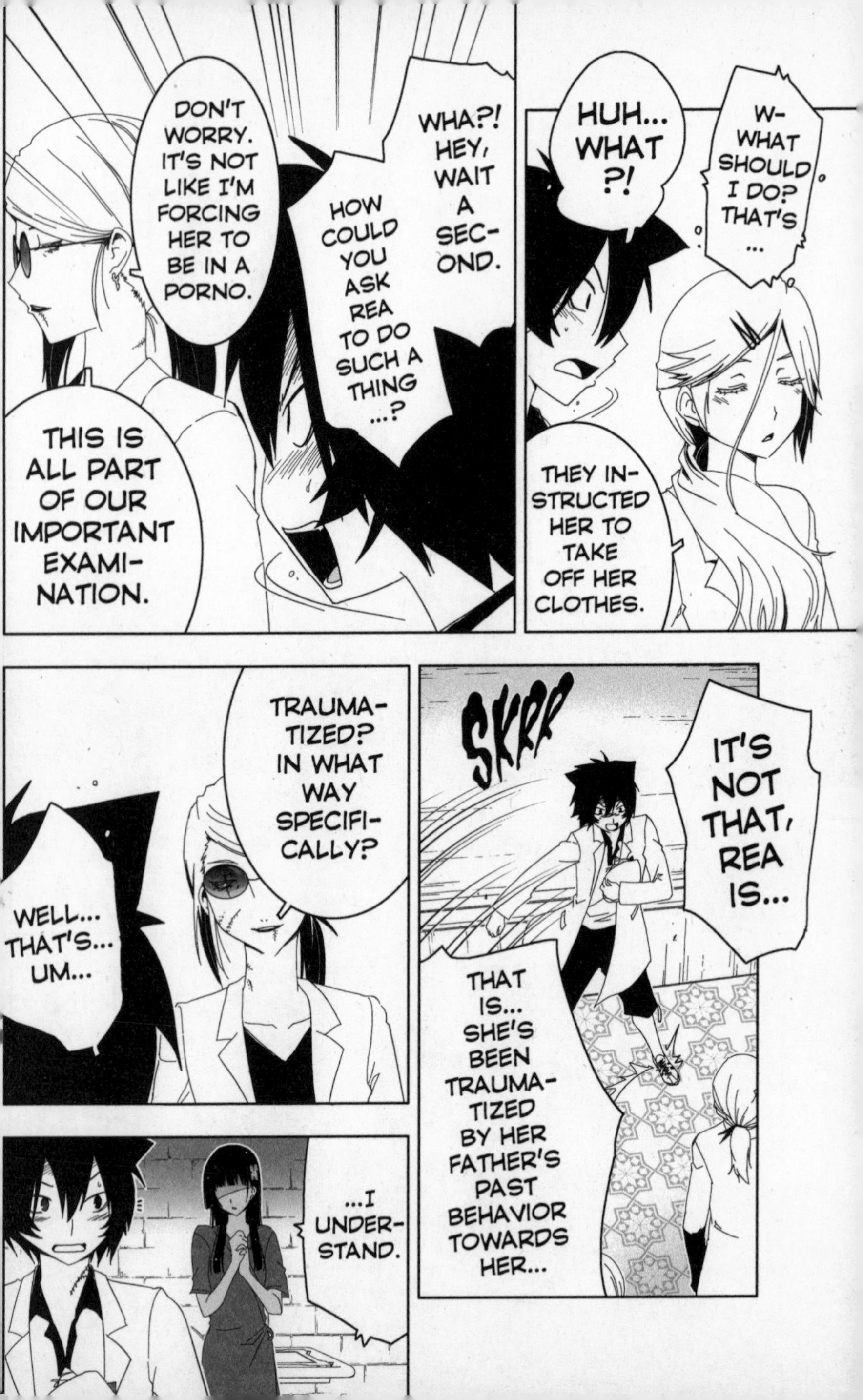
W- WHAT SHOULD I DO? THAT'S ...
HUH... WHAT ?!
THEY INSTRUCTED HER TO TAKE OFF HER CLOTHES.
WHA?! HEY, WAIT A SECOND.
HOW COULD YOU ASK REA TO DO SUCH A THING ...?
DON'T WORRY. IT'S NOT LIKE I'M FORCING HER TO BE IN A PORNO.
THIS IS ALL PART OF OUR IMPORTANT EXAMINATION.
SKRR
IT'S NOT THAT, REA IS...
THAT IS... SHE'S BEEN TRAUMATIZED BY HER FATHER'S PAST BEHAVIOR TOWARDS HER...
TRAUMATIZED? IN WHAT WAY SPECIFICALLY?
WELL... THAT'S... UM...
...I UNDERSTAND.

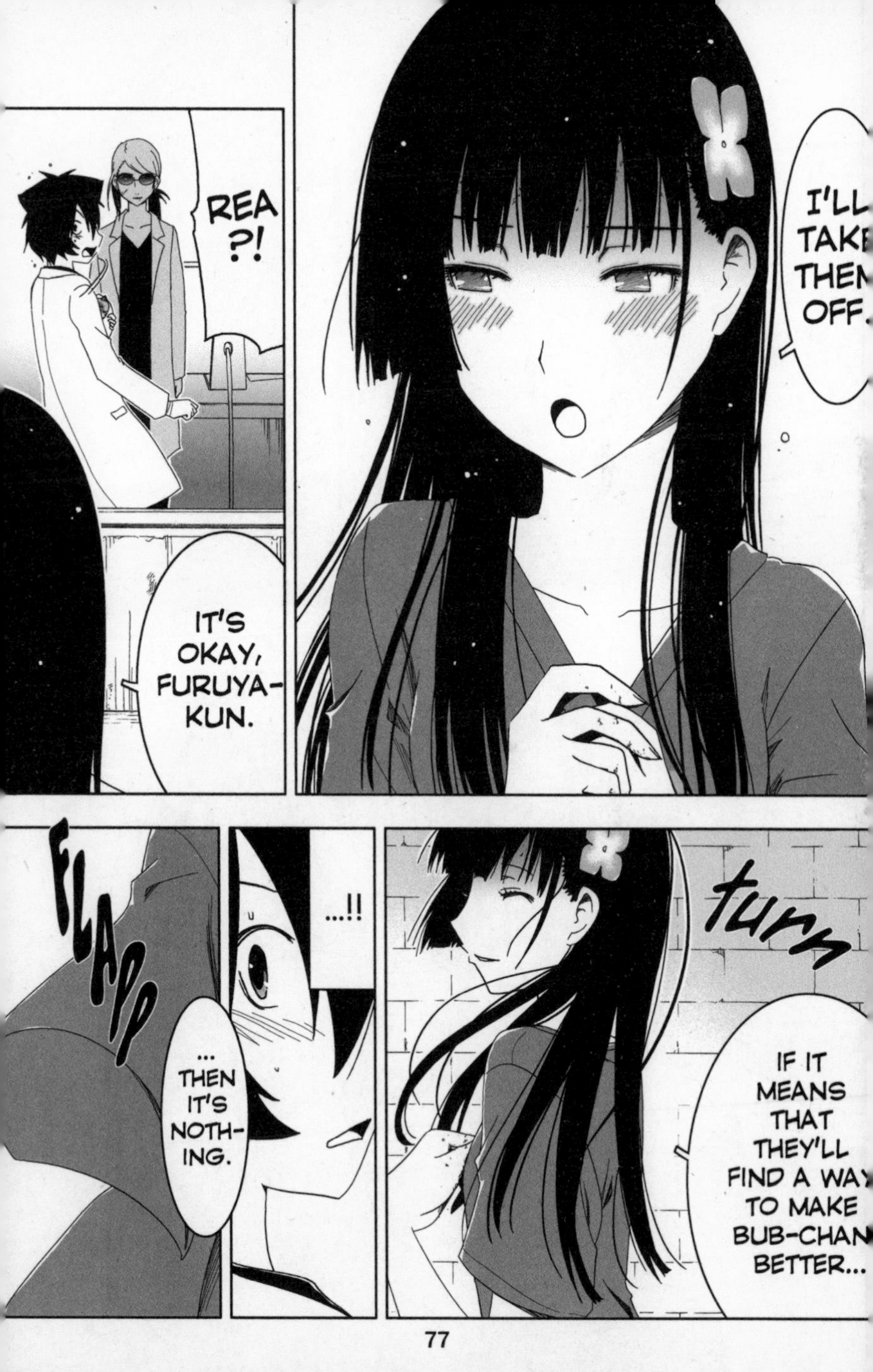
I'LL TAKE THEM OFF.
REA ?!
IT'S OKAY, FURUYA-KUN.
turn
IF IT MEANS THAT THEY'LL FIND A WAY TO MAKE BUB-CHAN BETTER...
...!!
... THEN IT'S NOTHING.
FLAP

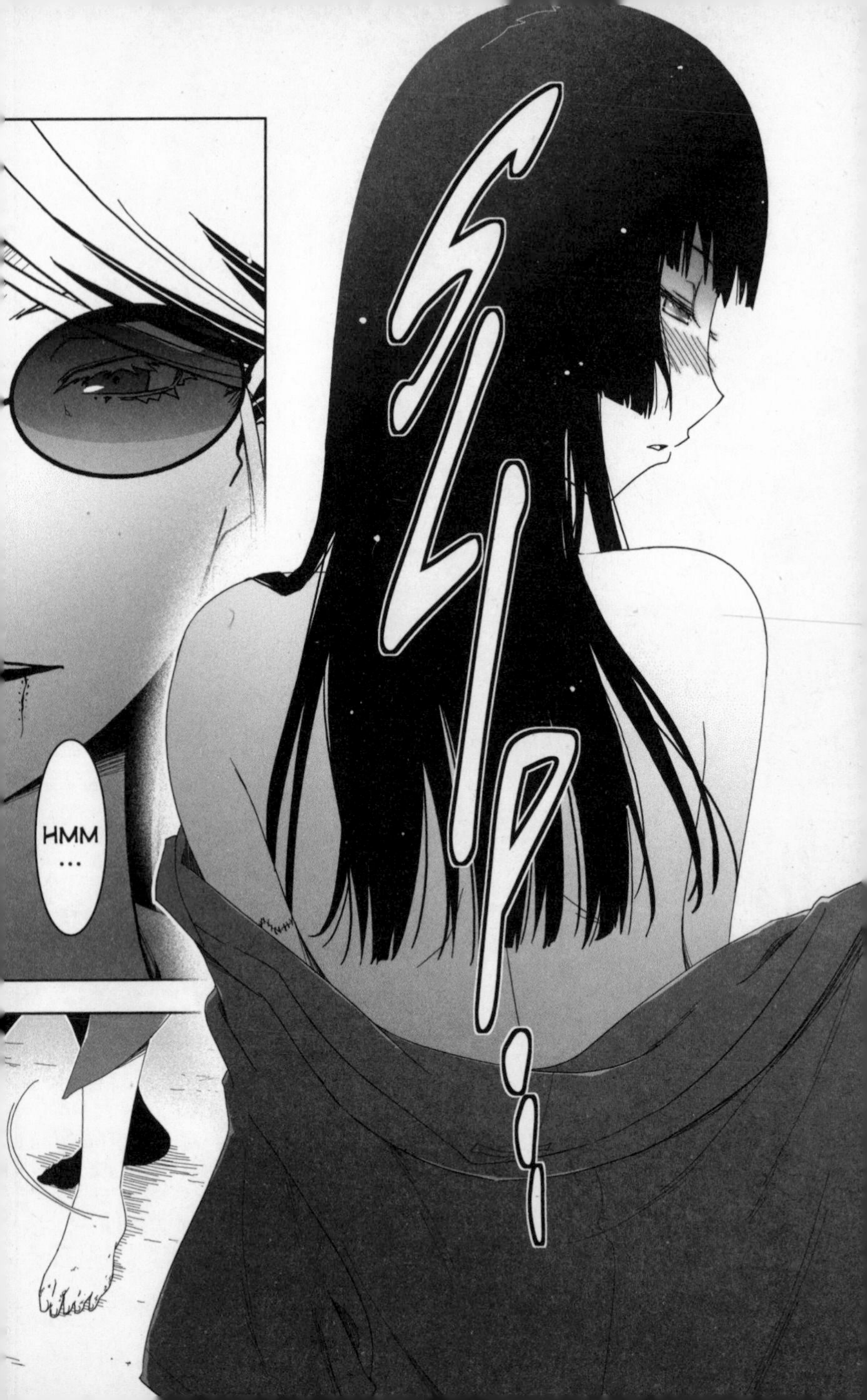
SLIP...
HMM
...

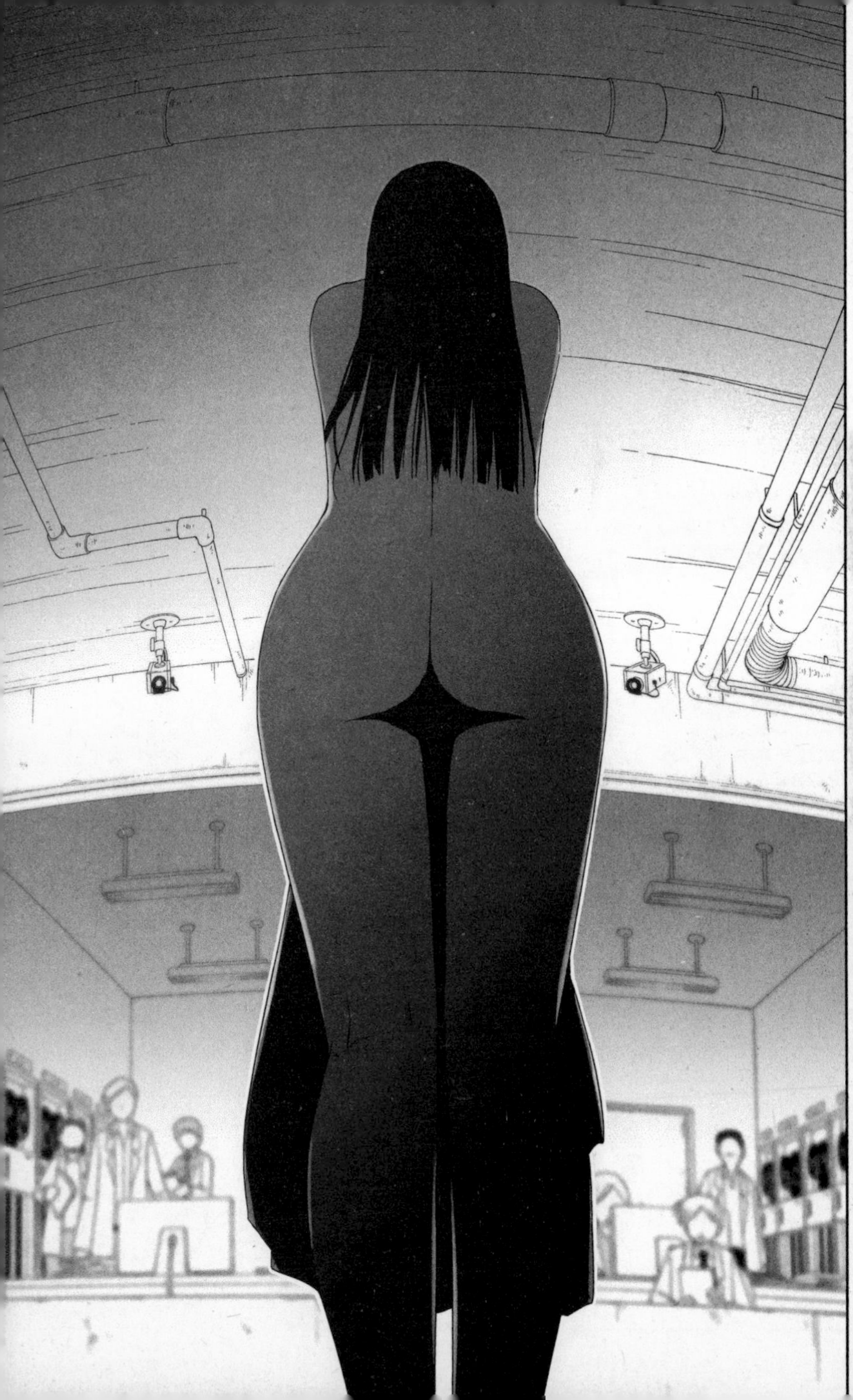

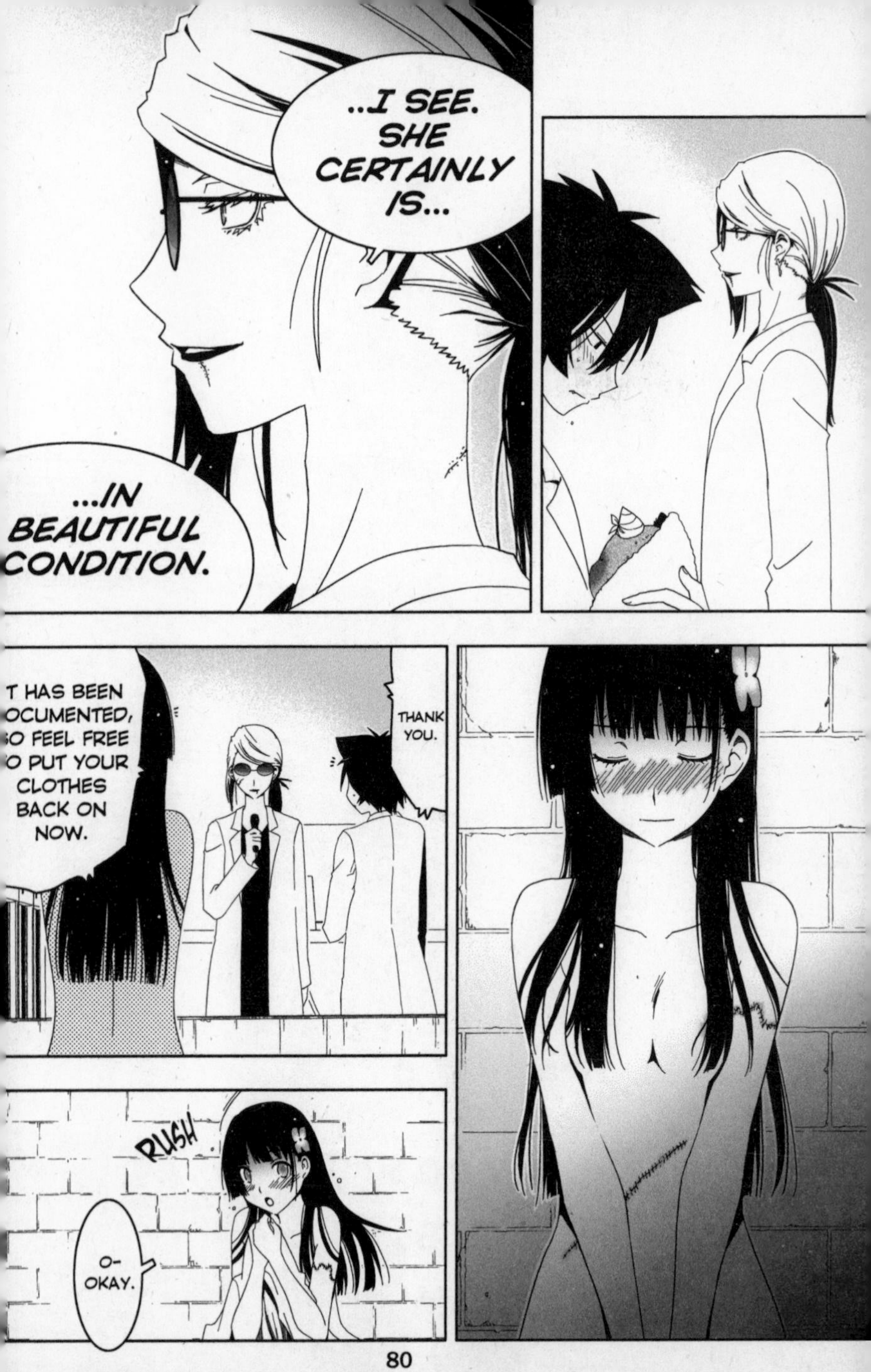

...I SEE. SHE CERTAINLY IS...
...IN BEAUTIFUL CONDITION.
THANK YOU.
T HAS BEEN OCUMENTED, O FEEL FREE O PUT YOUR CLOTHES BACK ON NOW.
RUSH
O- OKAY.

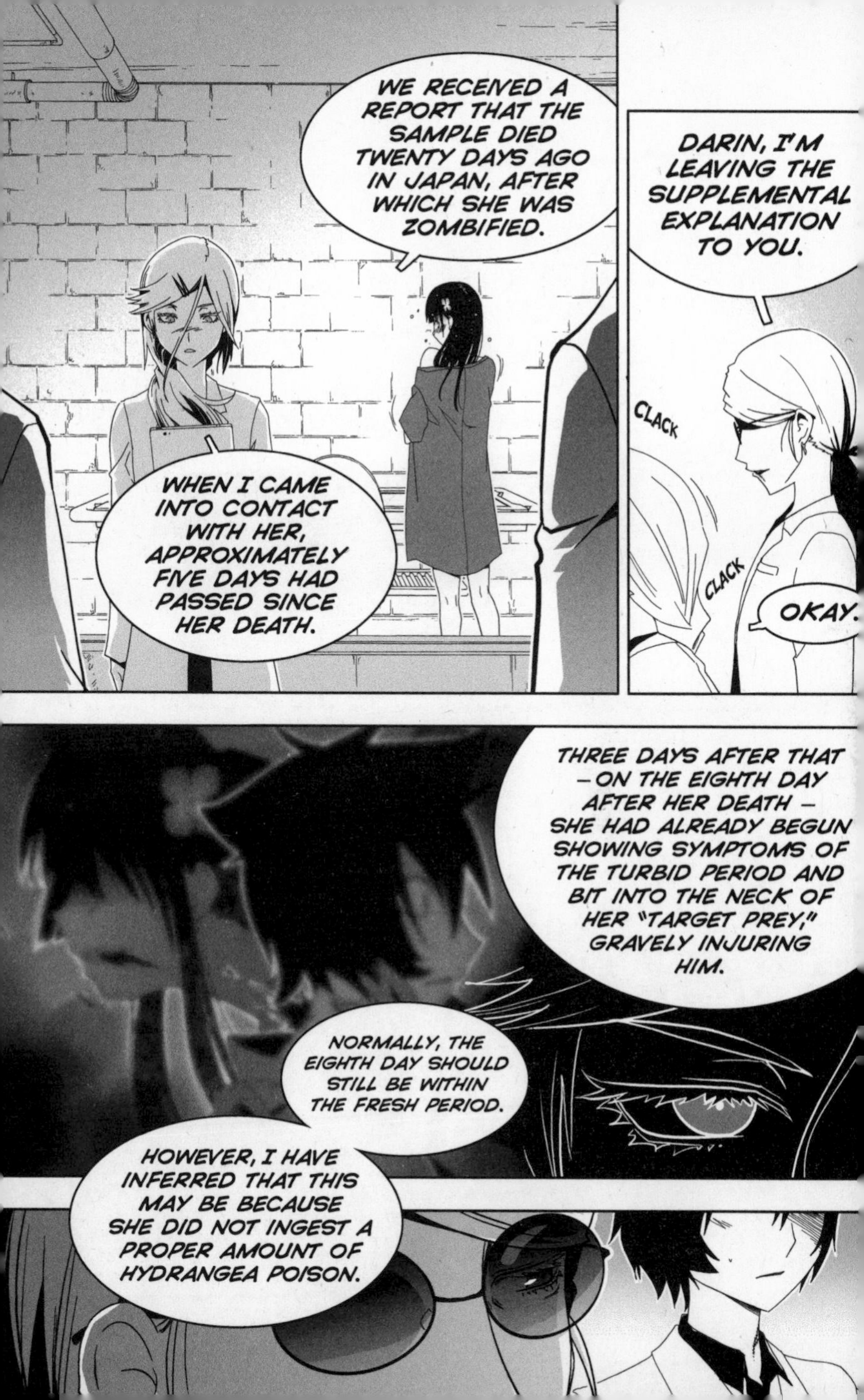
DARIN, I'M LEAVING THE SUPPLEMENTAL EXPLANATION TO YOU.
CLACK
CLACK
OKAY.
WE RECEIVED A REPORT THAT THE SAMPLE DIED TWENTY DAYS AGO IN JAPAN, AFTER WHICH SHE WAS ZOMBIFIED.
WHEN I CAME INTO CONTACT WITH HER, APPROXIMATELY FIVE DAYS HAD PASSED SINCE HER DEATH.
THREE DAYS AFTER THAT —ON THE EIGHTH DAY AFTER HER DEATH— SHE HAD ALREADY BEGUN SHOWING SYMPTOMS OF THE TURBID PERIOD AND BIT INTO THE NECK OF HER "TARGET PREY," GRAVELY INJURING HIM.
NORMALLY, THE EIGHTH DAY SHOULD STILL BE WITHIN THE FRESH PERIOD.
HOWEVER, I HAVE INFERRED THAT THIS MAY BE BECAUSE SHE DID NOT INGEST A PROPER AMOUNT OF HYDRANGEA POISON.

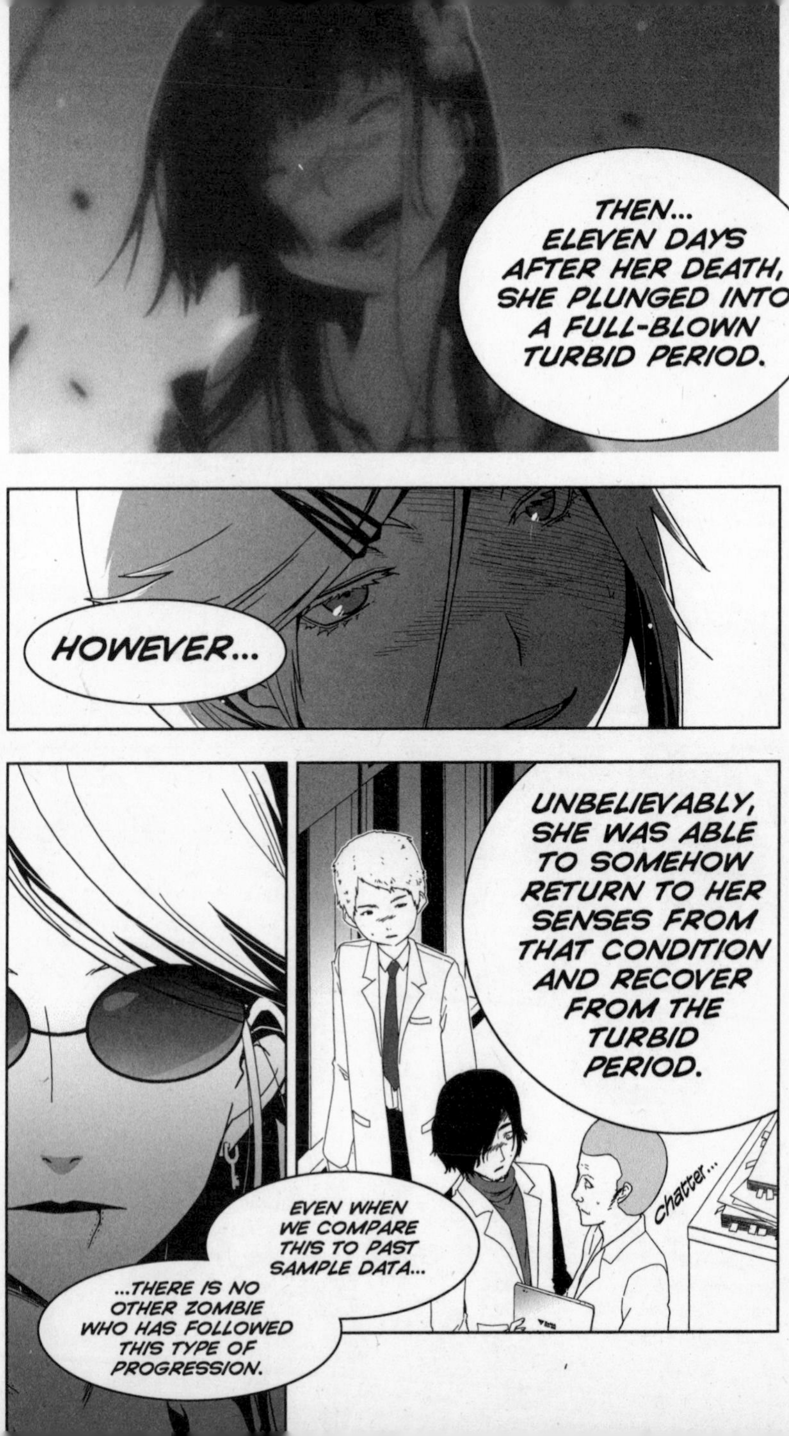
THEN... ELEVEN DAYS AFTER HER DEATH, SHE PLUNGED INTO A FULL-BLOWN TURBID PERIOD.
HOWEVER...
UNBELIEVABLY, SHE WAS ABLE TO SOMEHOW RETURN TO HER SENSES FROM THAT CONDITION AND RECOVER FROM THE TURBID PERIOD.
chatter...
EVEN WHEN WE COMPARE THIS TO PAST SAMPLE DATA...
...THERE IS NO OTHER ZOMBIE WHO HAS FOLLOWED THIS TYPE OF PROGRESSION.

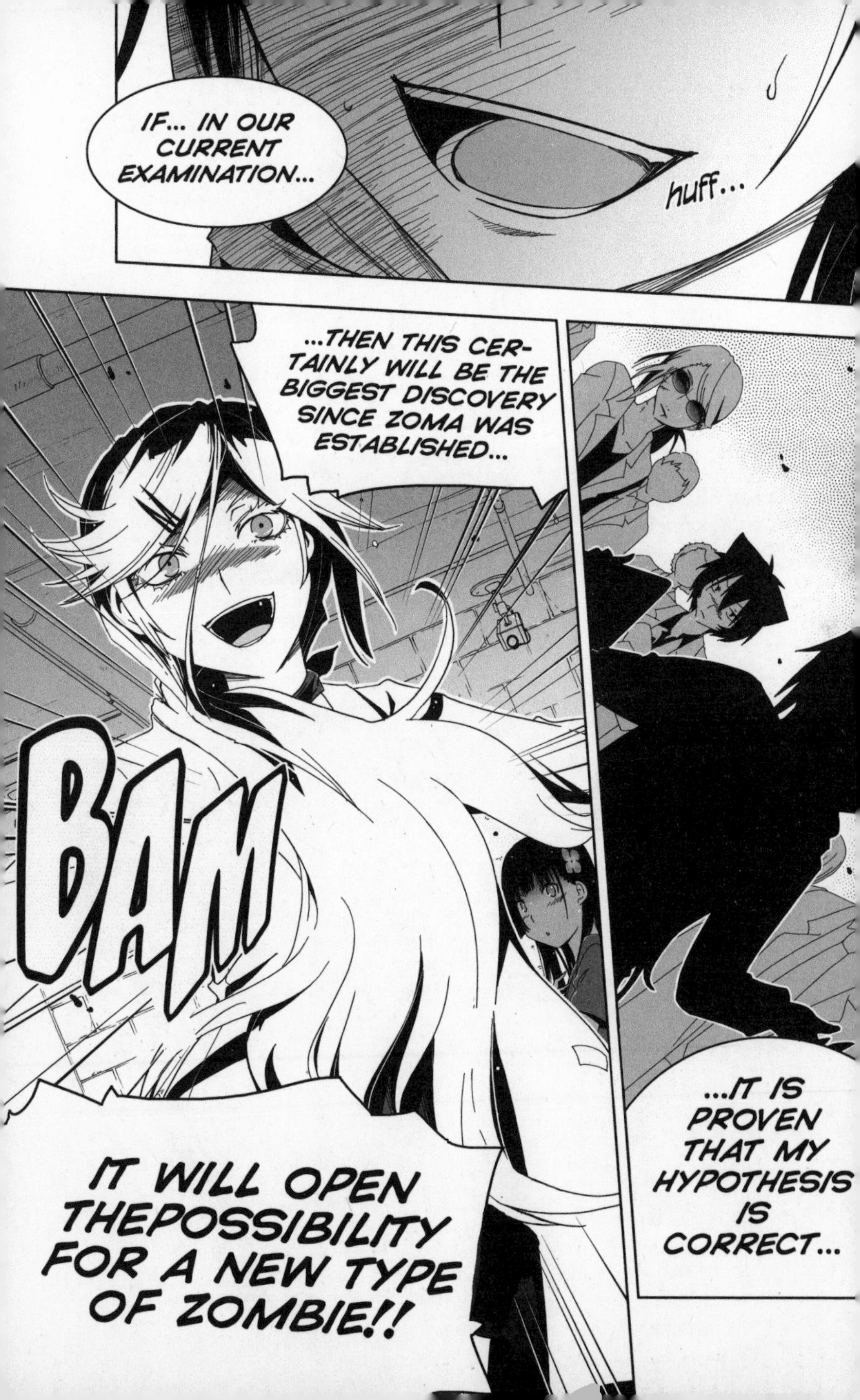
IF... IN OUR CURRENT EXAMINATION...
huff...
...IT IS PROVEN THAT MY HYPOTHESIS IS CORRECT...
...THEN THIS CER-TAINLY WILL BE THE BIGGEST DISCOVERY SINCE ZOMA WAS ESTABLISHED...
BAM
IT WILL OPEN THEPOSSIBILITY FOR A NEW TYPE OF ZOMBIE!!

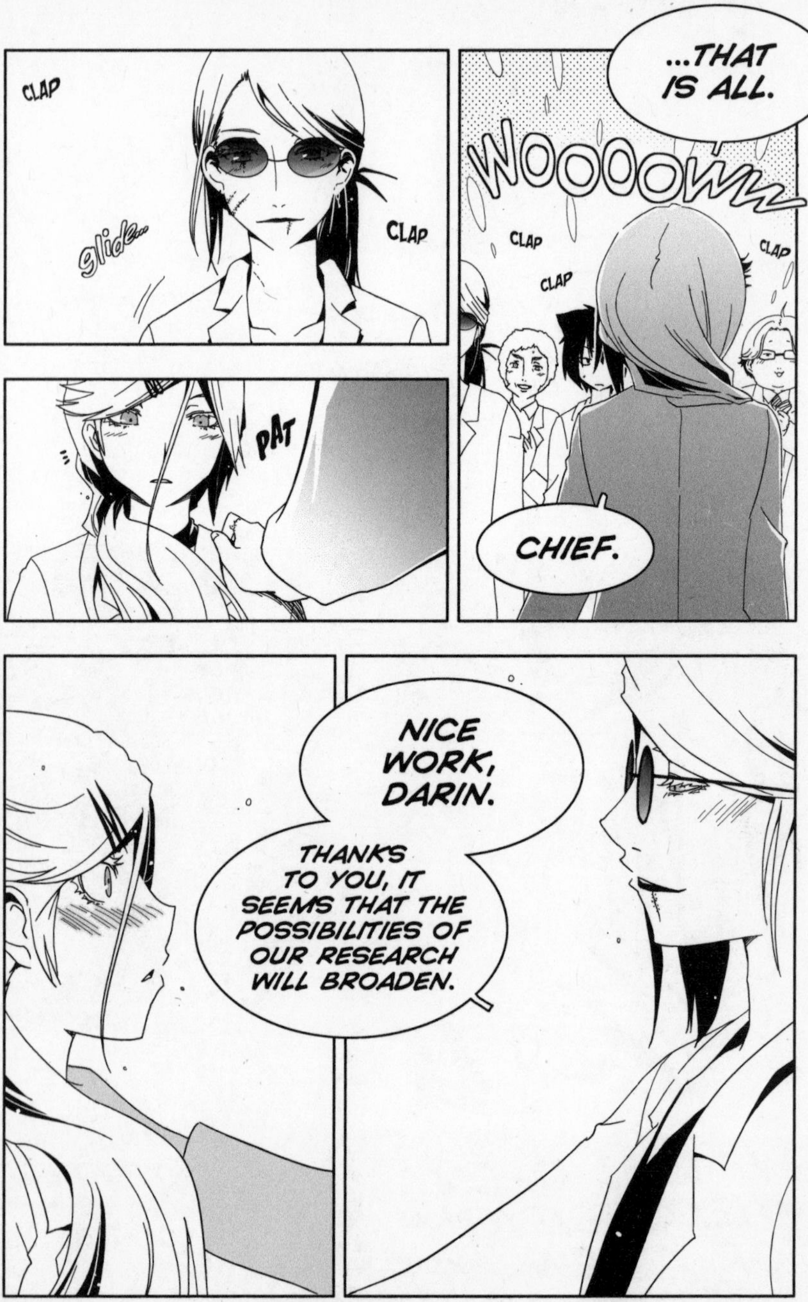
...THAT IS ALL.
WOOOOWW
CLAP
CLAP
CLAP
CHIEF.
CLAP
glide...
CLAP
PAT
NICE WORK, DARIN.
THANKS TO YOU, IT SEEMS THAT THE POSSIBILITIES OF OUR RESEARCH WILL BROADEN.

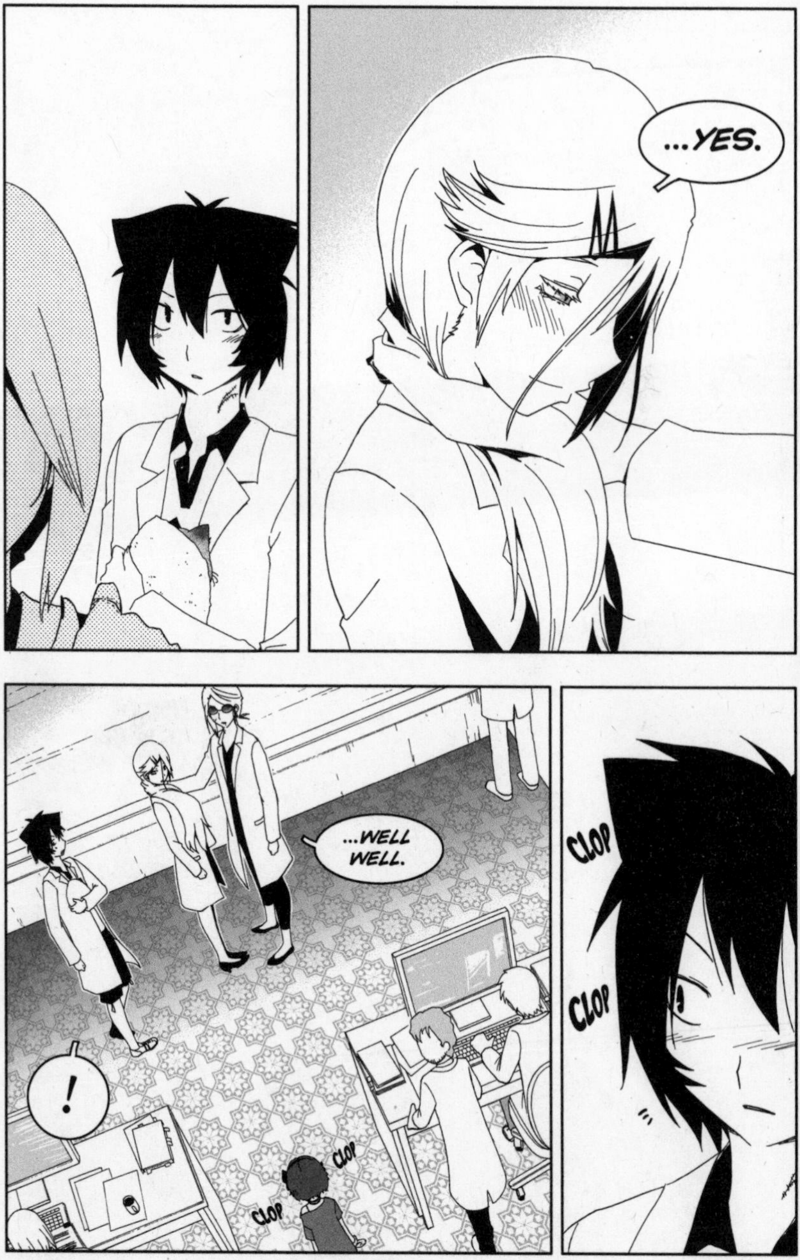
...YES.
CLOP
CLOP
...WELL WELL.
!
CLOP
CLOP

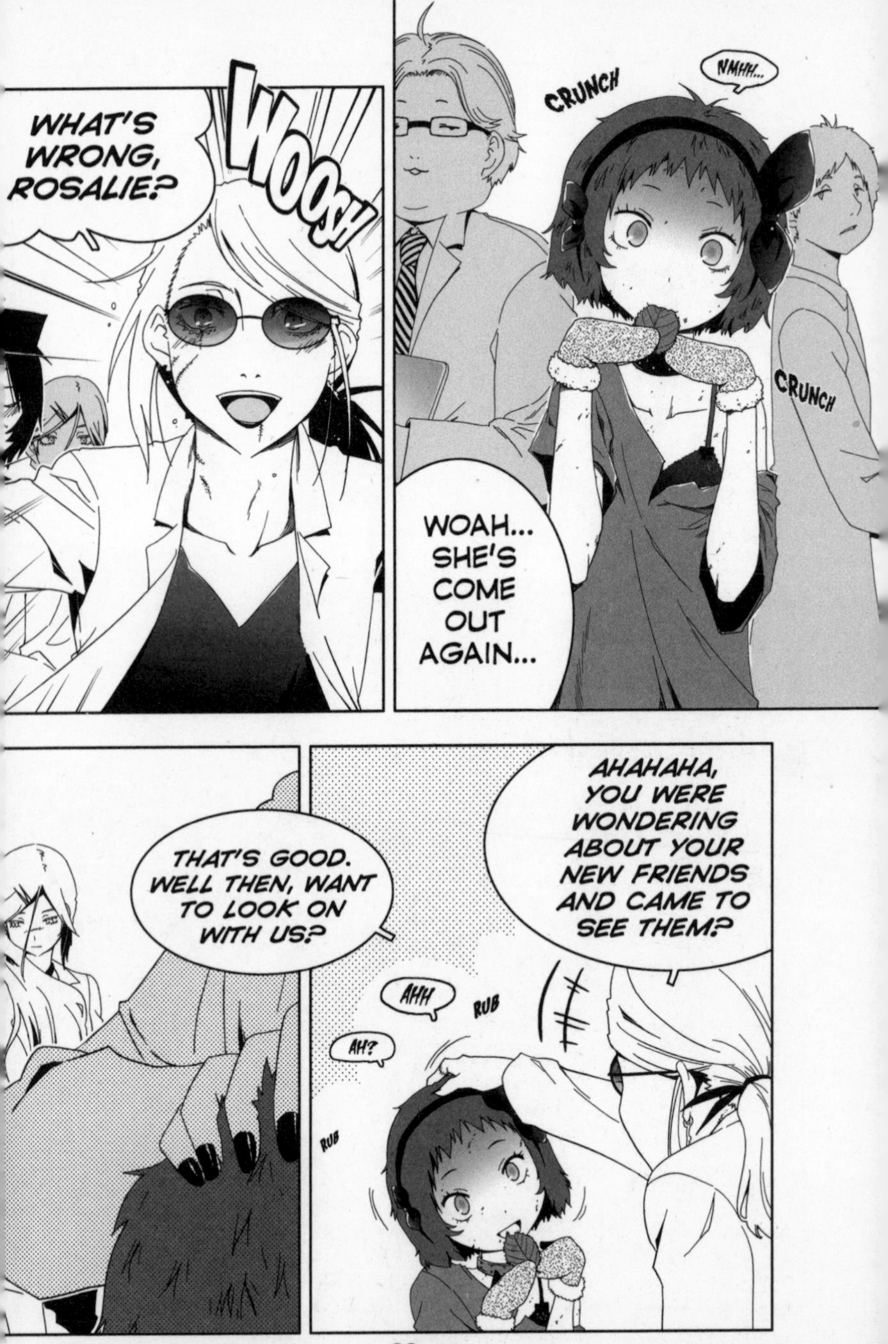
CRUNCH
NMHH...
CRUNCH
WOAH... SHE'S COME OUT AGAIN...
WOOSH
WHAT'S WRONG, ROSALIE?
AHAHAHA, YOU WERE WONDERING ABOUT YOUR NEW FRIENDS AND CAME TO SEE THEM?
AHH
RUB
AH?
RUB
THAT'S GOOD. WELL THEN, WANT TO LOOK ON WITH US?

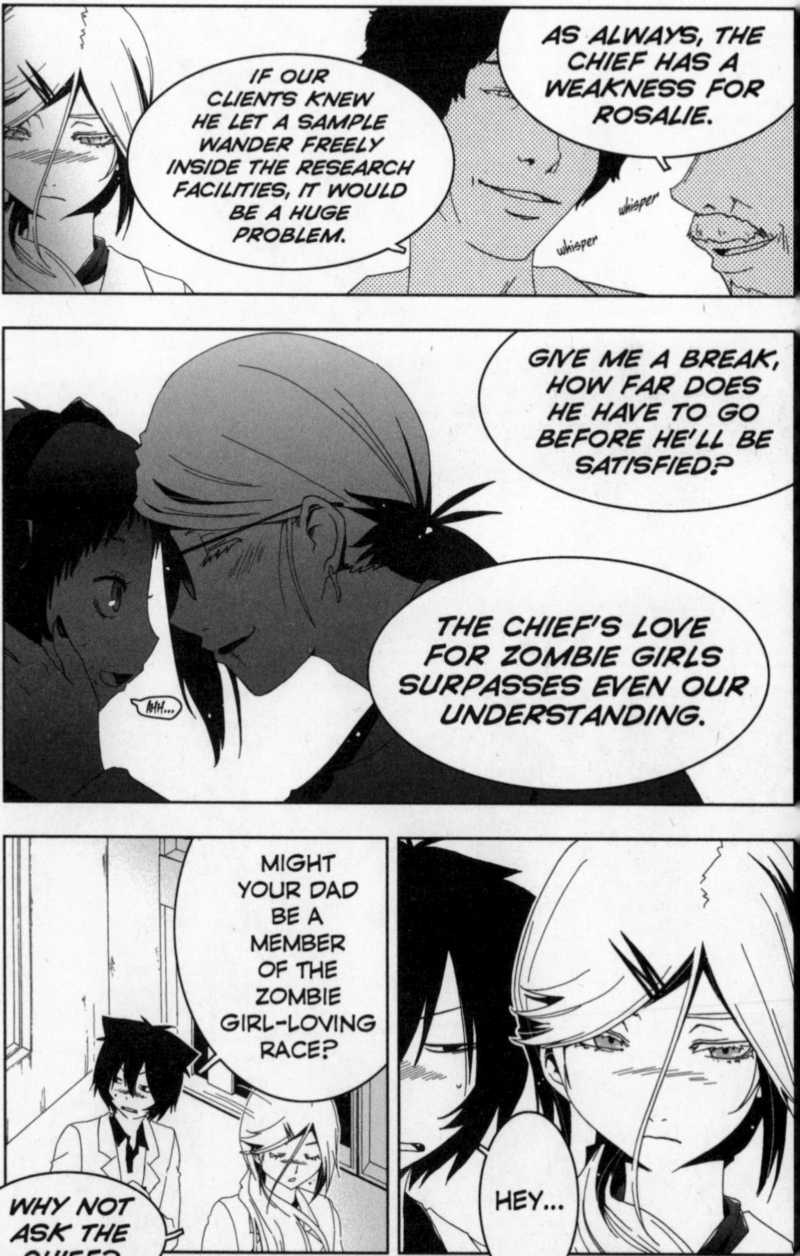
AS ALWAYS, THE CHIEF HAS A WEAKNESS FOR ROSALIE.
whisper
whisper
IF OUR CLIENTS KNEW HE LET A SAMPLE WANDER FREELY INSIDE THE RESEARCH FACILITIES, IT WOULD BE A HUGE PROBLEM.
GIVE ME A BREAK, HOW FAR DOES HE HAVE TO GO BEFORE HE'LL BE SATISFIED?
THE CHIEF'S LOVE FOR ZOMBIE GIRLS SURPASSES EVEN OUR UNDERSTANDING.
AHH...
HEY...
MIGHT YOUR DAD BE A MEMBER OF THE ZOMBIE GIRL-LOVING RACE?
WHY NOT ASK THE CHIEF?

WELL THEN, WE'LL BE TAKING SAMPLES OF YOUR BODILY FLUIDS AND TISSUE.

OKAY.

CLACK

CLACK

....?

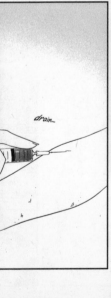

drain...

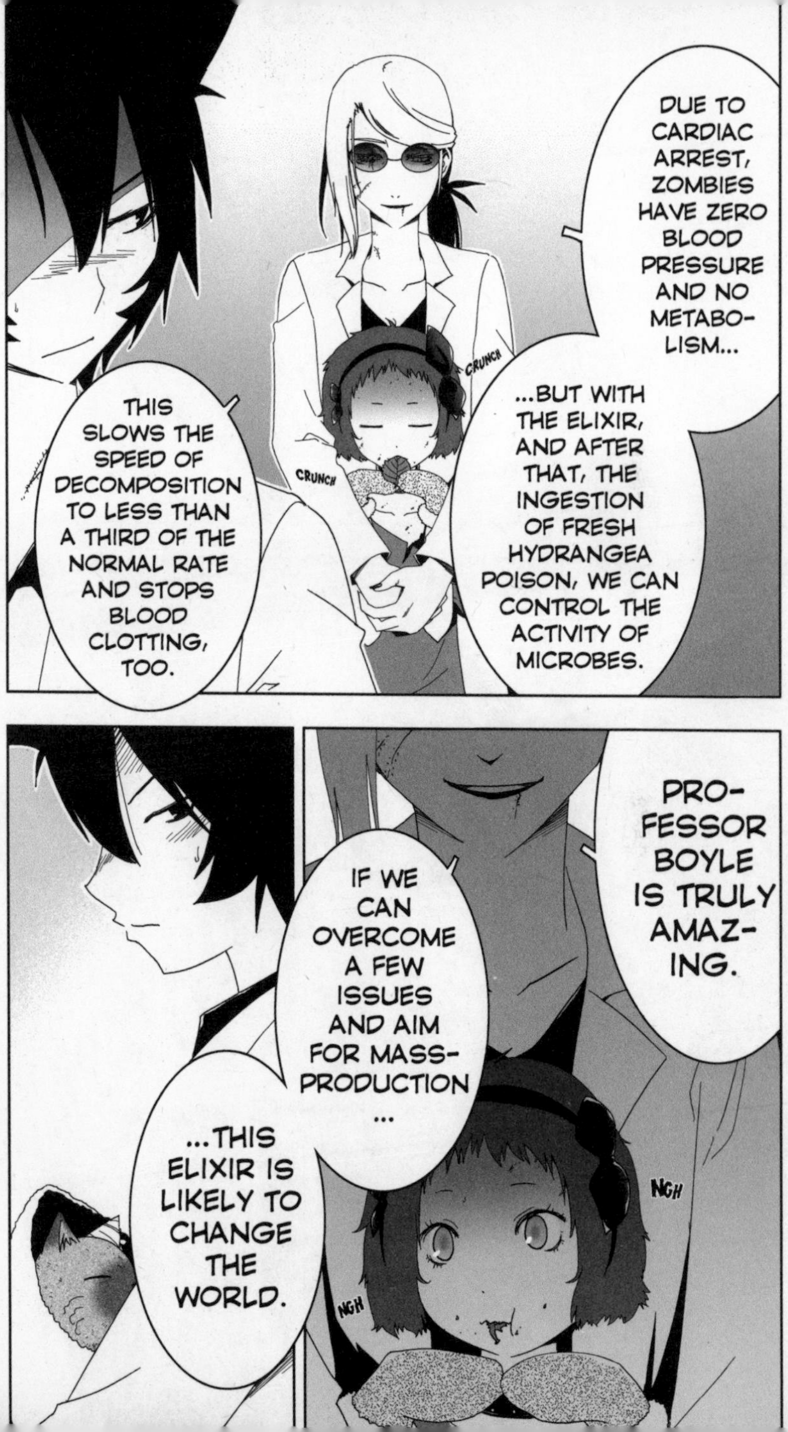
DUE TO CARDIAC ARREST, ZOMBIES HAVE ZERO BLOOD PRESSURE AND NO METABO-LISM...
CRUNCH
...BUT WITH THE ELIXIR, AND AFTER THAT, THE INGESTION OF FRESH HYDRANGEA POISON, WE CAN CONTROL THE ACTIVITY OF MICROBES.
CRUNCH
THIS SLOWS THE SPEED OF DECOMPOSITION TO LESS THAN A THIRD OF THE NORMAL RATE AND STOPS BLOOD CLOTTING, TOO.
PRO-FESSOR BOYLE IS TRULY AMAZ-ING.
IF WE CAN OVERCOME A FEW ISSUES AND AIM FOR MASS-PRODUCTION ...
NGH
NGH
...THIS ELIXIR IS LIKELY TO CHANGE THE WORLD.

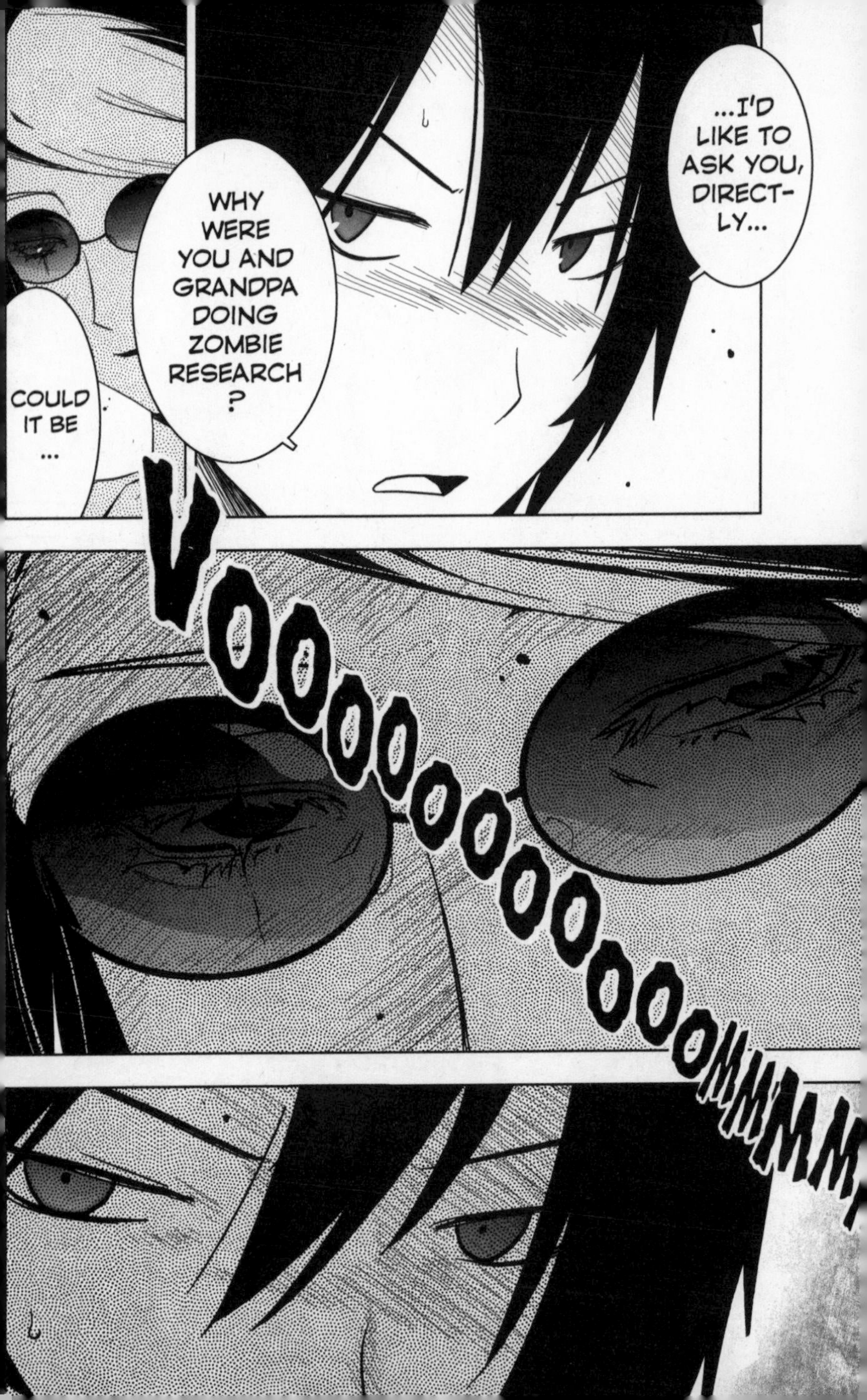
...I'D LIKE TO ASK YOU, DIRECT-LY...
WHY WERE YOU AND GRANDPA DOING ZOMBIE RESEARCH ?
COULD IT BE ...
VOOOOOOOOOOOOOOOMMMMM

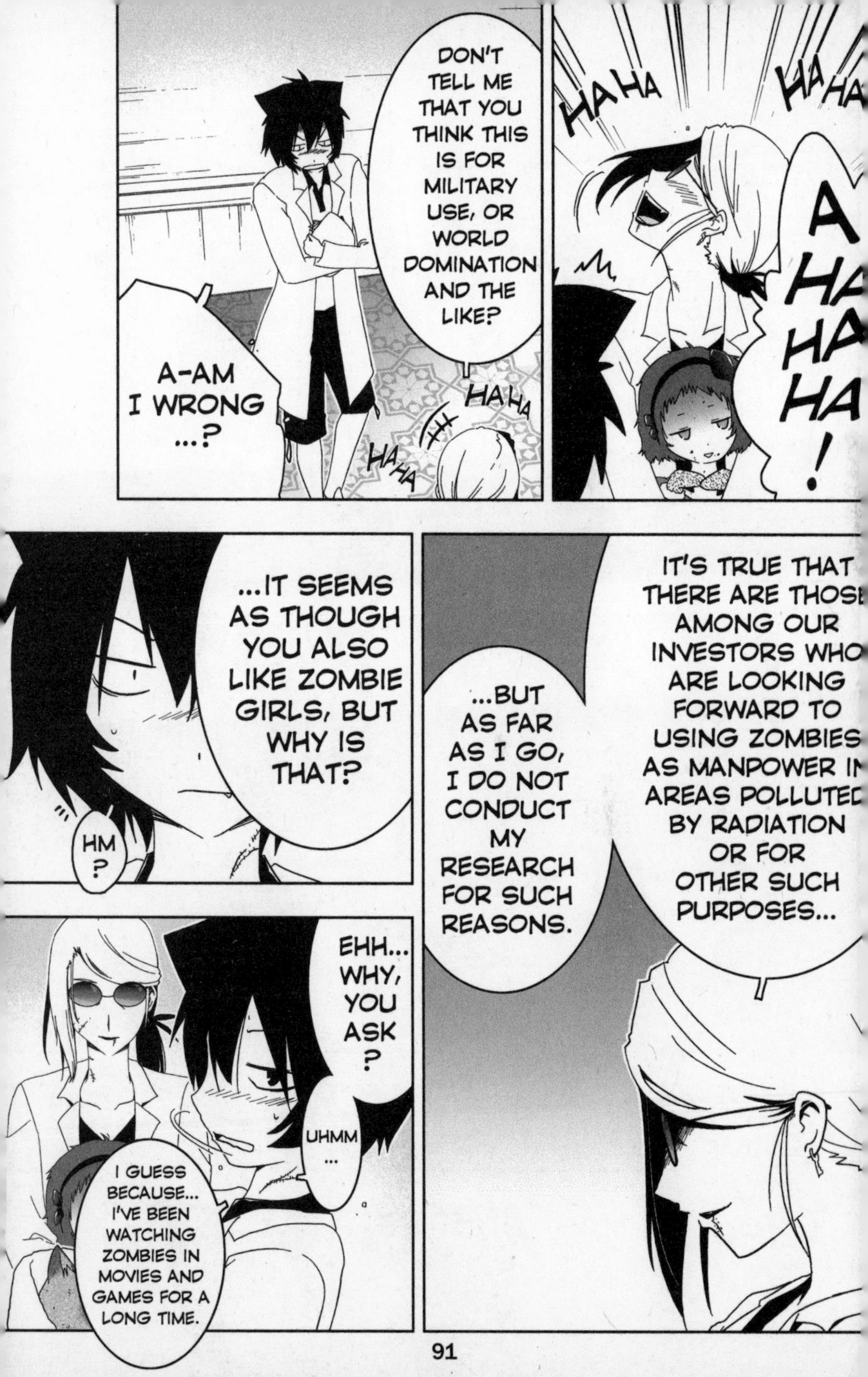
HA HA
HA HA
A HA HA HA!
DON'T TELL ME THAT YOU THINK THIS IS FOR MILITARY USE, OR WORLD DOMINATION AND THE LIKE?
HA HA
HA HA
A-AM I WRONG ...?
IT'S TRUE THAT THERE ARE THOSE AMONG OUR INVESTORS WHO ARE LOOKING FORWARD TO USING ZOMBIES AS MANPOWER IN AREAS POLLUTED BY RADIATION OR FOR OTHER SUCH PURPOSES...
...BUT AS FAR AS I GO, I DO NOT CONDUCT MY RESEARCH FOR SUCH REASONS.
...IT SEEMS AS THOUGH YOU ALSO LIKE ZOMBIE GIRLS, BUT WHY IS THAT?
HM?
EHH... WHY, YOU ASK?
UHMM...
I GUESS BECAUSE... I'VE BEEN WATCHING ZOMBIES IN MOVIES AND GAMES FOR A LONG TIME.

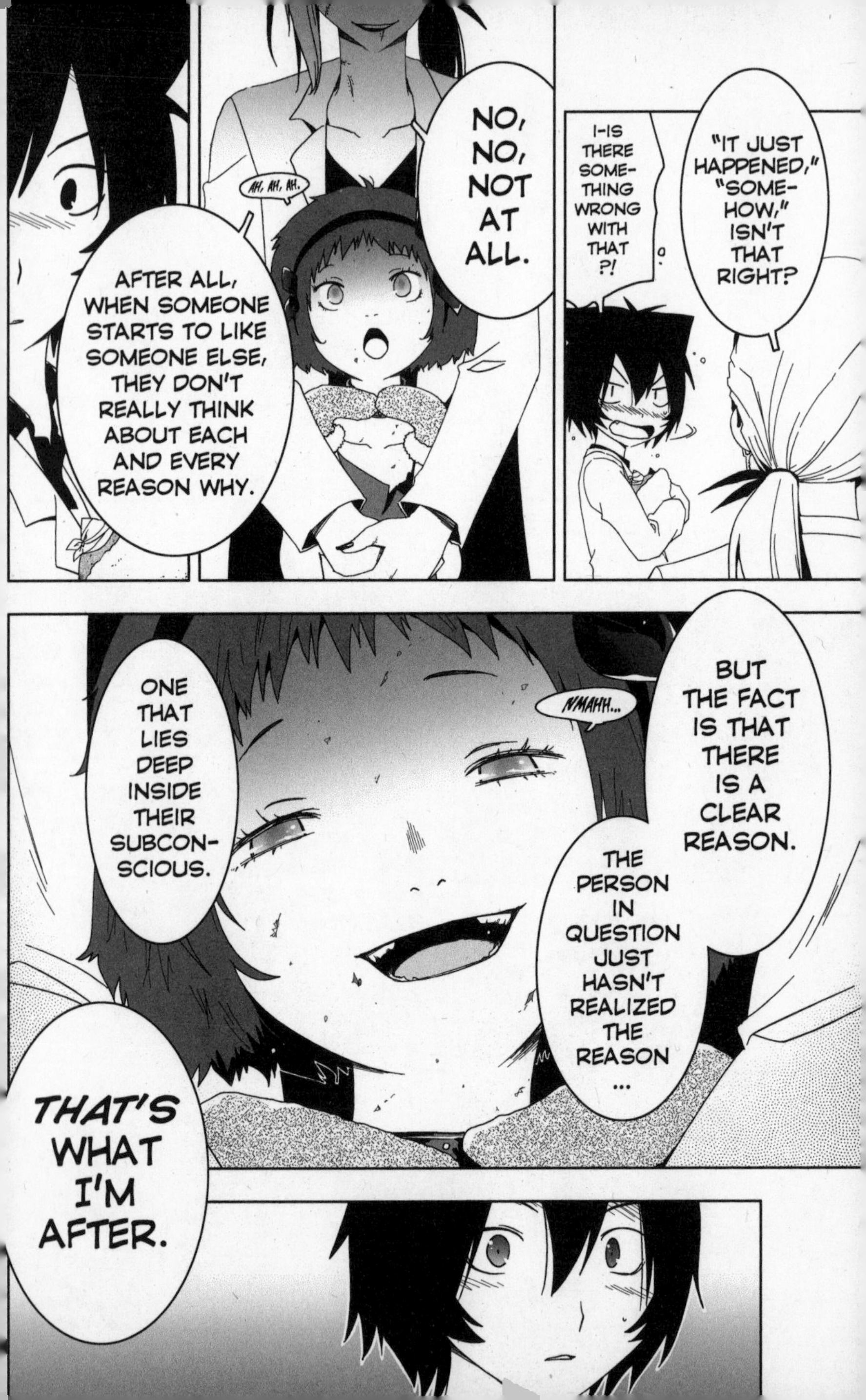

"IT JUST HAPPENED," "SOMEHOW," ISN'T THAT RIGHT?
I-IS THERE SOMETHING WRONG WITH THAT?!
NO, NO, NOT AT ALL.
AH, AH, AH.
AFTER ALL, WHEN SOMEONE STARTS TO LIKE SOMEONE ELSE, THEY DON'T REALLY THINK ABOUT EACH AND EVERY REASON WHY.
BUT THE FACT IS THAT THERE IS A CLEAR REASON.
N'MAHH...
ONE THAT LIES DEEP INSIDE THEIR SUBCONSCIOUS.
THE PERSON IN QUESTION JUST HASN'T REALIZED THE REASON...
THAT'S WHAT I'M AFTER.

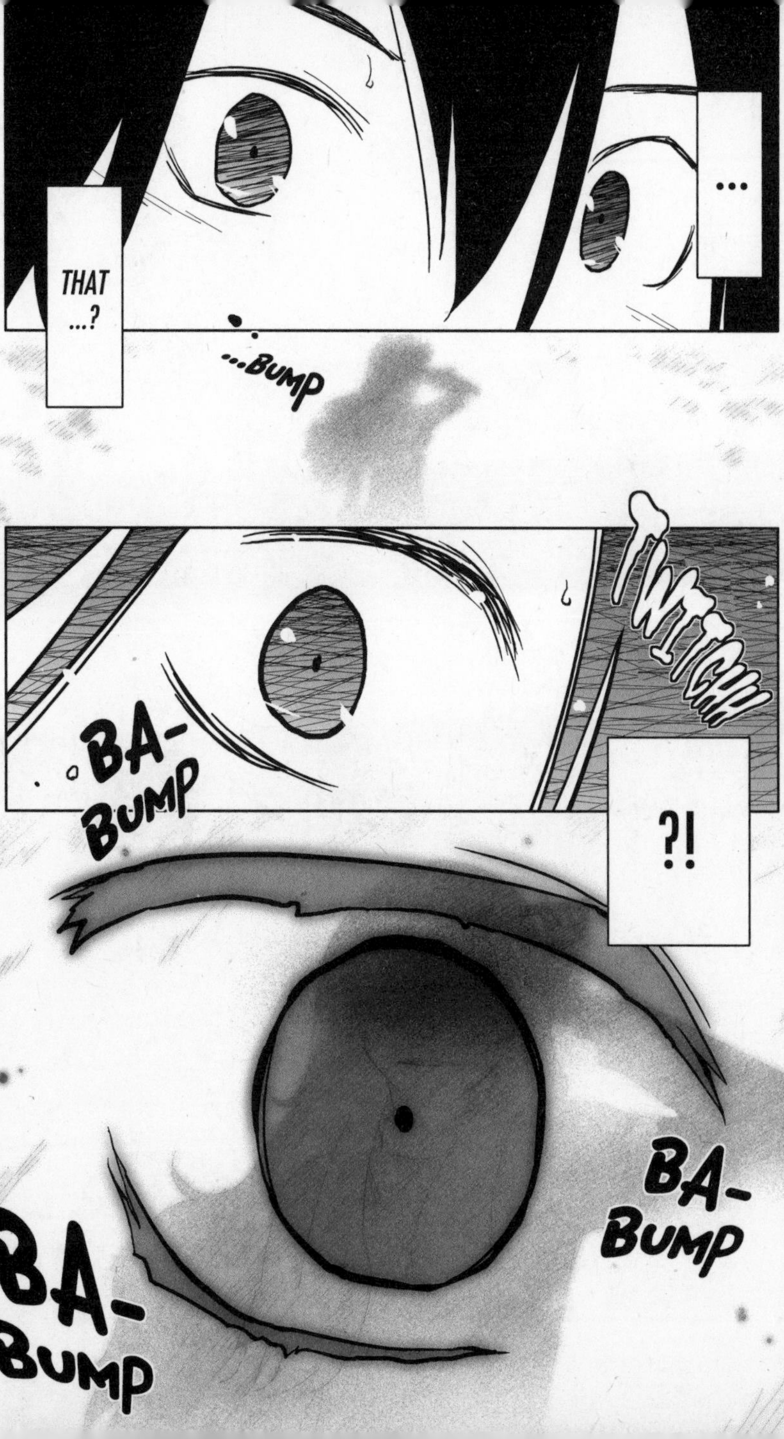
...
THAT ...?
...BUMP
TWITCH
BA-BUMP
?!
BA-BUMP
BA-BUMP

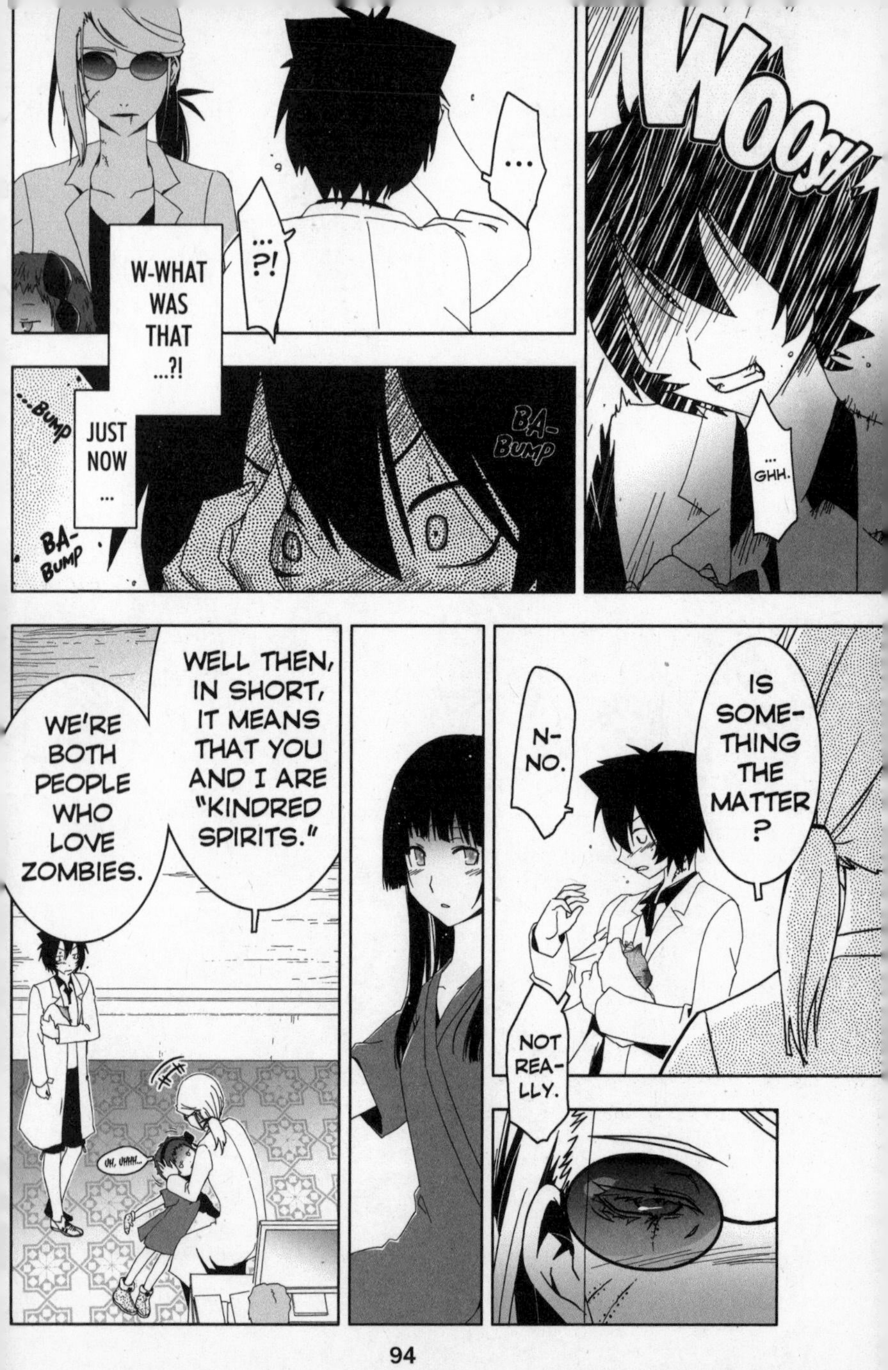
WOOSH
... GHH.
...
...?!
W-WHAT WAS THAT ...?!
JUST NOW ...
BA-BUMP
BA-BUMP
...BUMP
IS SOME-THING THE MATTER?
N-NO.
NOT REALLY.
WELL THEN, IN SHORT, IT MEANS THAT YOU AND I ARE "KINDRED SPIRITS."
WE'RE BOTH PEOPLE WHO LOVE ZOMBIES.
UH, UHHH...

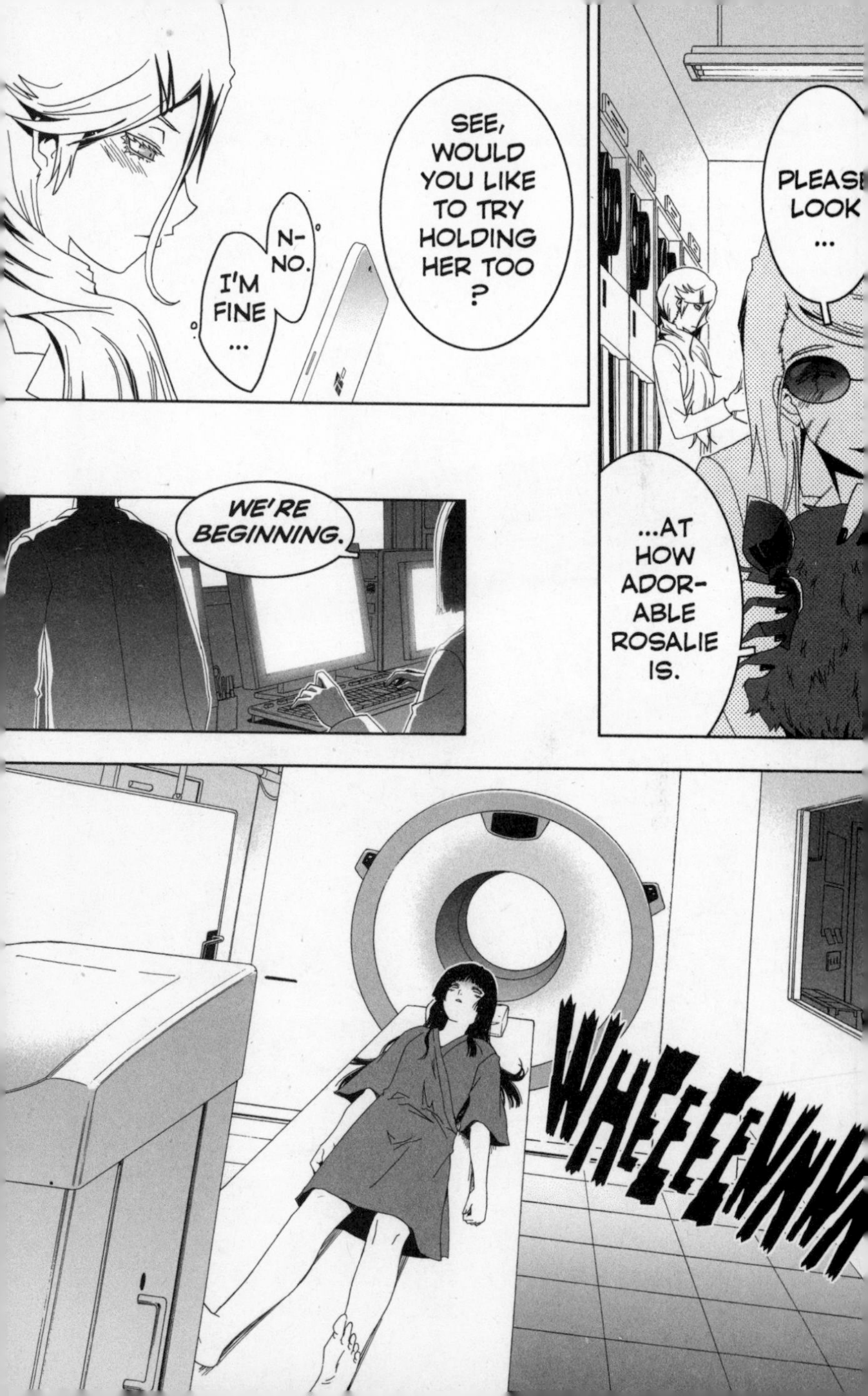
PLEASE LOOK ...
...AT HOW ADORABLE ROSALIE IS.
SEE, WOULD YOU LIKE TO TRY HOLDING HER TOO ?
N-NO. I'M FINE ...
WE'RE BEGINNING.
WHEEEENNNK

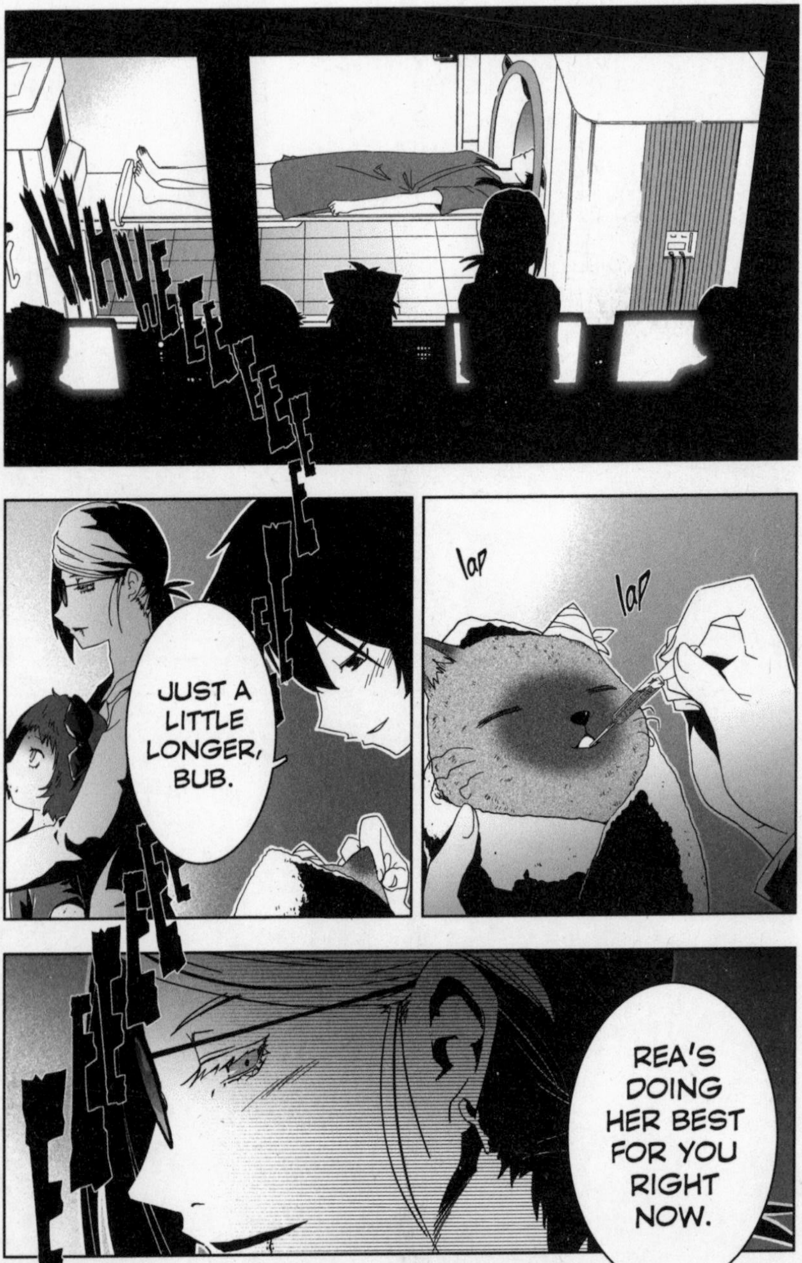
WHHEEEEEEEEEEEEE
lap
lap
JUST A LITTLE LONGER, BUB.
REA'S DOING HER BEST FOR YOU RIGHT NOW.

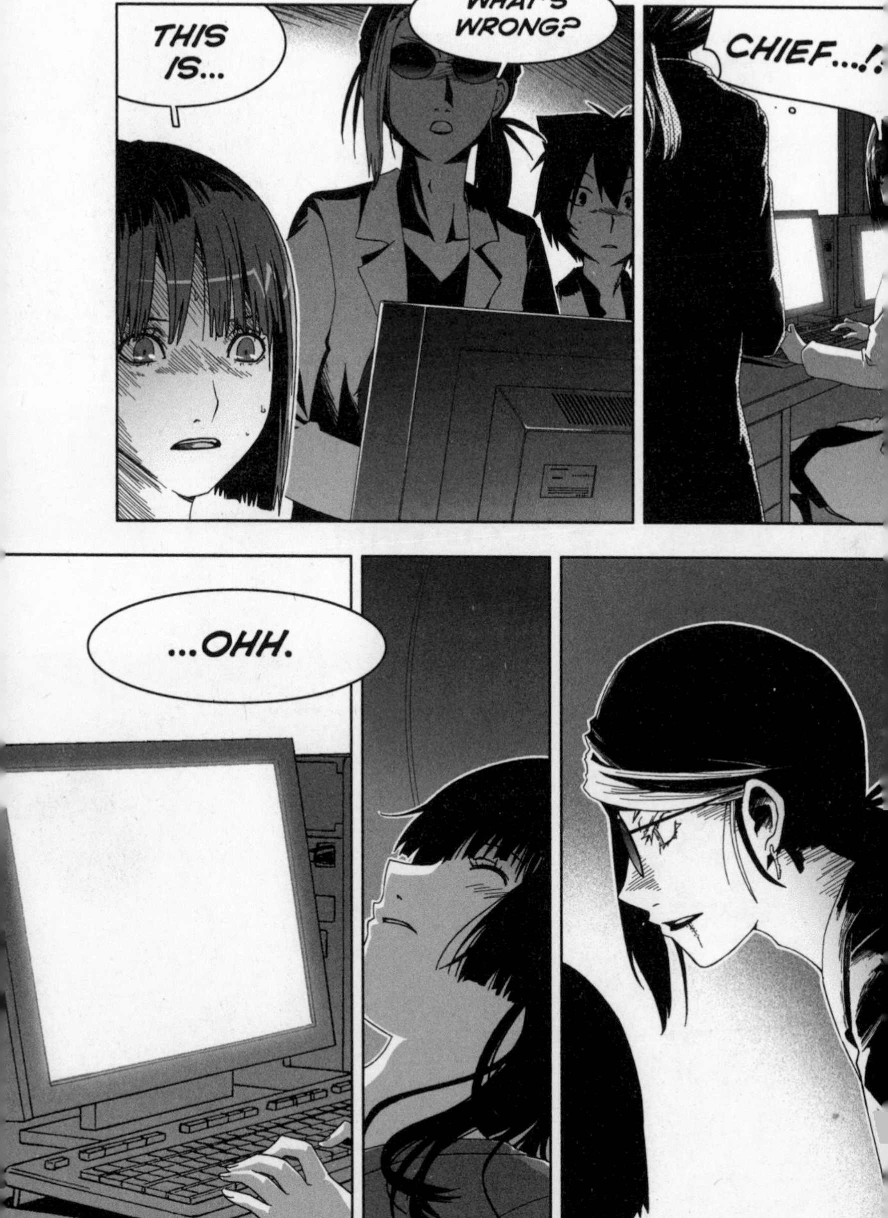
CHIEF...!
WHAT'S WRONG?
THIS IS...
...OHH.

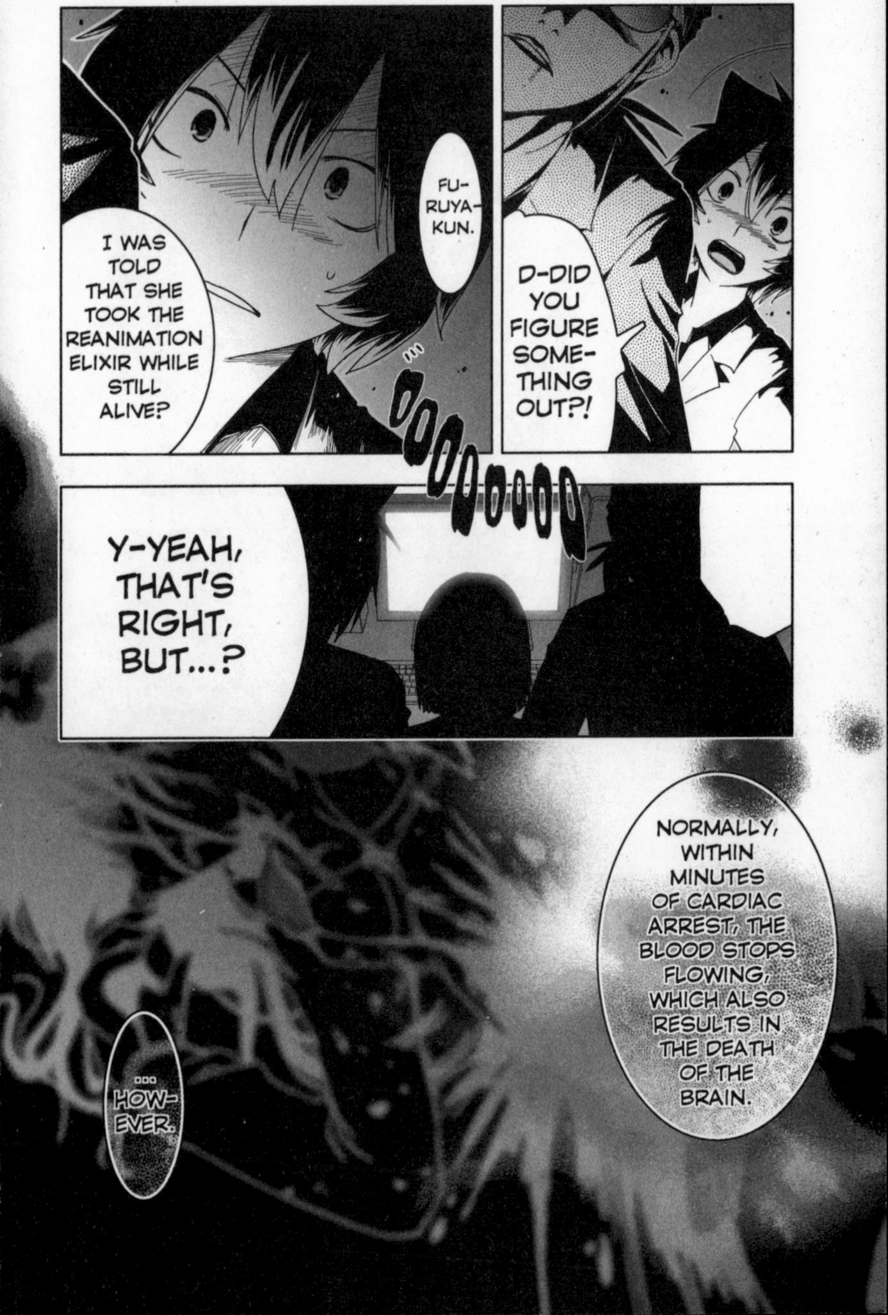
D-DID YOU FIGURE SOMETHING OUT?!
FURUYA-KUN.
I WAS TOLD THAT SHE TOOK THE REANIMATION ELIXIR WHILE STILL ALIVE?
Y-YEAH, THAT'S RIGHT, BUT...?
NORMALLY, WITHIN MINUTES OF CARDIAC ARREST, THE BLOOD STOPS FLOWING, WHICH ALSO RESULTS IN THE DEATH OF THE BRAIN.
...HOWEVER.

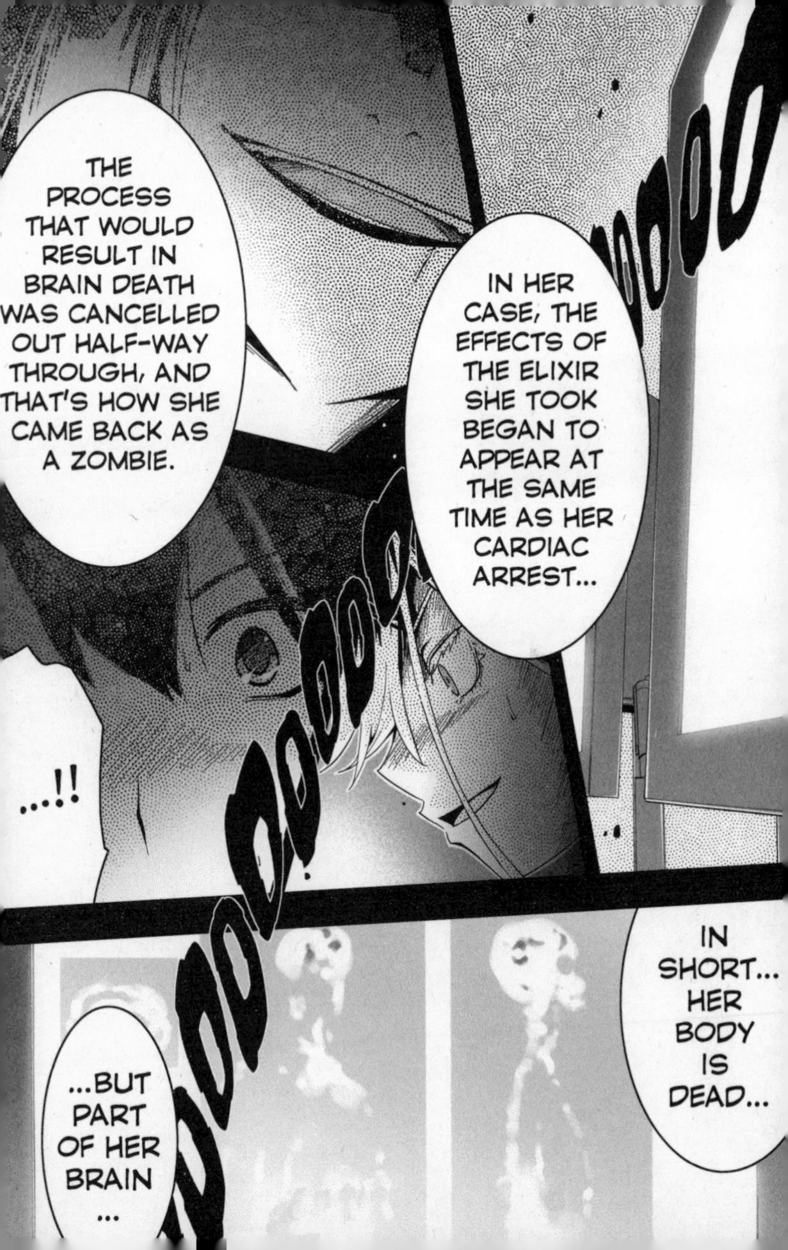
IN HER CASE, THE EFFECTS OF THE ELIXIR SHE TOOK BEGAN TO APPEAR AT THE SAME TIME AS HER CARDIAC ARREST...
THE PROCESS THAT WOULD RESULT IN BRAIN DEATH WAS CANCELLED OUT HALF-WAY THROUGH, AND THAT'S HOW SHE CAME BACK AS A ZOMBIE.
...!!
IN SHORT... HER BODY IS DEAD...
...BUT PART OF HER BRAIN ...

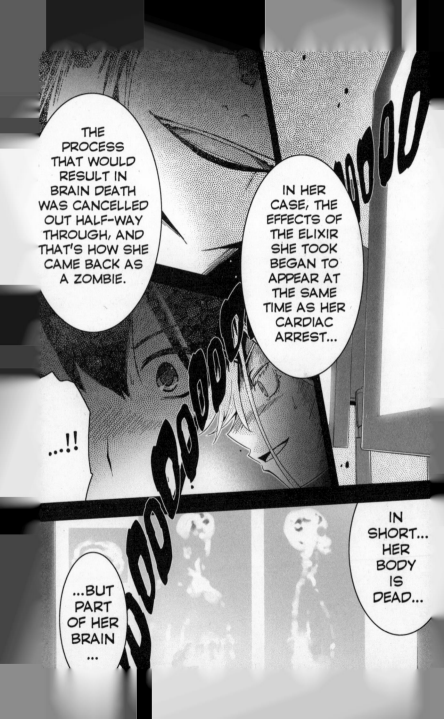

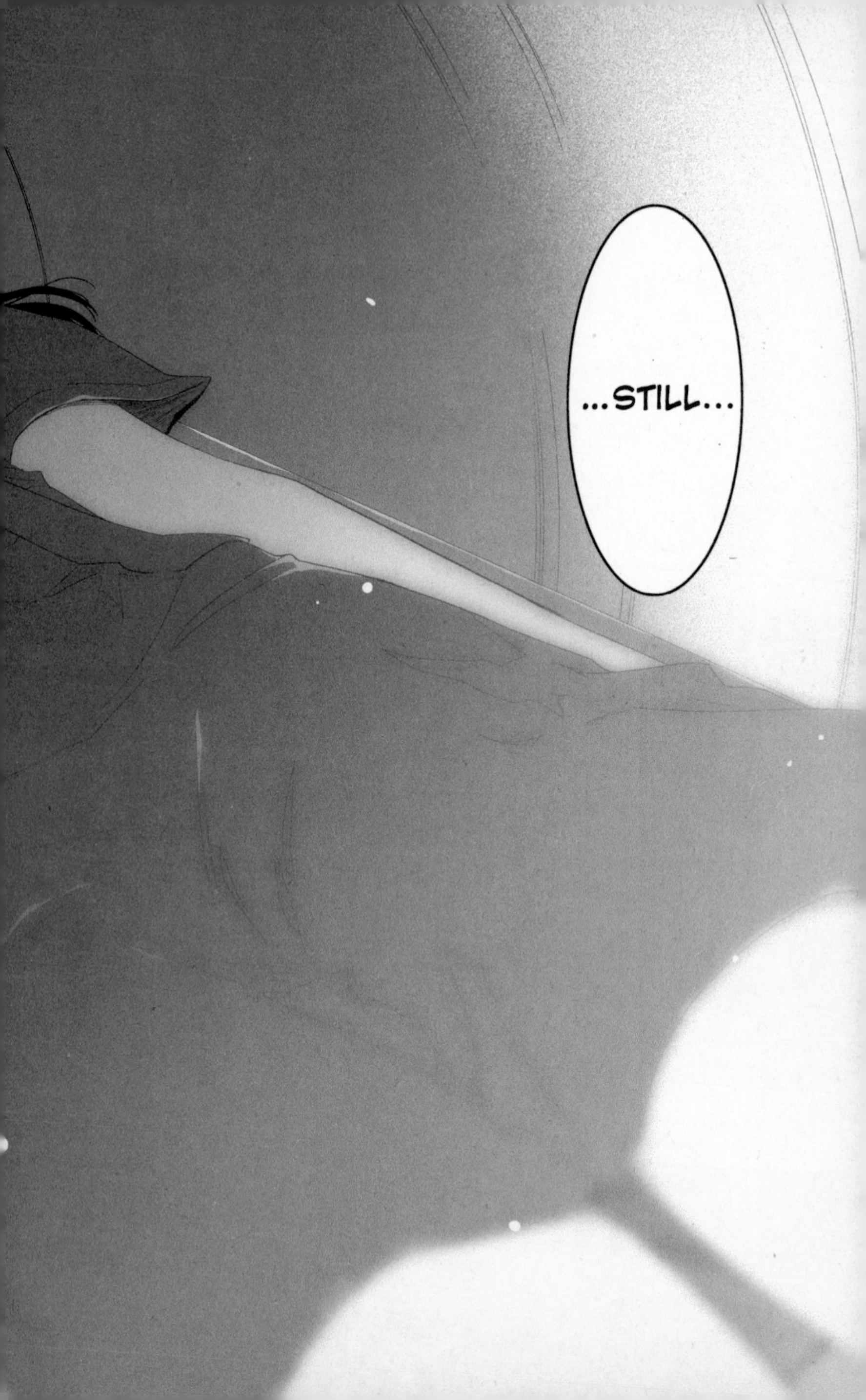
...STILL...

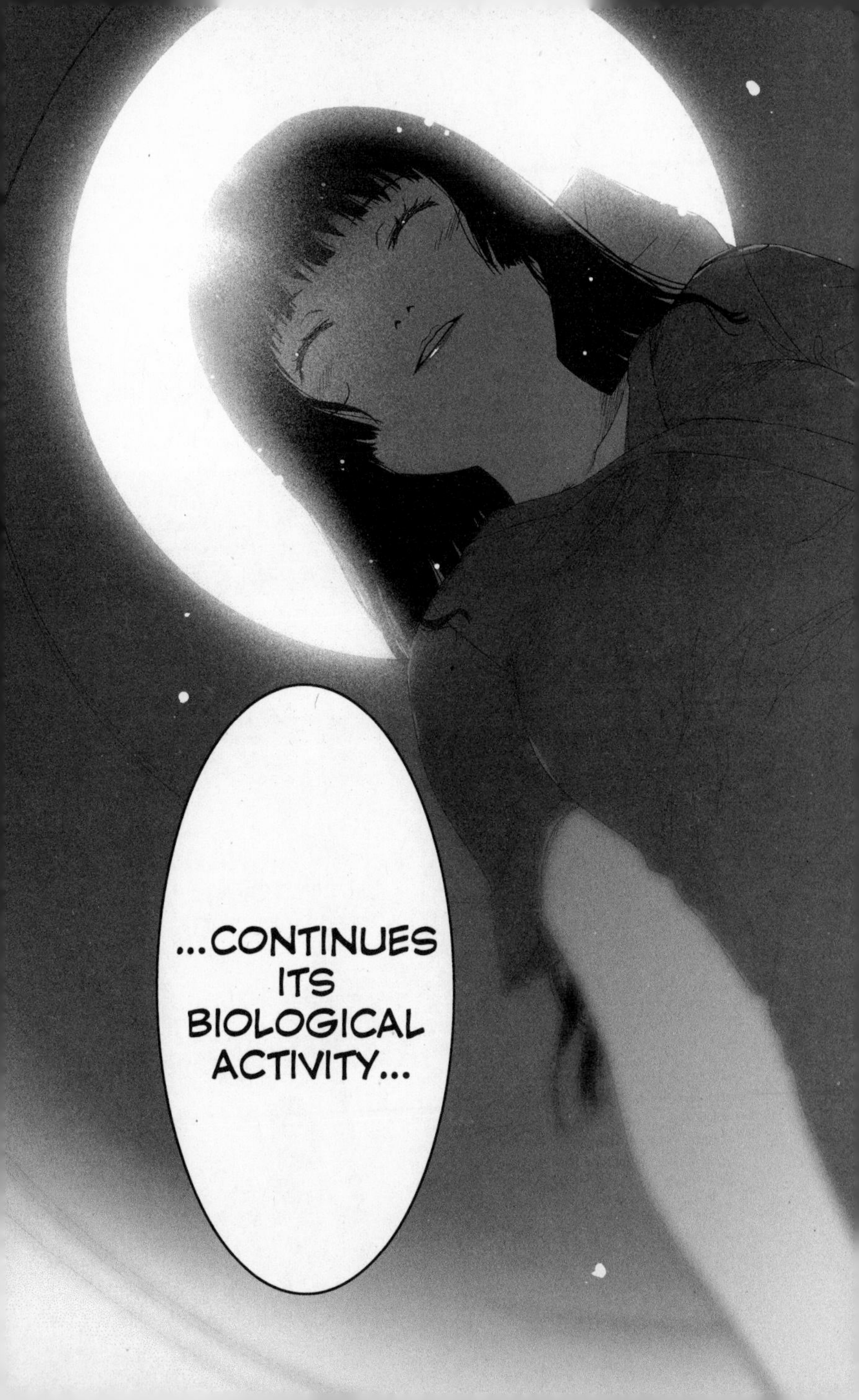
...CONTINUES ITS BIOLOGICAL ACTIVITY...

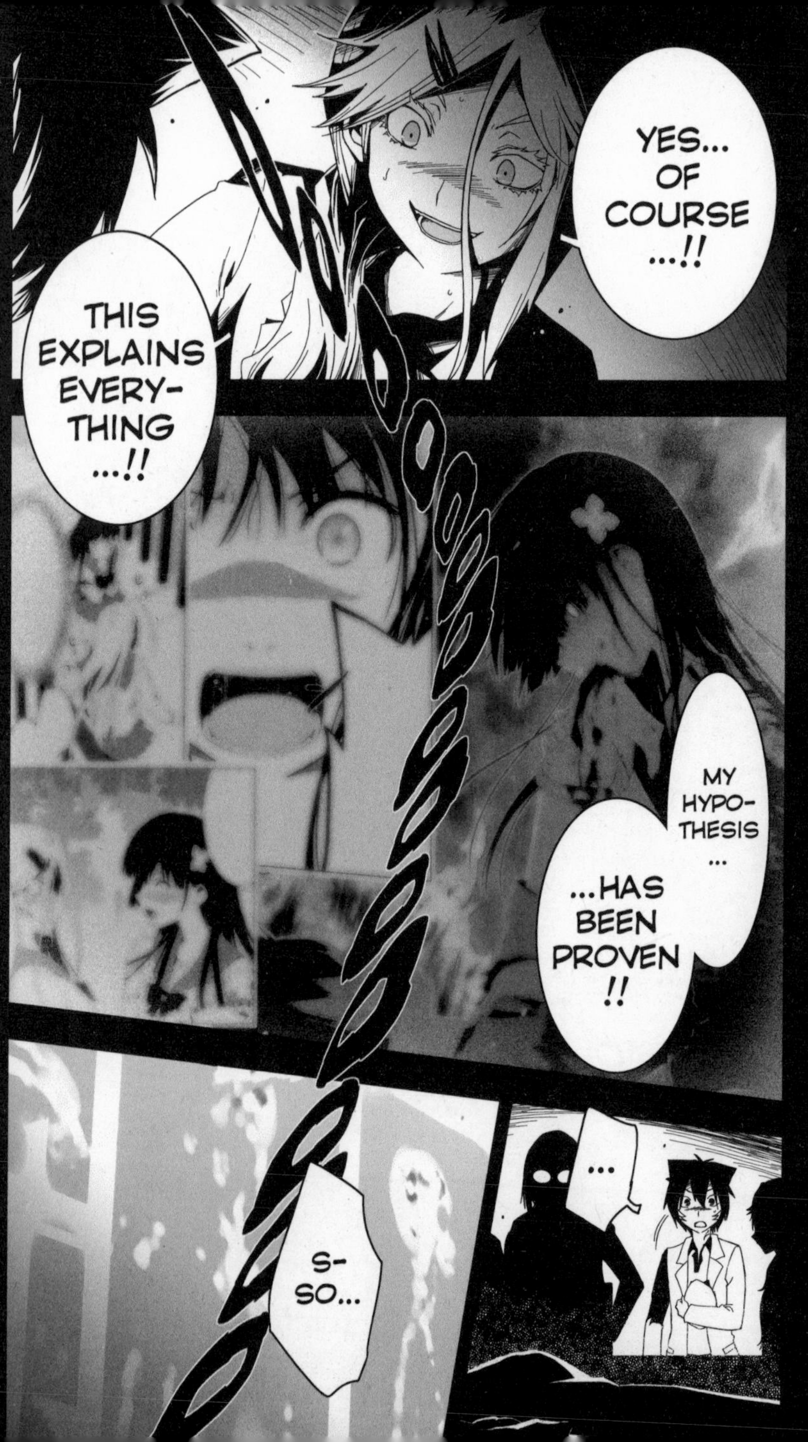
YES... OF COURSE ...!!
THIS EXPLAINS EVERY-THING ...!!
MY HYPO-THESIS ...
...HAS BEEN PROVEN !!
...
S- SO...

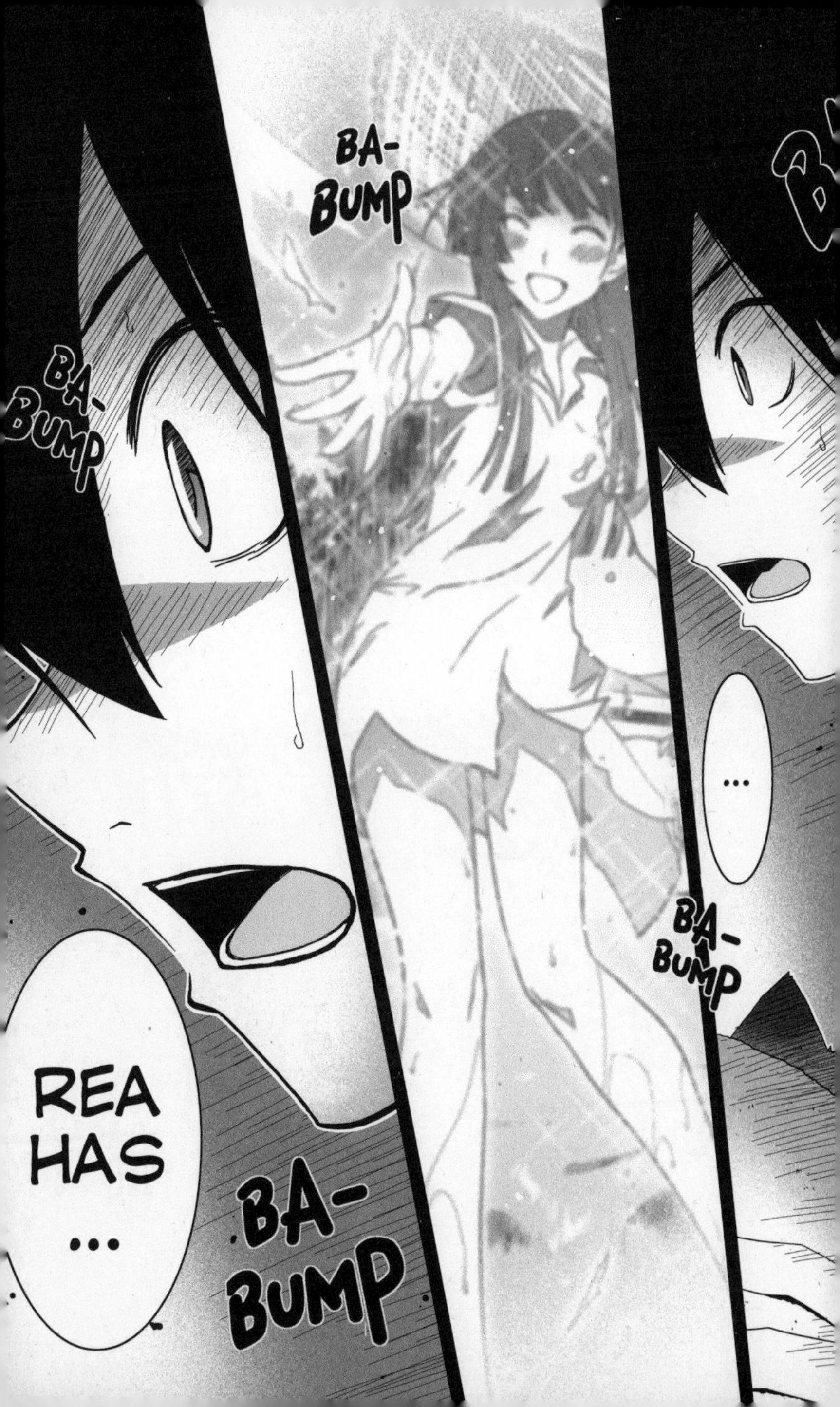
...
BA-BUMP
BA-BUMP
BA-BUMP
REA HAS ...
BA-BUMP

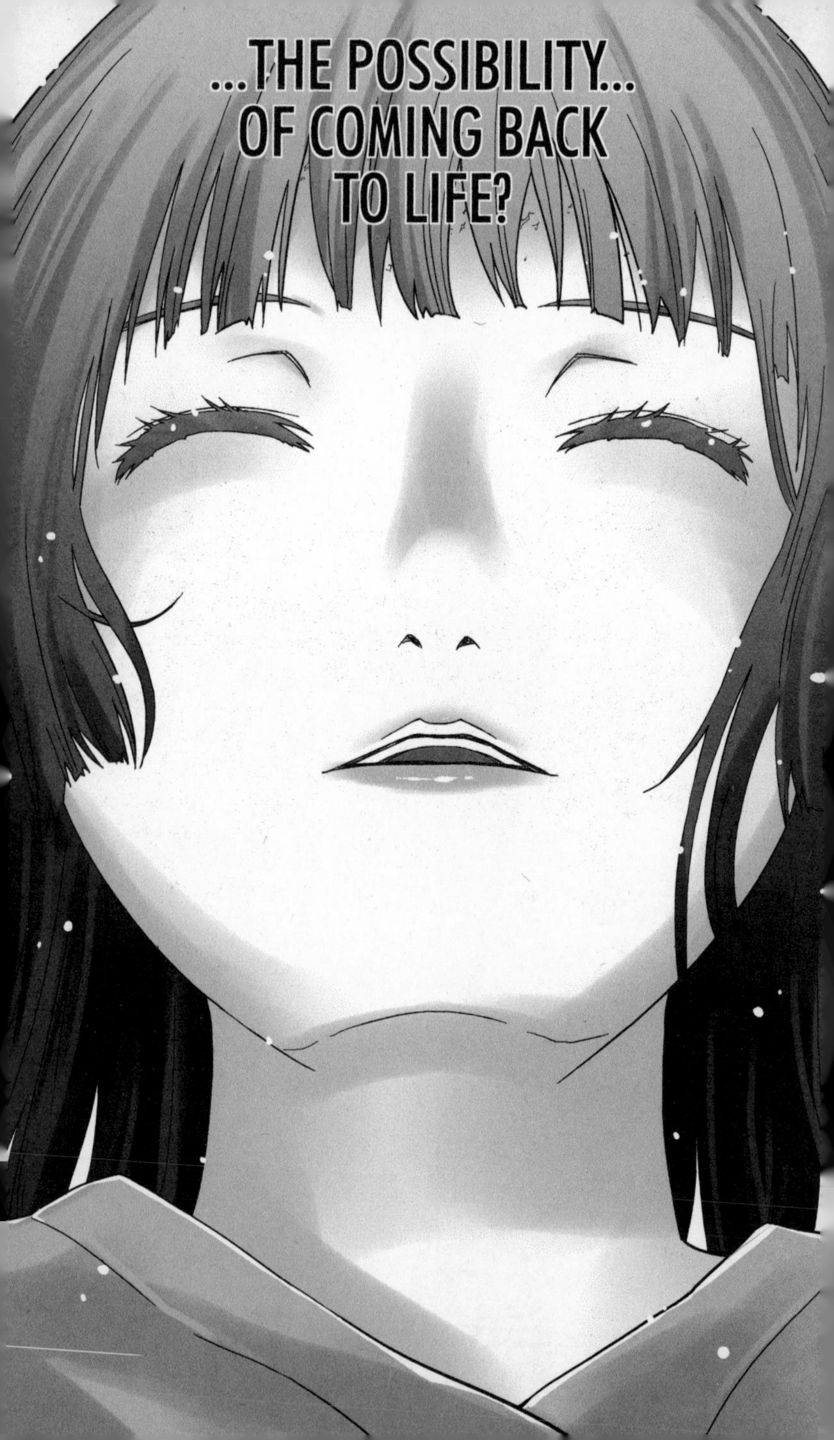
...THE POSSIBILITY... OF COMING BACK TO LIFE?

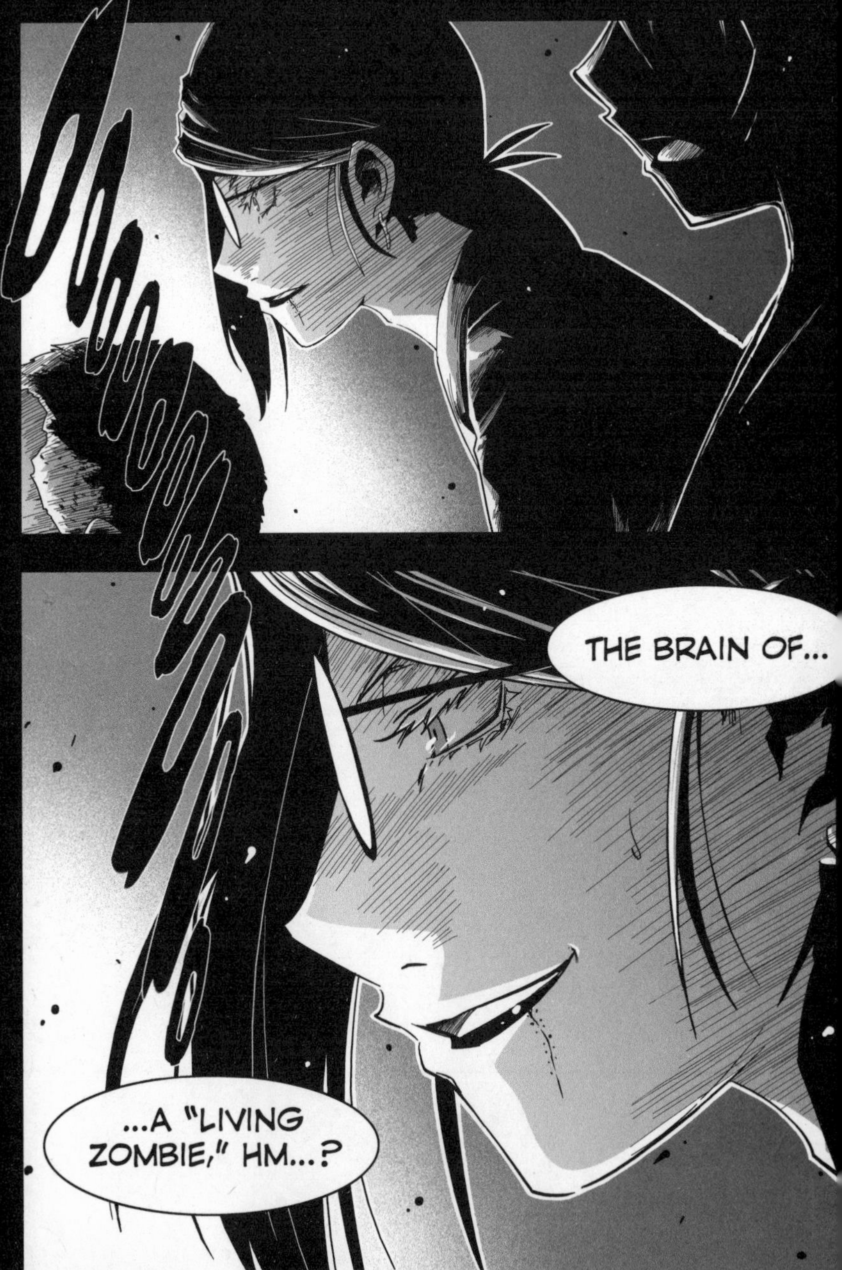
THE BRAIN OF...
...A "LIVING ZOMBIE," HM...?

SANKAREA

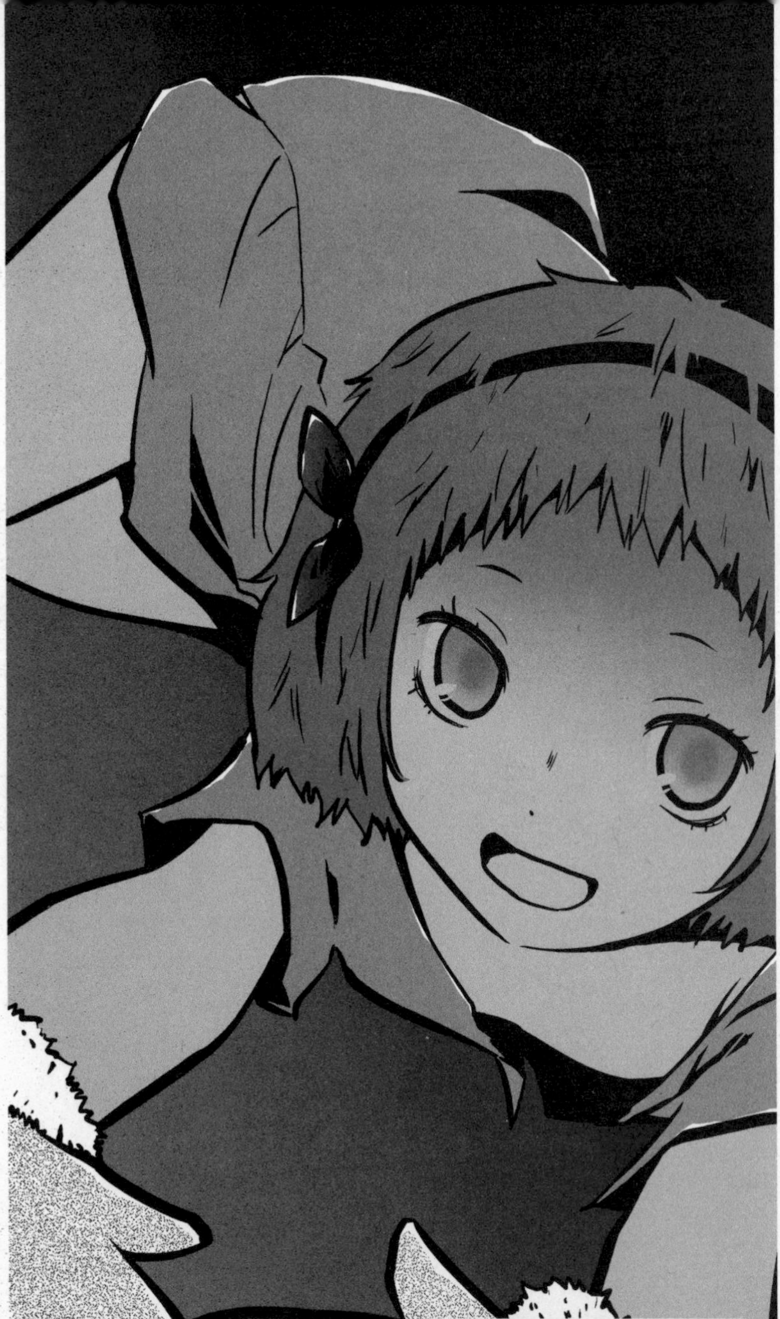

33 POSSI...BILITY...

✦ ✦ ✦ TOXIC ZOMBIES ✦ ✦ ✦

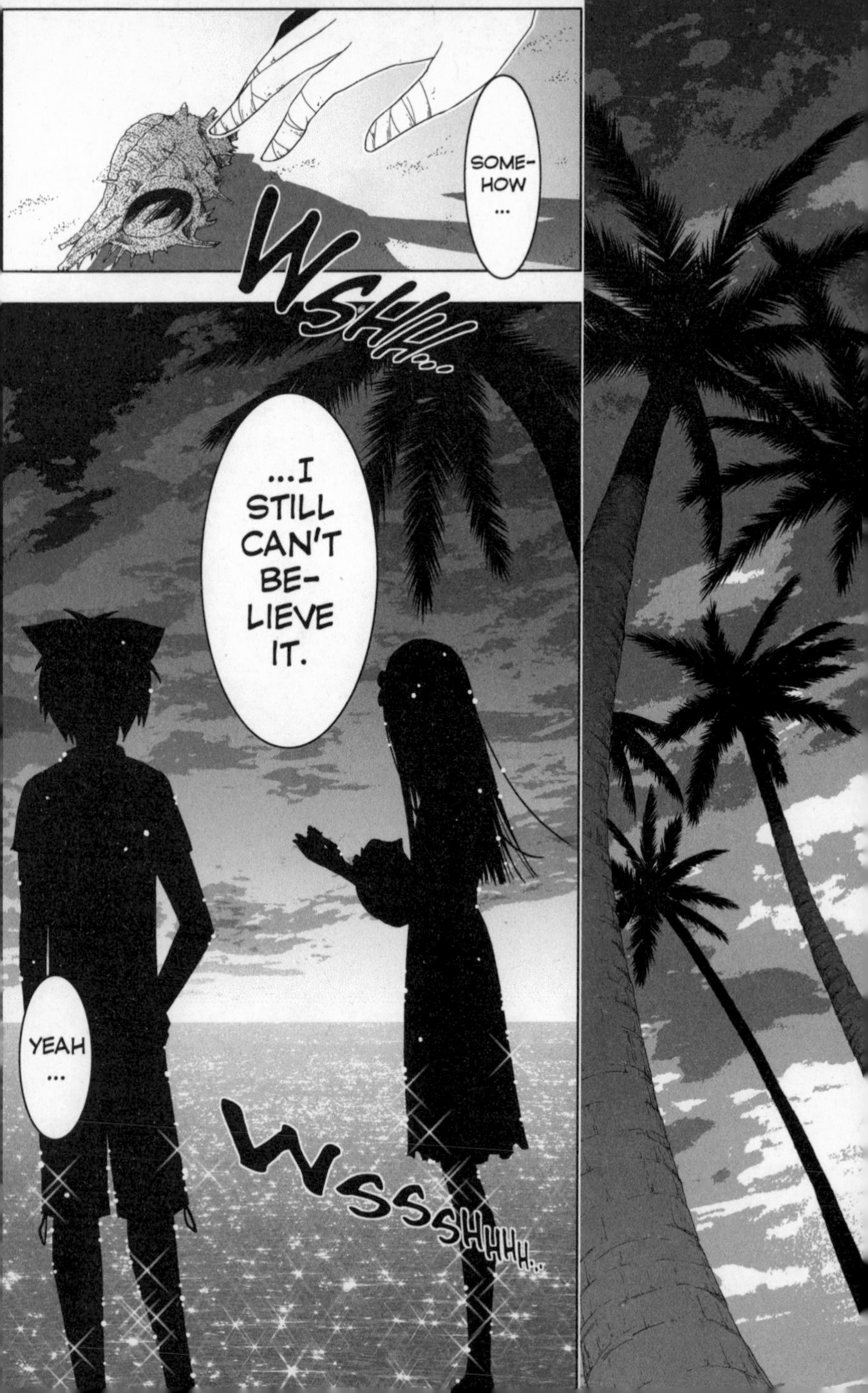
SOME-HOW ...
WSHH...
...I STILL CAN'T BE-LIEVE IT.
YEAH ...
WSSSHHHH..

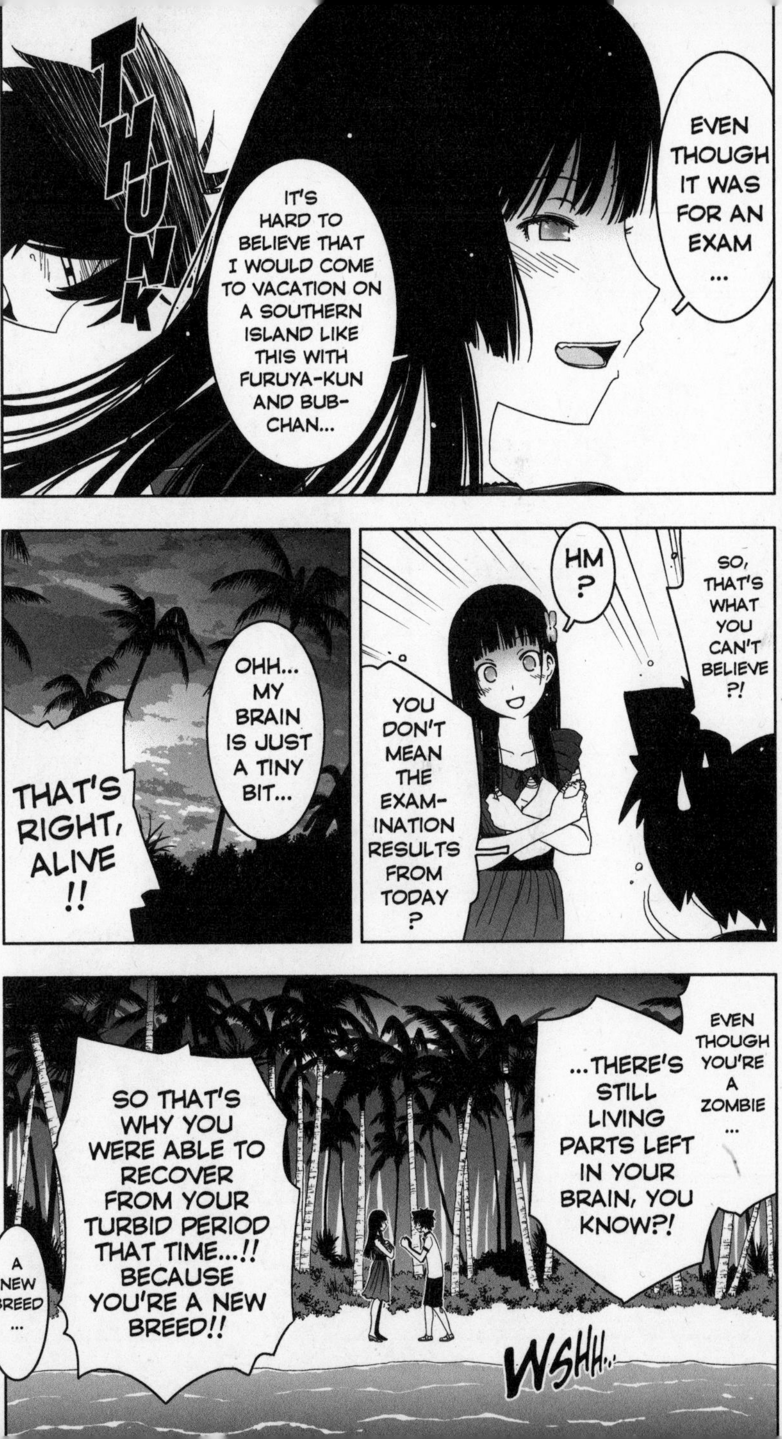
EVEN THOUGH IT WAS FOR AN EXAM ...
IT'S HARD TO BELIEVE THAT I WOULD COME TO VACATION ON A SOUTHERN ISLAND LIKE THIS WITH FURUYA-KUN AND BUB-CHAN...
THUNK
SO, THAT'S WHAT YOU CAN'T BELIEVE ?!
HM ?
YOU DON'T MEAN THE EXAM-INATION RESULTS FROM TODAY ?
OHH... MY BRAIN IS JUST A TINY BIT...
THAT'S RIGHT, ALIVE !!
EVEN THOUGH YOU'RE A ZOMBIE ...
...THERE'S STILL LIVING PARTS LEFT IN YOUR BRAIN, YOU KNOW?!
SO THAT'S WHY YOU WERE ABLE TO RECOVER FROM YOUR TURBID PERIOD THAT TIME...!! BECAUSE YOU'RE A NEW BREED!!
A NEW BREED ...
WSHH..

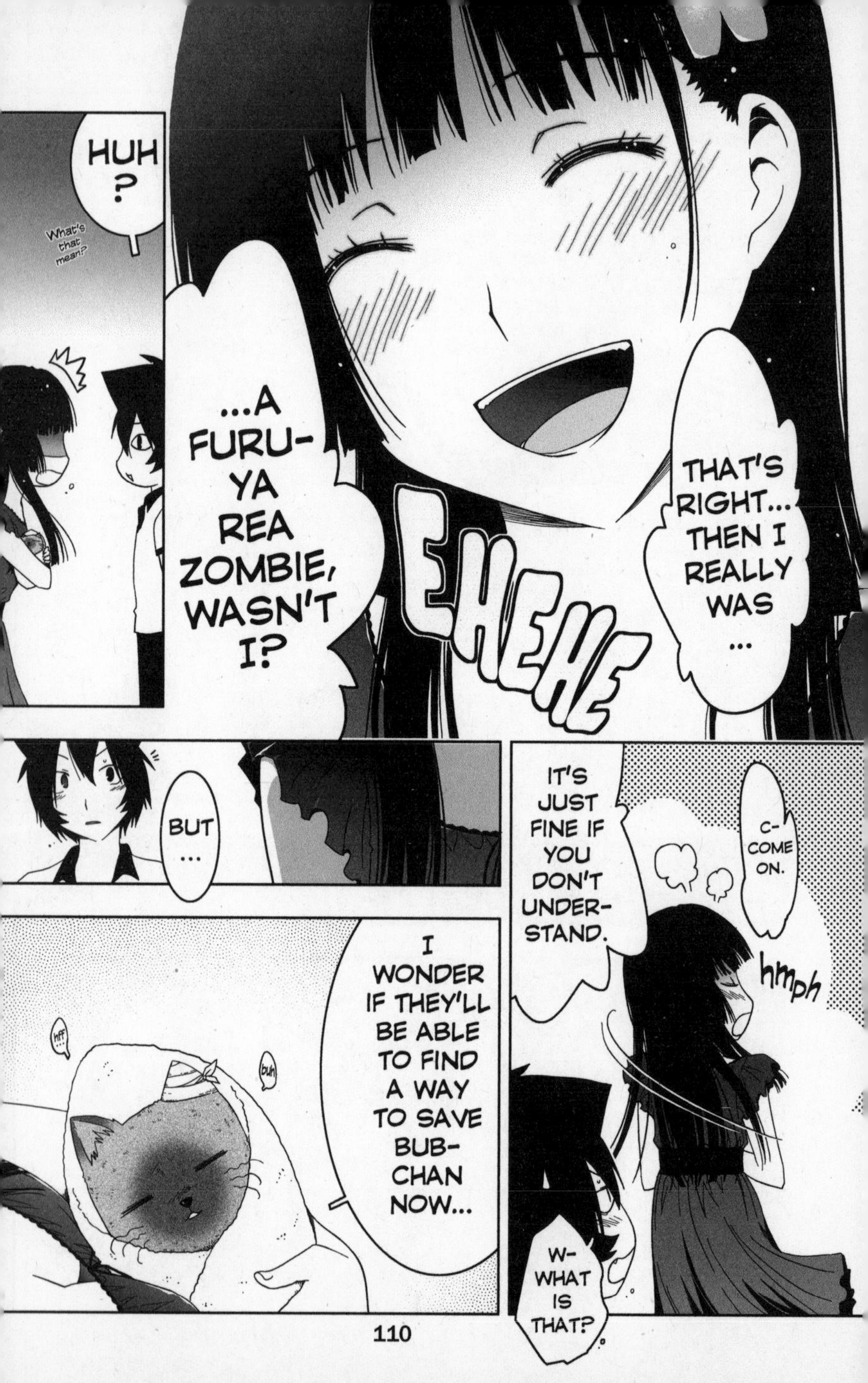
THAT'S RIGHT... THEN I REALLY WAS ...
EHEHE
...A FURUYA REA ZOMBIE, WASN'T I?
HUH ?
What's that mean?
C-COME ON.
IT'S JUST FINE IF YOU DON'T UNDERSTAND.
hmph
W-WHAT IS THAT?
BUT ...
I WONDER IF THEY'LL BE ABLE TO FIND A WAY TO SAVE BUB-CHAN NOW...
buh
hff ...

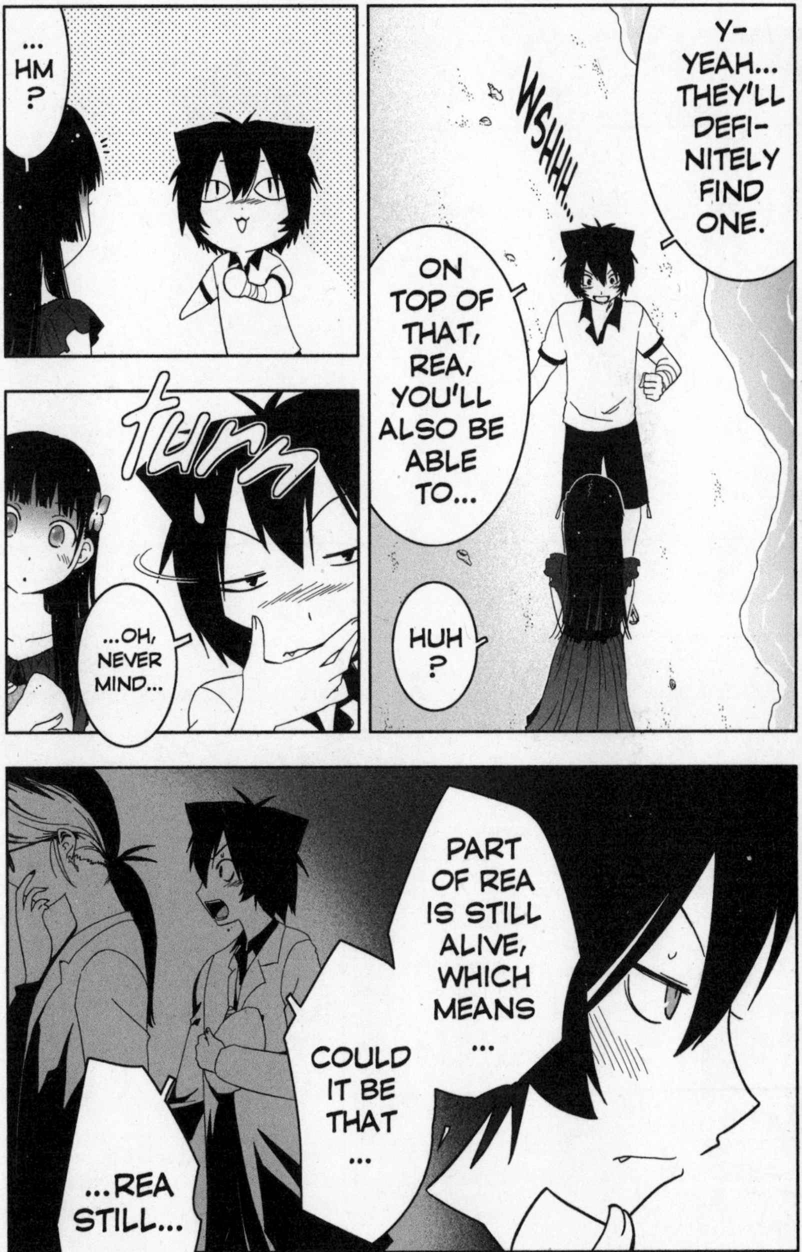
Y-YEAH... THEY'LL DEFINITELY FIND ONE.
WSHHH...
ON TOP OF THAT, REA, YOU'LL ALSO BE ABLE TO...
HUH?
...HM?
turn
...OH, NEVER MIND...
PART OF REA IS STILL ALIVE, WHICH MEANS...
COULD IT BE THAT...
...REA STILL...

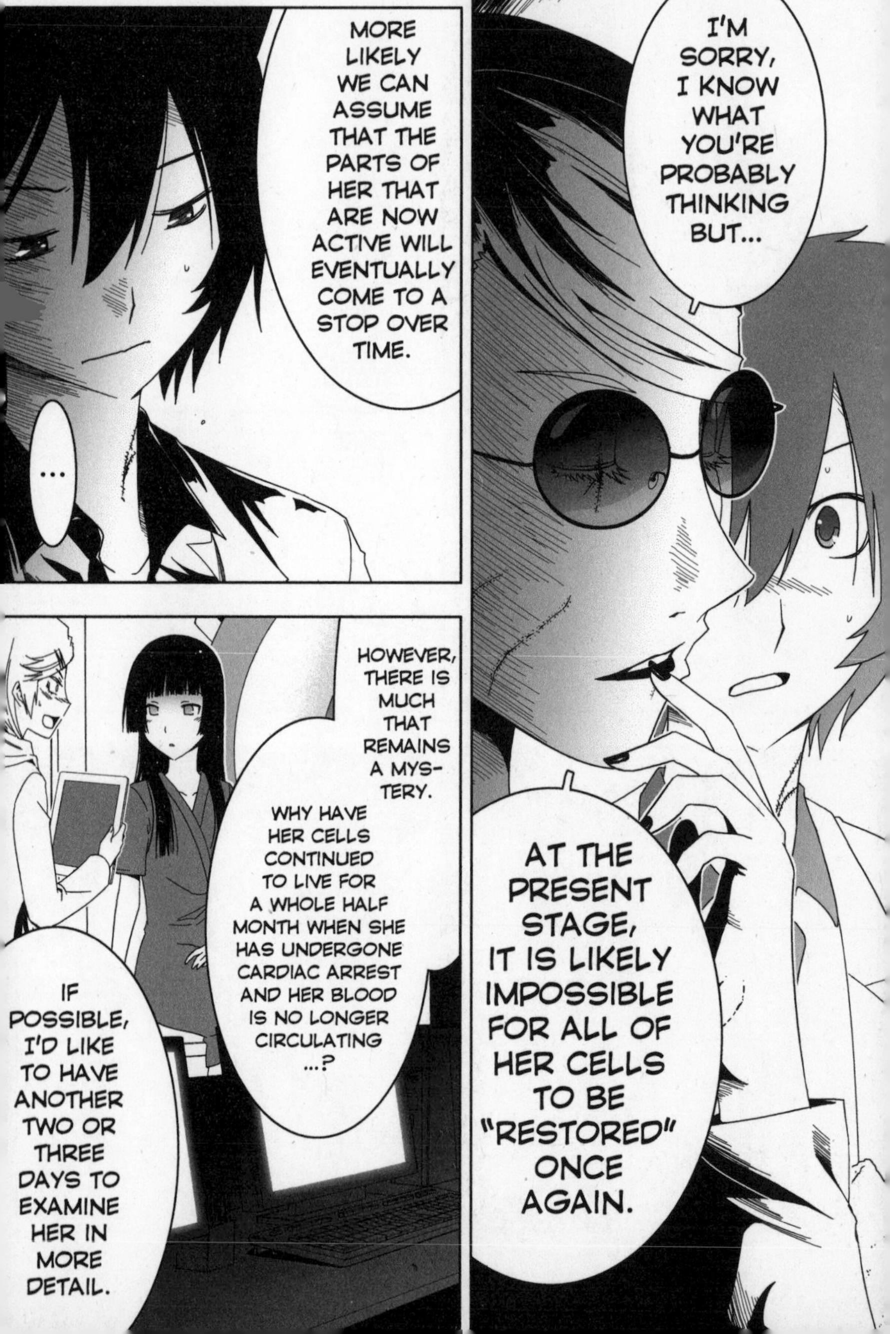
I'M SORRY, I KNOW WHAT YOU'RE PROBABLY THINKING BUT...
AT THE PRESENT STAGE, IT IS LIKELY IMPOSSIBLE FOR ALL OF HER CELLS TO BE "RESTORED" ONCE AGAIN.
MORE LIKELY WE CAN ASSUME THAT THE PARTS OF HER THAT ARE NOW ACTIVE WILL EVENTUALLY COME TO A STOP OVER TIME.
...
HOWEVER, THERE IS MUCH THAT REMAINS A MYSTERY.
WHY HAVE HER CELLS CONTINUED TO LIVE FOR A WHOLE HALF MONTH WHEN SHE HAS UNDERGONE CARDIAC ARREST AND HER BLOOD IS NO LONGER CIRCULATING ...?
IF POSSIBLE, I'D LIKE TO HAVE ANOTHER TWO OR THREE DAYS TO EXAMINE HER IN MORE DETAIL.

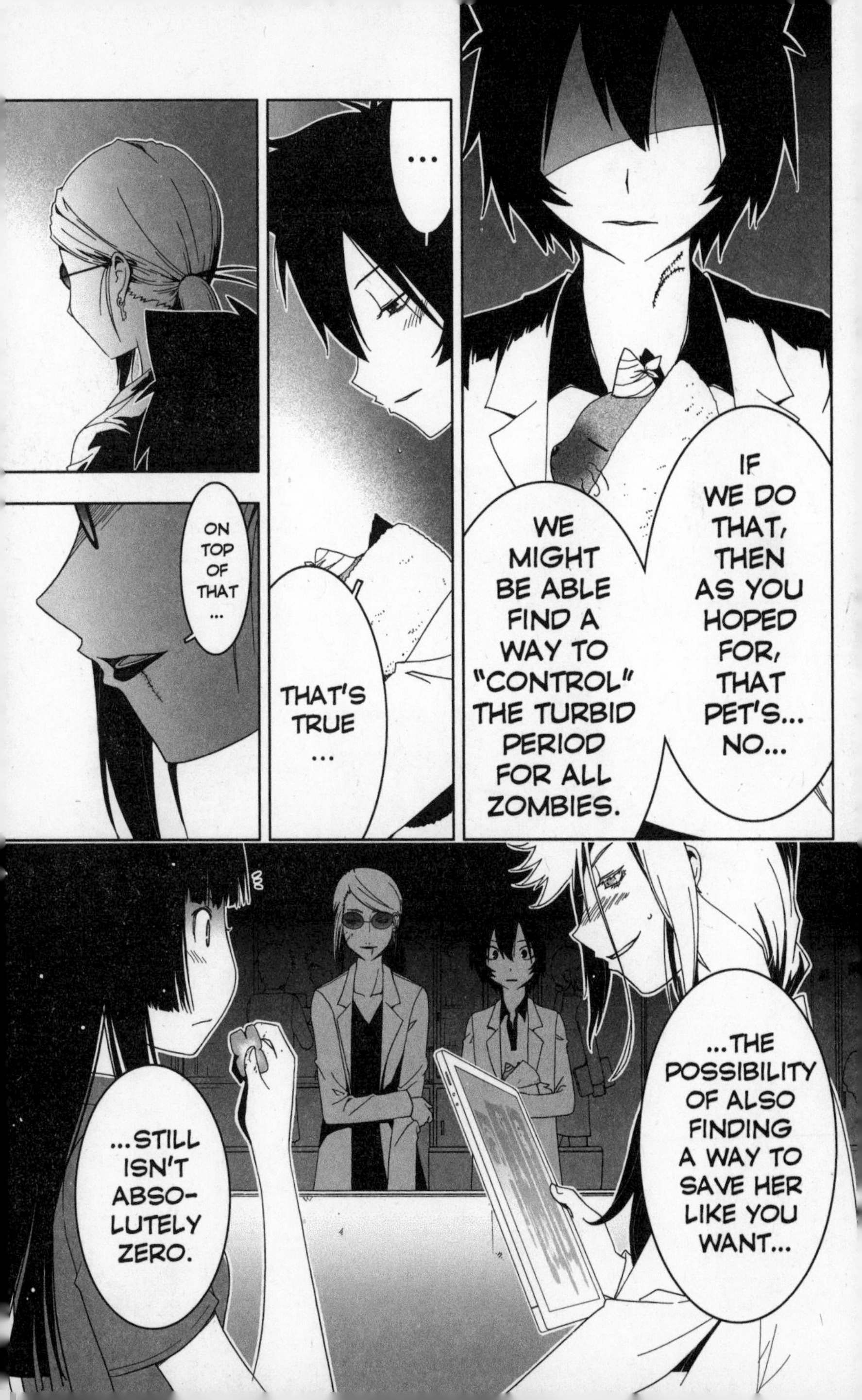

IF WE DO THAT, THEN AS YOU HOPED FOR, THAT PET'S... NO...
WE MIGHT BE ABLE FIND A WAY TO "CONTROL" THE TURBID PERIOD FOR ALL ZOMBIES.
...
THAT'S TRUE ...
ON TOP OF THAT ...
...THE POSSIBILITY OF ALSO FINDING A WAY TO SAVE HER LIKE YOU WANT...
...STILL ISN'T ABSO-LUTELY ZERO.

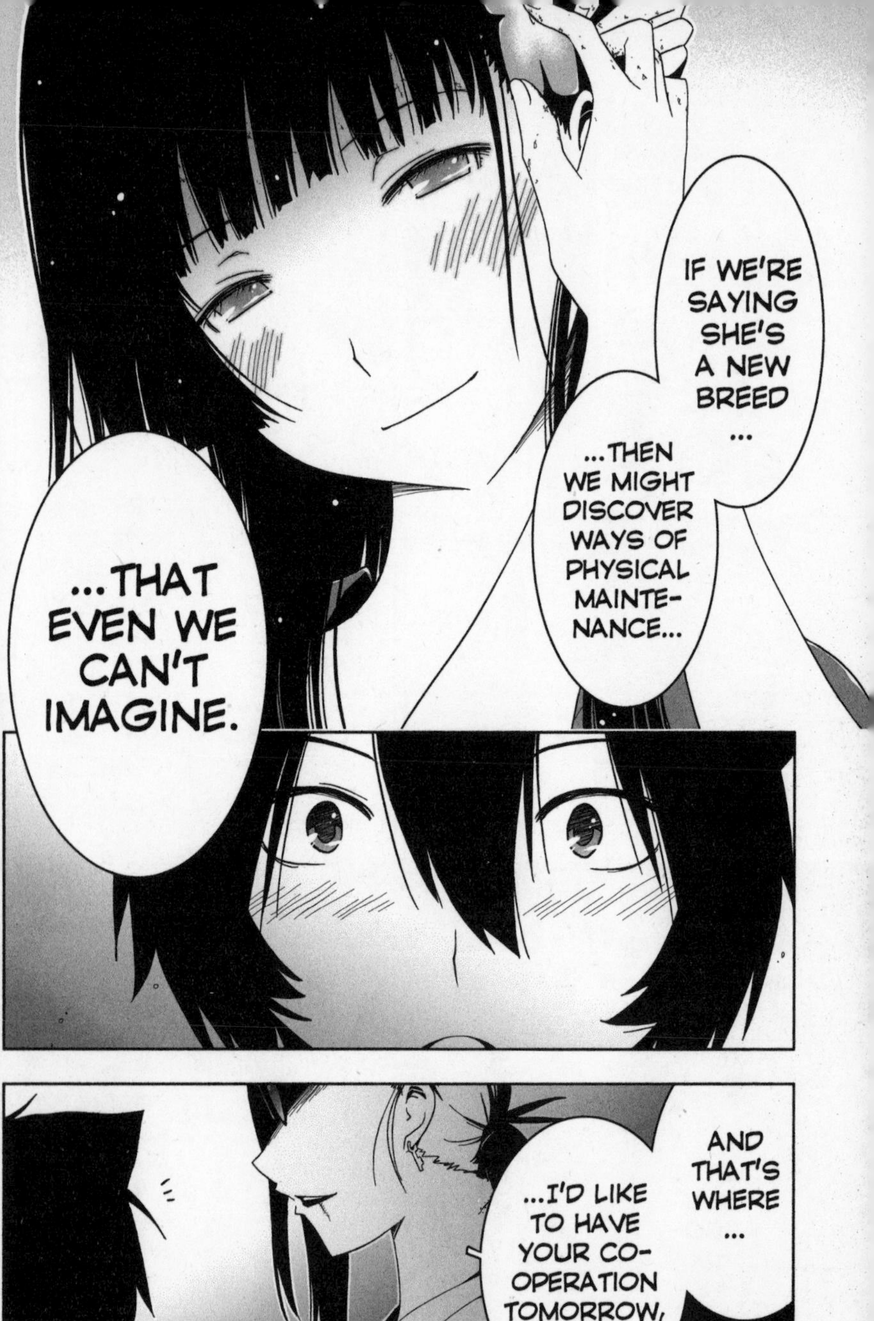
IF WE'RE SAYING SHE'S A NEW BREED ...
...THEN WE MIGHT DISCOVER WAYS OF PHYSICAL MAINTE-NANCE...
...THAT EVEN WE CAN'T IMAGINE.
AND THAT'S WHERE ...
...I'D LIKE TO HAVE YOUR CO-OPERATION TOMORROW, TOO.

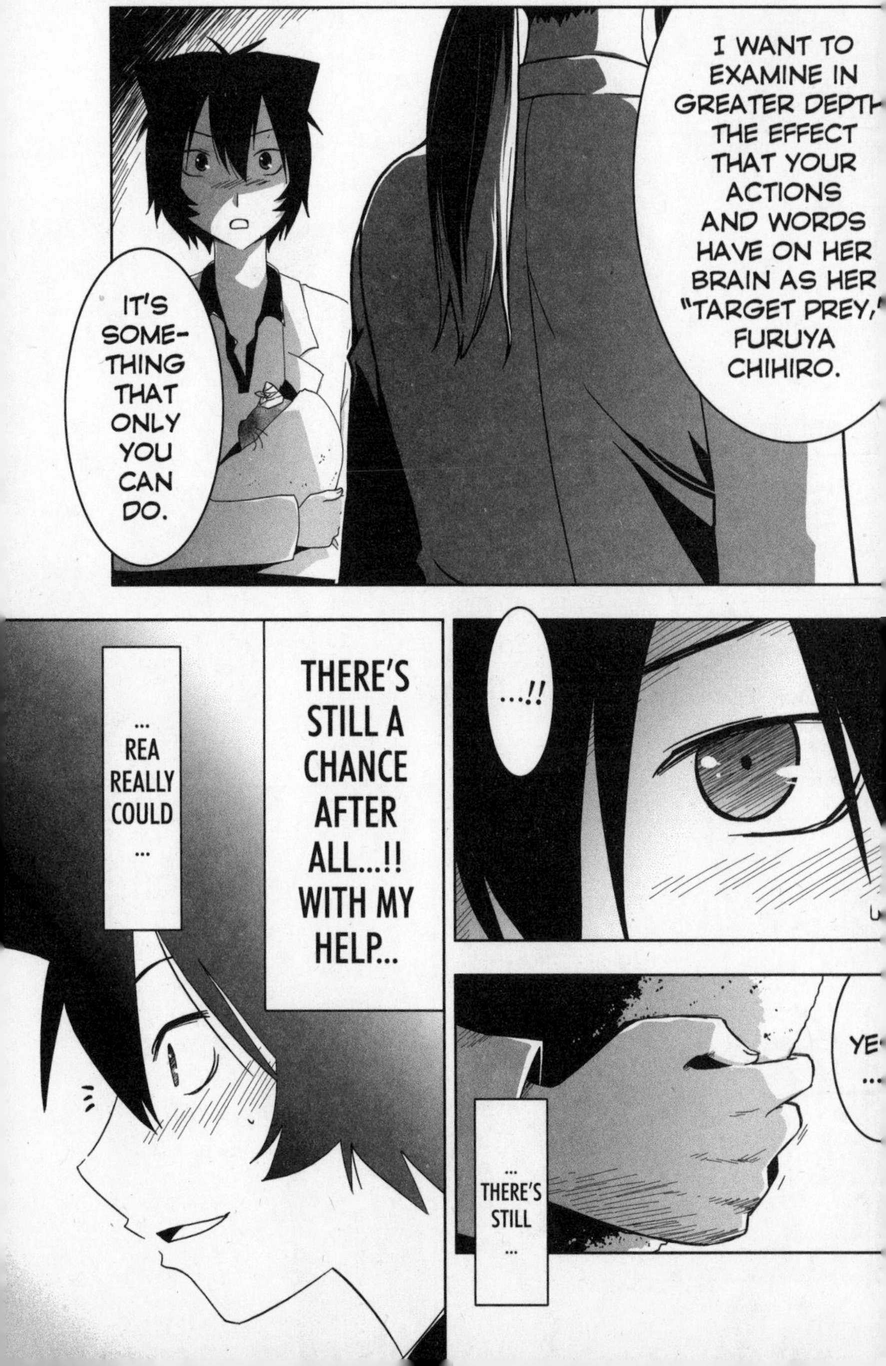
I WANT TO EXAMINE IN GREATER DEPTH THE EFFECT THAT YOUR ACTIONS AND WORDS HAVE ON HER BRAIN AS HER "TARGET PREY," FURUYA CHIHIRO.
IT'S SOMETHING THAT ONLY YOU CAN DO.
...!!
YE ...
... THERE'S STILL ...
THERE'S STILL A CHANCE AFTER ALL...!! WITH MY HELP...
... REA REALLY COULD ...

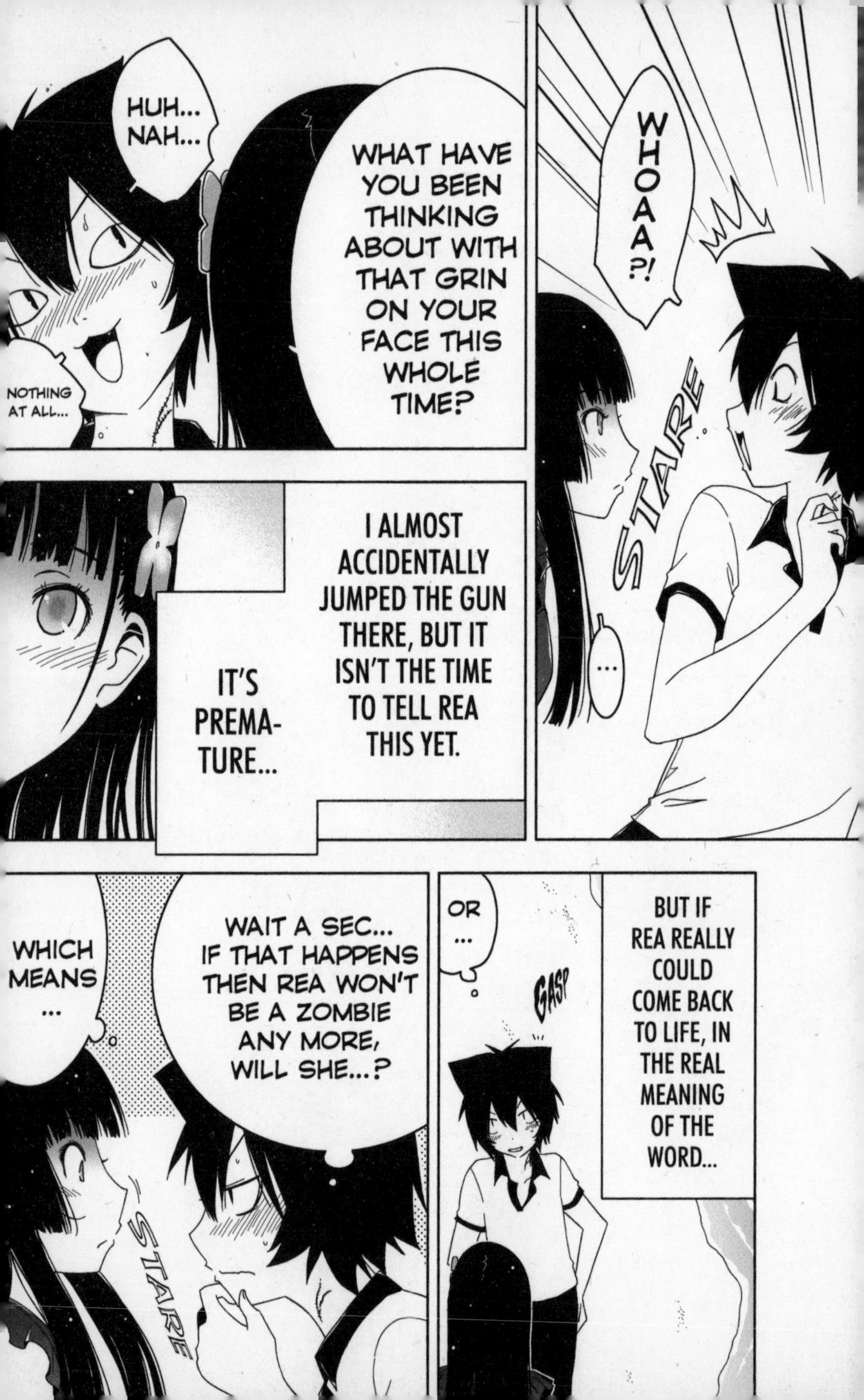
WHOAA?!
STARE
...
WHAT HAVE YOU BEEN THINKING ABOUT WITH THAT GRIN ON YOUR FACE THIS WHOLE TIME?
HUH... NAH...
NOTHING AT ALL...
I ALMOST ACCIDENTALLY JUMPED THE GUN THERE, BUT IT ISN'T THE TIME TO TELL REA THIS YET.
IT'S PREMA-TURE...
BUT IF REA REALLY COULD COME BACK TO LIFE, IN THE REAL MEANING OF THE WORD...
OR ...
GASP
WAIT A SEC... IF THAT HAPPENS THEN REA WON'T BE A ZOMBIE ANY MORE, WILL SHE...?
STARE
WHICH MEANS ...

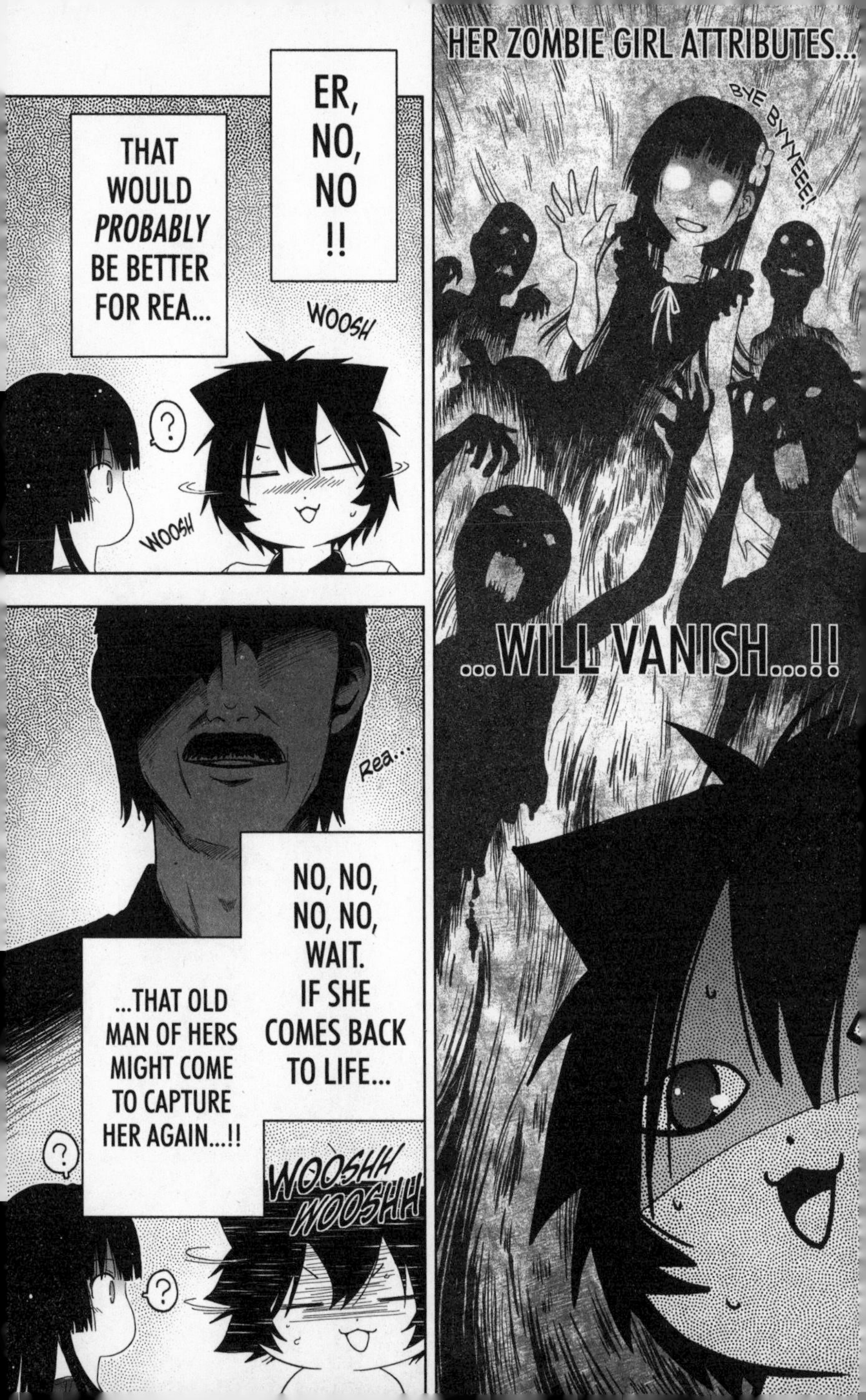
HER ZOMBIE GIRL ATTRIBUTES...
BYE BYYYEEE!
...WILL VANISH...!!
ER, NO, NO !!
THAT WOULD PROBABLY BE BETTER FOR REA...
WOOSH
?
WOOSH
Rea...
NO, NO, NO, NO, WAIT. IF SHE COMES BACK TO LIFE...
...THAT OLD MAN OF HERS MIGHT COME TO CAPTURE HER AGAIN...!!
?
WOOSHH WOOSHH
?

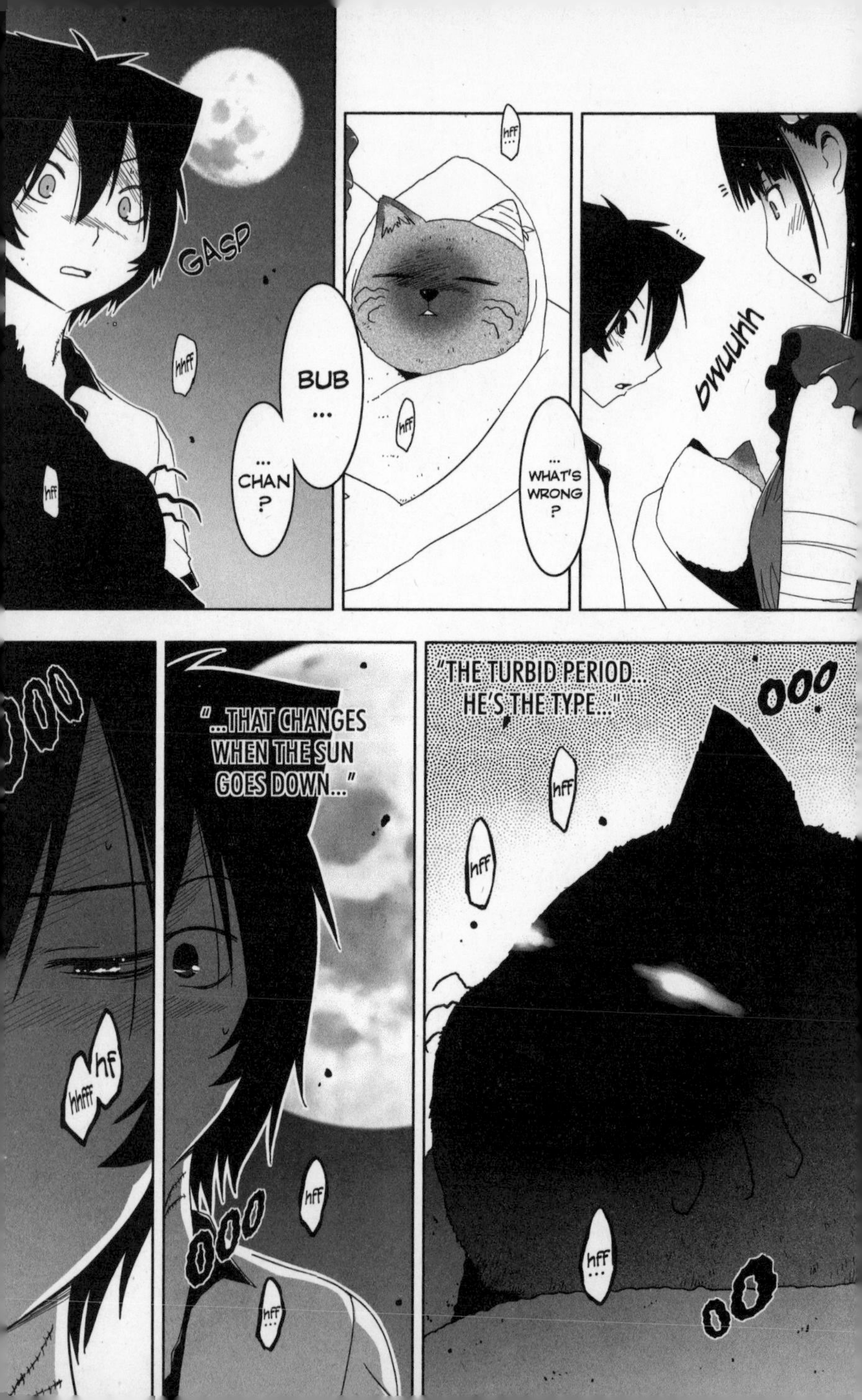
bwuuhh
...
WHAT'S
WRONG
?
hff
...
hff
BUB
...
...
CHAN
?
GASP
hhff
hff
"THE TURBID PERIOD...
HE'S THE TYPE..."
ooo
hff
hff
hff
...
oo
"...THAT CHANGES
WHEN THE SUN
GOES DOWN..."
hff
ooo
hff
...
ooo
hf
hhfff

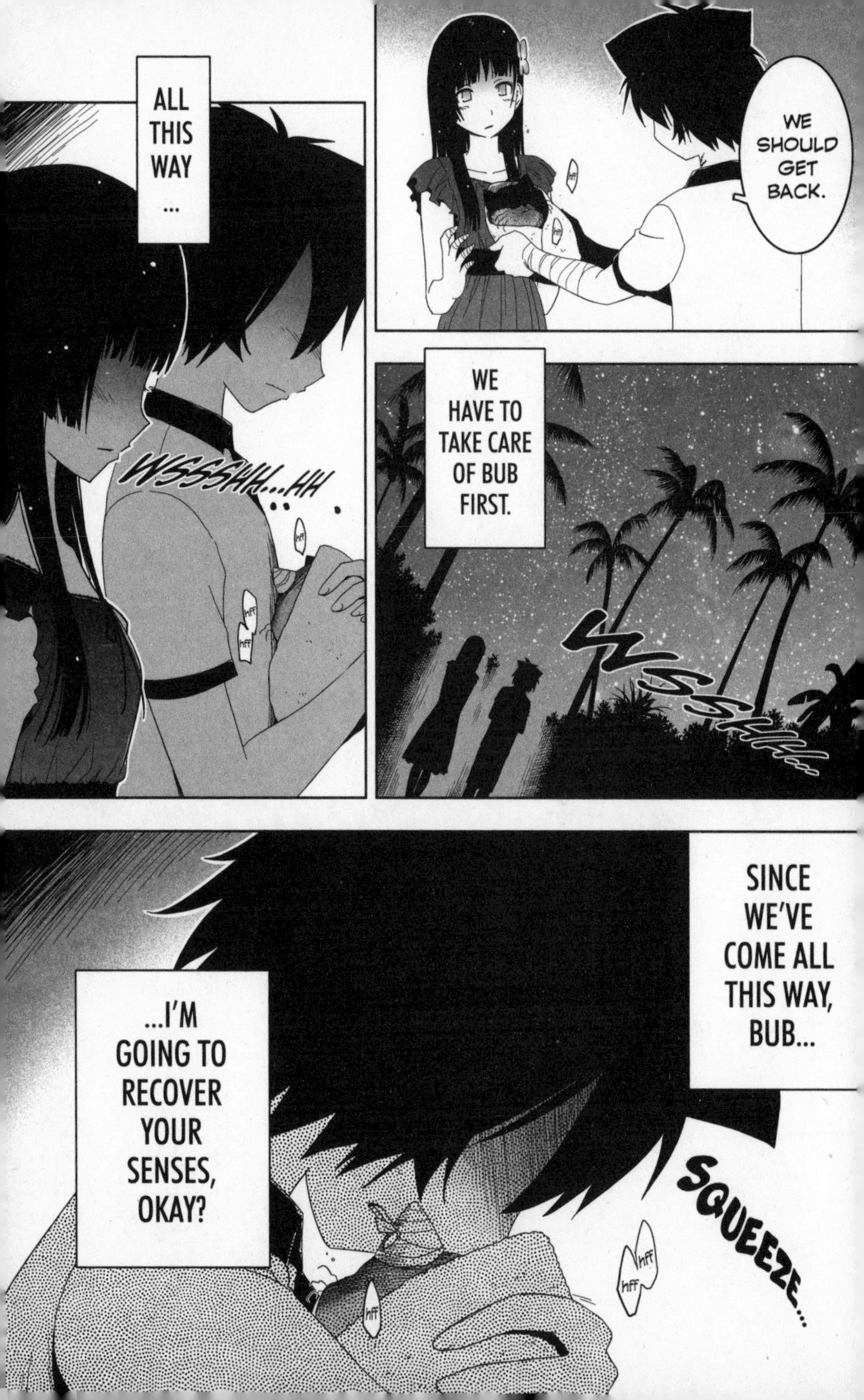
WE SHOULD GET BACK.
hff
hff
WE HAVE TO TAKE CARE OF BUB FIRST.
WSSHH...
ALL THIS WAY ...
WSSSHH...HH
hff
hff
hff
SINCE WE'VE COME ALL THIS WAY, BUB...
...I'M GOING TO RECOVER YOUR SENSES, OKAY?
SQUEEZE...
hff
hff
hff

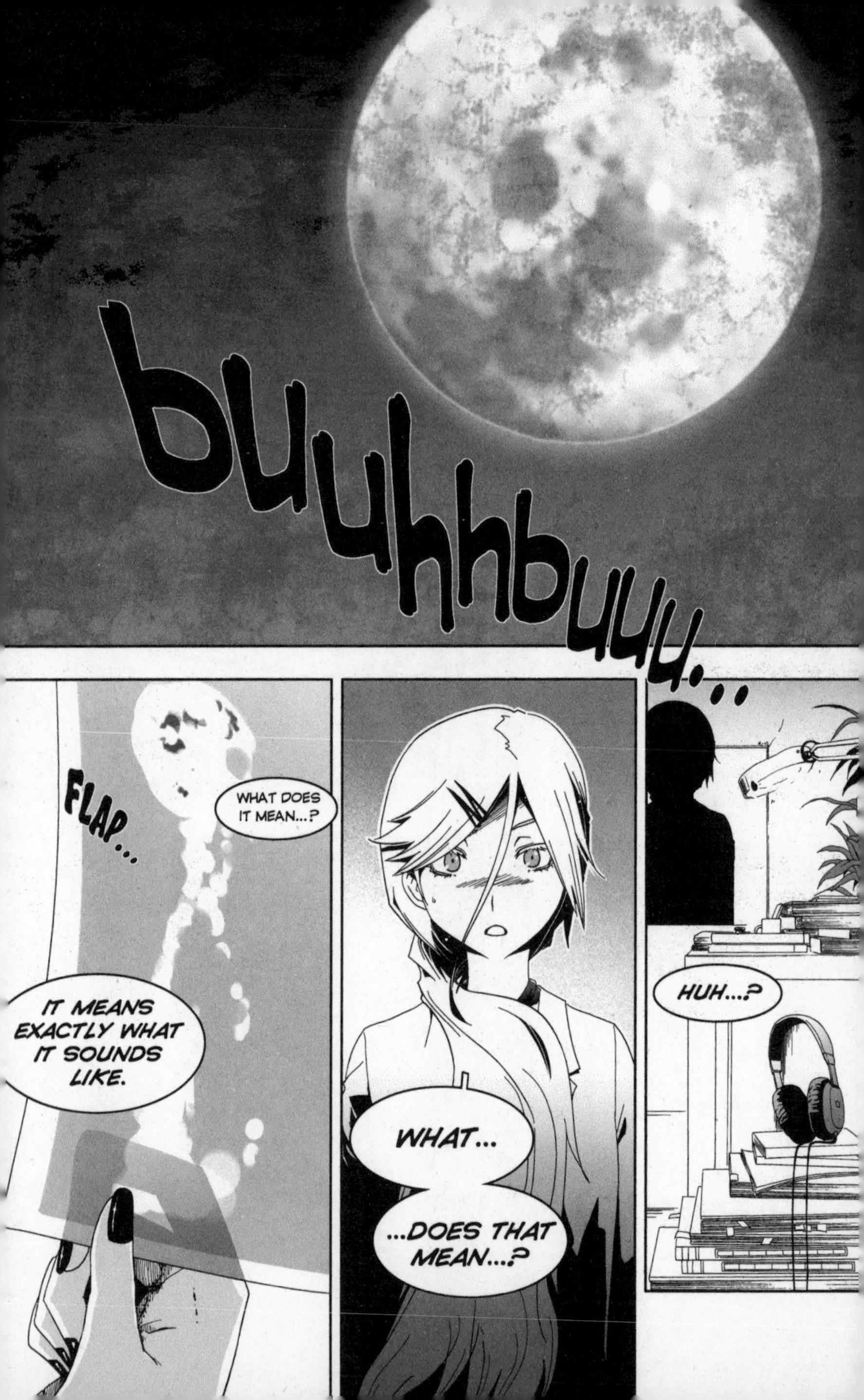
buuhhbuuuu...
HUH...?
WHAT...
...DOES THAT MEAN...?
WHAT DOES IT MEAN...?
FLAP...
IT MEANS EXACTLY WHAT IT SOUNDS LIKE.

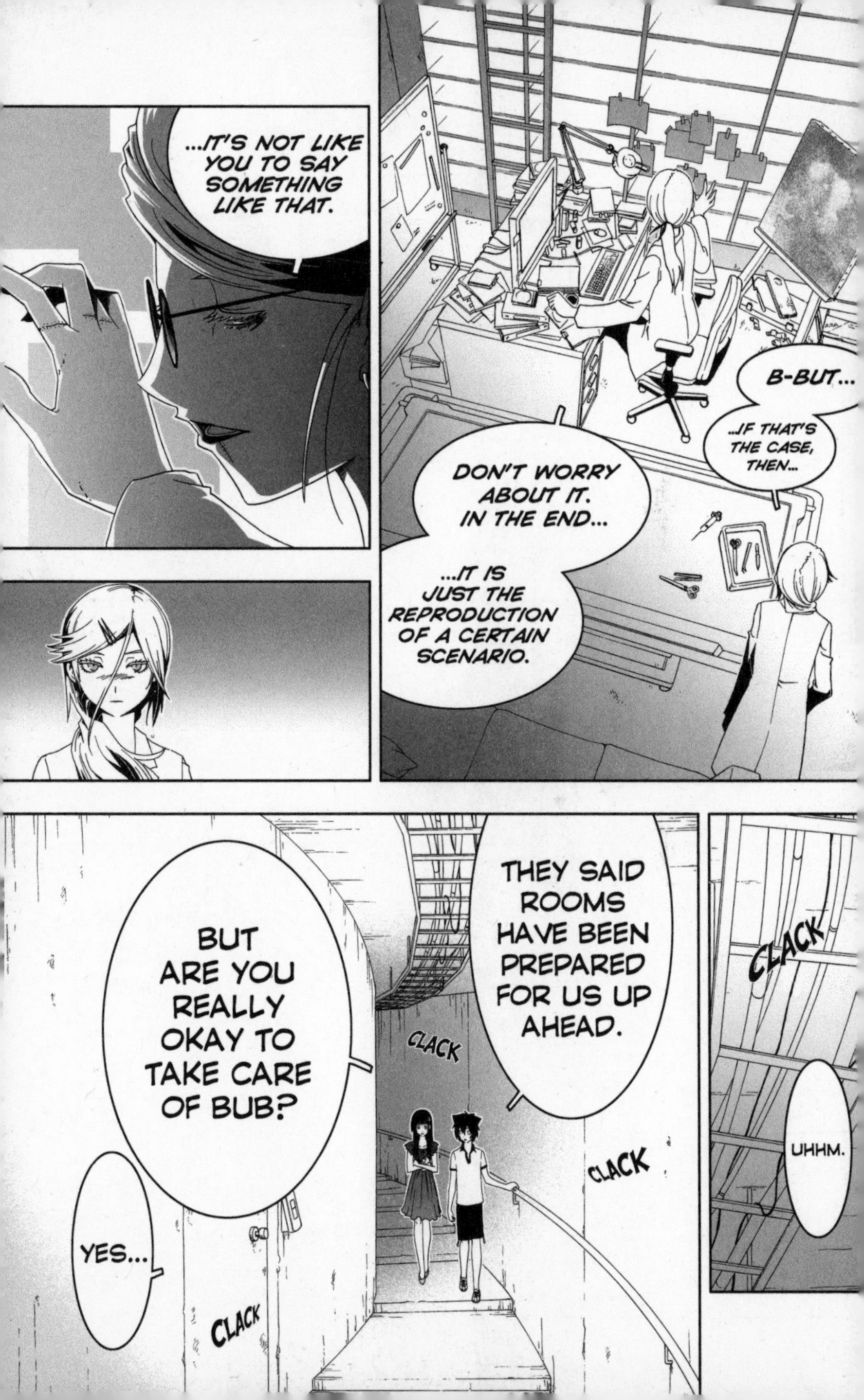
B-BUT...
...IF THAT'S THE CASE, THEN...
DON'T WORRY ABOUT IT. IN THE END...
...IT IS JUST THE REPRODUCTION OF A CERTAIN SCENARIO.
...IT'S NOT LIKE YOU TO SAY SOMETHING LIKE THAT.
CLACK
UHHM.
THEY SAID ROOMS HAVE BEEN PREPARED FOR US UP AHEAD.
BUT ARE YOU REALLY OKAY TO TAKE CARE OF BUB?
CLACK
CLACK
YES...
CLACK

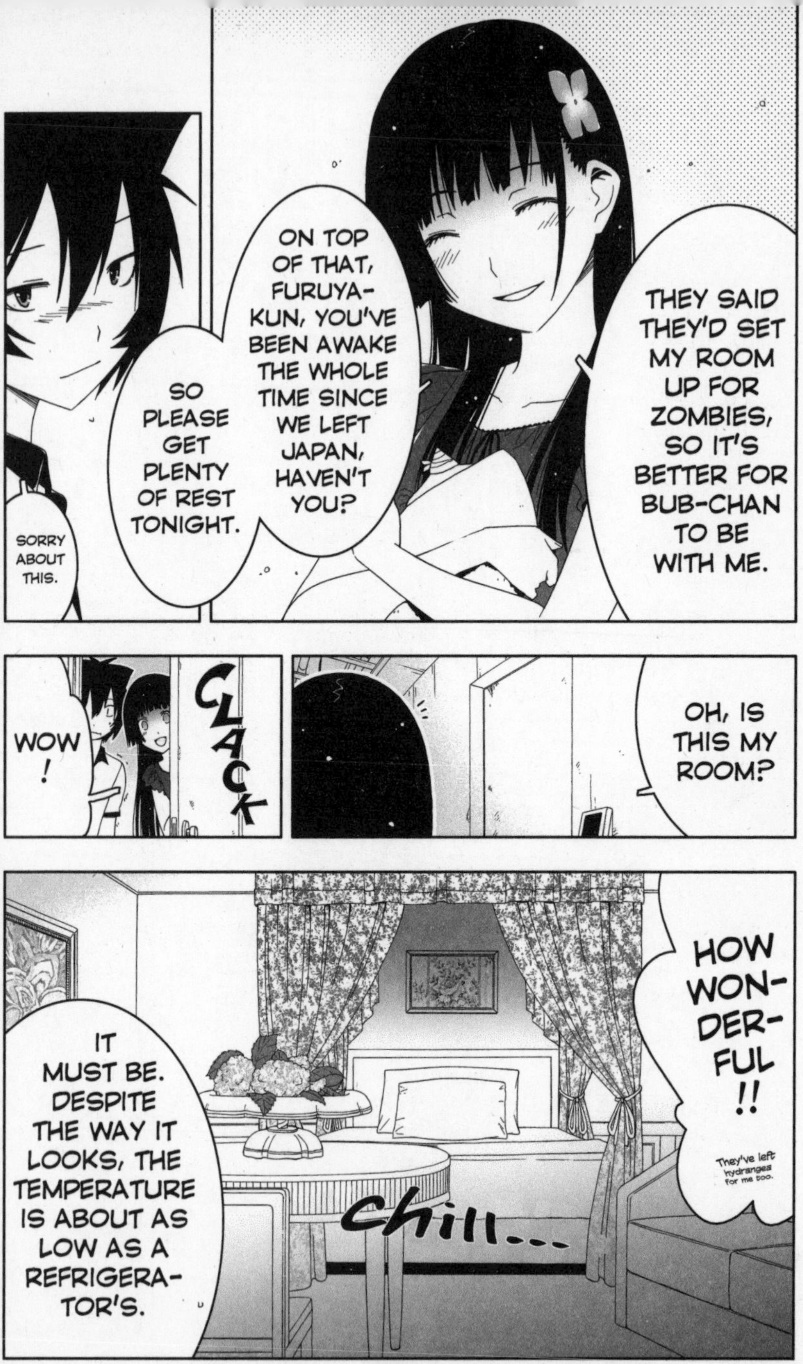
THEY SAID THEY'D SET MY ROOM UP FOR ZOMBIES, SO IT'S BETTER FOR BUB-CHAN TO BE WITH ME.
ON TOP OF THAT, FURUYA-KUN, YOU'VE BEEN AWAKE THE WHOLE TIME SINCE WE LEFT JAPAN, HAVEN'T YOU?
SO PLEASE GET PLENTY OF REST TONIGHT.
SORRY ABOUT THIS.
OH, IS THIS MY ROOM?
CLACK
WOW!
HOW WON-DER-FUL!!
They've left hydrangeas for me too.
IT MUST BE. DESPITE THE WAY IT LOOKS, THE TEMPERATURE IS ABOUT AS LOW AS A REFRIGERA-TOR'S.
Chill...

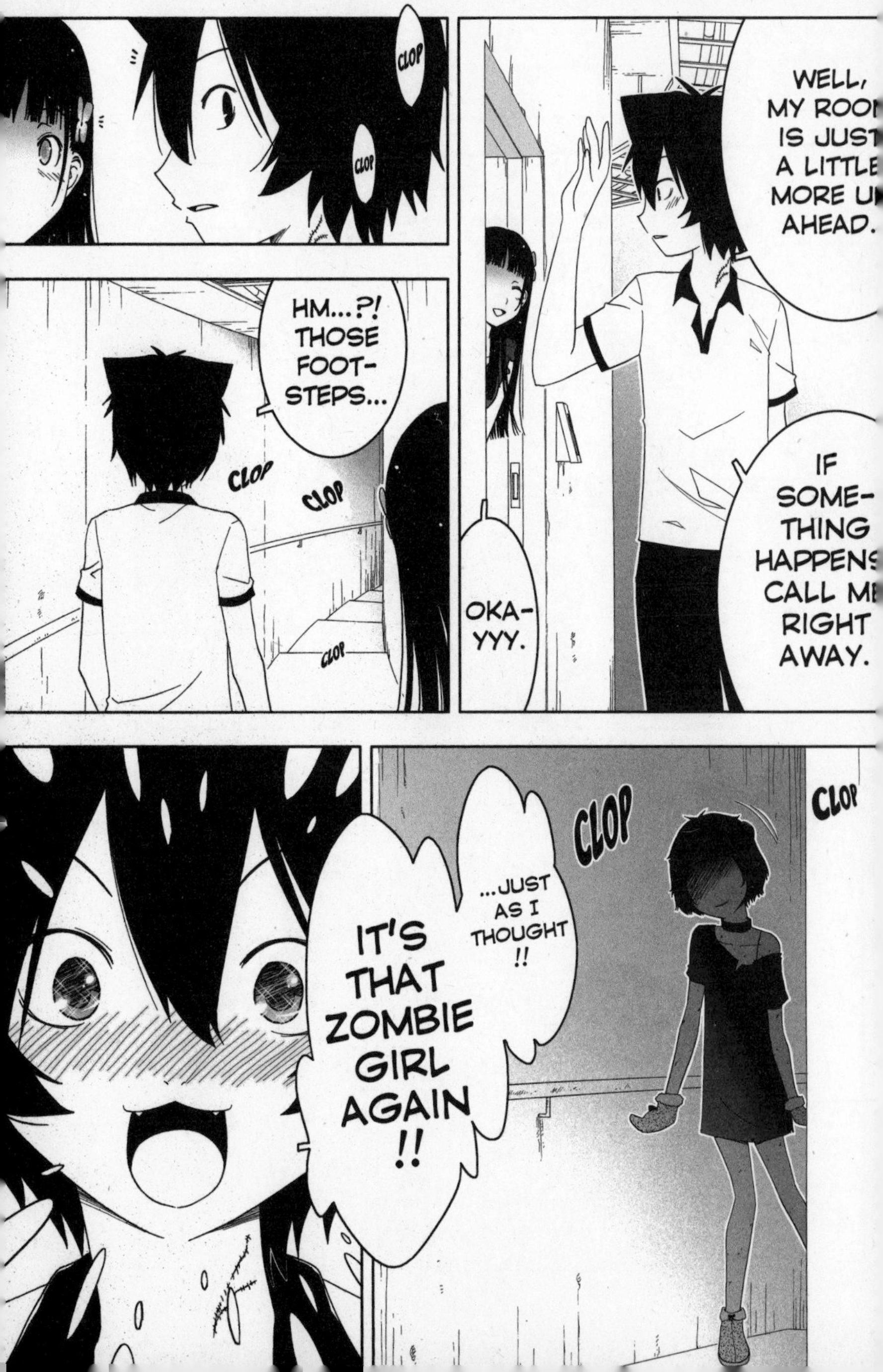
WELL, MY ROOM IS JUST A LITTLE MORE UP AHEAD.
IF SOMETHING HAPPENS CALL ME RIGHT AWAY.
OKA-YYY.
CLOP
CLOP
HM...?! THOSE FOOTSTEPS...
CLOP
CLOP
CLOP
CLOP
CLOP
...JUST AS I THOUGHT !!
IT'S THAT ZOMBIE GIRL AGAIN !!

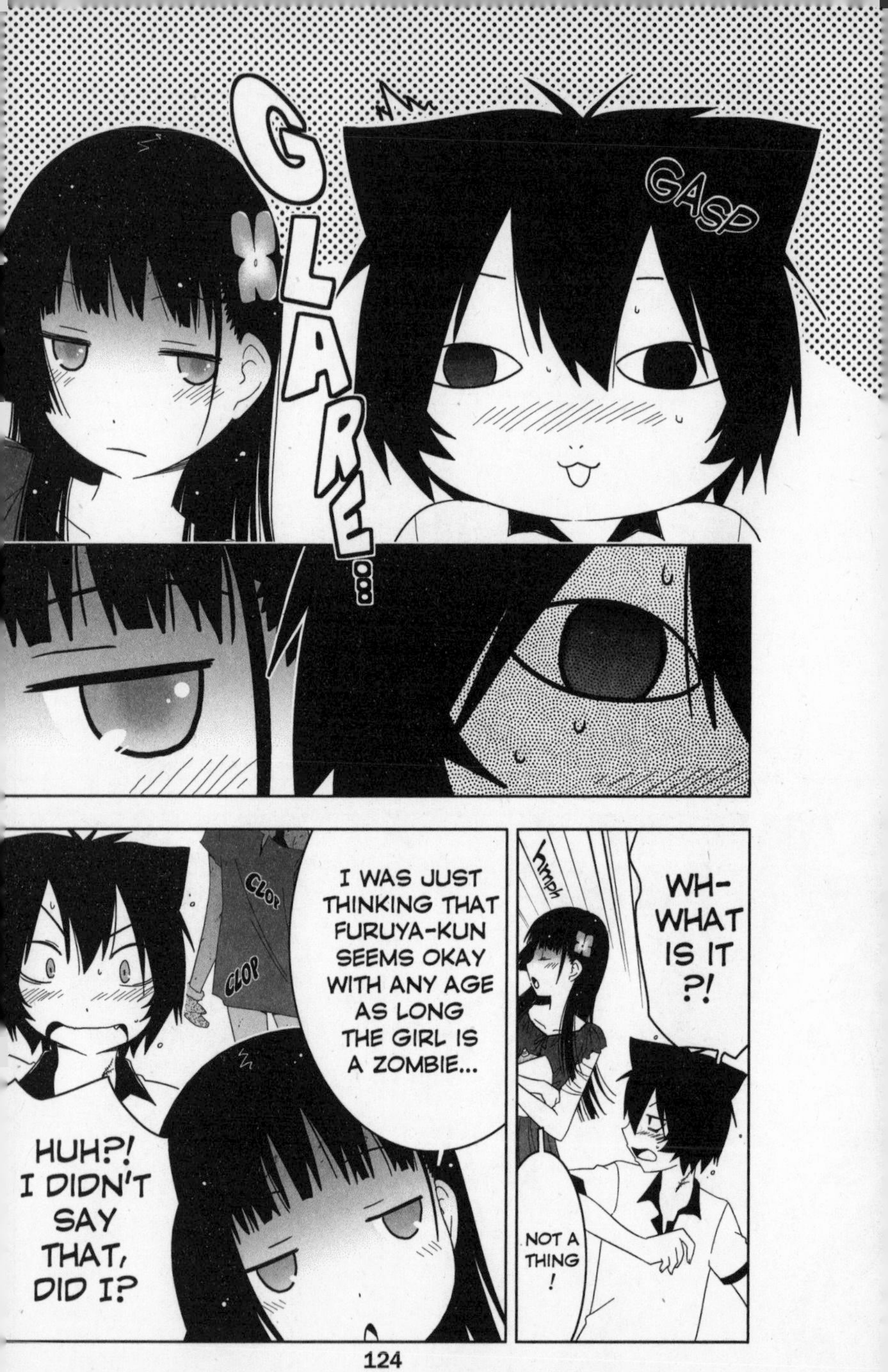
GASP
GLARE...
hmph
WH-WHAT IS IT?!
NOT A THING!
I WAS JUST THINKING THAT FURUYA-KUN SEEMS OKAY WITH ANY AGE AS LONG THE GIRL IS A ZOMBIE...
CLOP
CLOP
HUH?! I DIDN'T SAY THAT, DID I?

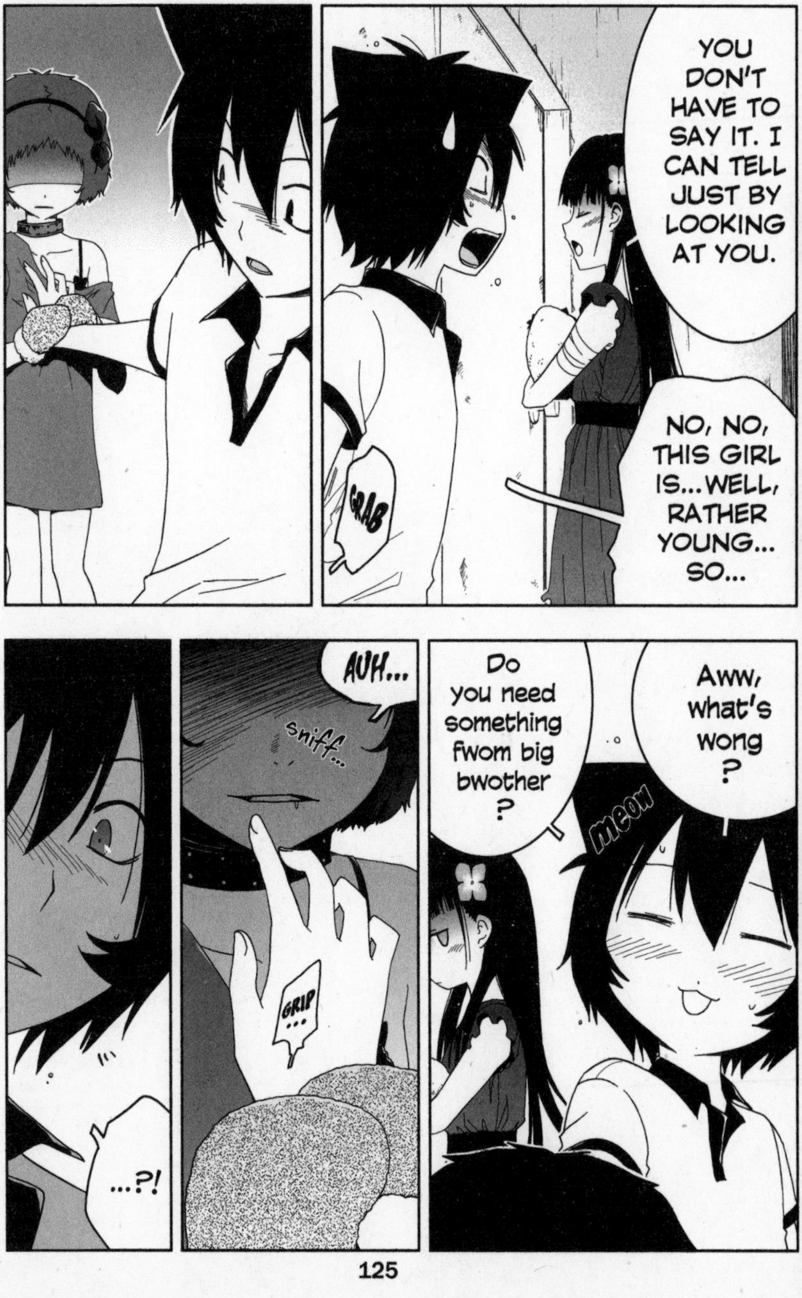
YOU DON'T HAVE TO SAY IT. I CAN TELL JUST BY LOOKING AT YOU.
NO, NO, THIS GIRL IS...WELL, RATHER YOUNG... SO...
GRAB
Aww, what's wong?
Do you need something fwom big bwother?
meow
AUH...
sniff...
GRIP...
...?!

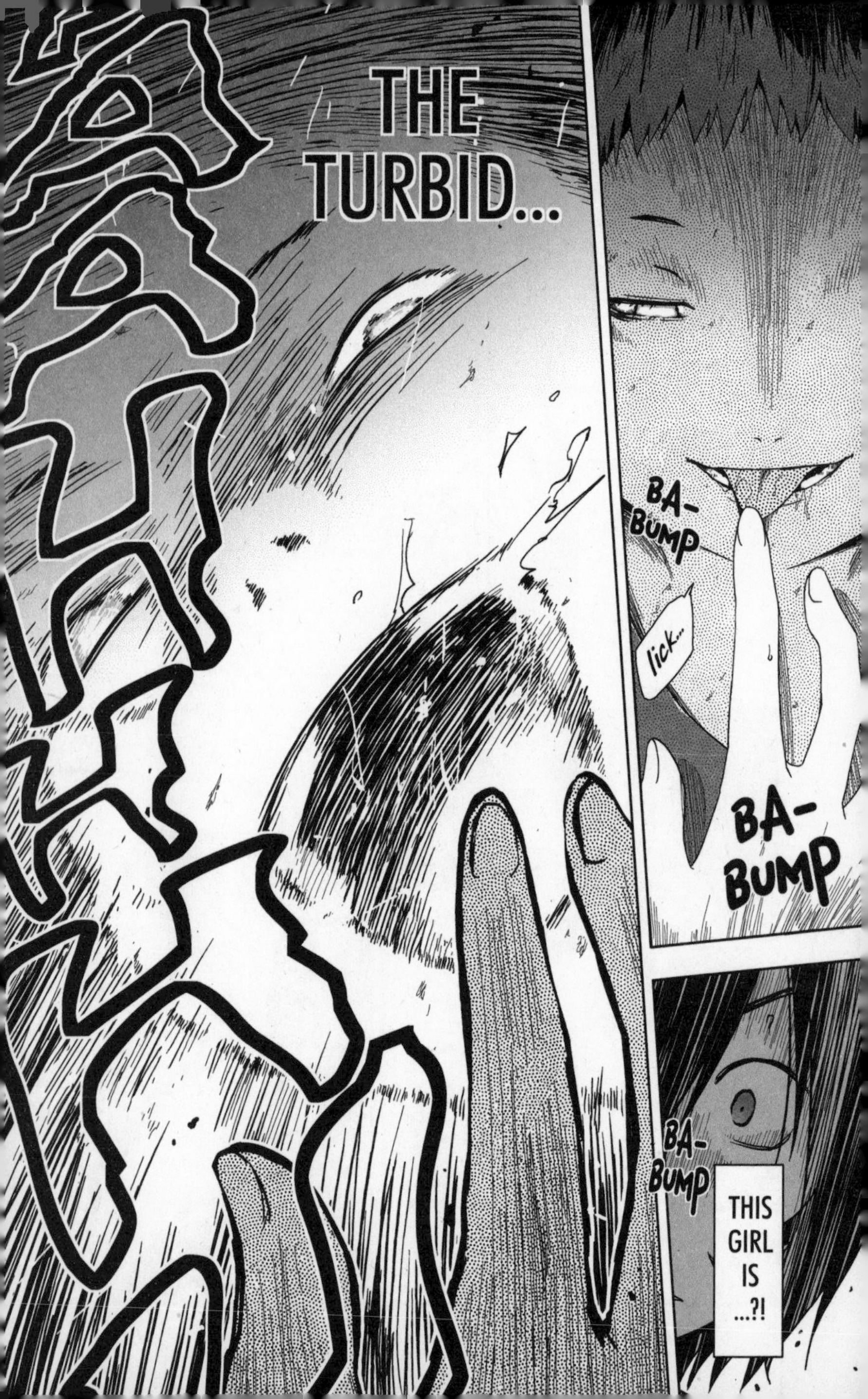
BA-BUMP
lick...
BA-BUMP
BA-BUMP
THIS GIRL IS ...?!
THE TURBID...

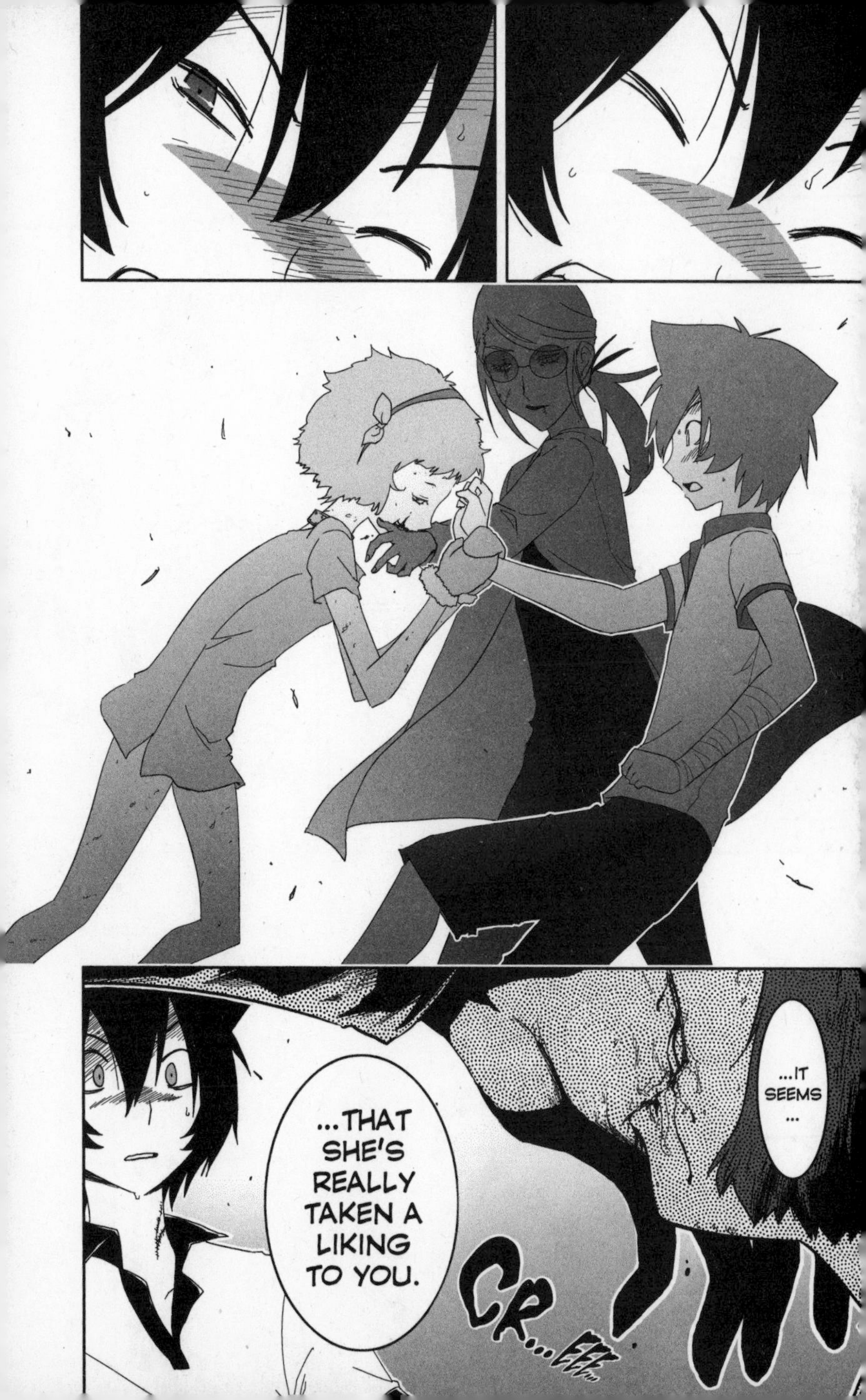
...IT SEEMS ...
...THAT SHE'S REALLY TAKEN A LIKING TO YOU.
CR...EEE

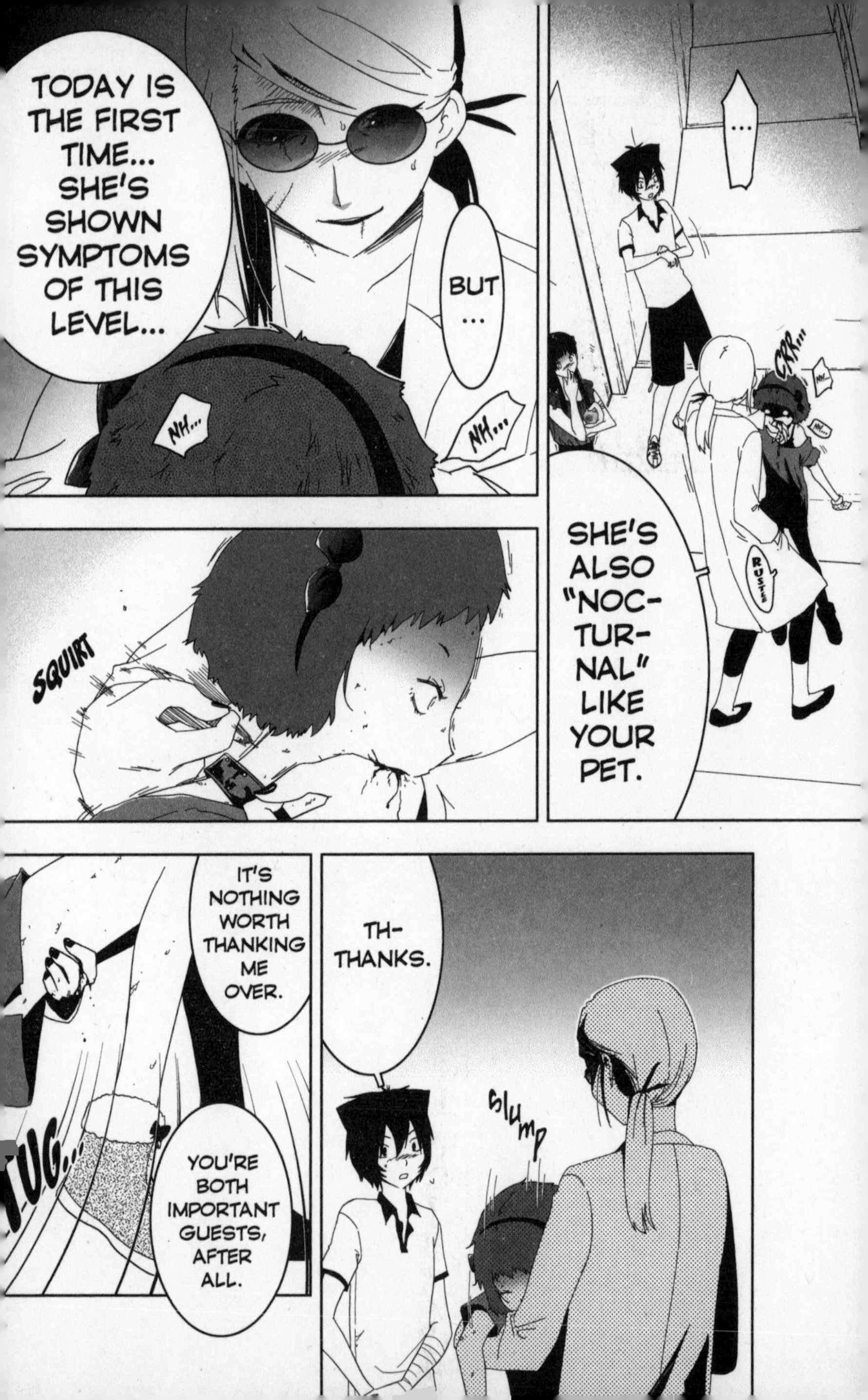
...
CRR...
RUSTLE
SHE'S ALSO "NOC-TUR-NAL" LIKE YOUR PET.
TODAY IS THE FIRST TIME... SHE'S SHOWN SYMPTOMS OF THIS LEVEL...
BUT ...
NH...
NH...
SQUIRT
TH-THANKS.
slump
IT'S NOTHING WORTH THANKING ME OVER.
YOU'RE BOTH IMPORTANT GUESTS, AFTER ALL.

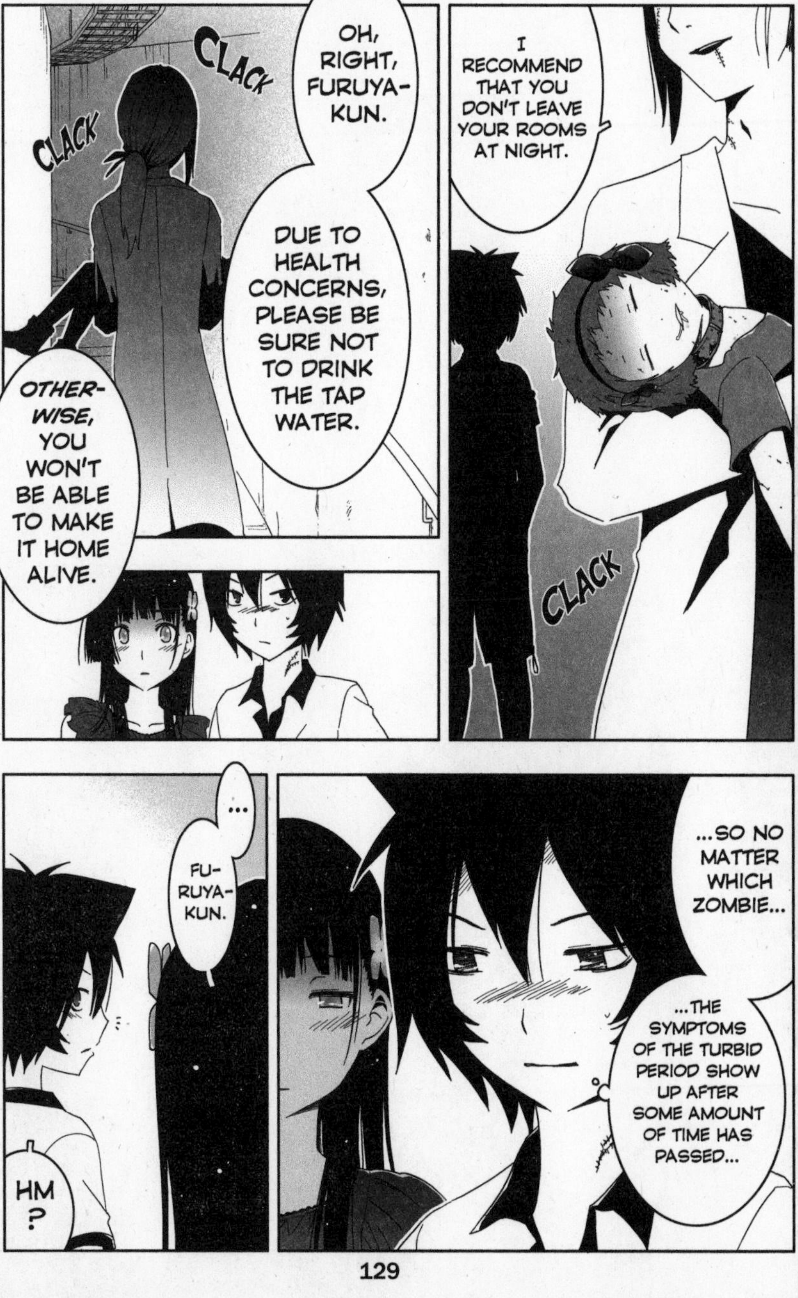
I RECOMMEND THAT YOU DON'T LEAVE YOUR ROOMS AT NIGHT.
CLACK
OH, RIGHT, FURUYA-KUN.
DUE TO HEALTH CONCERNS, PLEASE BE SURE NOT TO DRINK THE TAP WATER.
CLACK
CLACK
OTHER-WISE, YOU WON'T BE ABLE TO MAKE IT HOME ALIVE.
...SO NO MATTER WHICH ZOMBIE...
...THE SYMPTOMS OF THE TURBID PERIOD SHOW UP AFTER SOME AMOUNT OF TIME HAS PASSED...
...
FU-RUYA-KUN.
HM?

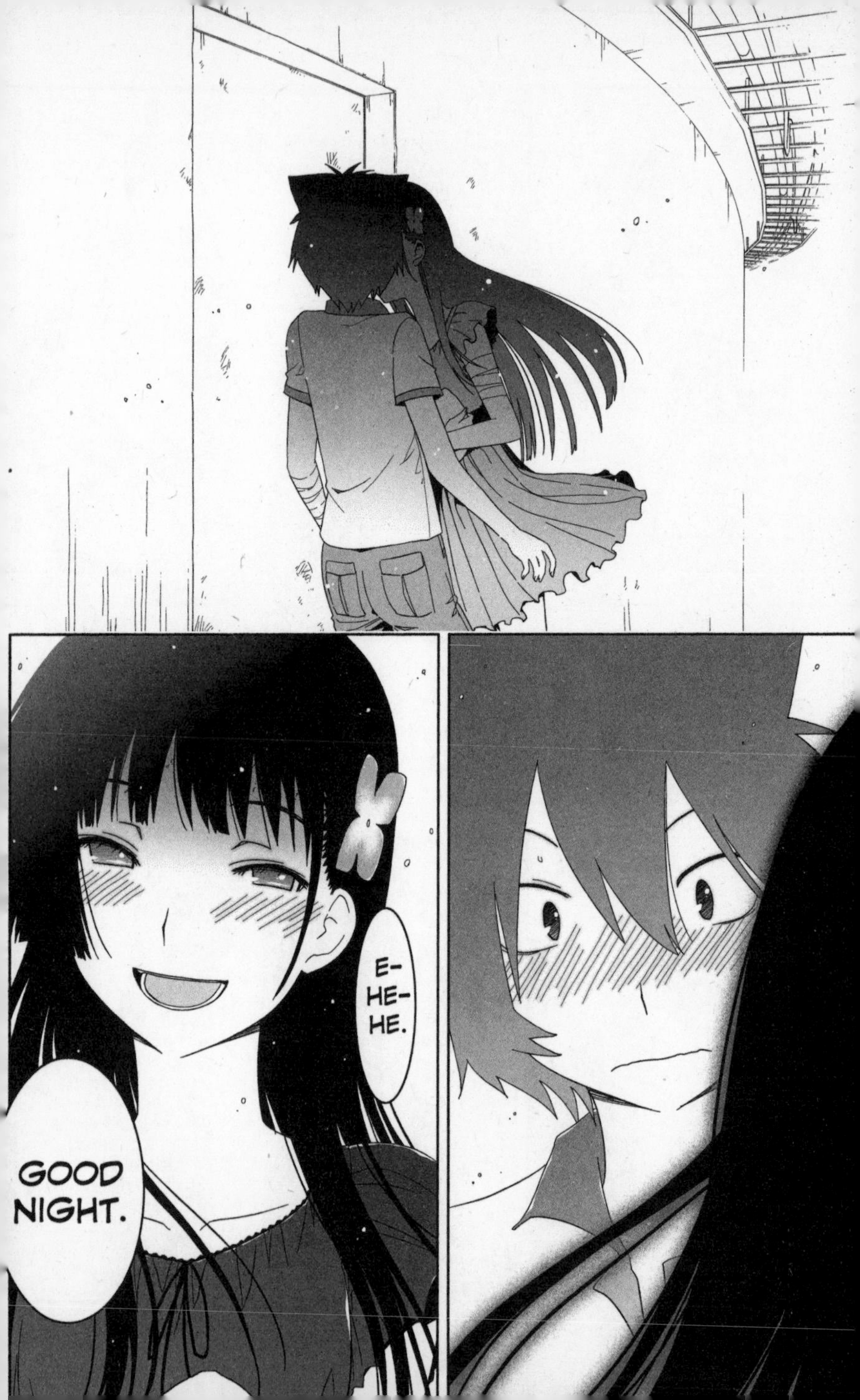
E-HE-HE.
GOOD NIGHT.

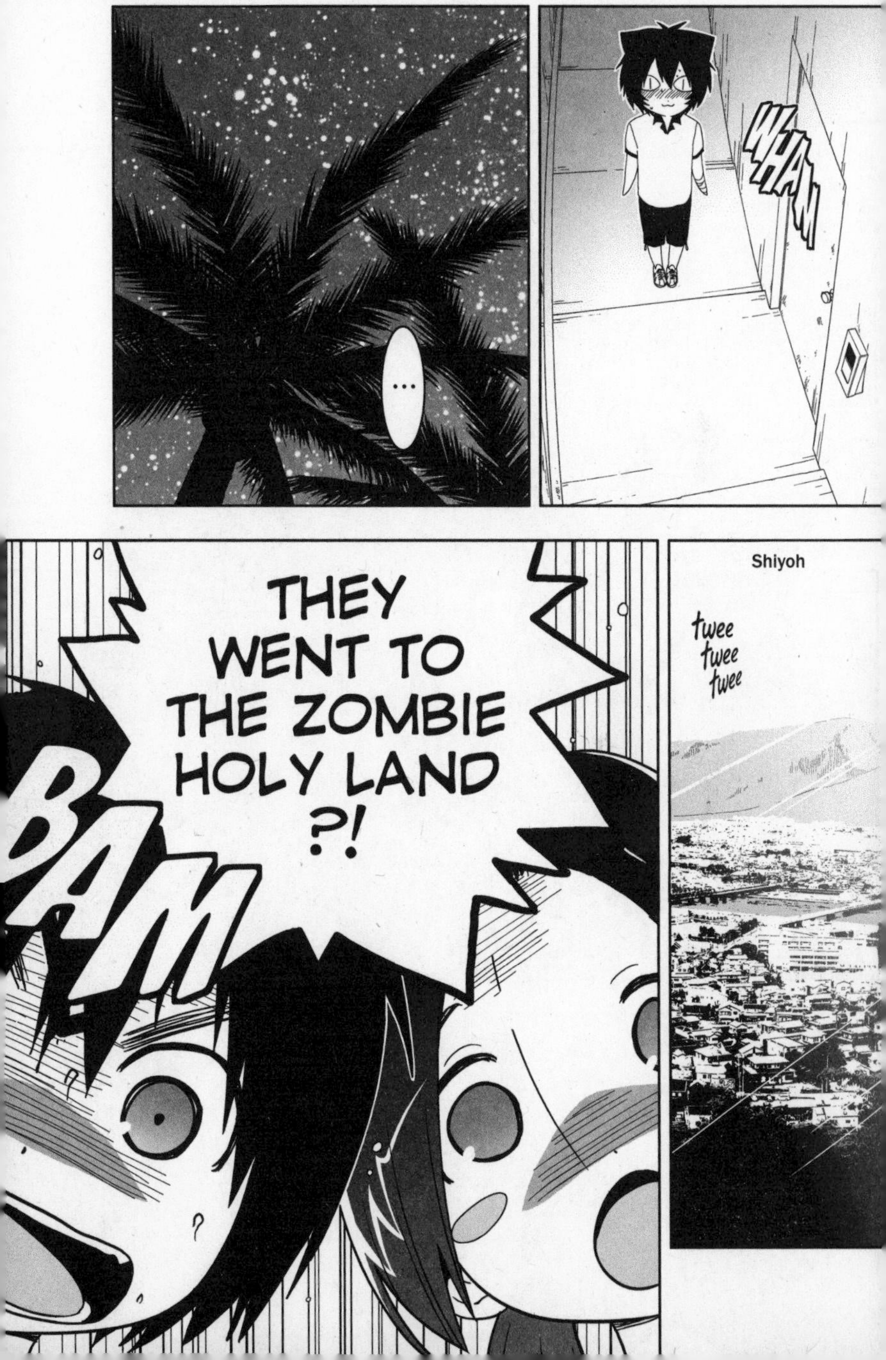
WHAM
...
Shiyoh
twee twee twee
THEY WENT TO THE ZOMBIE HOLY LAND ?!
BAM

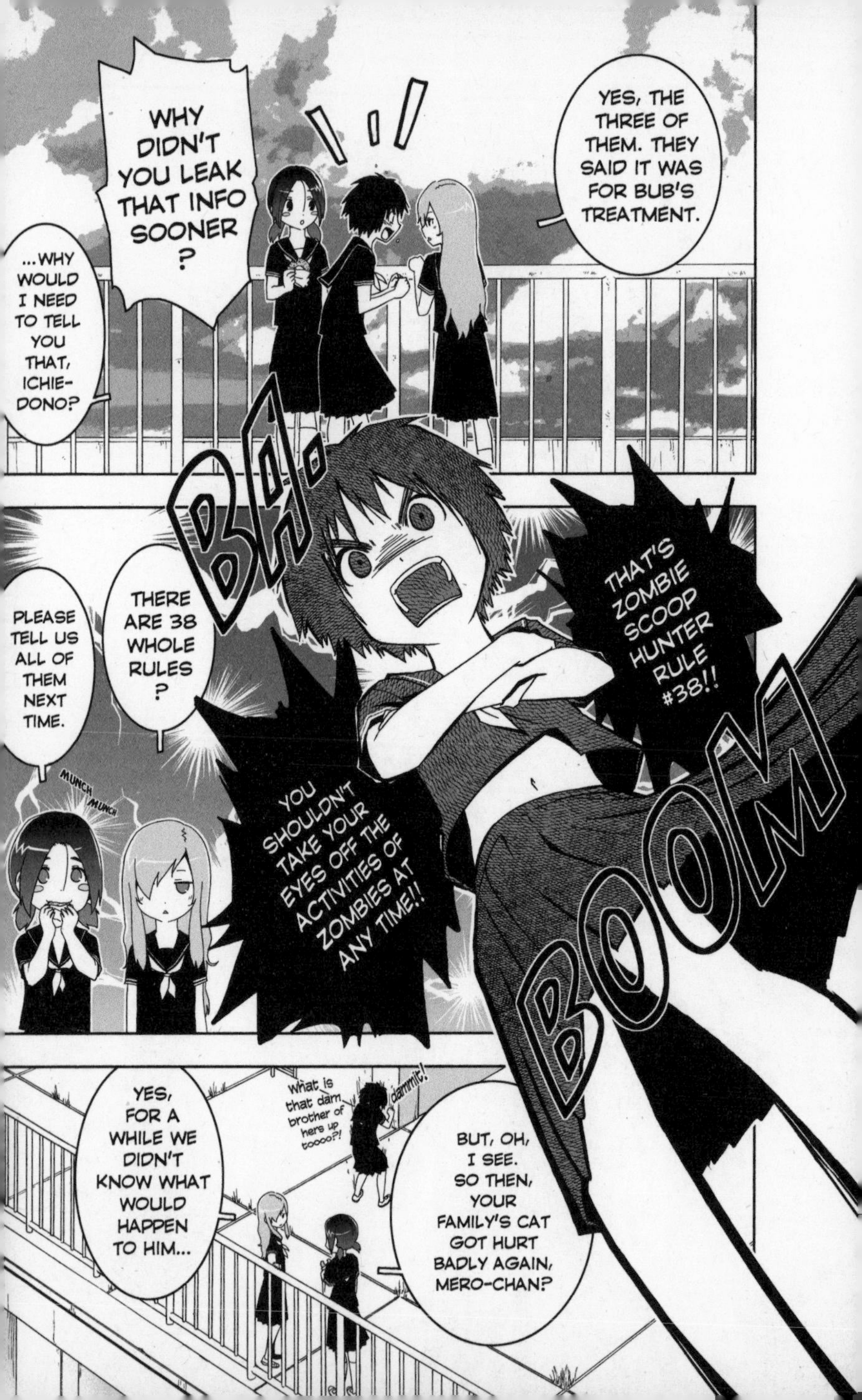
YES, THE THREE OF THEM. THEY SAID IT WAS FOR BUB'S TREATMENT.
WHY DIDN'T YOU LEAK THAT INFO SOONER?
!!
...WHY WOULD I NEED TO TELL YOU THAT, ICHIE-DONO?
THAT'S ZOMBIE SCOOP HUNTER RULE #38!!
YOU SHOULDN'T TAKE YOUR EYES OFF THE ACTIVITIES OF ZOMBIES AT ANY TIME!!
BOOM
THERE ARE 38 WHOLE RULES?
PLEASE TELL US ALL OF THEM NEXT TIME.
MUNCH MUNCH
BUT, OH, I SEE. SO THEN, YOUR FAMILY'S CAT GOT HURT BADLY AGAIN, MERO-CHAN?
dammit!
What is that darn brother of hers up toooo?!
YES, FOR A WHILE WE DIDN'T KNOW WHAT WOULD HAPPEN TO HIM...

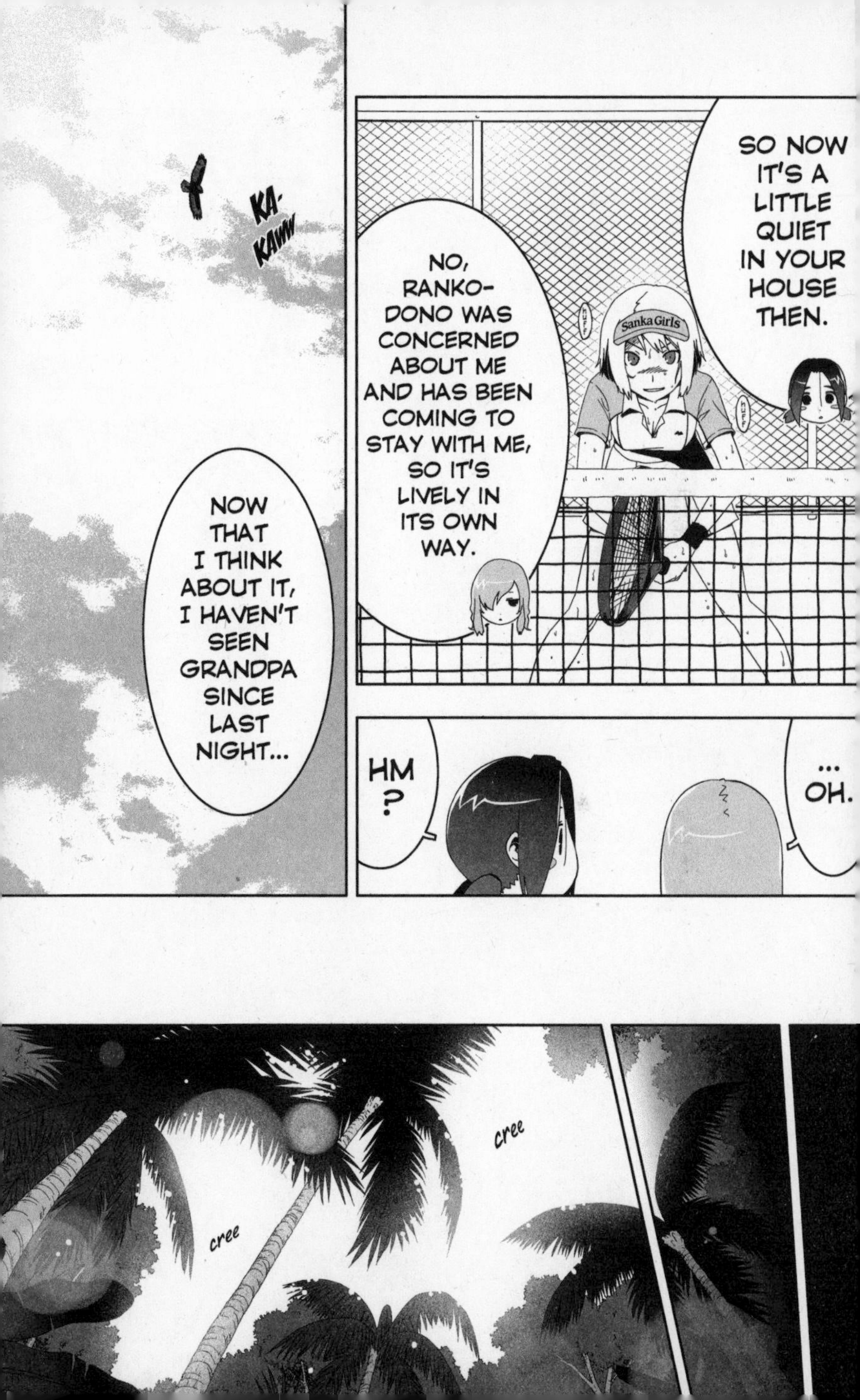
SO NOW IT'S A LITTLE QUIET IN YOUR HOUSE THEN.
NO, RANKO-DONO WAS CONCERNED ABOUT ME AND HAS BEEN COMING TO STAY WITH ME, SO IT'S LIVELY IN ITS OWN WAY.
Sanka Girls
... OH.
HM ?
KA-KAWW
NOW THAT I THINK ABOUT IT, I HAVEN'T SEEN GRANDPA SINCE LAST NIGHT...
cree
cree

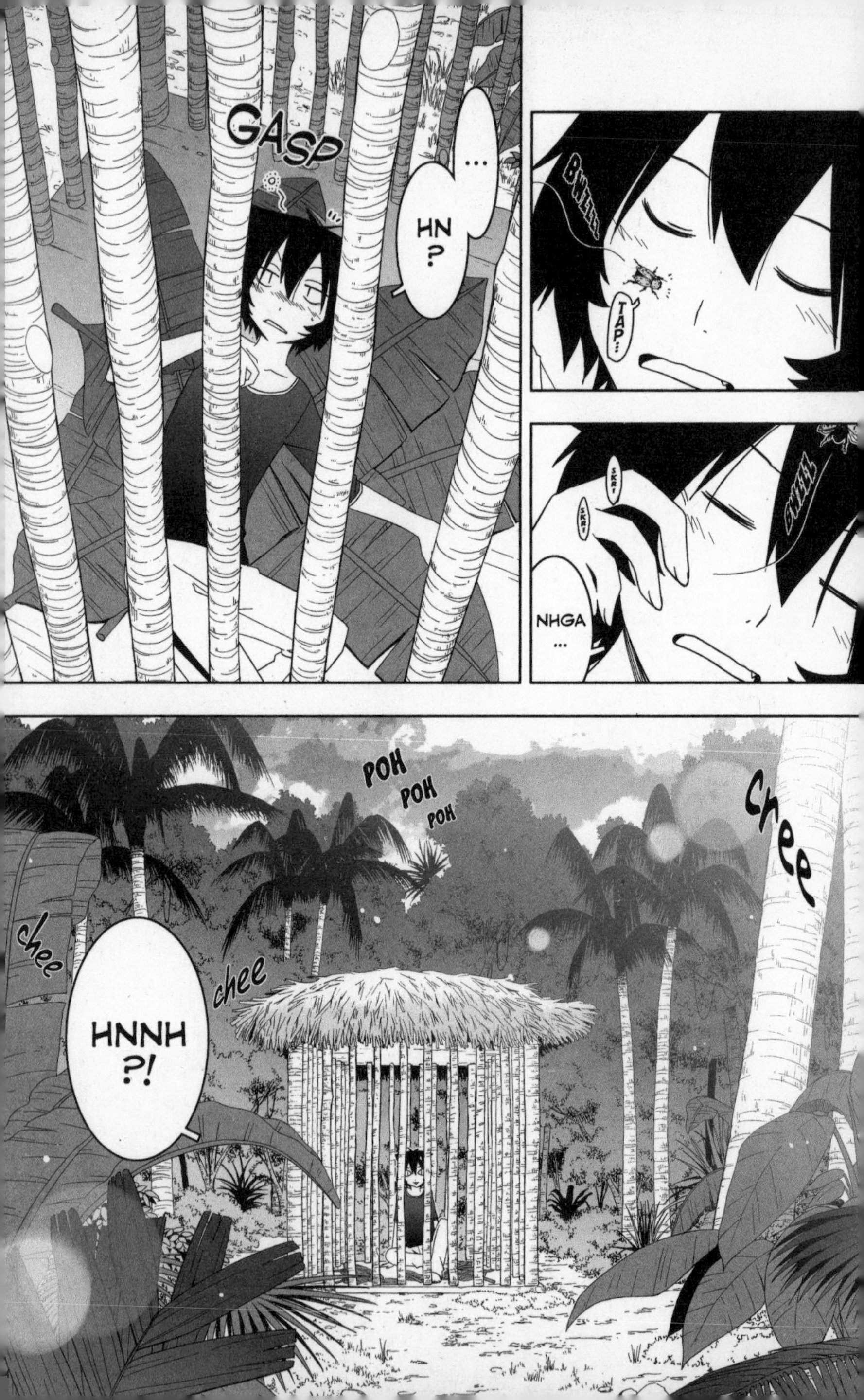

BWEEE
TAP...
SKRI
SKRI
BWEEE
NHGA ...
GASP
...
HN ?
POH POH POH
cree
chee
chee
HNNH ?!

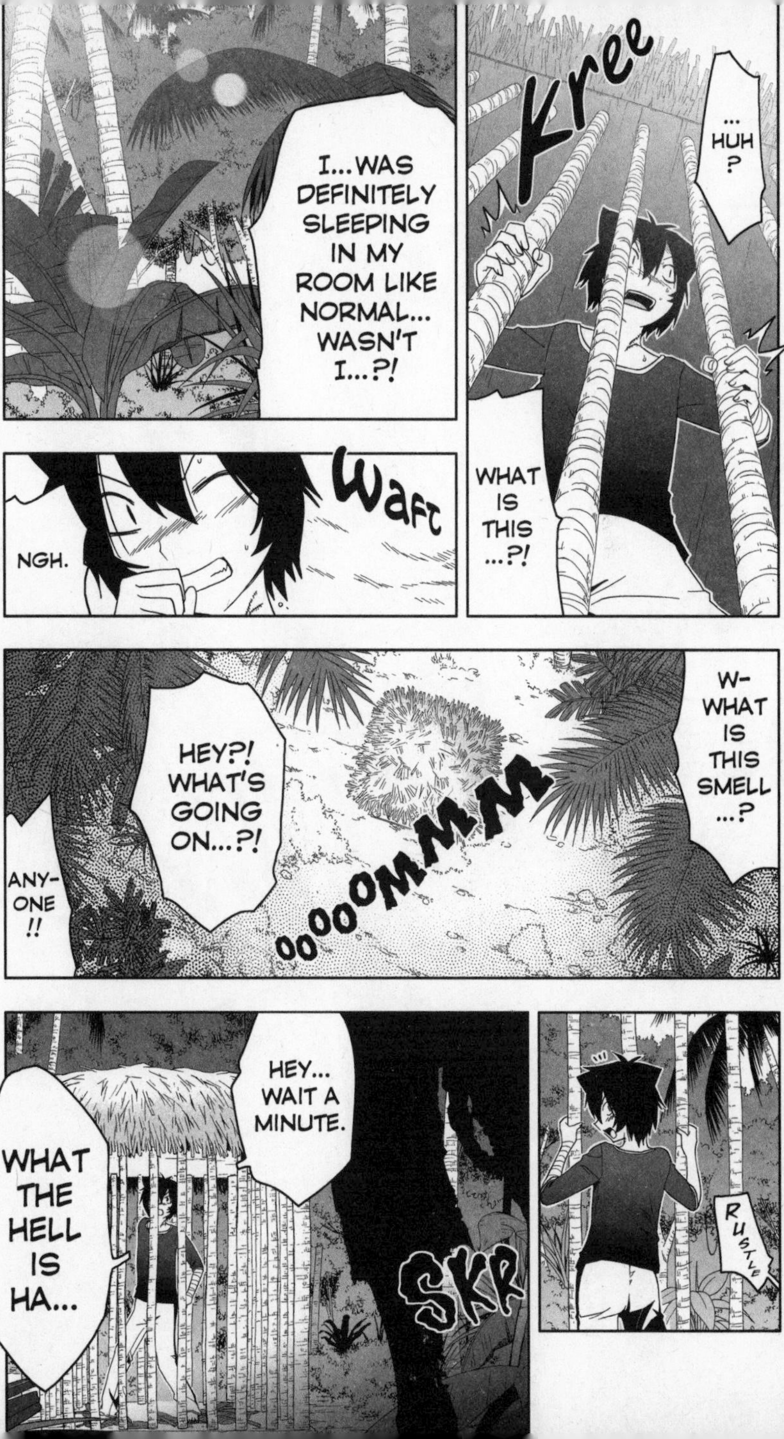
...HUH?
Kree
WHAT IS THIS...?!
I...WAS DEFINITELY SLEEPING IN MY ROOM LIKE NORMAL... WASN'T I...?!
Waft
NGH.
W-WHAT IS THIS SMELL...?
HEY?! WHAT'S GOING ON...?!
OOOOOMMMM
ANY-ONE!!
RUSTLE
HEY... WAIT A MINUTE.
SKR
WHAT THE HELL IS HA...

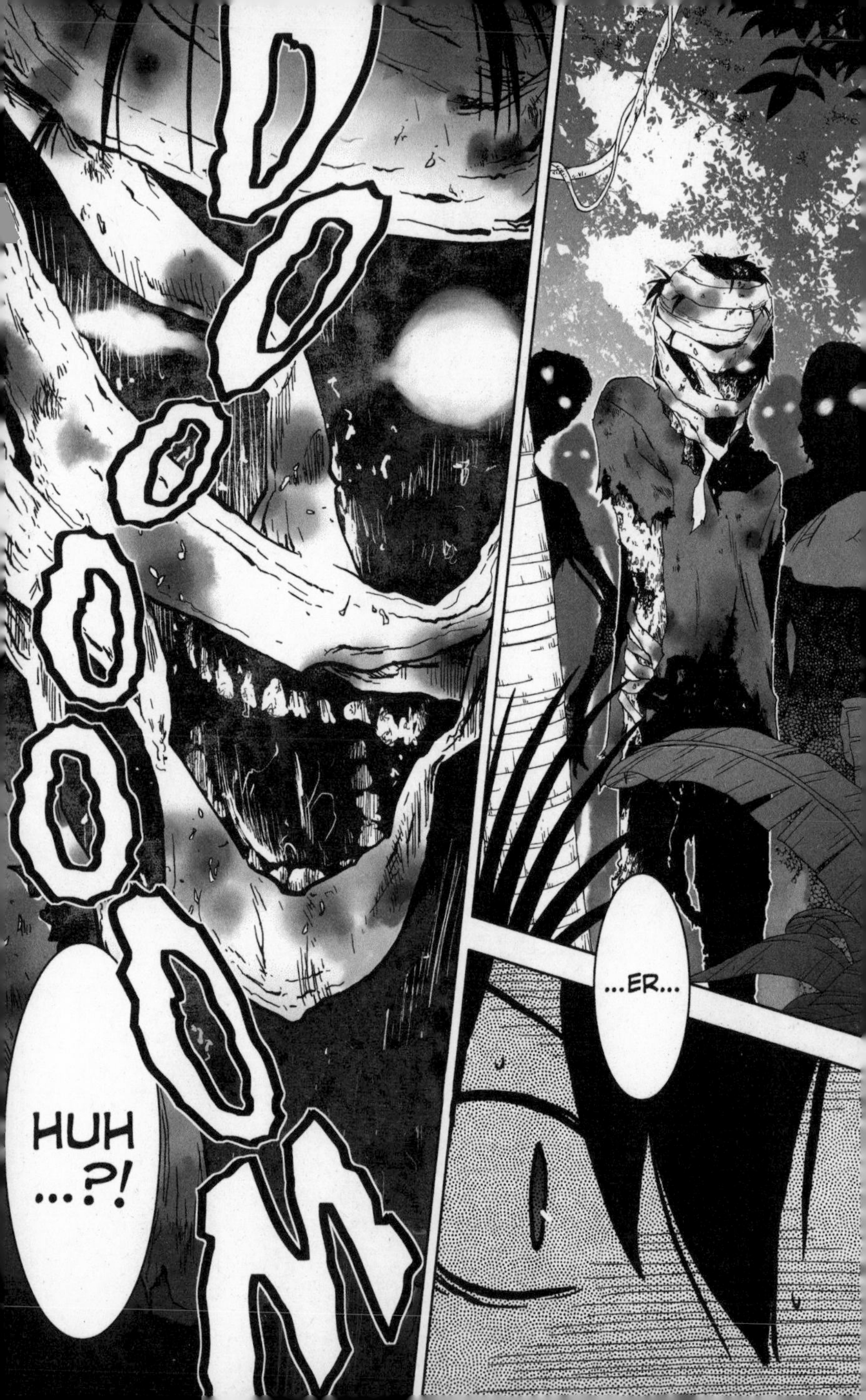
...ER...
DOOOOOM
HUH ...?!

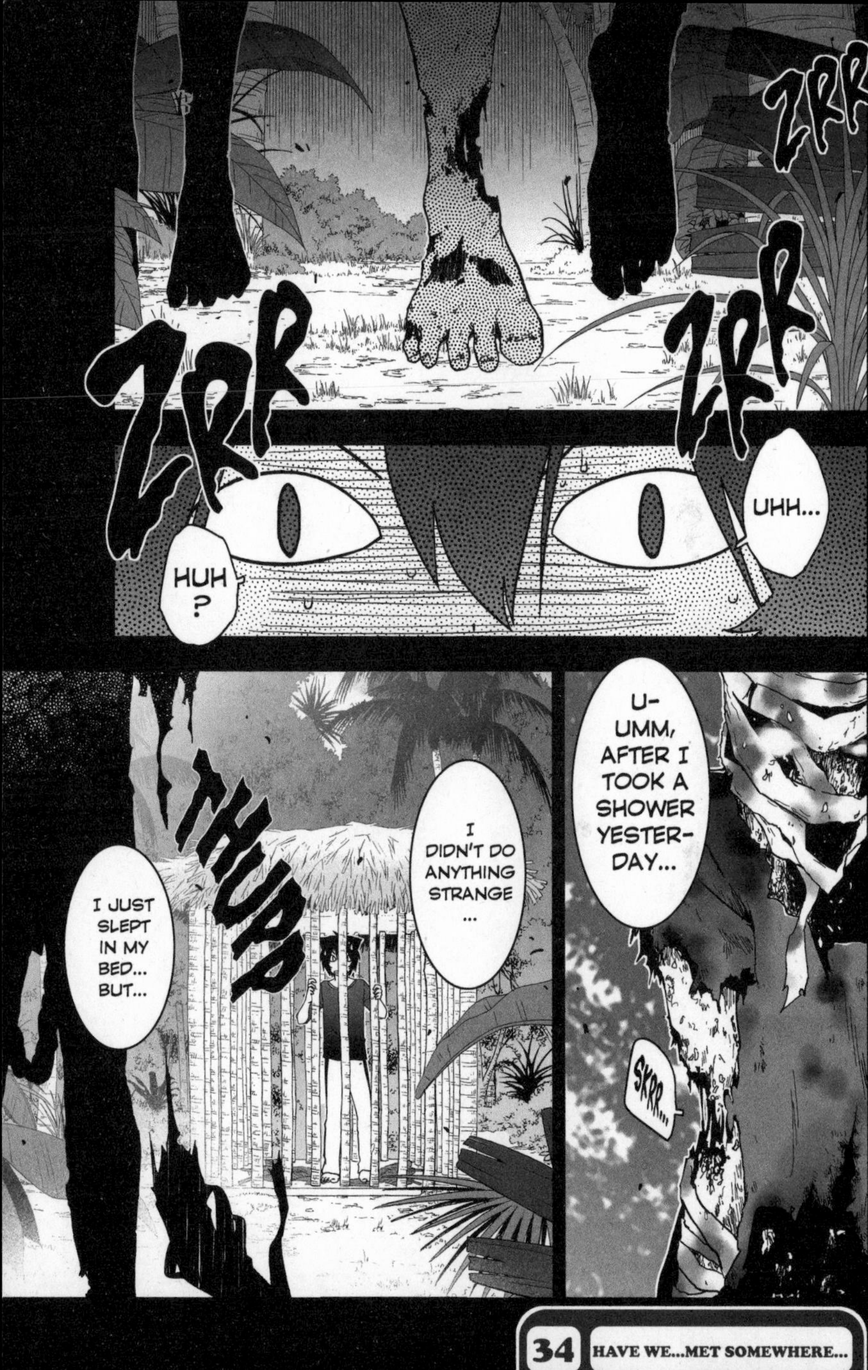
ZRR
ZRR
ZRR
UHH...
HUH?
U-UMM, AFTER I TOOK A SHOWER YESTER-DAY...
SKRR...
I DIDN'T DO ANYTHING STRANGE...
THUPP
I JUST SLEPT IN MY BED... BUT...

34 HAVE WE...MET SOMEWHERE...

✦ ✦ STEVE NILES' REMAINS ✦ ✦

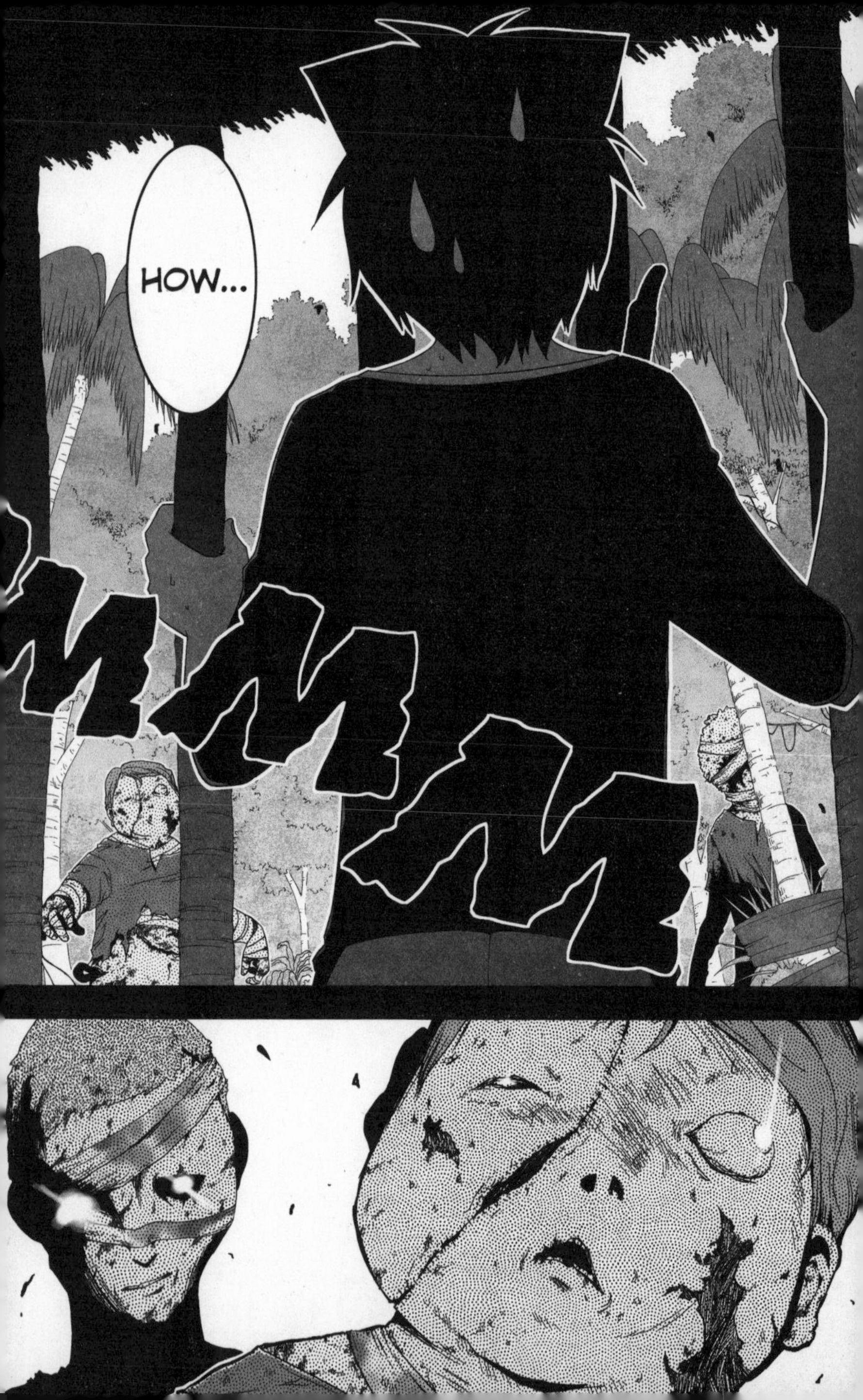
HOW...
MMMM

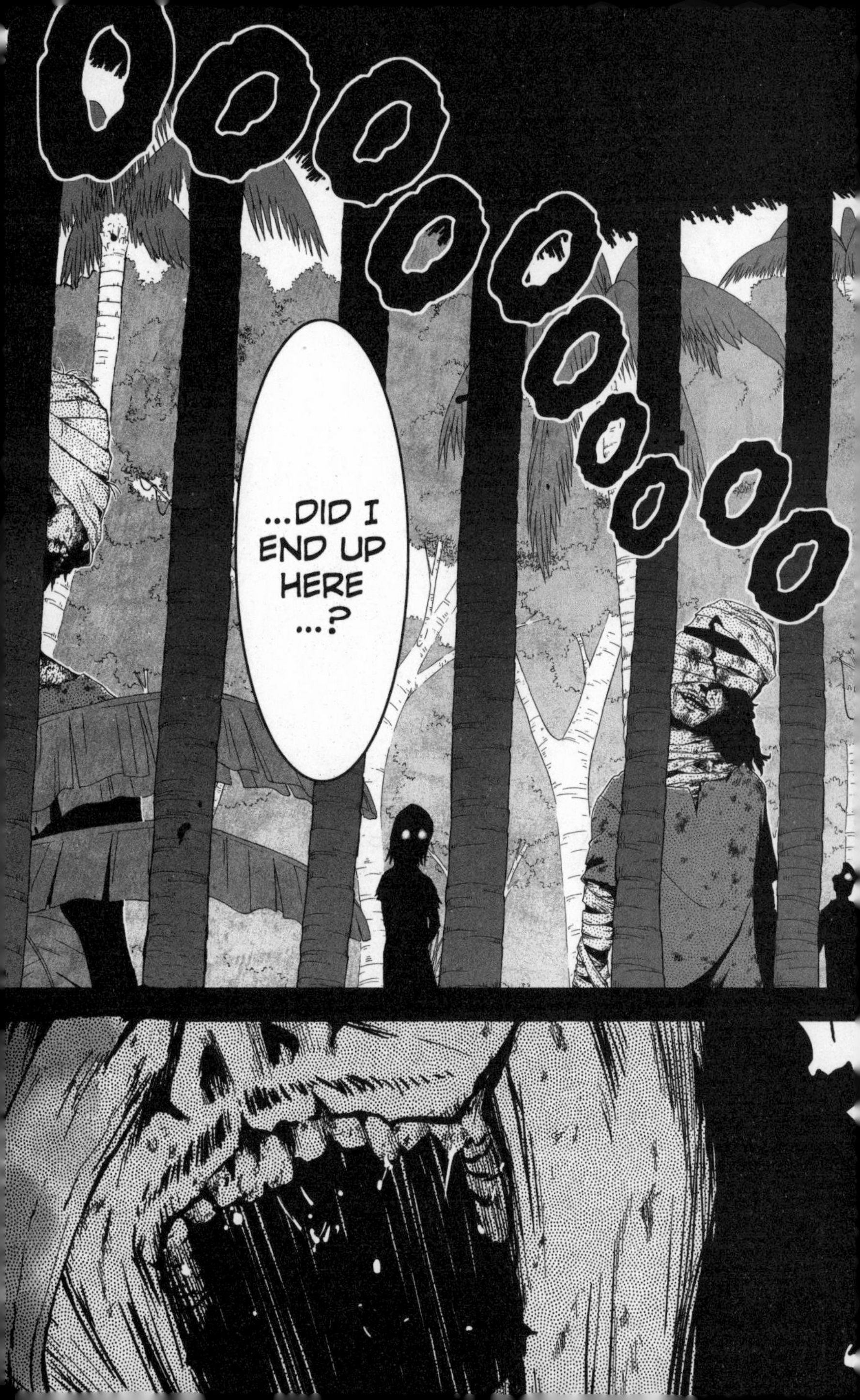
OOOOOOOOOO
...DID I END UP HERE ...?

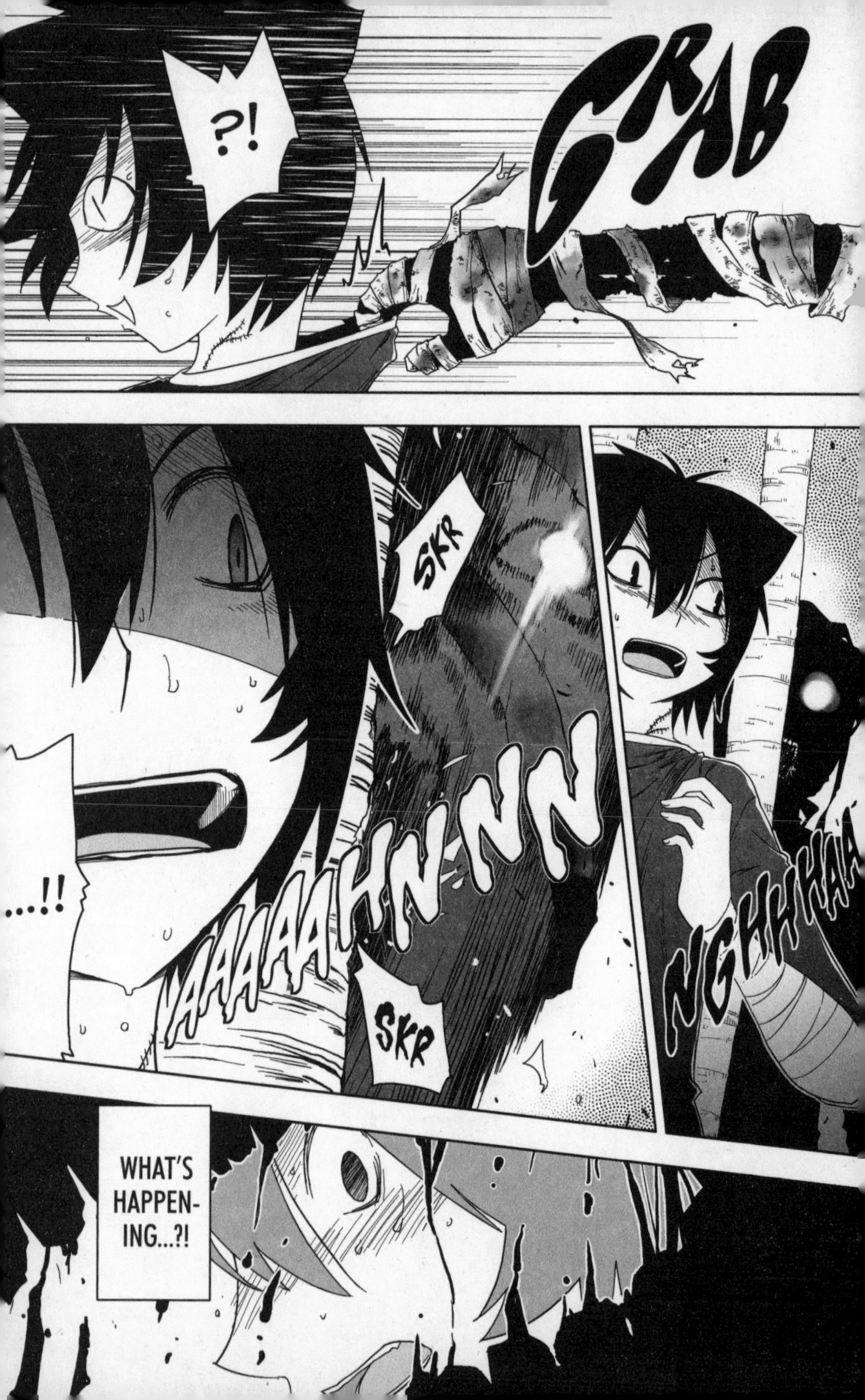
GRAB
?!
NGHHAA
SKR
AAAAAAHNNN
SKR
...!!
WHAT'S HAPPEN-ING...?!

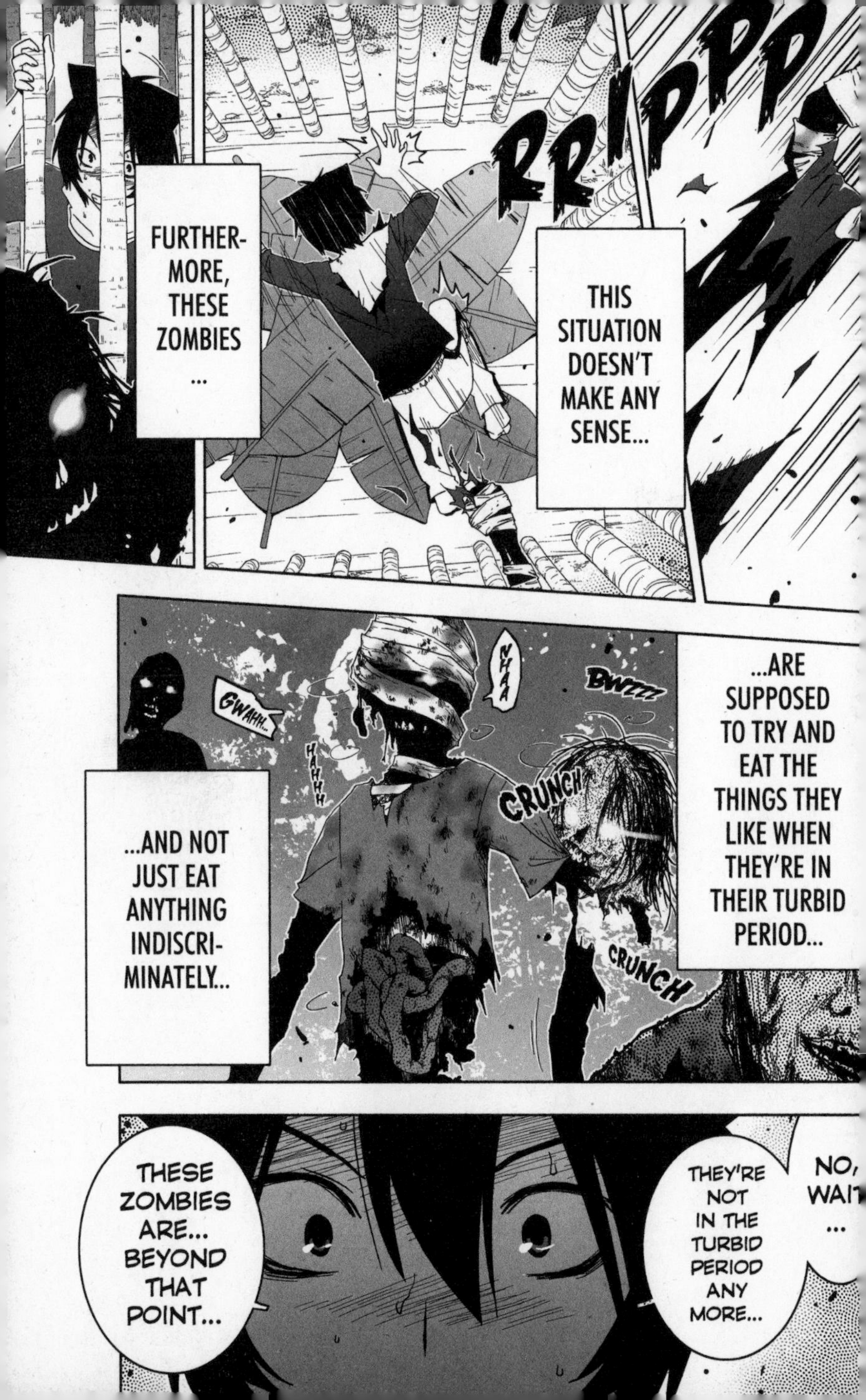
RRIPPP
THIS SITUATION DOESN'T MAKE ANY SENSE...
FURTHER-MORE, THESE ZOMBIES ...
...ARE SUPPOSED TO TRY AND EAT THE THINGS THEY LIKE WHEN THEY'RE IN THEIR TURBID PERIOD...
BWZZZ
NHAA
CRUNCH
CRUNCH
GWAHH..
HAHHH
...AND NOT JUST EAT ANYTHING INDISCRI-MINATELY...
NO, WAIT ...
THEY'RE NOT IN THE TURBID PERIOD ANY MORE...
THESE ZOMBIES ARE... BEYOND THAT POINT...

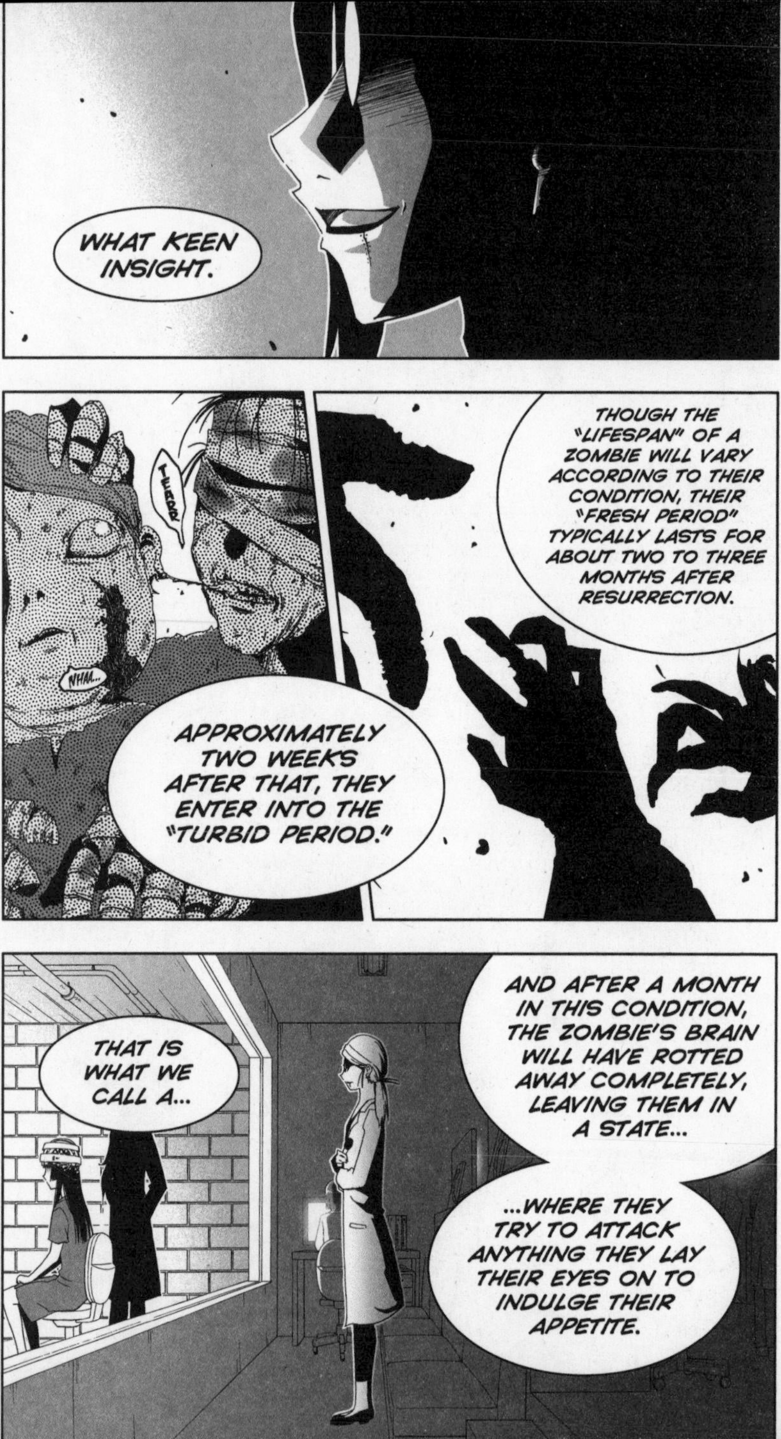
WHAT KEEN INSIGHT.
THOUGH THE "LIFESPAN" OF A ZOMBIE WILL VARY ACCORDING TO THEIR CONDITION, THEIR "FRESH PERIOD" TYPICALLY LASTS FOR ABOUT TWO TO THREE MONTHS AFTER RESURRECTION.
TEAR
NHAA...
APPROXIMATELY TWO WEEKS AFTER THAT, THEY ENTER INTO THE "TURBID PERIOD."
AND AFTER A MONTH IN THIS CONDITION, THE ZOMBIE'S BRAIN WILL HAVE ROTTED AWAY COMPLETELY, LEAVING THEM IN A STATE...
...WHERE THEY TRY TO ATTACK ANYTHING THEY LAY THEIR EYES ON TO INDULGE THEIR APPETITE.
THAT IS WHAT WE CALL A...

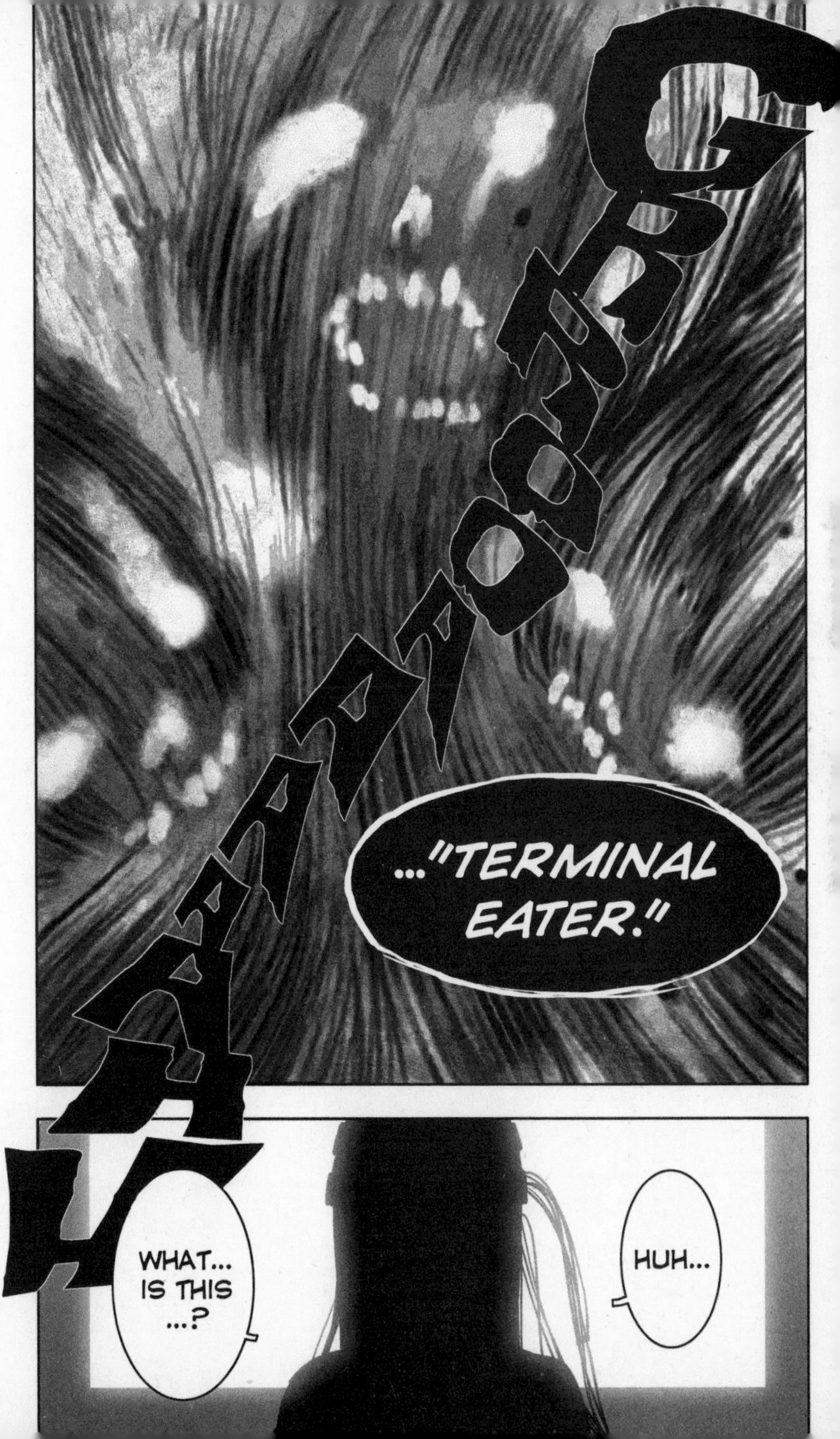
..."TERMINAL EATER."
HUH...
WHAT... IS THIS ...?

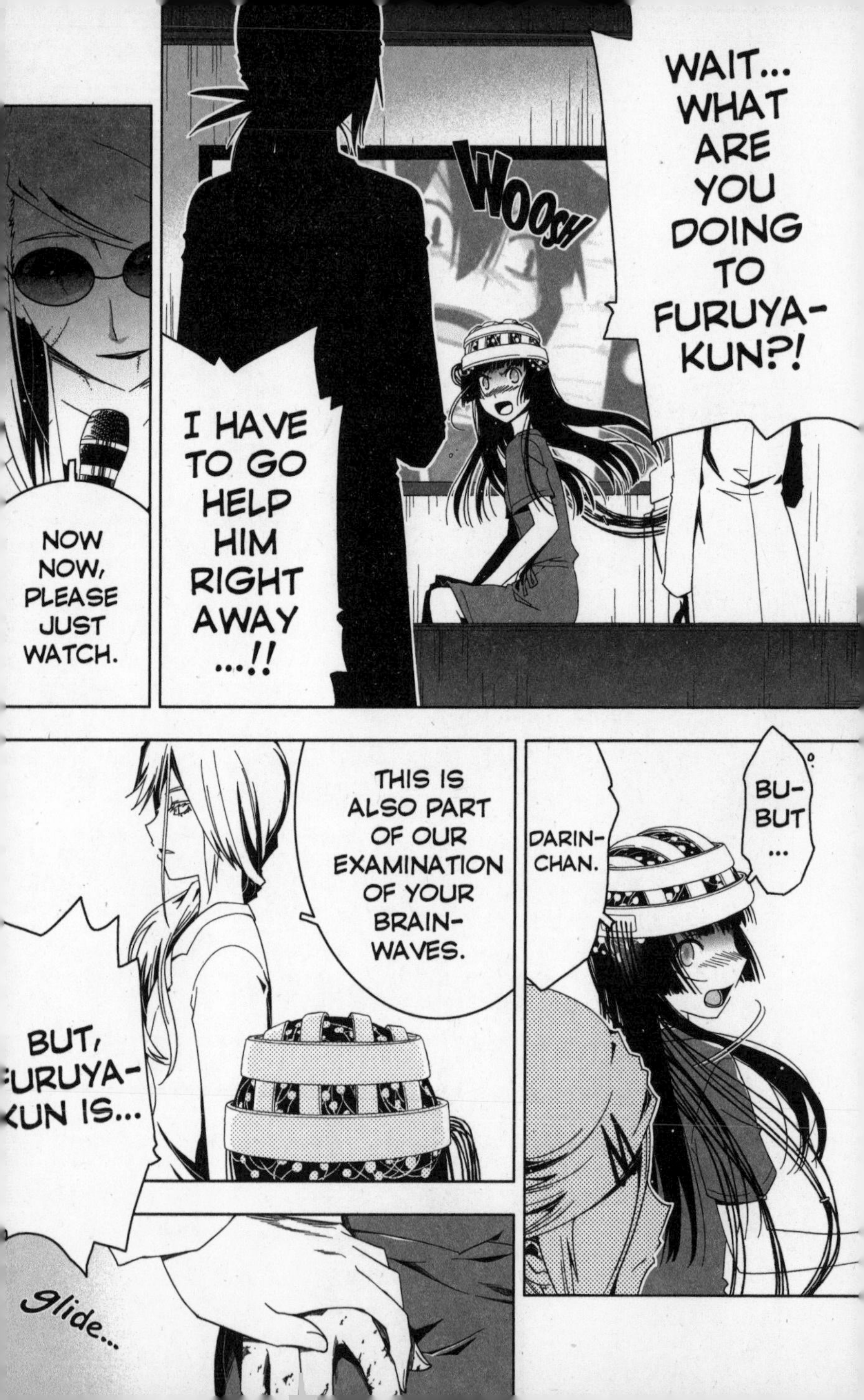
WAIT... WHAT ARE YOU DOING TO FURUYA-KUN?!
WOOSH
I HAVE TO GO HELP HIM RIGHT AWAY ...!!
NOW NOW, PLEASE JUST WATCH.
BU-BUT ...
DARIN-CHAN.
THIS IS ALSO PART OF OUR EXAMINATION OF YOUR BRAIN-WAVES.
BUT, FURUYA-KUN IS...
glide...

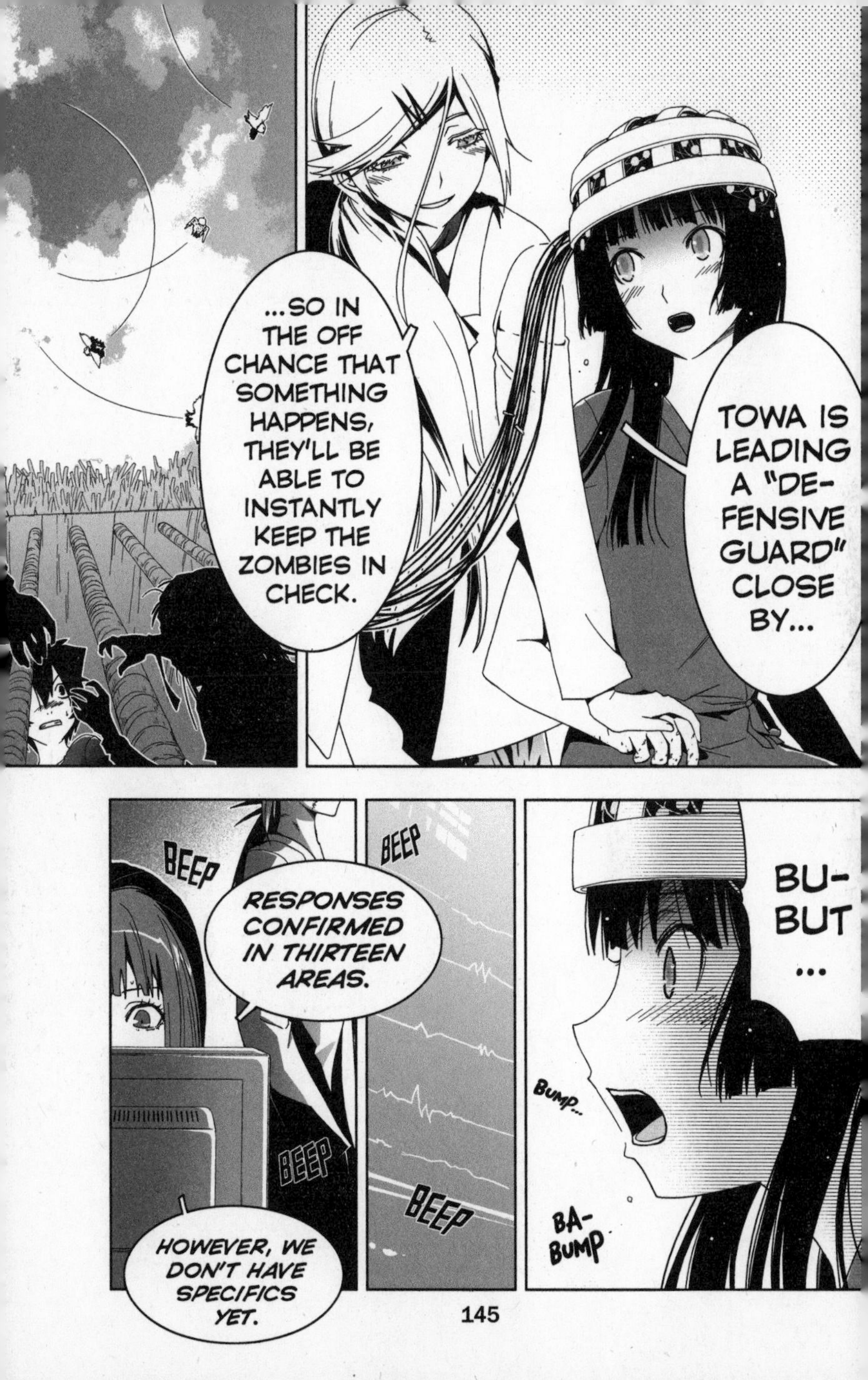
TOWA IS LEADING A "DE-FENSIVE GUARD" CLOSE BY...
...SO IN THE OFF CHANCE THAT SOMETHING HAPPENS, THEY'LL BE ABLE TO INSTANTLY KEEP THE ZOMBIES IN CHECK.
BU-BUT...
BUMP...
BA-BUMP
BEEP
BEEP
BEEP
RESPONSES CONFIRMED IN THIRTEEN AREAS.
BEEP
HOWEVER, WE DON'T HAVE SPECIFICS YET.

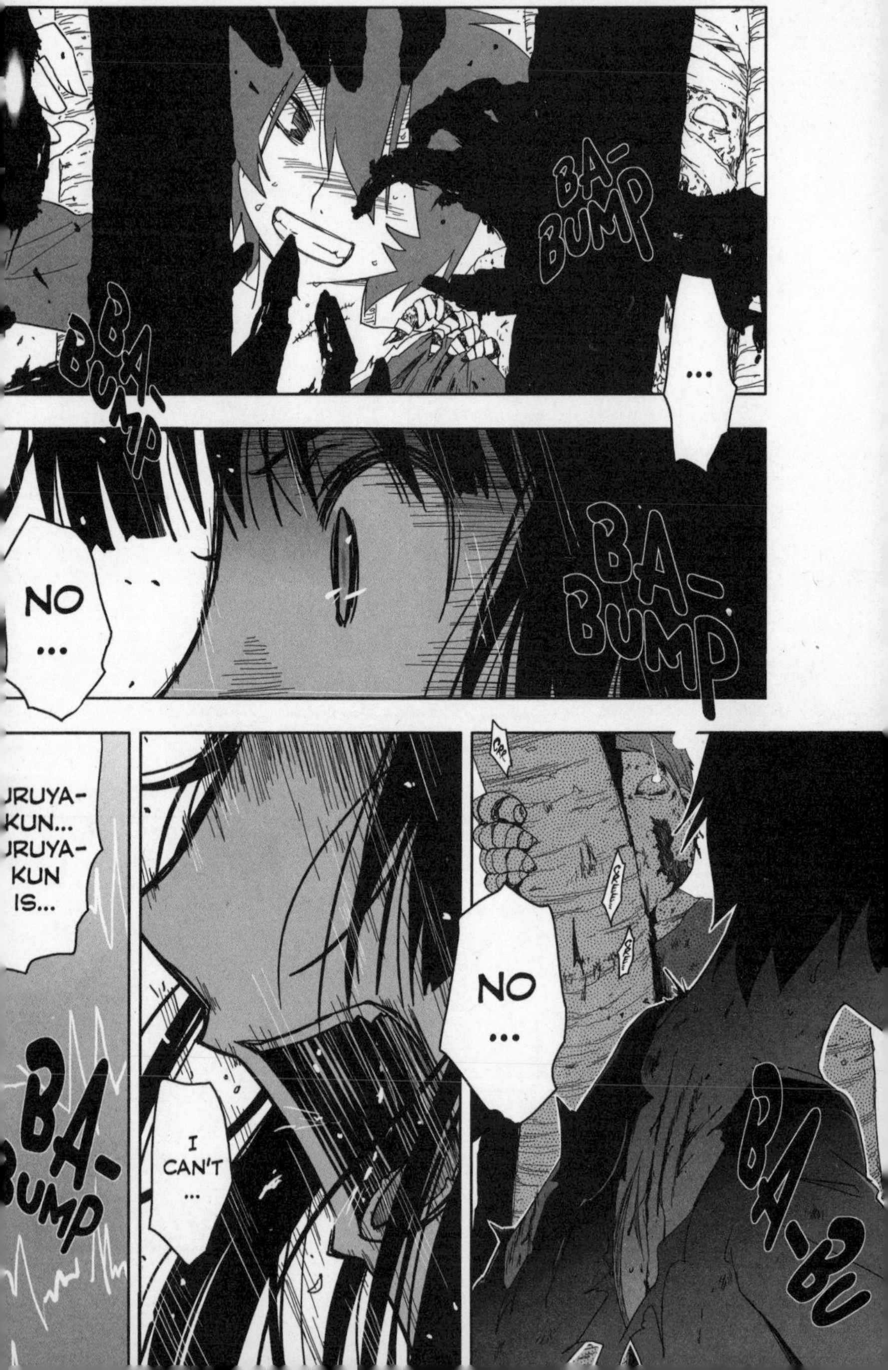
BA-BUMP
BA-BUMP
...
BA-BUMP
NO ...
BA-BU
NO ...
I CAN'T ...
URUYA-KUN... URUYA-KUN IS...
BA-BUMP

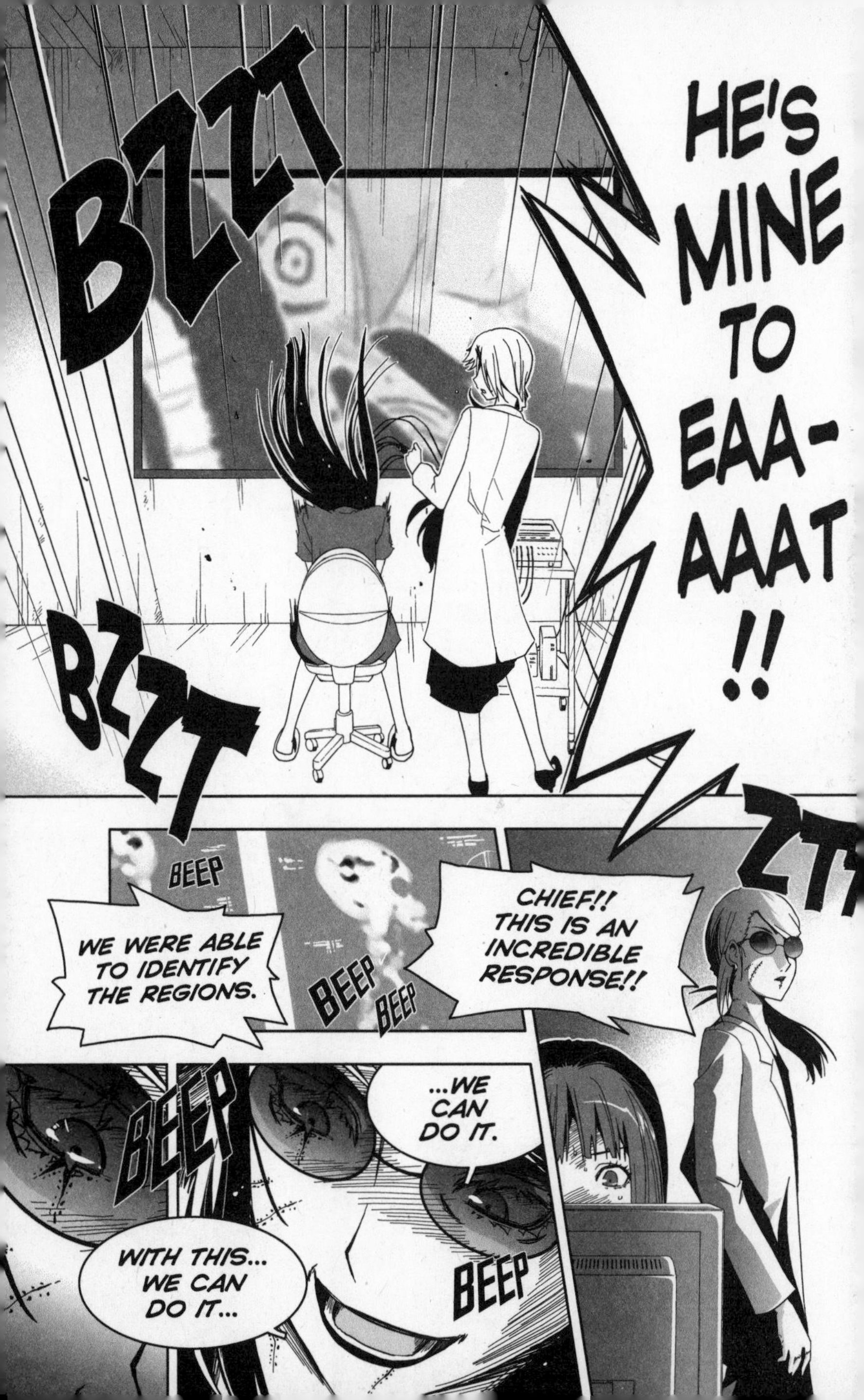
HE'S MINE TO EAAA-AAAT!!
BZZT
BZZT
ZZT
CHIEF!! THIS IS AN INCREDIBLE RESPONSE!!
BEEP
WE WERE ABLE TO IDENTIFY THE REGIONS.
BEEP
BEEP
...WE CAN DO IT.
BEEP
WITH THIS... WE CAN DO IT...
BEEP

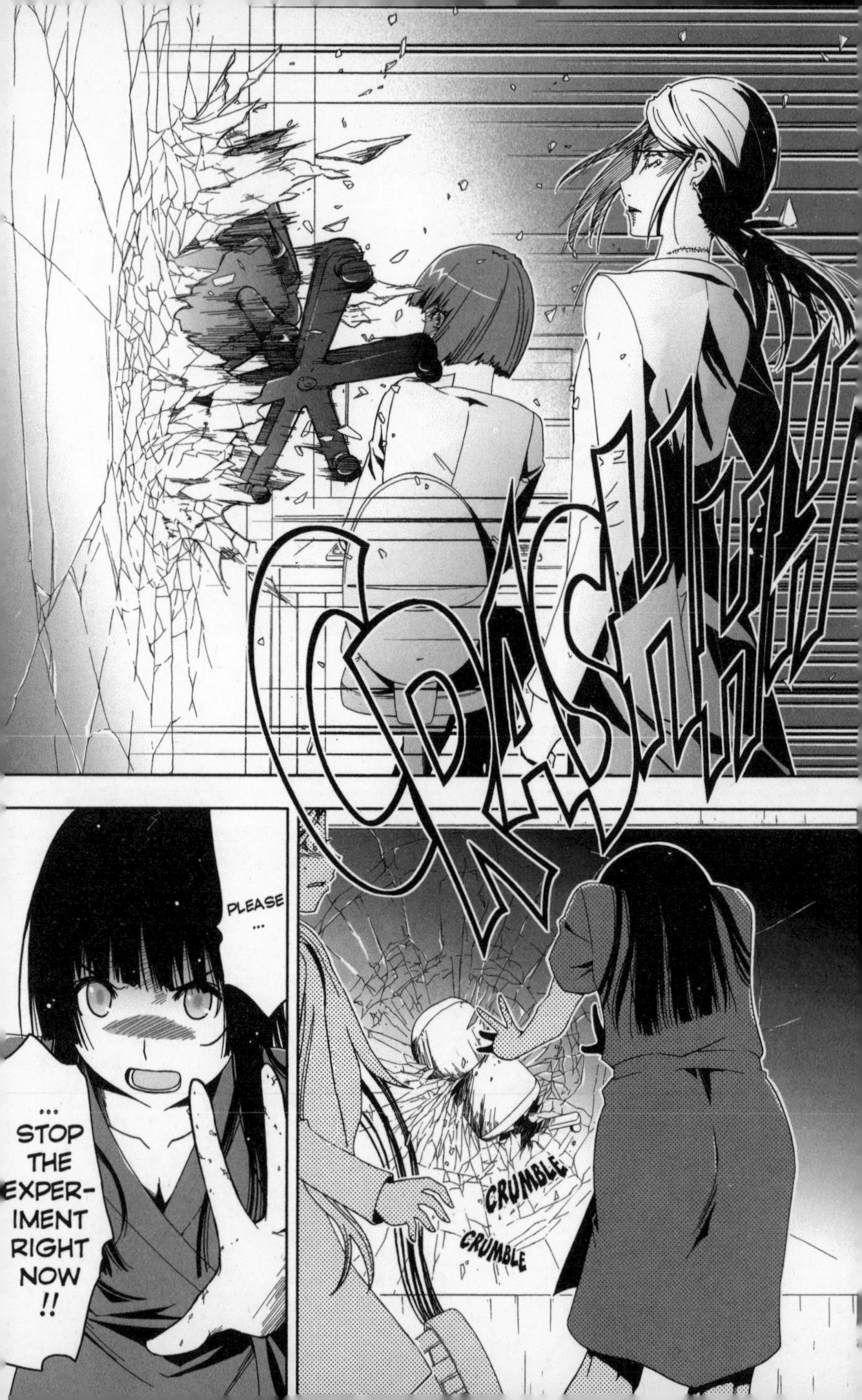
CRASH
CRUMBLE
CRUMBLE
PLEASE ...
... STOP THE EXPER-IMENT RIGHT NOW !!

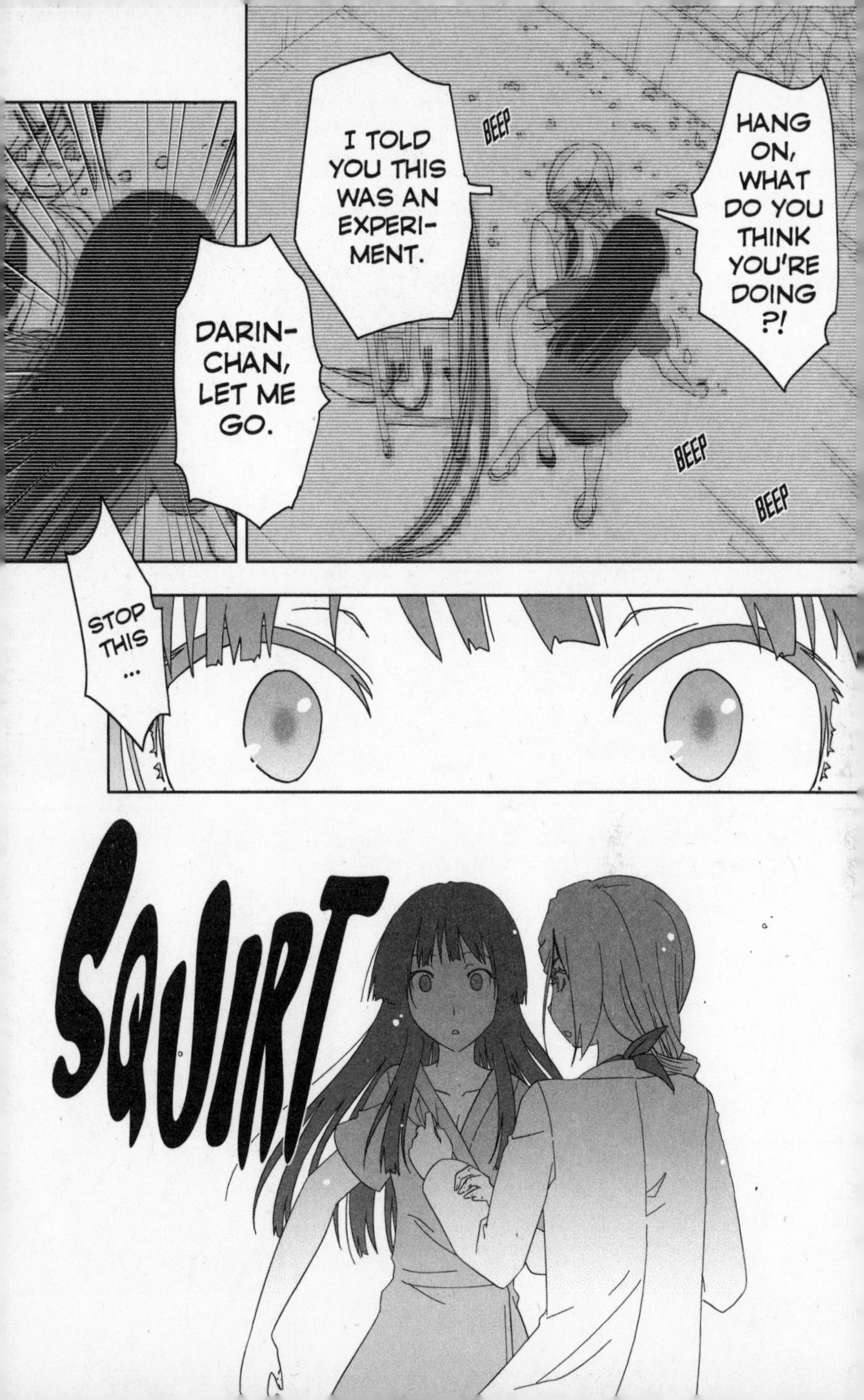
HANG ON, WHAT DO YOU THINK YOU'RE DOING?!
BEEP
I TOLD YOU THIS WAS AN EXPERI-MENT.
BEEP
BEEP
DARIN-CHAN, LET ME GO.
STOP THIS ...
SQUIRT

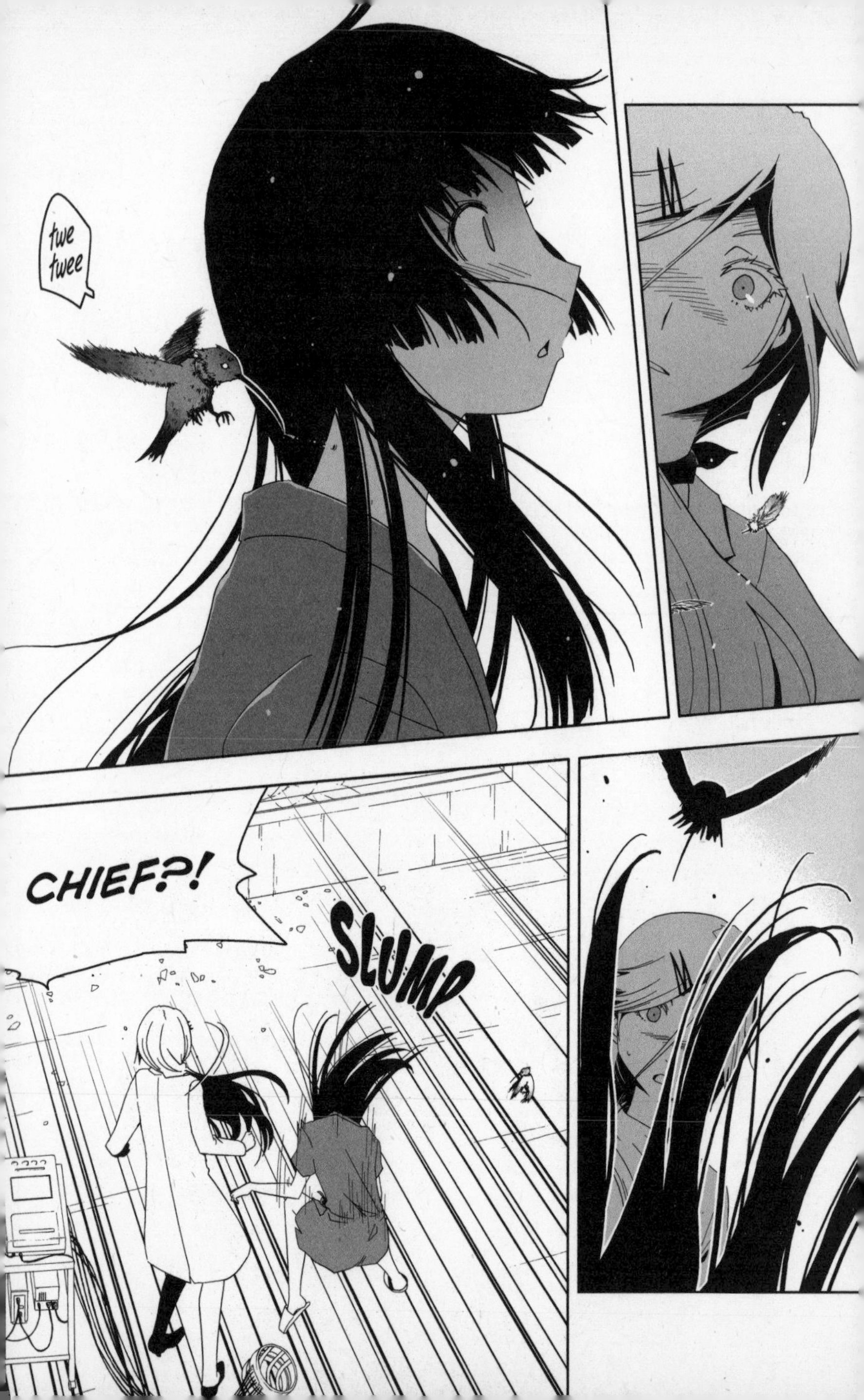
twe twee
SLUMP
CHIEF?!

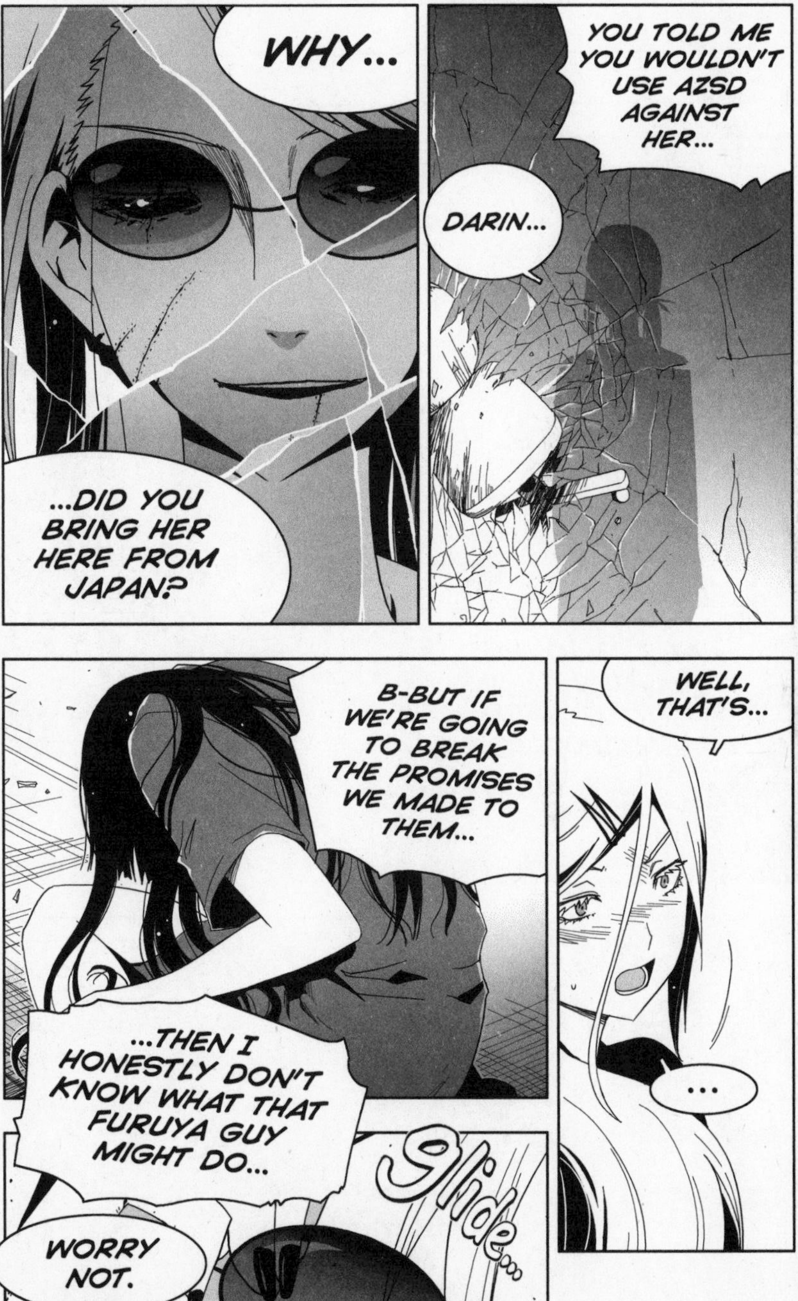
YOU TOLD ME YOU WOULDN'T USE AZSD AGAINST HER...
DARIN...
WHY...
...DID YOU BRING HER HERE FROM JAPAN?
WELL, THAT'S...
...
B-BUT IF WE'RE GOING TO BREAK THE PROMISES WE MADE TO THEM...
...THEN I HONESTLY DON'T KNOW WHAT THAT FURUYA GUY MIGHT DO...
glide...
WORRY NOT.

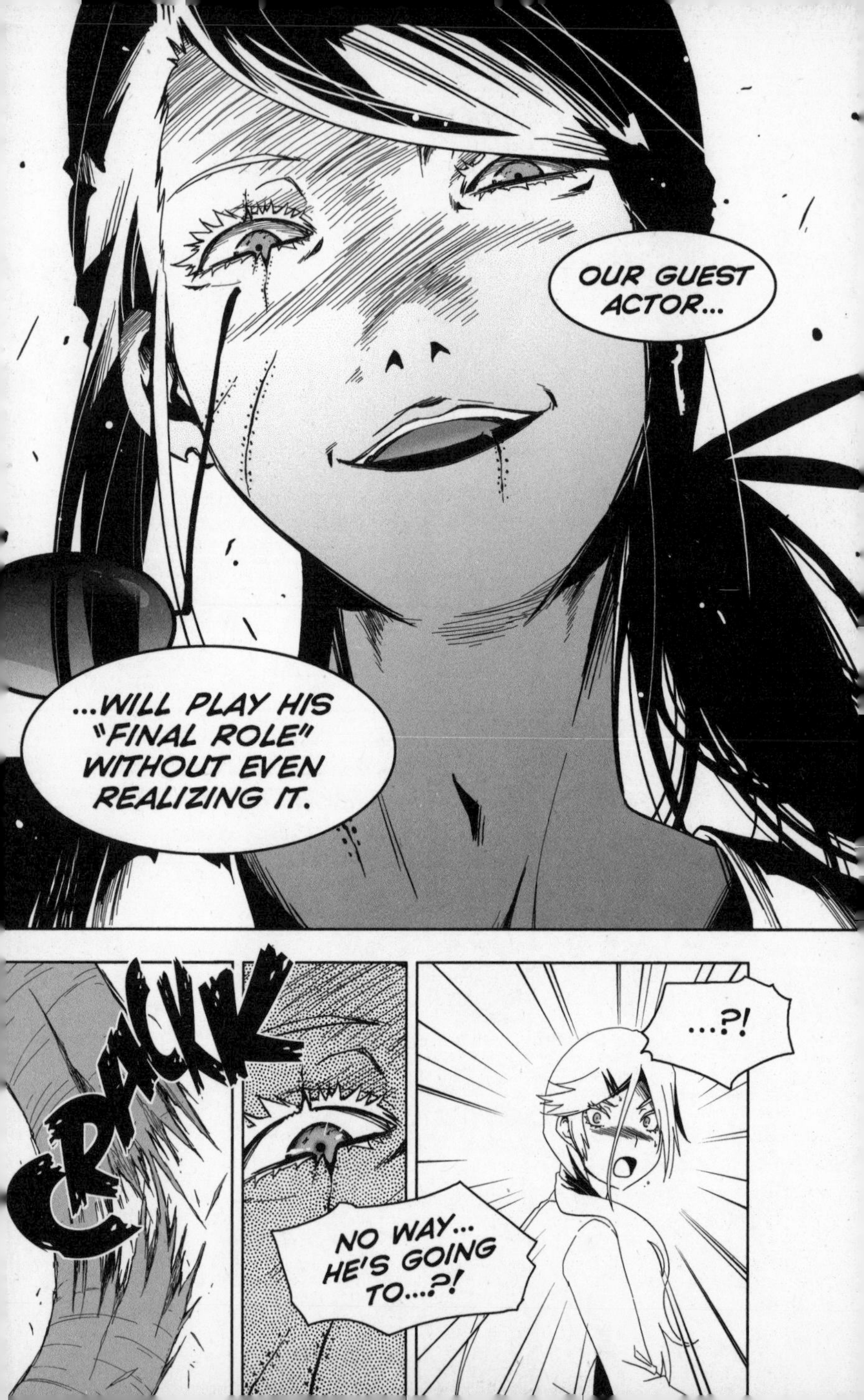
OUR GUEST ACTOR...
...WILL PLAY HIS "FINAL ROLE" WITHOUT EVEN REALIZING IT.
...?!
NO WAY... HE'S GOING TO...?!
CRACK

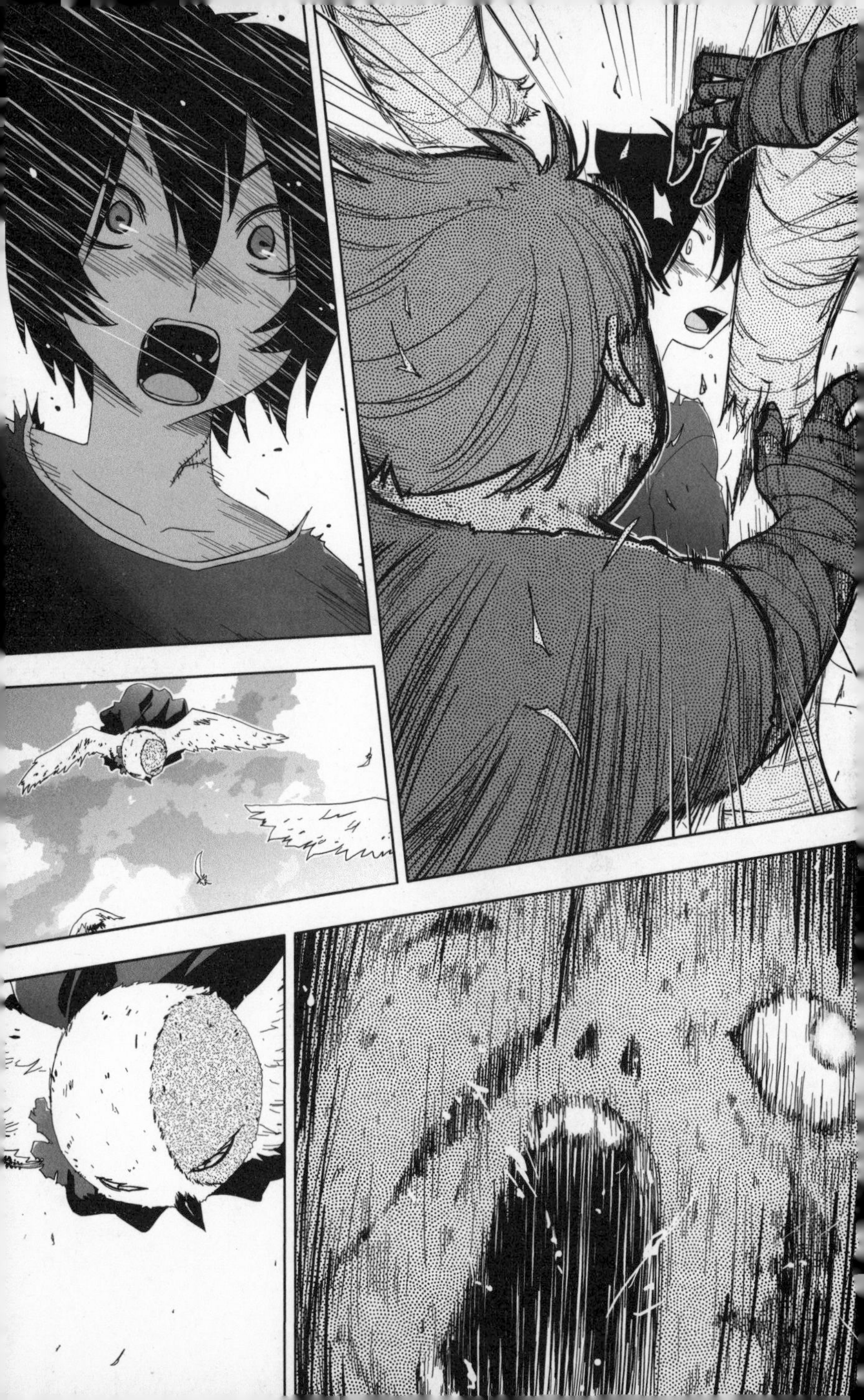

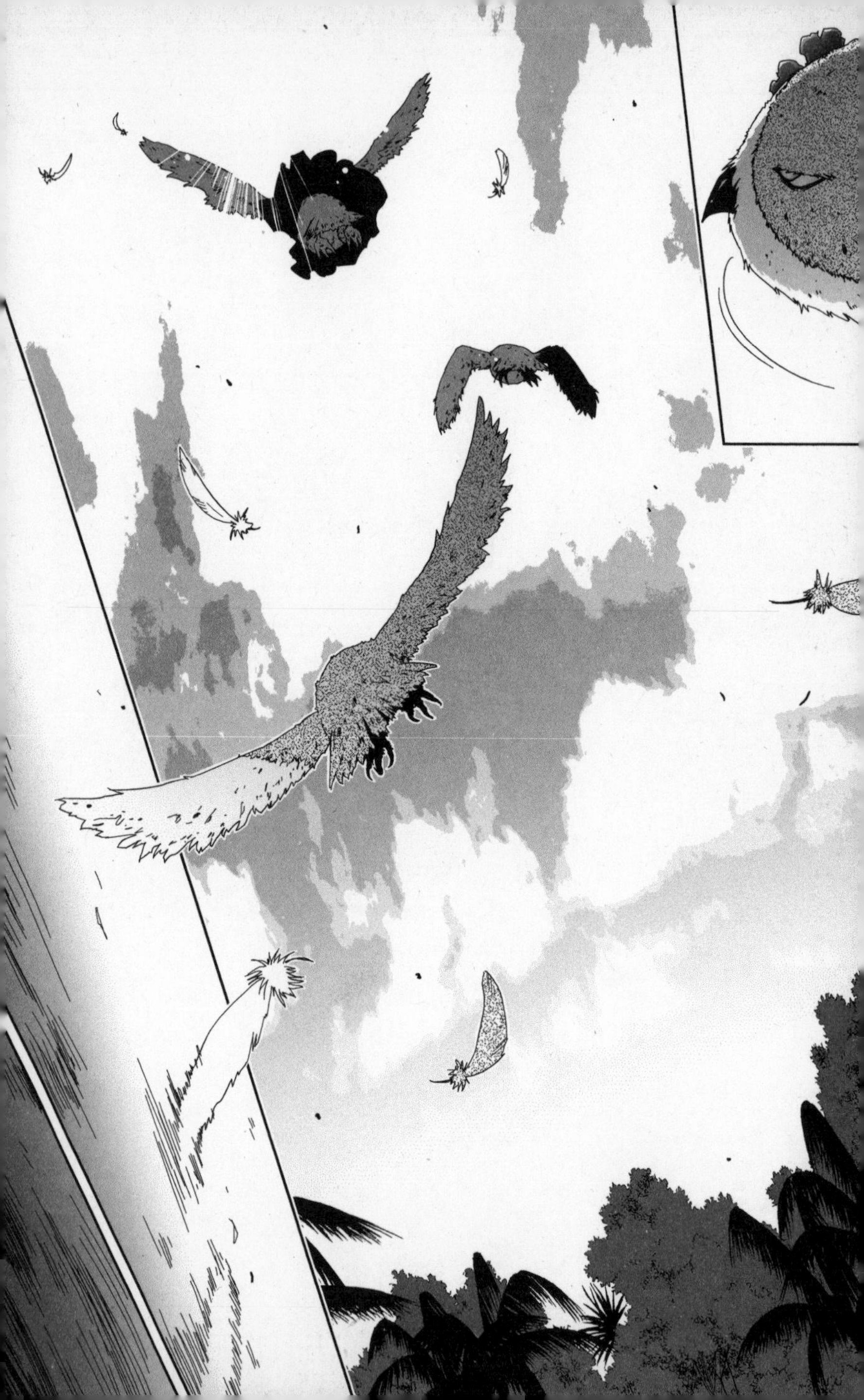

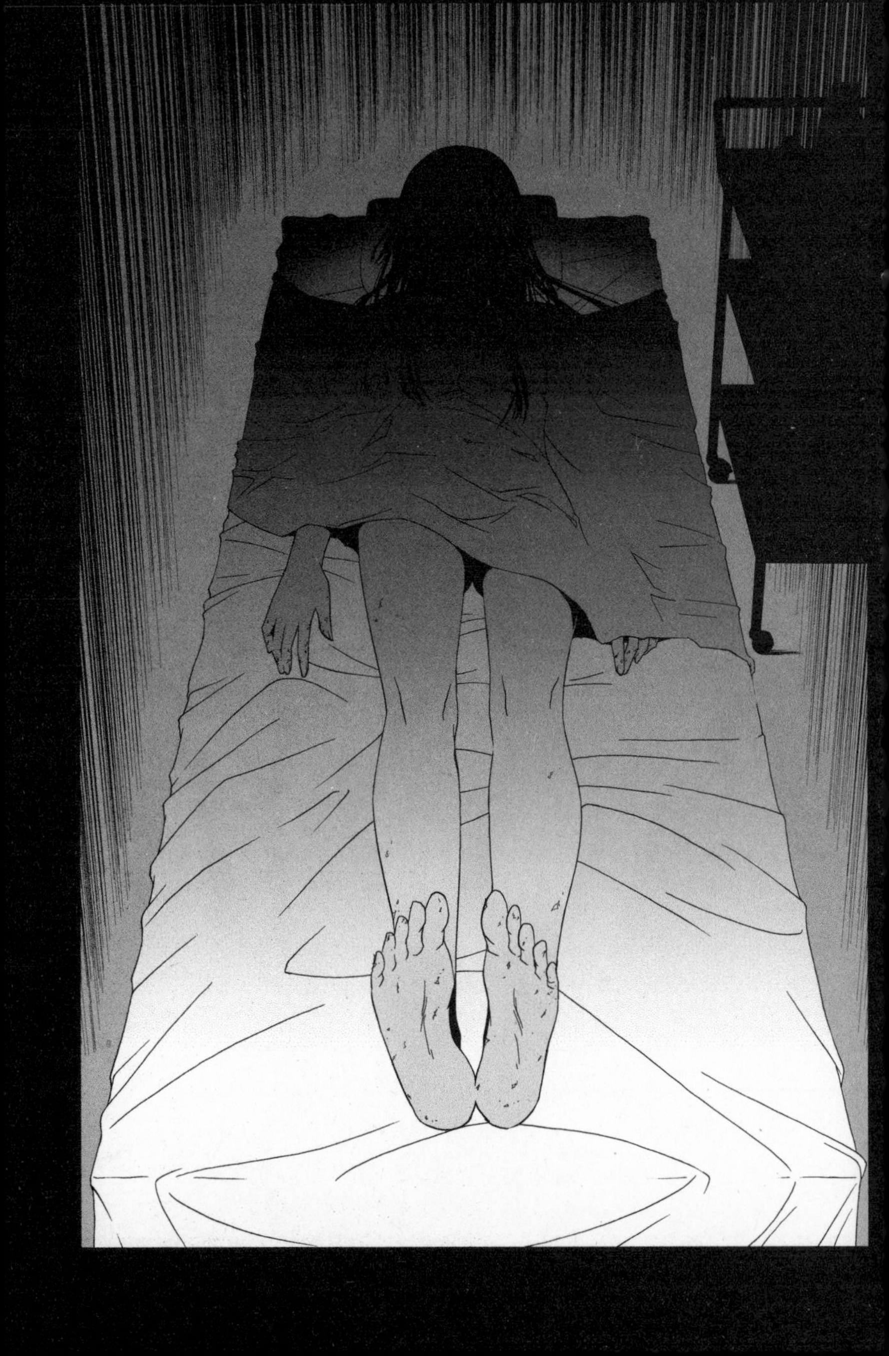

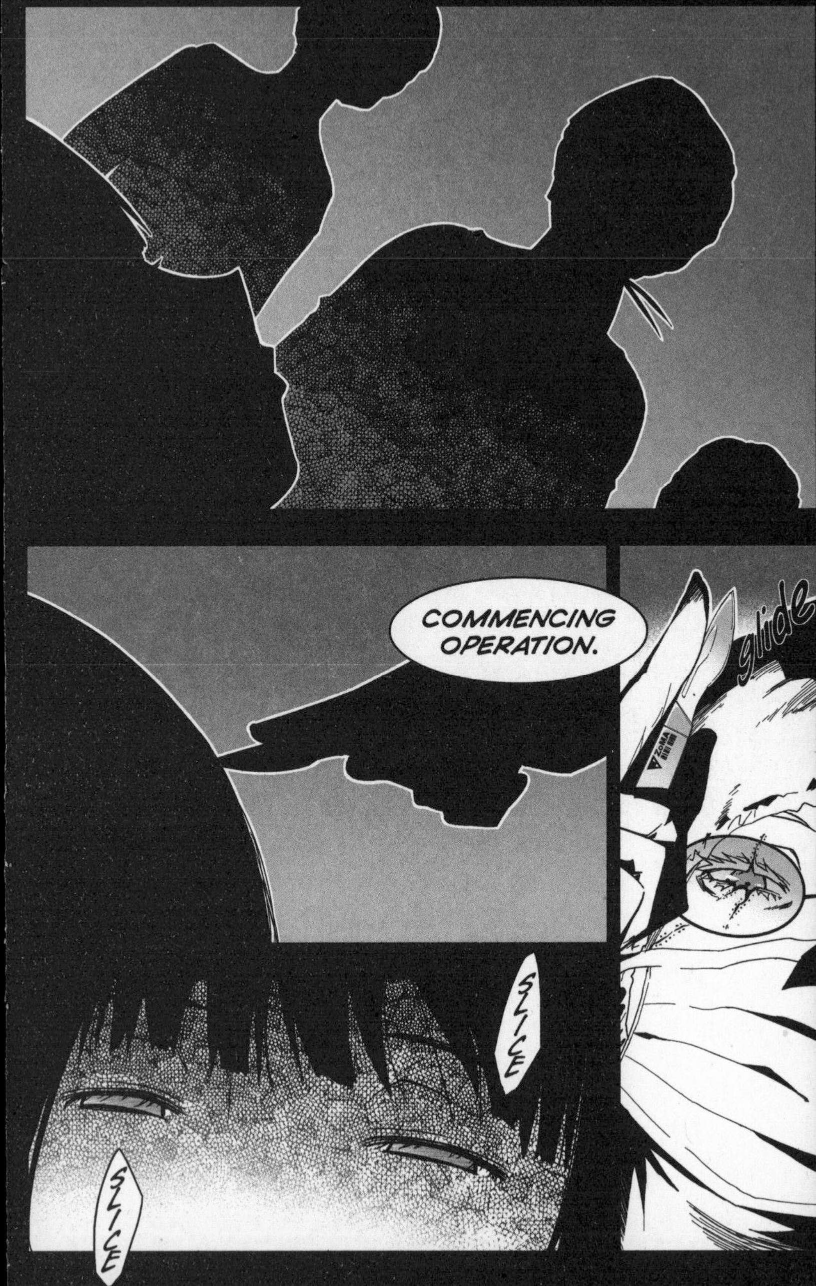
glide
ZOMA
COMMENCING OPERATION.
SLICE
SLICE

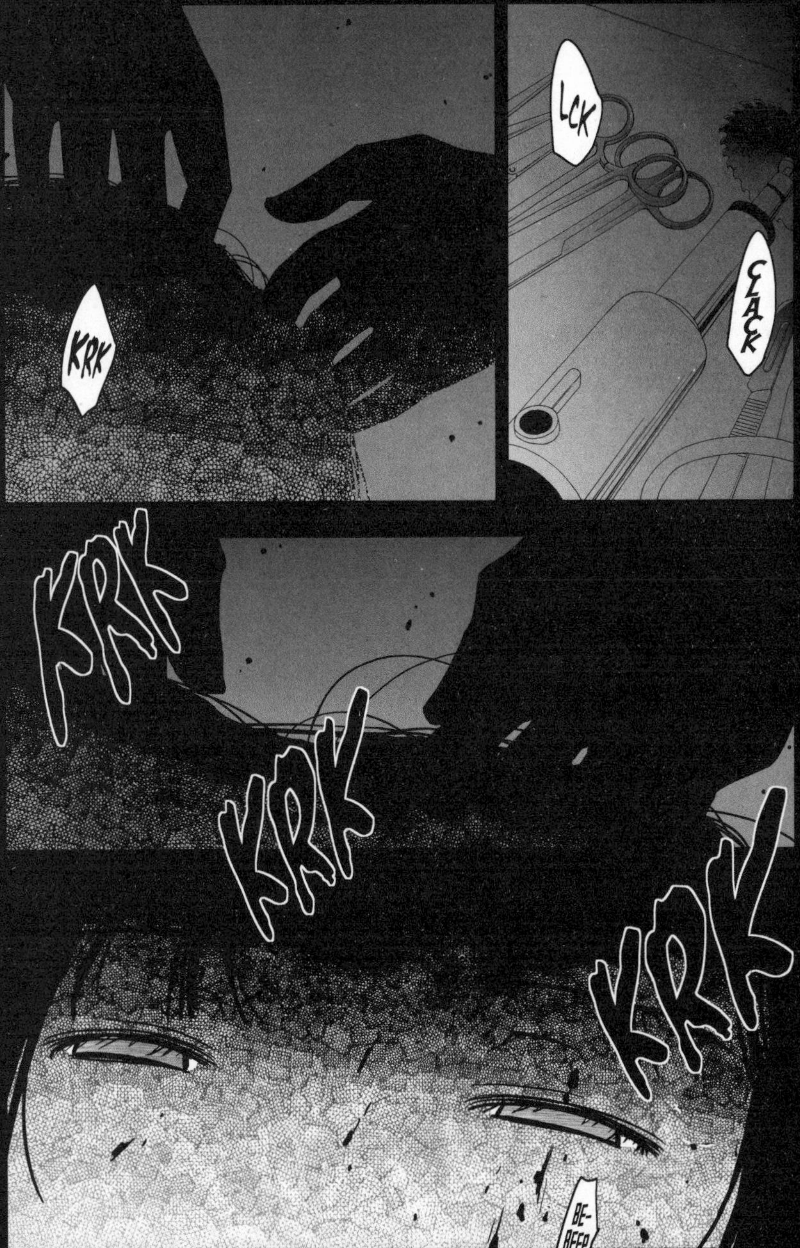
LCK
CLACK
KRK
KRK
KRK
KRK
BE-BEEP

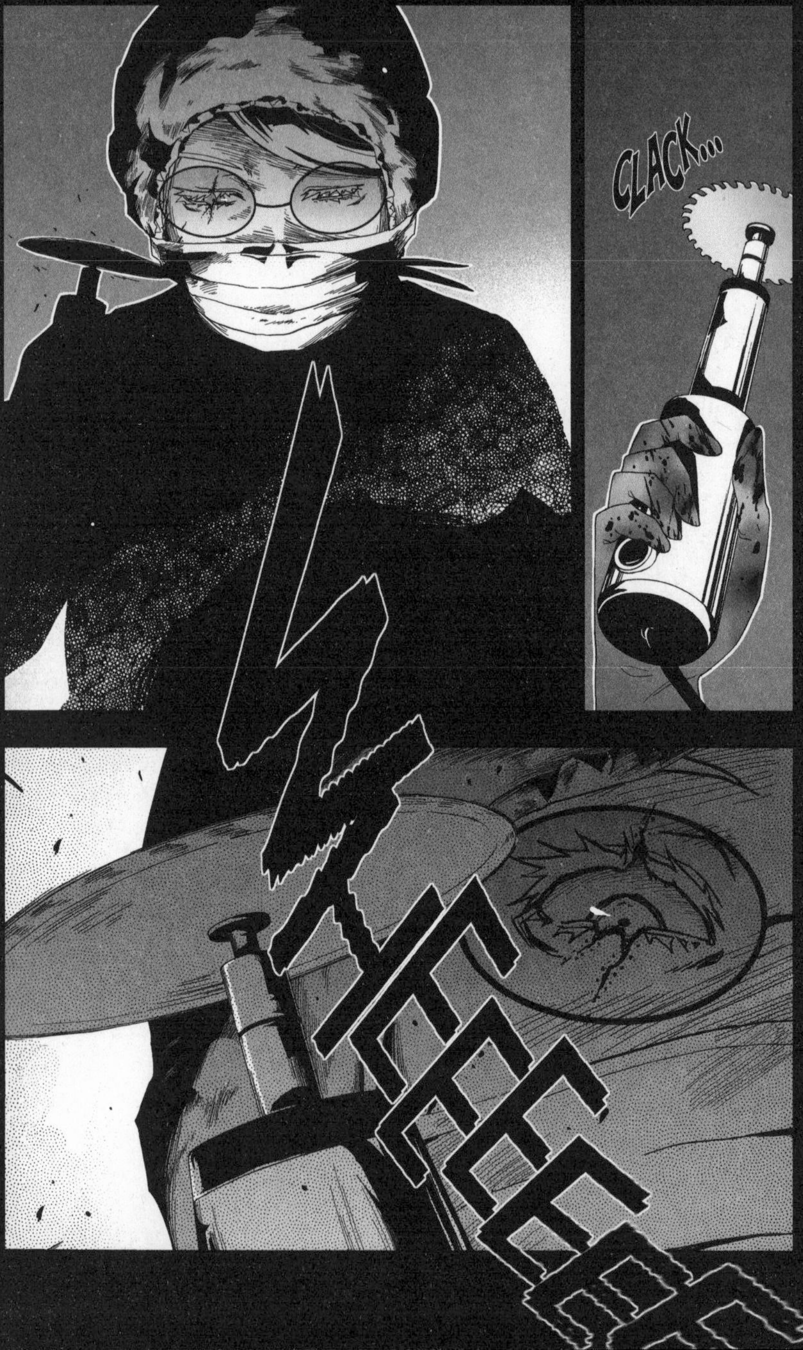
CLACK...

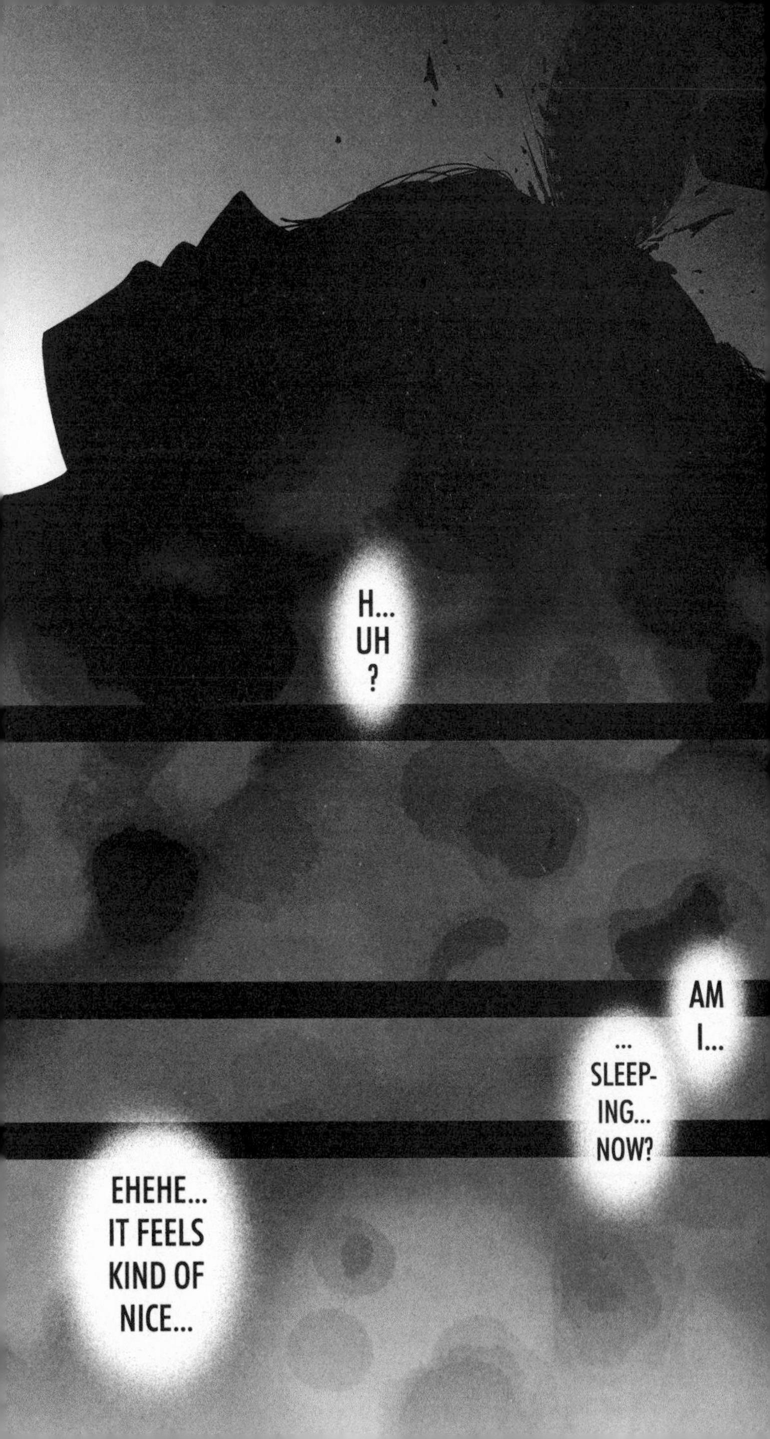
H... UH?
AM I...
...SLEEPING... NOW?
EHEHE... IT FEELS KIND OF NICE...

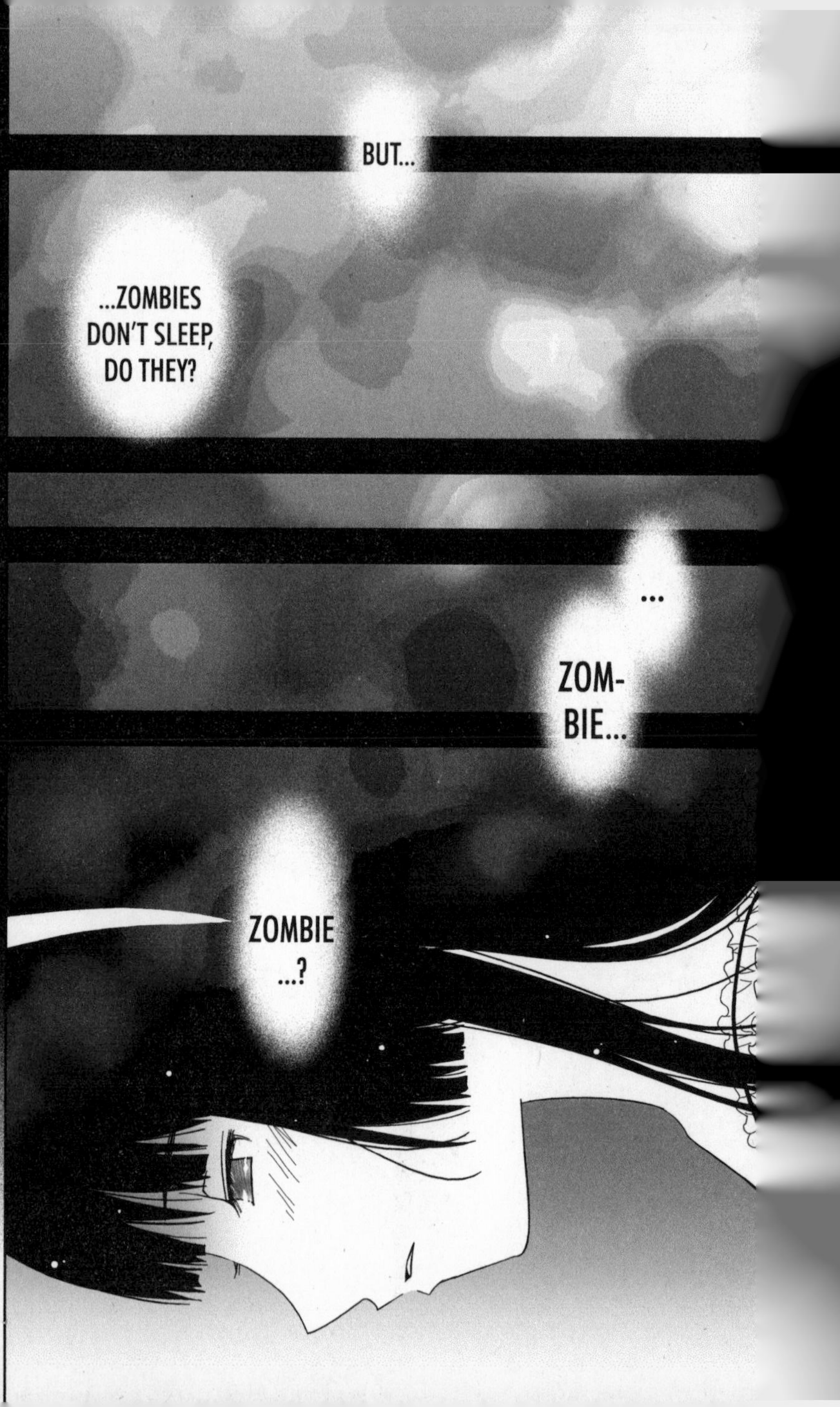
BUT...
...ZOMBIES DON'T SLEEP, DO THEY?
...
ZOM-BIE...
ZOMBIE ...?

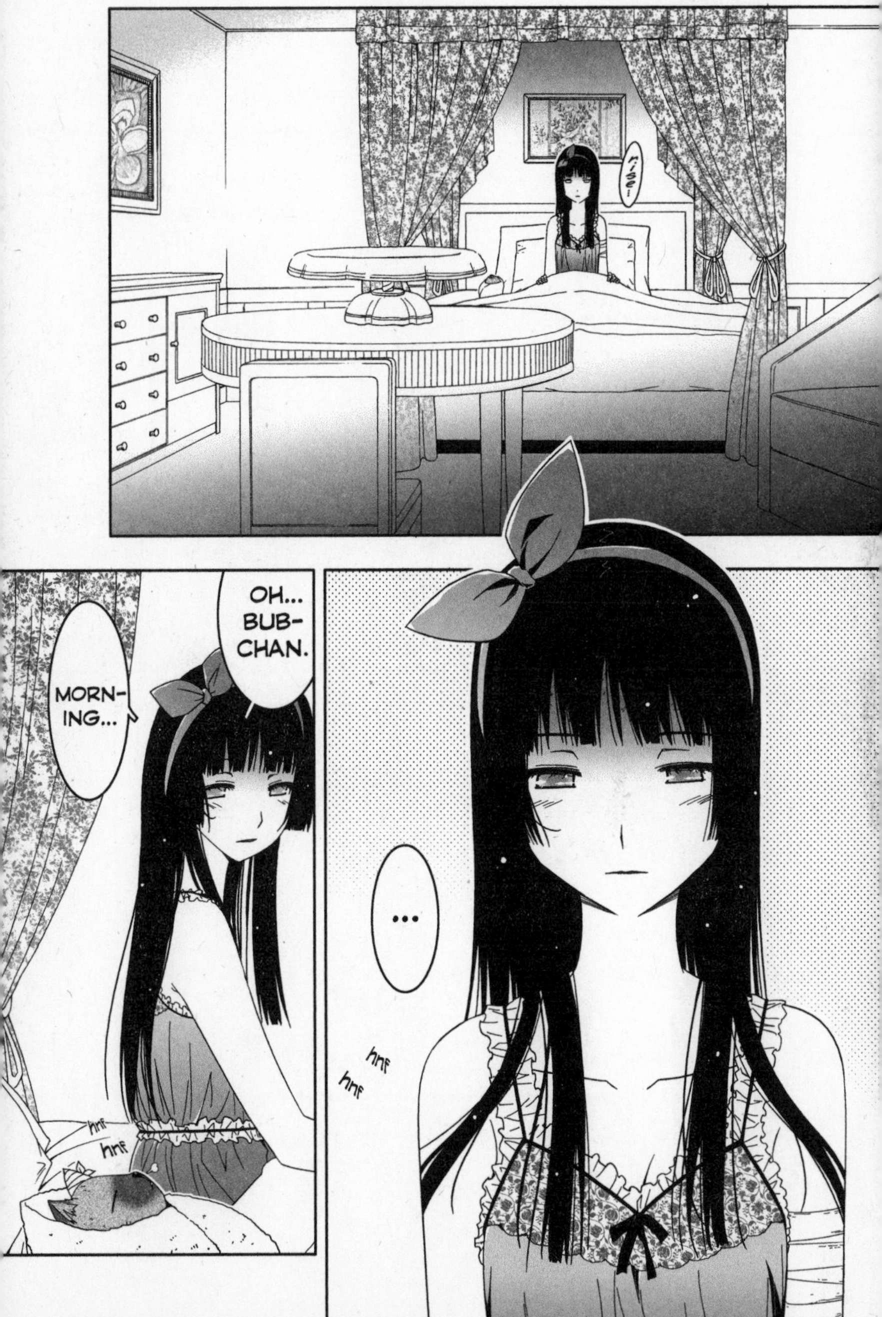
rise...
...
hnf
hnf
OH... BUB-CHAN.
MORN-ING...
hnf
hnf

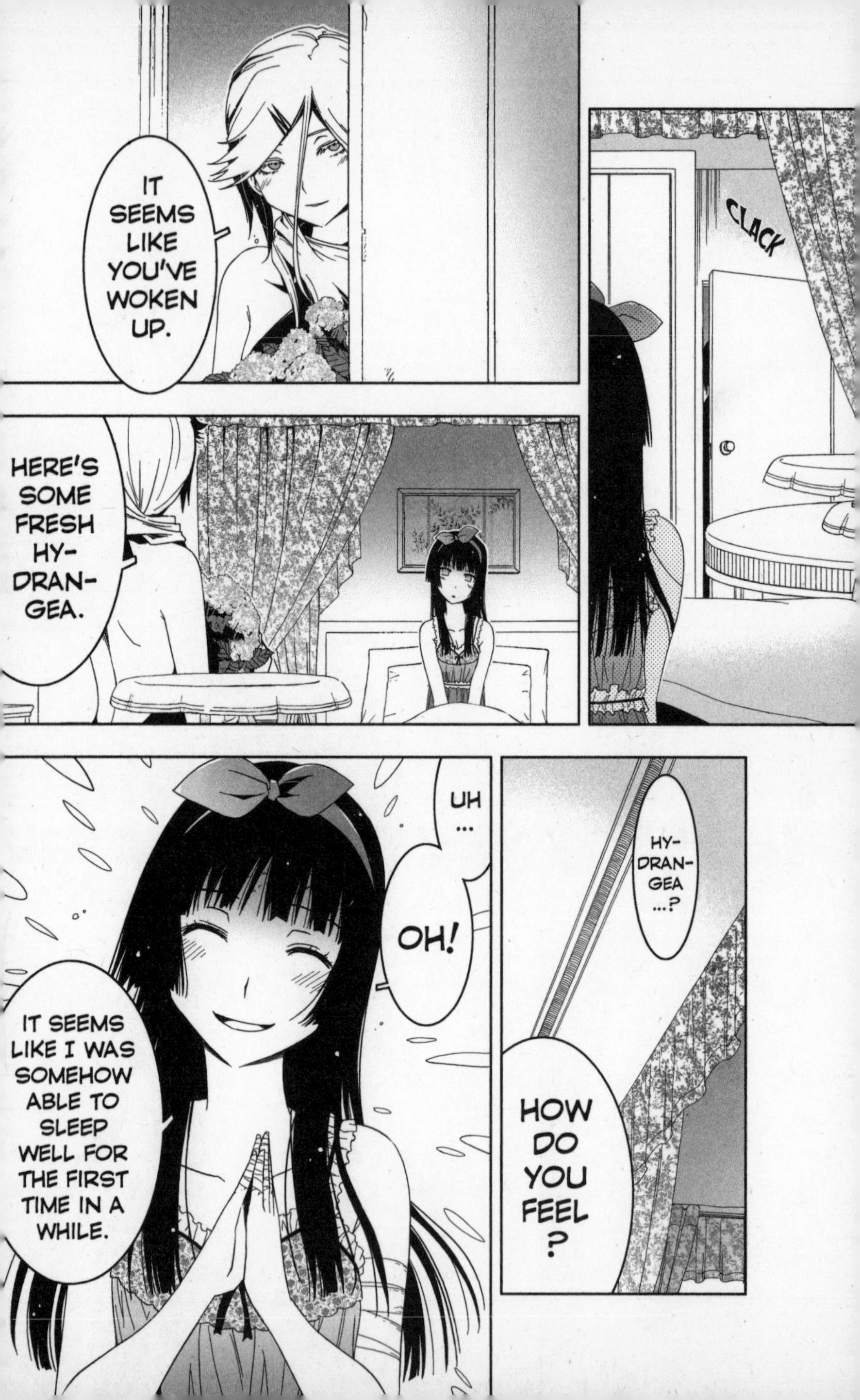
CLACK
IT SEEMS LIKE YOU'VE WOKEN UP.
HERE'S SOME FRESH HY-DRAN-GEA.
HY-DRAN-GEA ...?
HOW DO YOU FEEL?
UH ...
OH!
IT SEEMS LIKE I WAS SOMEHOW ABLE TO SLEEP WELL FOR THE FIRST TIME IN A WHILE.

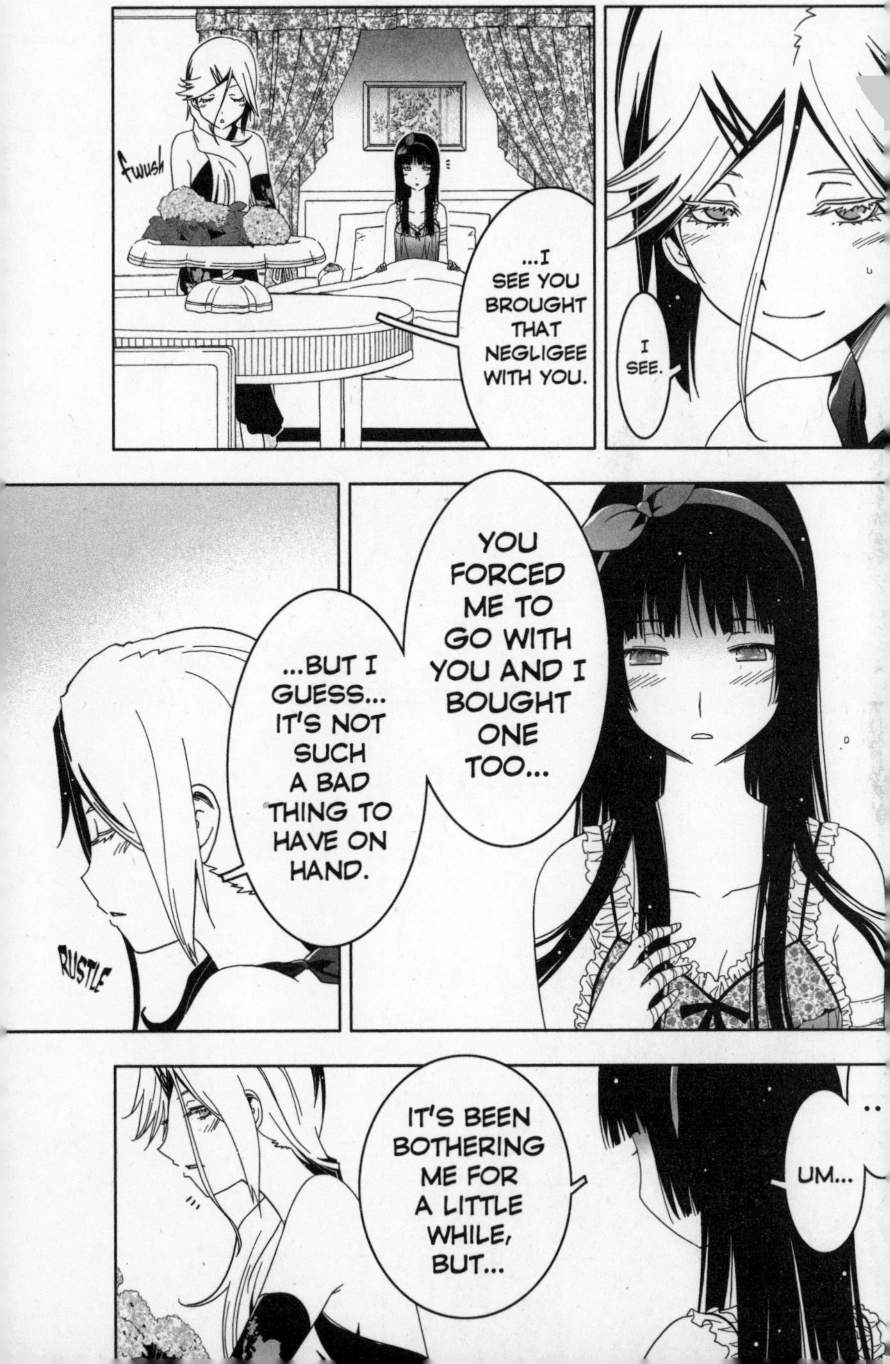
I SEE.
...I SEE YOU BROUGHT THAT NEGLIGEE WITH YOU.
fwush
YOU FORCED ME TO GO WITH YOU AND I BOUGHT ONE TOO...
...BUT I GUESS... IT'S NOT SUCH A BAD THING TO HAVE ON HAND.
RUSTLE
UM...
IT'S BEEN BOTHERING ME FOR A LITTLE WHILE, BUT...

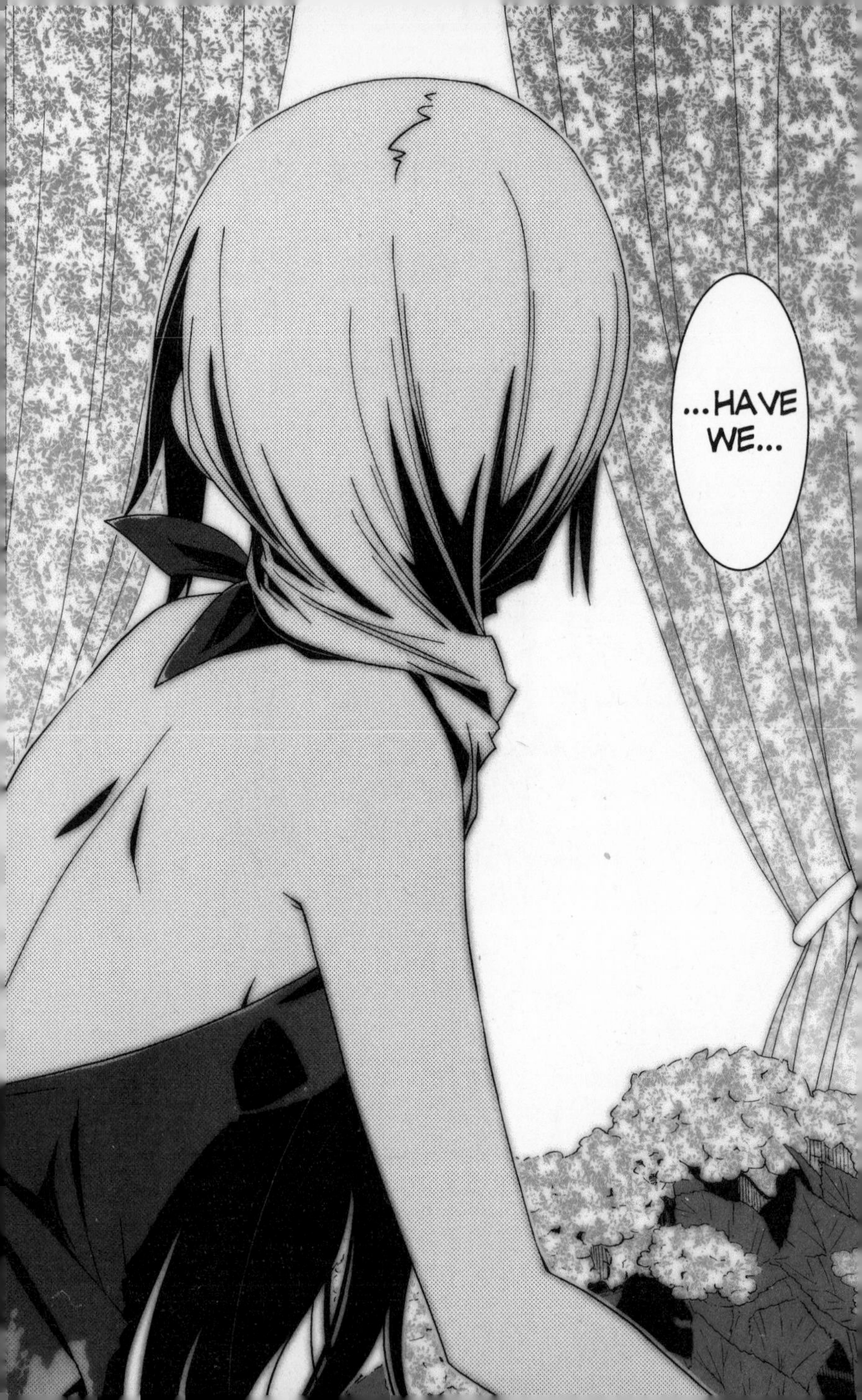
...HAVE WE...

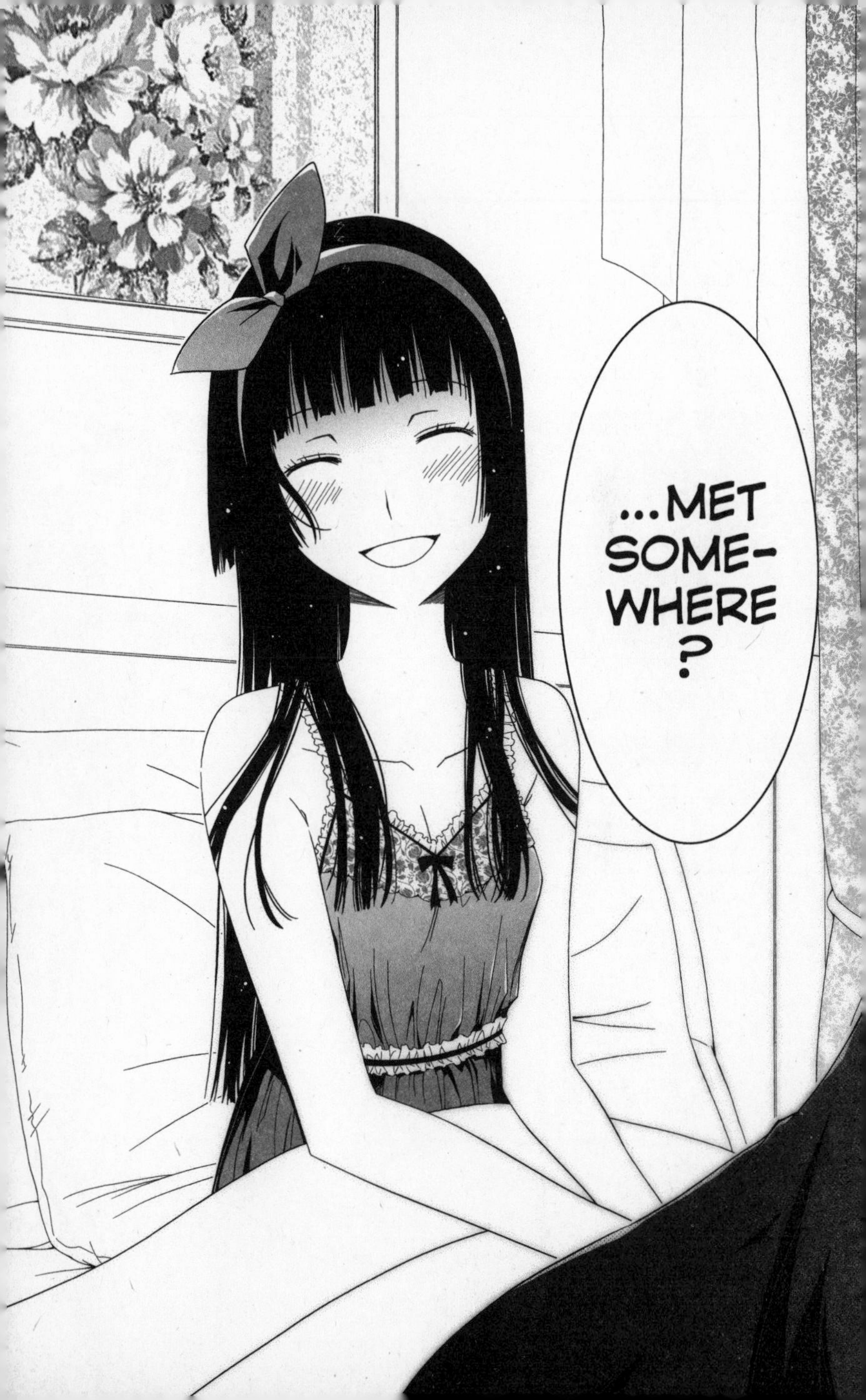
...MET SOMEWHERE?

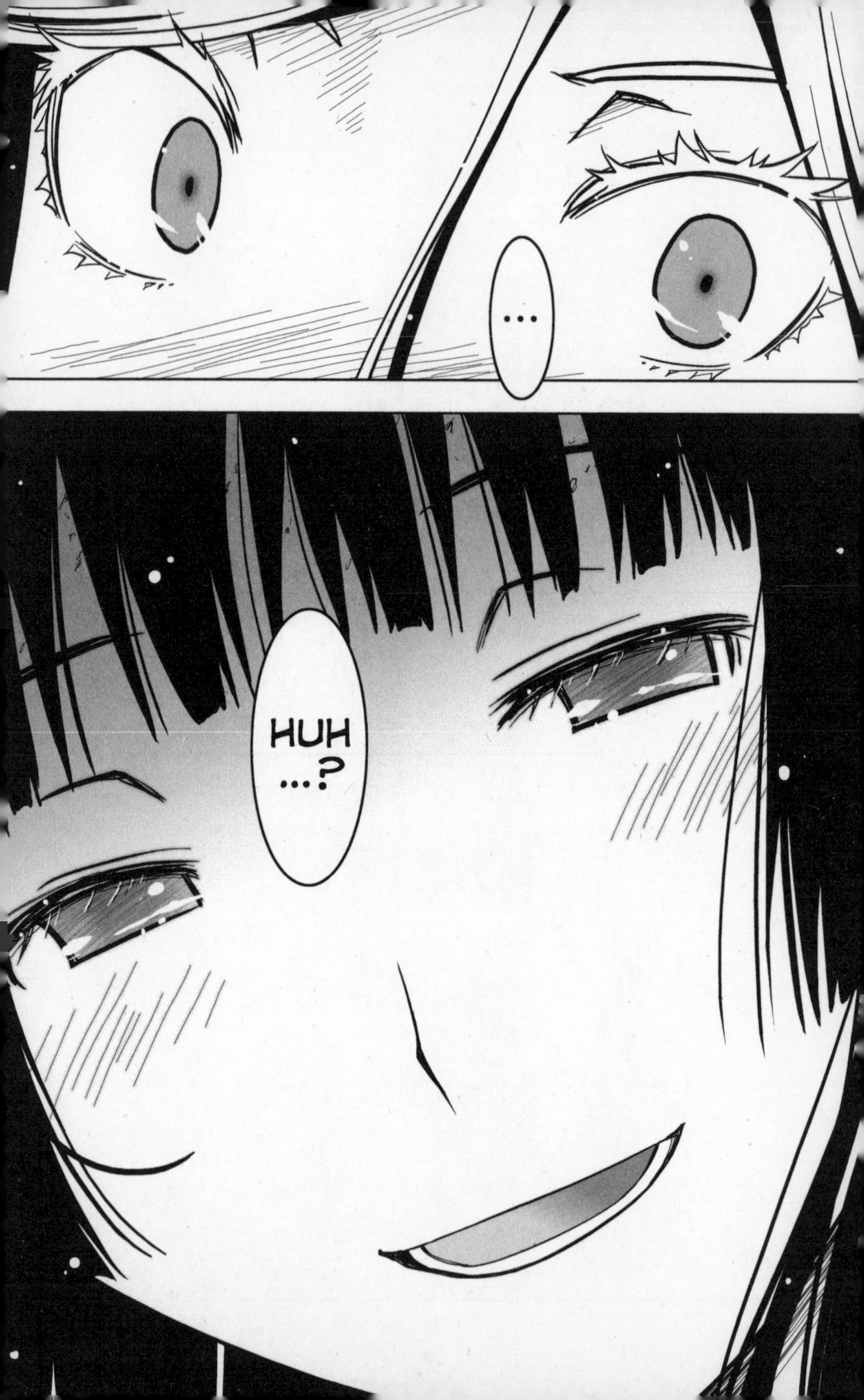
...
HUH ...?

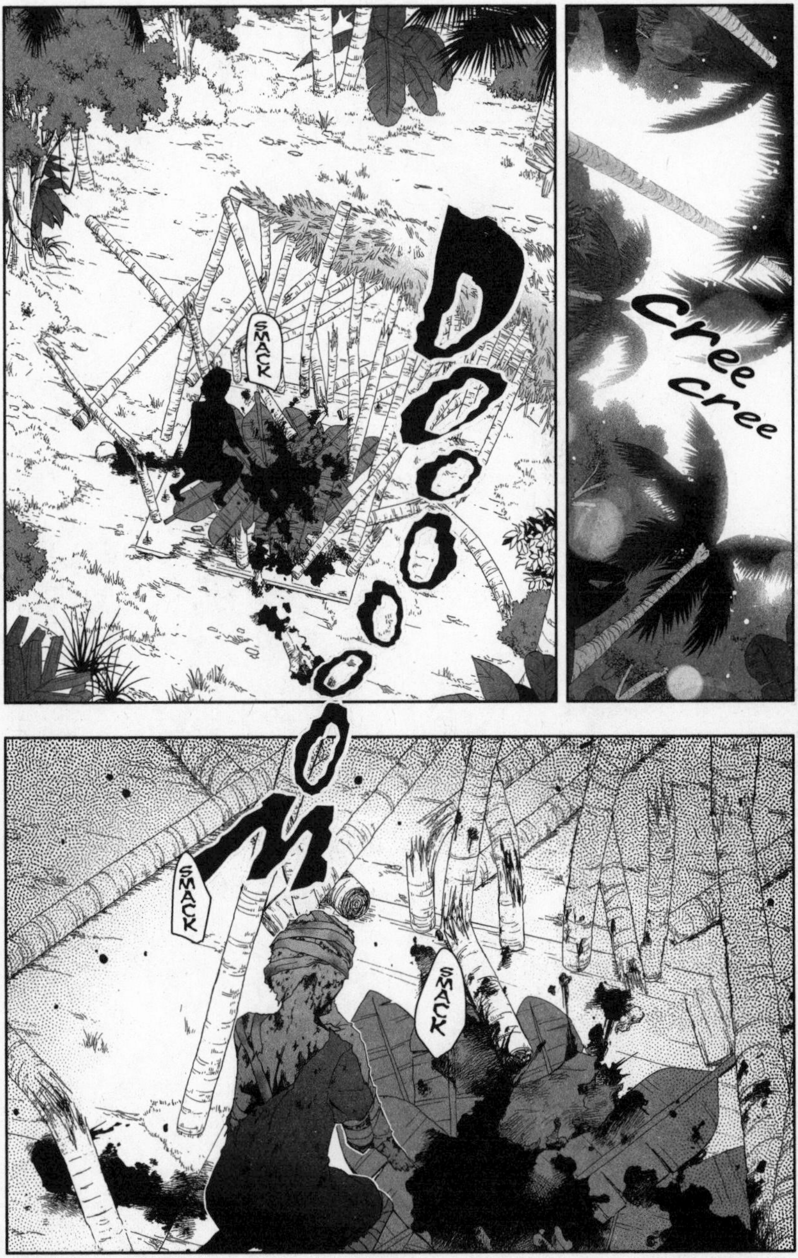
Cree cree
DOOOOOOM
SMACK
SMACK
SMACK

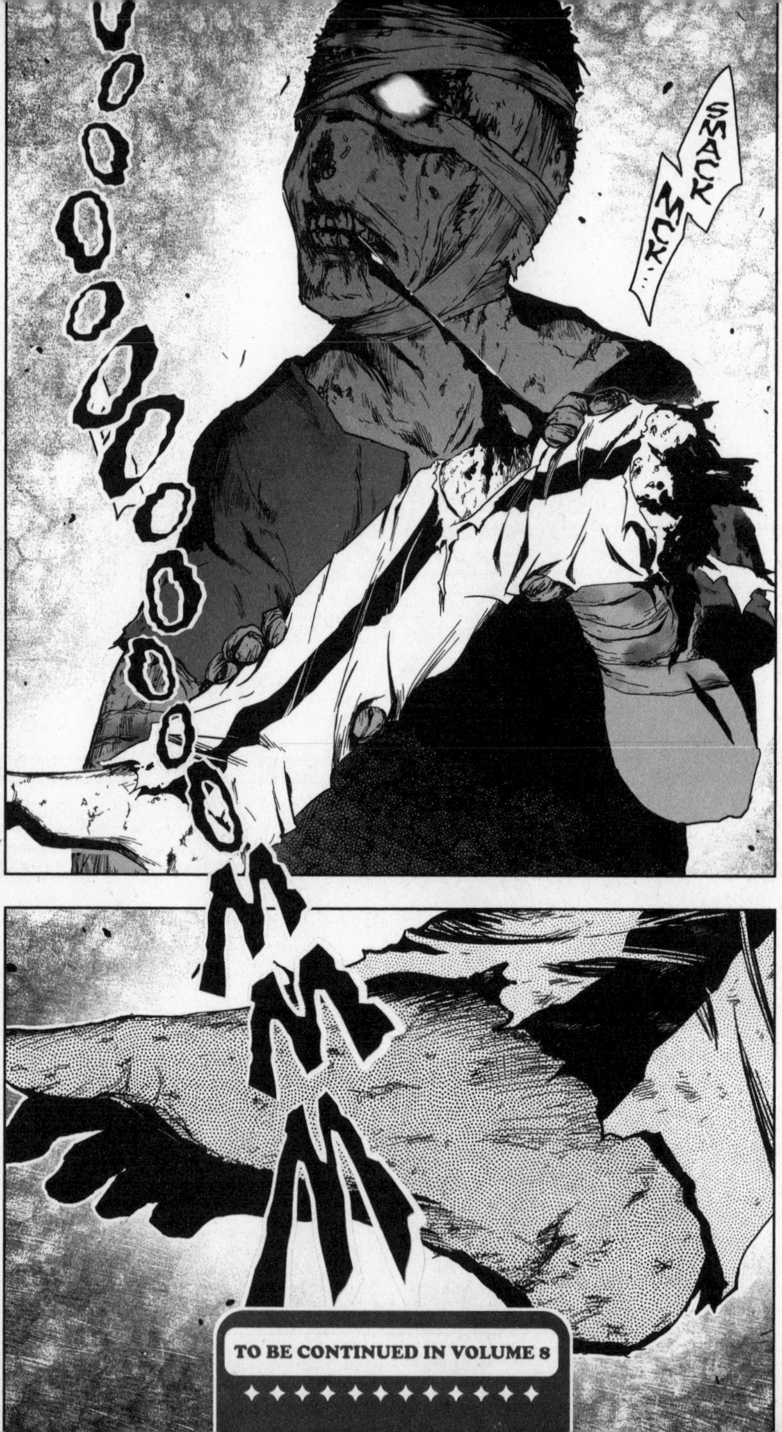
SMACK
MCK...
VOOOOOOOOOOOMMMM
TO BE CONTINUED IN VOLUME 8

SANKAREA

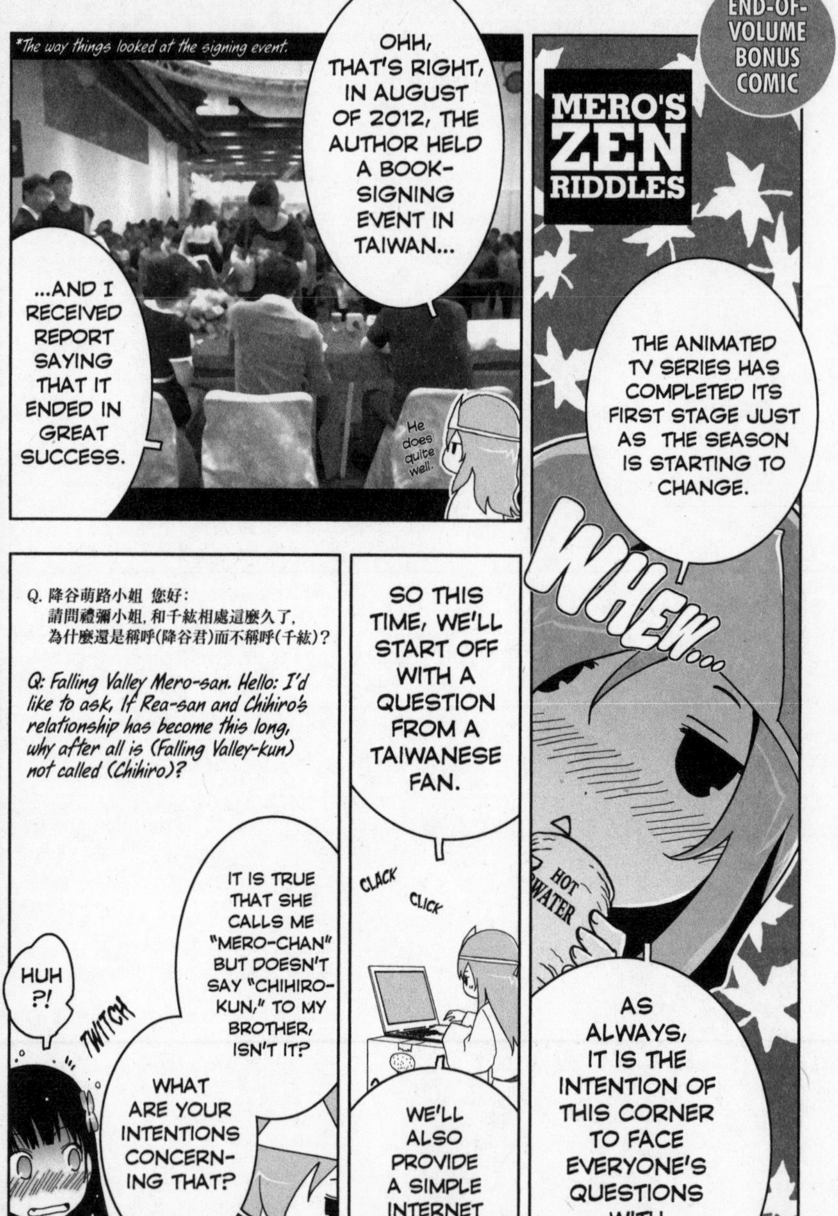
END-OF-VOLUME BONUS COMIC
MERO'S ZEN RIDDLES
THE ANIMATED TV SERIES HAS COMPLETED ITS FIRST STAGE JUST AS THE SEASON IS STARTING TO CHANGE.
WHEW...
HOT WATER
AS ALWAYS, IT IS THE INTENTION OF THIS CORNER TO FACE EVERYONE'S QUESTIONS WITH SINCERITY.
*The way things looked at the signing event.
OHH, THAT'S RIGHT, IN AUGUST OF 2012, THE AUTHOR HELD A BOOK-SIGNING EVENT IN TAIWAN...
...AND I RECEIVED REPORT SAYING THAT IT ENDED IN GREAT SUCCESS.
He does quite well.
SO THIS TIME, WE'LL START OFF WITH A QUESTION FROM A TAIWANESE FAN.
CLACK
CLICK
WE'LL ALSO PROVIDE A SIMPLE INTERNET TRANSLATION.
Q. 降谷萌路小姐 您好:
請問禮彌小姐,和千紘相處這麼久了,
為什麼還是稱呼(降谷君)而不稱呼(千紘)?
Q: Falling Valley Mero-san. Hello: I'd like to ask, If Rea-san and Chihiro's relationship has become this long, why after all is (Falling Valley-kun) not called (Chihiro)?
IT IS TRUE THAT SHE CALLS ME "MERO-CHAN" BUT DOESN'T SAY "CHIHIRO-KUN," TO MY BROTHER, ISN'T IT?
HUH?!
TWITCH
WHAT ARE YOUR INTENTIONS CONCERNING THAT?

TRANSLATION NOTES

Honorifics: This series retains the Japanese honorifics. Here's a guide:

-san: Polite, equivalent to "Mr." or "Ms."

-sama: A term of great respect.

-kun: Used for boys or people in a lower position.

-chan: A sometimes cutesy term of endearment for girls.

-dono: A very respectful and now old-fashioned term.

-senpai: Refers to a student who entered school before you, or a colleague who entered the company before you. (The equivalent for your juniors is "kohai.")

Page 149 onward:

Anywhere written in Italic is supposed to express that the researchers are speaking English. Chihiro doesn't know English, but Rea does.

Pages 159-60:

In the original Japanese, the examination that Chief Niiva speaks of is called "ningen dokku," which translates directly to "human dock." In Japan, after reaching a certain age, it is somewhat common to have a comprehensive examination of your entire body every now and then. This examination involves a litany of tests and goes far beyond what we in the United States might go through for a typical checkup or physical. The term "dock" part of the term comes from the idea that when a boat is docked at port, it goes through a series of thorough checks and tests.

Pages 170-171:

The Internet translations of the original Taiwanese are not perfect translation and have been further translated into English to evoke this sense. As an example, Falling Valley is literally the characters Furu and Ya.

Guidance

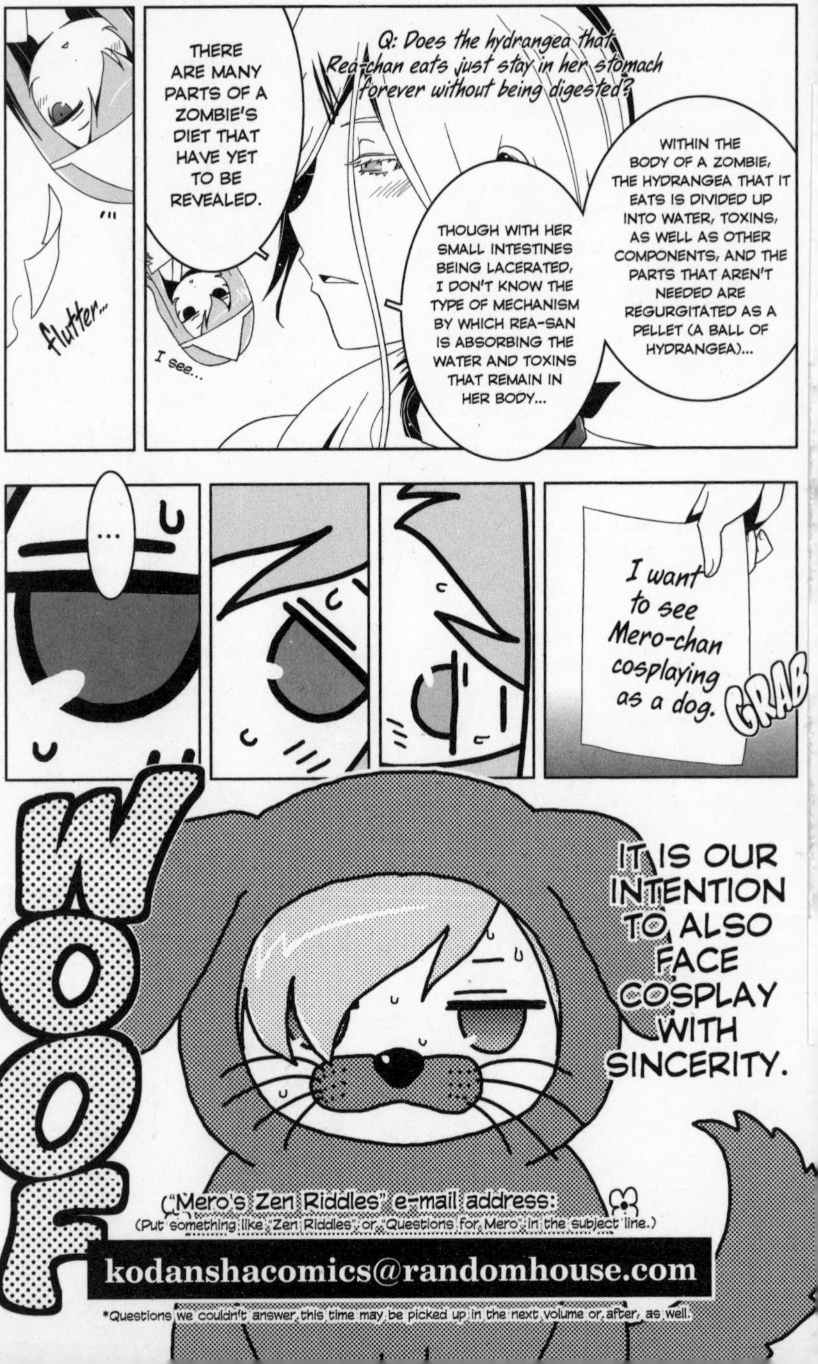

Q: Does the hydrangea that Rea-chan eats just stay in her stomach forever without being digested?
WITHIN THE BODY OF A ZOMBIE, THE HYDRANGEA THAT IT EATS IS DIVIDED UP INTO WATER, TOXINS, AS WELL AS OTHER COMPONENTS, AND THE PARTS THAT AREN'T NEEDED ARE REGURGITATED AS A PELLET (A BALL OF HYDRANGEA)...
THOUGH WITH HER SMALL INTESTINES BEING LACERATED, I DON'T KNOW THE TYPE OF MECHANISM BY WHICH REA-SAN IS ABSORBING THE WATER AND TOXINS THAT REMAIN IN HER BODY...
THERE ARE MANY PARTS OF A ZOMBIE'S DIET THAT HAVE YET TO BE REVEALED.
I see...
...
flutter...
I want to see Mero-chan cosplaying as a dog.
GRAB
...
IT IS OUR INTENTION TO ALSO FACE COSPLAY WITH SINCERITY.
WOOF
"Mero's Zen Riddles" e-mail address:
(Put something like "Zen Riddles" or "Questions for Mero" in the subject line.)
kodanshacomics@randomhouse.com
*Questions we couldn't answer this time may be picked up in the next volume or after, as well.

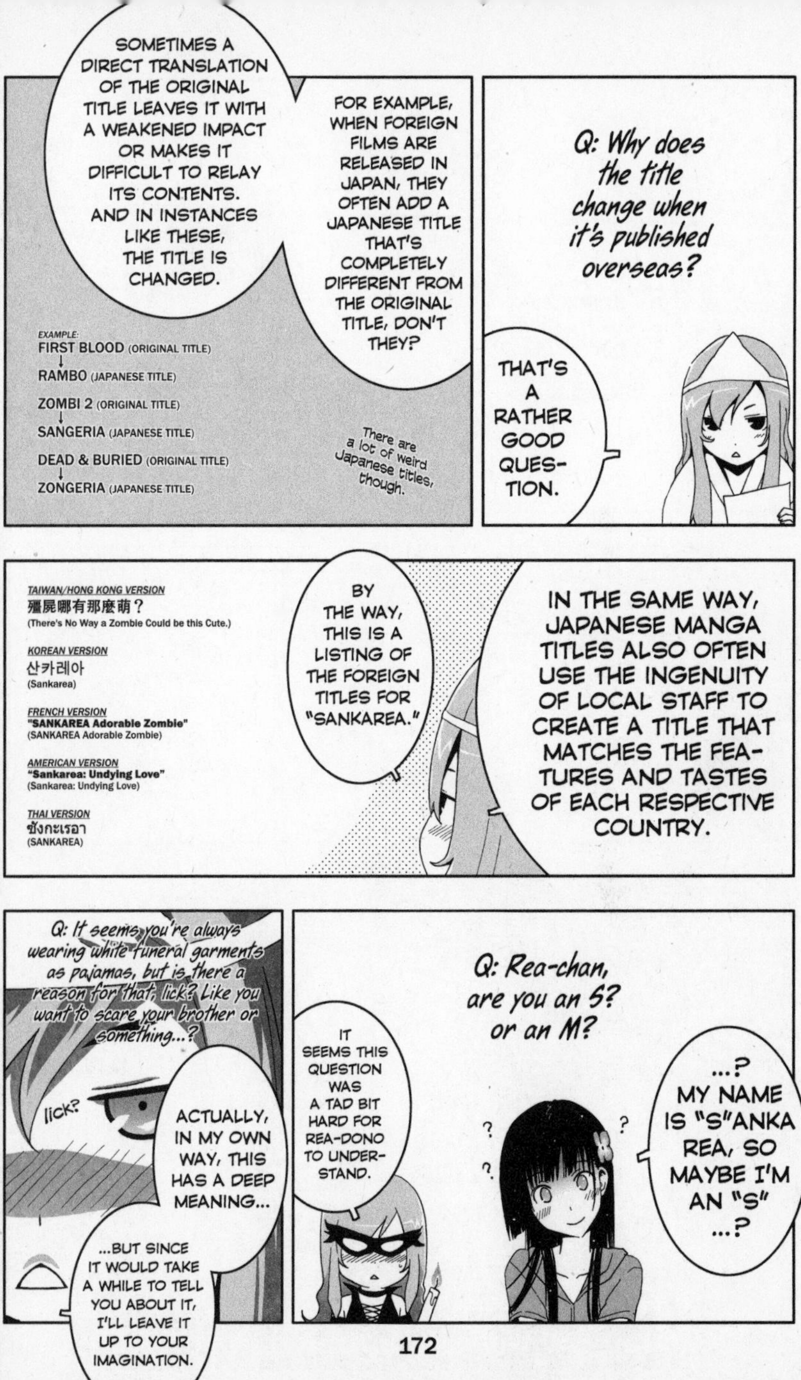
Q: Why does the title change when it's published overseas?
THAT'S A RATHER GOOD QUESTION.
FOR EXAMPLE, WHEN FOREIGN FILMS ARE RELEASED IN JAPAN, THEY OFTEN ADD A JAPANESE TITLE THAT'S COMPLETELY DIFFERENT FROM THE ORIGINAL TITLE, DON'T THEY?
SOMETIMES A DIRECT TRANSLATION OF THE ORIGINAL TITLE LEAVES IT WITH A WEAKENED IMPACT OR MAKES IT DIFFICULT TO RELAY ITS CONTENTS. AND IN INSTANCES LIKE THESE, THE TITLE IS CHANGED.
EXAMPLE:
FIRST BLOOD (ORIGINAL TITLE)
↓
RAMBO (JAPANESE TITLE)
ZOMBI 2 (ORIGINAL TITLE)
↓
SANGERIA (JAPANESE TITLE)
DEAD & BURIED (ORIGINAL TITLE)
↓
ZONGERIA (JAPANESE TITLE)
There are a lot of weird Japanese titles, though.
IN THE SAME WAY, JAPANESE MANGA TITLES ALSO OFTEN USE THE INGENUITY OF LOCAL STAFF TO CREATE A TITLE THAT MATCHES THE FEATURES AND TASTES OF EACH RESPECTIVE COUNTRY.
BY THE WAY, THIS IS A LISTING OF THE FOREIGN TITLES FOR "SANKAREA."
TAIWAN/HONG KONG VERSION
殭屍哪有那麼萌？
(There's No Way a Zombie Could be this Cute.)
KOREAN VERSION
산카레아
(Sankarea)
FRENCH VERSION
"SANKAREA Adorable Zombie"
(SANKAREA Adorable Zombie)
AMERICAN VERSION
"Sankarea: Undying Love"
(Sankarea: Undying Love)
THAI VERSION
ซังกะเรอา
(SANKAREA)
Q: Rea-chan, are you an S? or an M?
...? MY NAME IS "S"ANKA REA, SO MAYBE I'M AN "S" ...?
? ? ?
IT SEEMS THIS QUESTION WAS A TAD BIT HARD FOR REA-DONO TO UNDERSTAND.
Q: It seems you're always wearing white funeral garments as pajamas, but is there a reason for that, lick? Like you want to scare your brother or something...?
lick?
ACTUALLY, IN MY OWN WAY, THIS HAS A DEEP MEANING...
...BUT SINCE IT WOULD TAKE A WHILE TO TELL YOU ABOUT IT, I'LL LEAVE IT UP TO YOUR IMAGINATION.

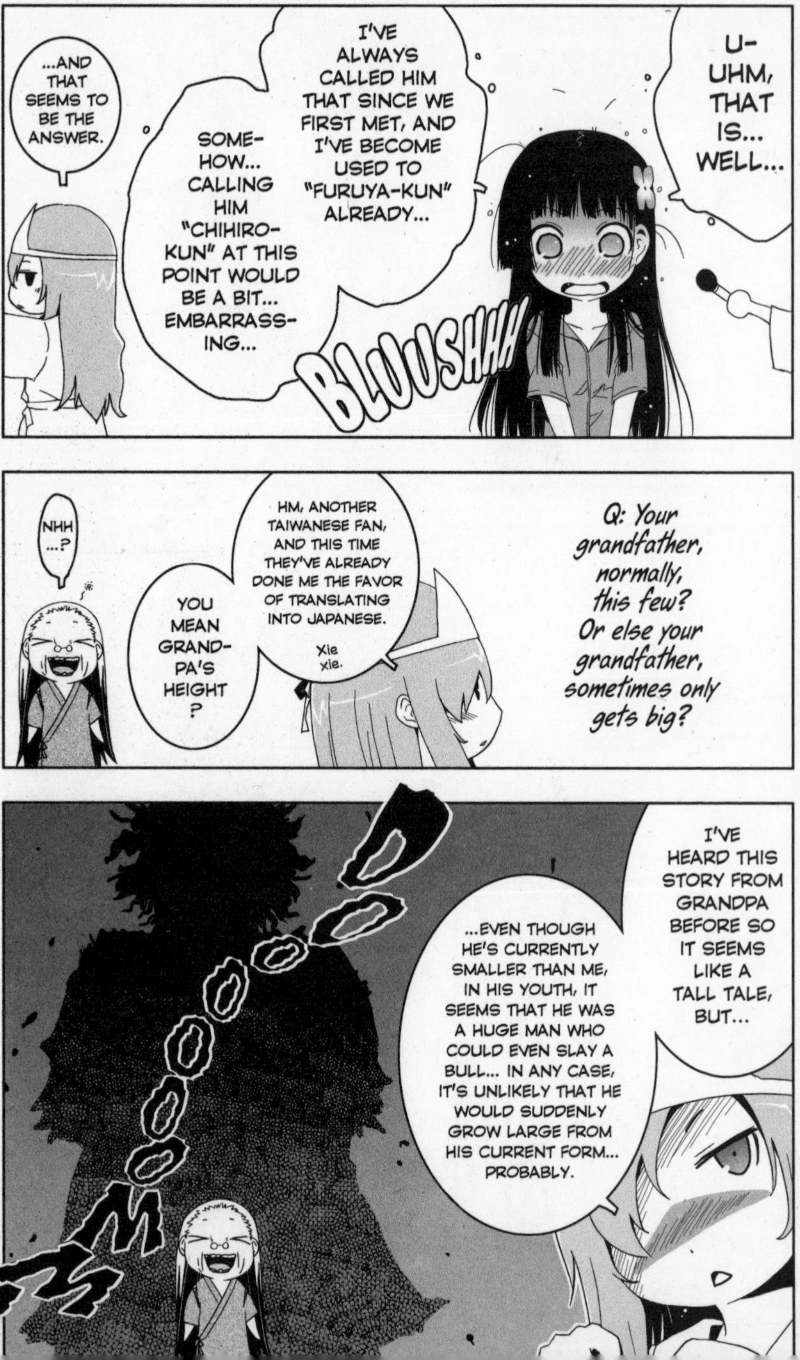
U-UHM, THAT IS... WELL...
I'VE ALWAYS CALLED HIM THAT SINCE WE FIRST MET, AND I'VE BECOME USED TO "FURUYA-KUN" ALREADY...
SOMEHOW... CALLING HIM "CHIHIRO-KUN" AT THIS POINT WOULD BE A BIT... EMBARRASSING...
BLOUSHHH
...AND THAT SEEMS TO BE THE ANSWER.
Q: Your grandfather, normally, this few? Or else your grandfather, sometimes only gets big?
HM, ANOTHER TAIWANESE FAN, AND THIS TIME THEY'VE ALREADY DONE ME THE FAVOR OF TRANSLATING INTO JAPANESE.
Xie xie.
YOU MEAN GRANDPA'S HEIGHT?
NHH...?
I'VE HEARD THIS STORY FROM GRANDPA BEFORE SO IT SEEMS LIKE A TALL TALE, BUT...
...EVEN THOUGH HE'S CURRENTLY SMALLER THAN ME, IN HIS YOUTH, IT SEEMS THAT HE WAS A HUGE MAN WHO COULD EVEN SLAY A BULL... IN ANY CASE, IT'S UNLIKELY THAT HE WOULD SUDDENLY GROW LARGE FROM HIS CURRENT FORM... PROBABLY.
DOOOOOOOOOMMM